The Island Race

WINSTON S. CHURCHILL

The Island Race

Webb & Bower
EXETER, ENGLAND

THE ISLAND RACE

is an abridgement by Timothy Baker
of the four volumes of
A History of the English-Speaking Peoples
by Sir Winston Churchill

© Cassell & Co. Ltd, 1964

This edition published in 1985 by
Webb & Bower (Publishers) Limited,
9 Colleton Crescent, Exeter, Devon EX2 4BY.

British Library Cataloguing in Publication Data

Churchill, Winston S. (Winston Spencer)
   A history of the English-speaking peoples
   The island race.
   1. Great Britain – History – Chronology
   I.   A history of the English-speaking peoples
   II. Title   III. Baker, Timothy
   941′.002′02   DA34

   ISBN 0-86350-113-3

Printed and bound in Italy by Grafiche Editoriali Padane

Contents

Our story centres in an island, not widely sundered from the Continent, and so tilted that its mountains lie all to the west and north, while south and east is a gently undulating landscape of wooded valleys, open downs, and slow rivers. It is very accessible to the invader, whether he comes in peace or war, as pirate or merchant, conqueror or missionary. Those who dwell there are not insensitive to any shift of power, any change of faith, or even fashion, on the mainland, but they give to every practice, every doctrine that comes to it from abroad, its peculiar turn and imprint. . . .

CHAPTER ONE

The Island Race

IN the summer of the Roman year 699, now described as the year 55 before the birth of Christ, the Proconsul of Gaul, Gaius Julius Cæsar, turned his gaze upon Britain. He knew that it was inhabited by the same type of tribesmen who confronted the Roman arms in Germany, Gaul, and Spain. To Cæsar the Island presented itself as an integral part of his task of subjugating the Northern barbarians to the rule and system of Rome. All that mattered was to choose a good day in the fine August weather, throw a few legions on to the nearest shore, and see what there was in this strange Island. Cæsar's vision pierced the centuries, and where he conquered civilisation dwelt.

What was, in fact, this Island which now for the first time in coherent history was to be linked with the great world? We have dug up in the present age from the gravel of Swanscombe a human skull which is certainly a quarter of a million years old. It is said that the whole of Southern Britain could in this period support upon its game no more than seven hundred families. Already man had found out that a flint was better than a fist. His descendants would burrow deep in the chalk and gravel for battle-axe flints of the best size and quality, and gain survival thereby. But so far he had only learned to chip his flints into rough tools.

At the close of the Ice Age changes in climate brought about the collapse of the hunting civilisations of Old Stone Age Man, and after a very long period of time the tides of invasion brought Neolithic culture into the Western forests. The newcomers had a primitive agriculture. Presently they constructed earthwork enclosures on the hill-tops, into which they drove their cattle at night-time. Moreover, Neolithic man had developed a means of polishing his flints into perfect shape for killing. This betokened a great advance; but others were in prospect.

In early days Britain was part of the Continent. A wide plain joined England and Holland, in which the Thames and the Rhine met together and poured their waters northward. In some slight movement of the earth's surface this plain sank a few hundred feet, and admitted the ocean to the North Sea and the Baltic. Another tremor, important for our story, sundered the cliffs of Dover from those of Cape Gris Nez, and the scour of the ocean and its tides made the Straits of Dover and the English Channel. Britain was still little more than a promontory of Europe, or divided from it by a narrow tide race which has gradually enlarged into the Straits of Dover, when the Pyramids were a-building, and when learned Egyptians were laboriously exploring the ancient ruins of Sakkara.

While what is now our Island was still joined to the Continent another great improvement was made in human methods of destruction. Copper and tin were discovered and worried out of the earth; the one too soft and the other too brittle for the main purpose, but, blended by human genius, they opened the Age of Bronze. Other things being equal, the men with bronze could beat the men with flints. The discovery was hailed, and the Bronze Age began. The Late Bronze Age in the southern parts of Britain, according

A bronze shield boss, circa *250–150* B.C., *found in the Thames at Wandsworth*. BRITISH MUSEUM

to most authorities, began about 1000 B.C. and lasted until about 400 B.C.

At this point the march of invention brought a new factor upon the scene. Iron was dug and forged. Men armed with iron entered Britain from the Continent and killed the men of bronze. The Iron Age immigrations brought with them a revival of the hill-top camps, which had ceased to be constructed since the Neolithic Age.

The last of the successive waves of Celtic inroad and supersession which marked the Iron Age came in the early part of the first century B.C. There is no doubt that the Belgæ were by far the most enlightened invaders who had hitherto penetrated the recesses of the Island. This active, alert, conquering, and ruling race established themselves wherever they went with ease and celerity, and might have looked forward to a long dominion. But the tramp of the legions had followed hard behind them, and they must soon defend the prize they had won against still better men and higher systems of government and war.

Meanwhile, in Rome, at the centre and summit, only vague ideas prevailed about the Western islands. These were the ultimate fringes of the world. Still, there was the tin trade, in which important interests were concerned, and Polybius, writing about 140

Left: *Julius Cæsar*

Facing page. Above: *Cunobelinus* (d. circa *43*)

Below: *Vespasian*

B.C., shows that this aspect at least had been fully discussed by commercial writers.

Late in August 55 B.C. Cæsar sailed with eighty transports and two legions at midnight, and descended upon Albion on the low, shelving beach between Deal and Walmer. There was a short, ferocious fight amid the waves, but the Romans reached the shore, and, once arrayed, forced the Britons to flight. Cæsar's landing, however, was only the first of his troubles. His cavalry, in eighteen transports, caught by a sudden gale, drifted far down the Channel, and were thankful to regain the Continent. The high tide of the full moon wrought grievous damage to his fleet at anchor. The Britons had sued for peace after the battle on the beach, but now in great numbers they attacked the Roman foragers. Discipline and armour once again told their tale. The British submitted. Their conqueror imposed only nominal terms. He never even pretended that his expedition had been a success.

To supersede the record of it he came again the next year, this time with five legions and some cavalry conveyed in eight hundred ships. The landing was unimpeded, but again the sea assailed him. He was forced to spend ten days in hauling all his ships on to the shore, and in fortifying the camp of which they then formed part. This done he renewed his invasion and crossed the Thames near Brentford. But the British had found a leader in the chief Cassivellaunus, who was a master of war under the prevailing conditions. Dismissing to their homes the mass of untrained foot-soldiers and peasantry, he kept pace with the invaders march by march with his chariots and horsemen. None the less Cæsar captured his first stronghold; the tribes began to make terms for themselves; a well-conceived plan for destroying Cæsar's base on the Kentish shore was defeated. Cassivellaunus negotiated a further surrender of hostages and a promise of tribute and submission, in return for which Cæsar was again content to quit the Island. Cæsar had his triumph, and British captives trod their dreary path at his tail through the streets of Rome; but for

Maiden Castle, near Dorchester, the great hill-fort town assaulted and taken by the Romans during the Claudian invasion campaign, 43. AEROFILMS

nearly a hundred years no invading army landed upon the Island coasts.

In the year A.D. 41 the murder of the Emperor Caligula, and a chapter of accidents, brought his uncle, the clownish scholar Claudius, to the throne of the world. He was attracted by the idea of gaining a military reputation. In the year 43, almost one hundred years after Julius Cæsar's evacuation, a powerful, well-organised Roman army of some twenty thousand men was prepared for the subjugation of Britain.

The internal situation favoured the invaders. Cunobelinus (Shakespeare's Cymbeline) had established an overlordship over the South-East of the Island, with his capital at Colchester. But in his old age dissensions had begun to impair his authority, and on his death the kingdom was ruled jointly by his sons Caractacus and Togodumnus. They were not everywhere recognised, and they had no time to form a union of the tribal

kingdom before the Roman commander, Plautius, and his legions arrived. The people of Kent fell back on the tactics of Cassivellaunus, and Plautius had much trouble in searching them out; but when he did find them he first defeated Caractacus, and then his brother somewhere in East Kent. Then, advancing along Cæsar's old line of march, he came on a river he had not heard of, the Medway. "The barbarians thought that the Romans would not be able to cross without a bridge, and consequently bivouacked in rather careless fashion on the opposite bank";[1] nevertheless, the Britons faced them on the second day, and were only broken by a flank attack, Vespasian—some day to be Emperor himself—having discovered a ford higher up. This victory marred the stage-management of the campaign. Plautius won his battle too soon, and in the wrong place. Something had to be done to show that the Emperor's presence was necessary to victory.

[1] Dio Cassius, Book LX.

So Claudius, who had been waiting on events in France, crossed the seas, bringing substantial reinforcements, including a number of elephants. A battle was procured, and the Romans won. Claudius returned to Rome to receive from the Senate the title of "Britannicus" and permission to celebrate a triumph. But the British war continued. Caractacus escaped to the Welsh border, and, rousing its tribes, maintained an indomitable resistance for more than six years.

"In this year A.D. 61", according to Tacitus,[1] "a severe disaster was sustained in Britain." Suetonius, the new Governor, had engaged himself deeply in the West. The King of the East Anglian Iceni had died. "His kingdom was plundered by centurions, and his private property by slaves, as if they had been captured in war; his widow Boadicea [relished by the learned as Boudicca] was flogged, and his daughters outraged; the chiefs of the Iceni were robbed of their ancestral properties as if the Romans had received the whole country as a gift, and the king's own relatives were reduced to slavery."

In all Britain there were only four legions, at most twenty thousand men. The Fourteenth and Twentieth were with Suetonius on his Welsh campaign. The Ninth was at Lincoln, and the Second at Gloucester. The

Claudius

first target of the revolt was Camulodunum (Colchester), the centre of Roman authority and Roman religion. The town was burned to ashes. Everyone, Roman or Romanised, was massacred and everything destroyed. Meanwhile, the Ninth Legion was marching to the rescue. The victorious Britons advanced from the sack of Colchester to meet it. By sheer force of numbers they overcame the Roman infantry and slaughtered them to a man, and the commander, Petilius Cerialis, was content to escape with his cavalry. Such were the tidings which reached Suetonius in Anglesey. He, "undaunted, made his way through a hostile country to Londinium, a town which, though not dignified by the title of colony, was a busy emporium for traders". This is the first mention of London in literature. The citizens implored Suetonius to protect them, but when he heard that Boadicea, having chased Cerialis towards Lincoln, had turned and was marching south he took the hard but right decision to leave them to their fate. The slaughter which fell upon London was universal. Boadicea then turned upon Verulamium (St Albans). A like total slaughter and obliteration was inflicted. "No less", according to Tacitus, "than seventy thousand citizens and allies were slain" in these three cities. This is probably the most horrible episode which our Island has known.

"And now Suetonius, having with him the Fourteenth Legion, with the veterans of the Twentieth, and the auxiliaries nearest at hand, making up a force of about ten thousand fully armed men, resolved . . . for battle." At heavy adverse odds Roman discipline and tactical skill triumphed. Boadicea poisoned herself.

Suetonius now thought only of vengeance, and the extermination of the entire ancient British race might have followed but for the remonstrances of a new Procurator, supported by his Treasury seniors at Rome, who saw themselves about to be possessed of a desert instead of a province. In the end it was resolved to make the best of the Britons. The Emperor Nero sent a new Governor, who made a peace with the desperate

The Roman theatre at Verulamium (St Albans). Verulamium was founded by the Romans after the Claudian conquest of 43, possibly on the actual site of the Belgic Verulam, and was sacked by Boadicea in the revolt of 61. The theatre itself, the only one to have been discovered in Britain, is thought to have been built circa 300. BRITISH TRAVEL ASSOCIATION

[1] Extracts from Tacitus' *Annals* are from G. G. Ramsay's translation; passages from the *Agricola* come from the translation of Church and Brodribb.

The monument to Queen Boadicea (d. 62) and her two daughters on the Thames Embankment, opposite the Houses of Parliament. JOHN R. FREEMAN

tribesmen which enabled their blood to be perpetuated in the Island race.

In A.D. 78 Agricola, a Governor of talent and energy, was sent to Britannia. With military ability Agricola united a statesman-like humanity and showed "such a preference for the natural powers of the Britons over the more laboured style of the Gauls" that the well-to-do classes were conciliated and became willing to adopt the toga and other Roman fashions. Although in the Senate and governing circles in Rome it was constantly explained that the Imperial policy adhered to the principle of the great Augustus, that the frontiers should be maintained but not extended, Agricola was permitted to conduct six campaigns of expansion in Britannia. But there was no safety or permanent peace for the British province unless he could subdue the powerful tribes and large bands of desperate warriors who had been driven northwards by his advance. The decisive battle was fought in A.D. 83 at Mons Graupius, a place unidentified, though some suggest the Pass of Killiecrankie. Here, according to the Roman account, "ten thousand of the enemy were slain, and on our side there were about three hundred and sixty men". The way to the entire subjugation of the Island was now

open, and had Agricola been encouraged or at least supported by the Imperial Government the course of history might have been altered. But Caledonia was to Rome only a sensation: the real strain was between the Rhine and the Danube. Counsels of prudence prevailed, and the remnants of the British

fighting men were left to moulder in the Northern mists. In the wild North and West freedom found refuge among the mountains, but elsewhere the conquest and pacification were at length complete and Britannia became one of the forty-five provinces of the Roman Empire.

For nearly three hundred years Britain, reconciled to the Roman system, enjoyed in many respects the happiest, most comfortable, and most enlightened times its inhabitants have had. In all, the army of occupation numbered less than forty thousand men, and after a few generations was locally recruited and almost of purely British birth. In this period, almost equal to that which separates us from the reign of Queen Elizabeth I, well-to-do persons in Britain lived better than they ever did until Late Victorian times. In culture and learning Britain was a pale reflection of the Roman scene, not so lively as the Gallic. But there was law; there was order; there was peace; there was warmth; there was food, and a long-established custom of life. The population was free from barbarism without being sunk in sloth or luxury. Indeed, it may be said that of all the provinces few assimilated the Roman system with more aptitude than the Islanders. A poll in the fourth century would have declared for an indefinite continuance of the Roman régime.

Towns were planned in chessboard squares for communities dwelling under orderly government. During the first century the builders evidently took a sanguine view of the resources and future of Britannia, and all their towns were projected to meet an increasing population. We may assume a population of at least a million in the Romanised area. But there are no signs that any large increase of population accompanied the Roman system. The conquerors who so easily subdued and rallied the Britons to their method of social life brought with them no means, apart from stopping tribal war, of increasing the annual income derived from the productivity of the soil. The cultivated ground was still for the most part confined to the lighter and more easily cultivated upland soils, which had for thousands of years been worked in a primitive fashion. Such mining of lead and tin, such smelting, as had existed from time immemorial may have gained something from orderly administration; but there was no new science, no new thrust of power and knowledge in the material sphere. These conditions soon cast their shadows upon the boldly planned towns. The surrounding agricultural prosperity was not sufficient to support the hopes of their designers. Nevertheless, men dwelt safely, and what property they had was secured by iron laws. Urban life in Britannia was a failure, not of existence, but of expansion.

We owe London to Rome. An extensive and well-planned city with mighty walls took the place of the wooden trading settlement of A.D. 61, and soon achieved a leading place in the life of the Roman province of Britain, superseding the old Belgic capital, Colchester, as the commercial centre. The comparative unsuccess of urban life led the better-class Roman Britons to establish themselves in the country, and thus the villa system was the dominant feature of Roman Britain in its heyday. A very large number of comfortable dwellings, each with its lands around it, rose and thrived. At least five hundred have been explored in the Southern counties. None is found farther north than Yorkshire or farther west than the Glamorgan sea-plain. The towns were shrunken after the third century. The villas still flourished in the fourth, and in some cases lingered on into the darkening days of the fifth.

The work of Agricola in Northern Britain had been left unfinished and the position which he had won in Scotland had to be gradually abandoned. The accession of Hadrian was marked by a serious disaster. Hadrian came himself to Britain in 122, and the reorganisation of the frontier began.

should find ourselves in the presence of a theme as well founded, as inspired, and as inalienable from the inheritance of mankind as the *Odyssey* or the Old Testament. It is all true, or it ought to be; and more and better besides. And wherever men are fighting against barbarism, tyranny, and massacre, for freedom, law, and honour, let them remember that the fame of their deeds, even though they themselves be exterminated, may perhaps be celebrated as long as the world rolls round. Let us then declare that King Arthur and his noble knights, guarding the Sacred Flame of Christianity and the theme of a world order, sustained by valour, physical strength, and good horses and armour, slaughtered innumerable hosts of foul barbarians and set decent folk an example for all time.

Did the invaders exterminate the native population, or did they superimpose themselves upon them and become to some extent blended with them? The invaders themselves were not without their yearnings for settled security. Their hard laws, the rigours they endured, were but the results of the immense pressures behind them as the hordes of avid humanity spread westward from Central Asia. To these savage swords Britain seemed a refuge. In the wake of the raiders there grew steadily the plan and system of settlement.

Serious writers contend that the Anglo-Saxon conquest was for the bulk of the British community mainly a change of masters. The rich were slaughtered; the brave and proud fell back in large numbers upon the Western mountains. The Saxon was moreover a valley-settler. But in many places a long time must have passed before these lower grounds could be cleared and drained, and while this work was in progress what did he live on but the produce of the upland British farms? It is more natural to suppose that he would keep his natives working as serfs on the land with which they were familiar until the valley was ready for sowing. Then the old British farms would go down to grass, and the whole population would cluster in the village by the stream or the spring. But the language of

Tintagel Castle, Cornwall, built between the twelfth and fourteenth centuries on the site of an earlier Celtic monastery and the legendary castle of King Arthur in the fifth century.
J. ALLAN CASH

the valley-settlers, living in compact groups, would be dominant over that of the hill-cultivators, scattered in small and isolated holdings. The study of modern English place-names has shown that hill, wood, and stream names are often Celtic in origin, even in regions where the village names are Anglo-Saxon. In this way, without assuming any wholesale extermination, the disappearance of the British language can be explained even in areas where we know a British population to have survived. No uniformity of practice prevailed in the Island. There was no colour bar. In physical type the two races resembled each other; and the probabilities are that in many districts a substantial British element was incorporated in the Saxon stock.

Of all the tribes of the Germanic race none was more cruel than the Saxons. Although tradition and the Venerable Bede assign the

9

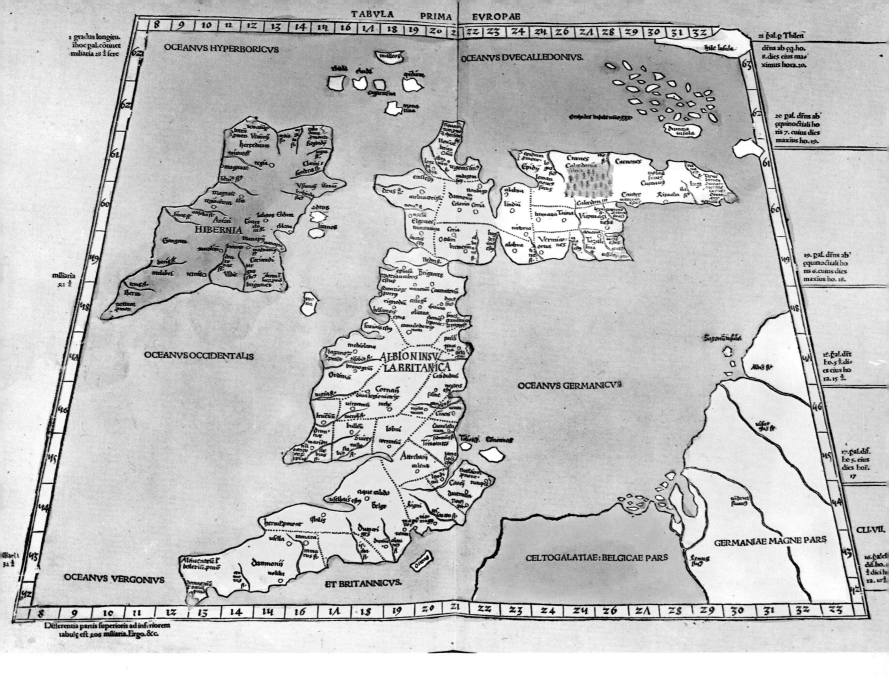

A fifteenth-century copy of a Ptolemy map of Britain, circa 150. BRITISH MUSEUM

Left: *Stonehenge (circa 1850–1500 B.C.), the circle of megaliths. The outer circle of standing stones (circa 1600–1500 B.C.) is twenty feet high and some hundred feet in diameter.* JOHN R. FREEMAN

conquest of Britain to the Angles, Jutes, and Saxons together, and although the various settlements have tribal peculiarities, it is probable that before their general exodus from Schleswig-Holstein the Saxons had virtually incorporated the other two strains.

In the tribal conceptions of the Germanic nation lie, no doubt, many of those principles which are now admired, and which have formed a recognisable part of the message which the English-speaking peoples have given to the world. But the conquerors of Roman Britain, far from practising these ideals, introduced a whole scheme of society which was fundamentally sordid and vicious. The invaders brought into Britain a principle common to all Germanic tribes, namely, the use of the money power to regulate all the legal relations of men. An elaborate tariff prescribed in shillings the "wergild" or exact value or worth of every man. The life of a slaughtered man could be compounded for cash. With money all was possible; without it only retribution or loss of liberty.

The great transition which we witness among the emigrants is the abandonment of blood and kin as the theme of their society and its replacement by local societies and lordship based on the ownership of land. The armed farmer-colonists found themselves forced to accept a stronger State authority owing to the stresses of continued military action. In Germany they had no kings. They developed them in Britain from leaders who claimed descent from the ancient gods. The position of the king continually increased in importance, and his supporters or companions gradually formed a new class in society, which carried with it the germ of feudalism, and was in the end to dominate all other conventions. The spoils of war were soon consumed, but the land remained for ever. Insensibly, at first, but with growing speed from the seventh century onwards, a landed aristocracy was created owing all it had to the king.

But with this movement towards a more coherent policy or structure of society there came also a welter of conflicting minor powers. For a long time the Island presented only the spectacle of a chaos arising from the strife of small fiercely organised entities. Although from the time of the immigration the people south of the Humber were generally subject to a common overlord, they were never able to carry the evolution of kingship forward to a national throne.

Christianity had not been established as the religion of the Empire during the first two centuries of the Roman occupation of Britain. There arose, however, a British Christian Church which sent its bishops to the early councils, and fell back with other survivors upon the Western parts of the Island. Such was the gulf between the warring races that no attempt was made at anytime by the British bishops to Christianise the invaders.

After an interval one of their leading luminaries, afterwards known as St David, accomplished the general conversion of what is now Wales. St Patrick sailed back in 432 to the wild regions which he had quitted, converted kingdoms which were still pagan, and brought Ireland into touch with the Church of Western Europe. Columba, born half a century after St Patrick's death, but an offspring of his Church, and imbued with his grace and fire, proved a new champion of the faith. From the monastery which he established in the island of Iona his disciples went forth to the British kingdom of Strathclyde, to the Pictish tribes of the North, and to the Anglian kingdom of Northumbria. He is the founder of the Scottish Christian Church. There was, however, a distinction in the form of Christianity which reached England through the mission of St Columba and that which was more generally accepted throughout the Christianised countries of Europe. It was monastic in its form, and it travelled from the East through Northern Ireland to its new home without touching at any moment the Roman centre.

These were the days when it was the first care of the Bishop of Rome that all Christ's sheep should be gathered into one fold. It was decided in the closing decade of the sixth century that a guide and teacher should be sent to England to diffuse and stimulate the faith, to convert the heathen, and also to bring about an effective working union between British Christians and the main body of the Church. The King of Kent had married Bertha, a daughter of the Frankish King, the descendant of Clovis, now enthroned in Paris. St Augustine, as he is known to history, began his mission in 596 under hopeful auspices. With the aid of the Frankish Princess he converted King Ethelbert, who had for reasons of policy long meditated this step. Ethelbert, as overlord of England, exercised an effective authority over the kingdoms of the South and West. He was himself, as the only English Christian ruler, in a position where he might hold out the hand to the British princes, and, by using the Christian faith as a bond of union, establish his supremacy over the whole country. This, no doubt, was also in accordance with the ideas which Augustine had carried from Rome. Thus, at the opening of the seventh century, Ethelbert and Augustine summoned a conference of the British Christian bishops. It failed for two separate reasons: first, the sullen and jealous temper of the British bishops, and, secondly, the tactless arrogance of St Augustine. All further efforts by Rome through Ethelbert and the Kentish kingdom to establish even the slightest contact with Christian Britain were inexorably repulsed. Augustine's mission therefore drew to a dignified but curtailed end.

Almost a generation passed before envoys from Rome began to penetrate into Northern England and rally its peoples to Christianity, and then it came about in the wake of political and dynastic developments. The Crown of Northumbria was gained by an exiled prince, Edwin, who by his abilities won his way, step by step, to the foremost position in England. Edwin married a Christian princess of Kent, whose religion he had promised to respect. Consequently, in her train from Canterbury to Edwin's capital at York there rode in 625 the first Roman missionary to Northern England, Paulinus, an envoy who had first come to Britain in the days of St Augustine, twenty-four years before. Paulinus converted Edwin, and the ample kingdom of Northumbria, shaped like England itself in miniature, became Christian. But this blessed event brought with it swift and dire consequences. The overlordship of Northumbria was fiercely resented by King Penda of Mercia, or, as we should now say, of the Midlands. In 633 Penda, the heathen, made an unnatural alliance with Cadwallon, the Christian British King of North Wales, with the object of overthrowing the suzerainty of Edwin and breaking the Northumbrian power. Here for the first time noticed in history British and English fought side by side. In a savage battle near Doncaster Edwin was defeated and slain, and his head —not the last—was exhibited on the ramparts of captured York. But the inherent power of Northumbria was great. The

The eighth-century Anglo-Saxon Runic Cross in Ruthwell Church, Dumfriesshire. It stands some eighteen feet high. J. ALLAN CASH

destruction of Cadwallon and the clearance from Northumbria of the wild Western Britons, whose atrocities had united all the Saxon forces in the North, was the prelude to the struggle with King Penda. Much of Mercia and East Anglia, as well as Northumbria, was recovered to Christianity by the Celtic missionaries. With the defeat and death of Penda, and upon the surge of all the passions which had been loosed, Anglo-Saxon England was definitely rallied to the Christian faith.

Henceforward the issue is no longer whether the Island shall be Christian or

13

Roman mosaic of the first half of the third century, found in Leadenhall Street, London. BRITISH MUSEUM

Right: *The legend of King Arthur and the Knights of the Round Table became an ever-popular subject for storytellers and artists. From the fourteenth-century* Waresbrut MS *in the British Museum comes the illustration of the King asleep in a boat. The thirteenth-century* Flores Historiarum *in Westminster Abbey provides an illustration depicting his Coronation.*
COURTESY: THE DEAN AND CHAPTER

Efuncto autem rege que
neruur wntifices cu clero reg

A roundel from the twelfth-century Guthlac Roll shows St Guthlac, the "comforter" of King Ethelbald's exile, being taken by Tetwine up the River Welland to Crowland, in the Fen District, to begin his hermitage in 699. Crowland Abbey was built over the Saint's earthly remains. BRITISH MUSEUM

pagan, but whether the Roman or the Celtic view of Christianity shall prevail. These differences persisted across the centuries, much debated by all the parties concerned. The celebrated and largely successful attempt to solve them took place at the Synod of Whitby in 663. The issues hung in the balance, but in the end after much pious dissertation the decision was taken that the Church of Northumbria should be a definite part of the Church of Rome and of the Catholic system. Mercia soon afterwards conformed. These events brought Northumbria to her zenith. In Britain for the first time there was achieved a unity of faith, morals, and Church government covering five-sixths of the Island.

The Papacy realised that its efforts to guide and govern British Christianity through the kingdom of Kent had been misplaced. Two fresh emissaries were chosen in 668 to carry the light into the Northern mists, the first a native of Asia Minor, Theodore of Tarsus, the second an African named Hadrian from Carthage. When their work was finished

the Anglican Church raised its mitred front in a majesty which has not yet been dimmed. Before he died in 690 Theodore had increased the number of bishoprics from seven to fourteen, and by his administrative skill he gave the Church a new cohesion. This remarkable Asiatic was the earliest of the statesmen of England, and guided her steps with fruitful wisdom.

There followed a long and intricate rivalry for leadership between the various Anglo-Saxon kings which occupied the seventh and eighth centuries. Bede, a monk of high ability, alone attempts to paint for us, and, so far as he can, explain the spectacle of Anglo-Saxon England in its first phase: seven kingdoms of varying strength, all professing the Gospel of Christ, and striving over each other for mastery by force and fraud.

The leadership of Saxon England passed to Mercia. For nearly eighty years two Mercian kings asserted or maintained their ascendancy over all England south of the Humber. Ethelbald took to styling himself "King of the Southern English" and "King of Britain". Little is known of Offa, who reigned for the second forty years, but the imprint of his power is visible not only throughout England but upon the Continent; he was reputed to be the first "King of all the English", and he had the first quarrel since Roman times with the mainland. Charlemagne wished one of his sons to marry one of Offa's daughters. Here we have an important proof of the esteem in which the Englishman was held. Offa stipulated that his son must simultaneously marry a daughter of Charlemagne. The founder of the Holy Roman Empire appeared at first incensed at this assumption of equality, but after a while he found it expedient to renew his friendship with Offa. It seems that "the King of the English" had placed an embargo upon Continental merchandise, and the inconvenience of this retaliation speedily overcame all points of pride and sentiment. Here was an English king who ruled over the greatest part of the Island, whose trade was important, and whose daughters were fit consorts for the

monasteries were the home, and of which only fragments have come down to us, had come into being. Bede was universally honoured as the greatest scholar of his day. In the eighth century indeed England had claims to stand in the van of Western culture. England, with an independent character and personality, might scarcely yet be a part of a world civilisation as in Roman times, but there was a new England, closer than ever before to national unity, and with a native genius of her own.

Measure for measure, what the Saxon pirates had given to the Britons was meted out to the English after the lapse of four hundred years. In the eighth century a vehement manifestation of conquering energy appeared in Scandinavia. Norway, Sweden, and Denmark threw up bands of formidable fighting men, who, in addition to all their other martial qualities, were the hardy rovers of the sea. The relations between the Danes and the Norwegians were tangled and vary-ing. Sometimes they raided in collusion; sometimes they fought each other in desper-ate battles; but to Saxon England they presented themselves in the common guise of a merciless scourge.

In 793, on a January morning, the wealthy monastic settlement of Lindisfarne (or Holy Island), off the Northumbrian coast, was suddenly attacked by a powerful fleet from Denmark. The news of the atrocity travelled far and wide, not only in England but throughout Europe, and the loud cry of the Church sounded a general alarm. The Vikings, having a large choice of action, allowed an interval of recovery before paying another visit. It was not till 835 that the

sons of Charles the Great. We have a tangible monument of Offa in the immense dyke which he caused to be built between con-verted Saxon England and the still uncon-quered British. It conveys to us an idea of the magnitude and force of Offa's kingdom.

Art and culture grew in the track of order. The English had brought with them from their Continental home a vigorous barbaric art and a primitive poetry. Once established in the Island, this art was profoundly affected by the Celtic genius for curve and colour, a genius suppressed by Roman provincialism, but breaking out again as soon as the Roman hand was removed. Christianity gave them a new range of subjects to adorn. The results are seen in such masterpieces as the Lindis-farne Gospels and the sculptured crosses of Northern England. A whole world of refinement and civilisation of which the

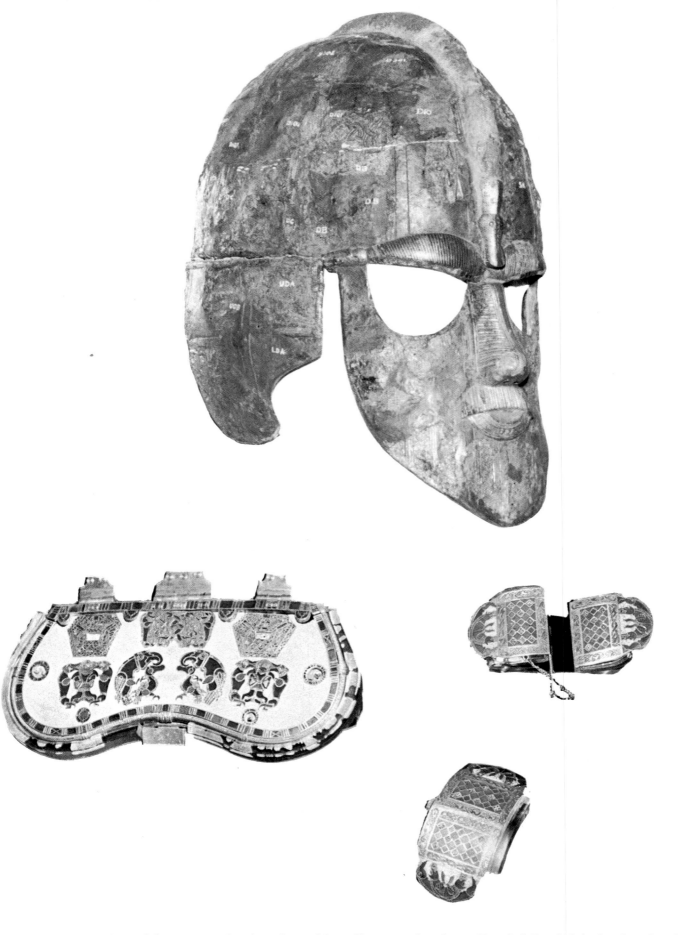

Some of the treasures taken from the royal long-ship excavated at Sutton Hoo, Suffolk, which is thought to have been interred circa 650. At the top is the reconstructed royal helmet; on the left the gold frame and the ornamental plaques with garnets and "millefiori" enamels of a purse lid; and on the right two gold shoulder-clasps, both hinged, and again with garnets and "millefiori" enamels. BRITISH MUSEUM

Right: A decorative initial from the eighth-century Lindisfarne Gospels. BRITISH MUSEUM

+ Lucas uitulus ·

on ginneð godspell

INCIPIT EUANGELIUM

æft lucas

SECUNDUM LUCAM ...

forðon

QUONIAM

aec soð

QUIDEM

monigo cunnendo

MULTI CONATI

woeron ðte hiu ge

SUNT ORDINA

endebrednadon ðiu gesaga

RE NARRATIONEM

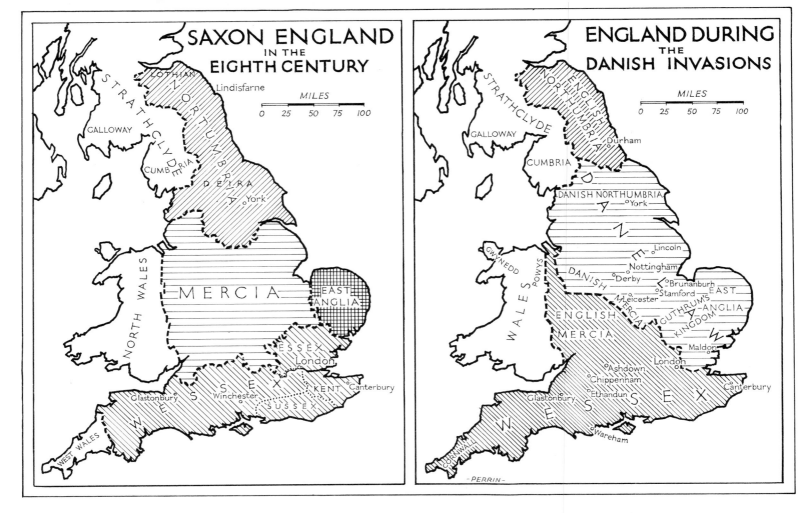

SAXON ENGLAND IN THE EIGHTH CENTURY

ENGLAND DURING THE DANISH INVASIONS

storm broke in fury, and fleets, sometimes of three or four hundred vessels, rowed up the rivers of England, France, and Russia in predatory enterprises on the greatest scale. For thirty years Southern England was constantly attacked. Paris was more than once besieged. Constantinople was assaulted. The harbour towns in Ireland were captured and held. The Swedish element penetrated into the heart of Russia, ruling the river towns and holding the trade to ransom. The Norwegian Vikings, coming from a still more severe climate, found the Scottish islands good for settlement. They reached Greenland and Stoneland (Labrador). They sailed up the St Lawrence. They discovered America; but they set little store by the achievement.

For a long time no permanent foothold was gained in Britain or France. It was not until 865, when resistance on the Continent had temporarily stiffened, that the great Danish invasion of Northumbria and Eastern England began. Saxon England was at this time ripe for the sickle. On all sides were abbeys and monasteries, churches, and even

cathedrals, possessed in that starveling age of treasures of gold and silver, of jewels, and also large stores of food, wine, and such luxuries as were known. To an undue subservience to the Church the English at this time added military mismanagement. The local noble, upon the summons of his chief or king, could call upon the able-bodied cultivators of the soil to serve in their own district for about forty days. This service, in the "fyrd", was grudgingly given, and when it was over the army dispersed without paying regard to the enemies who might be afoot or the purposes for which the campaign had been undertaken. The Danes and Norsemen had not only the advantages of surprise which sea-power so long imparted, but they showed both mobility and skill on land. Their stratagems have been highly praised. Among these "feigned flight" was foremost. They were, in fact, the most audacious and treacherous type of pirate and shark that had ever yet appeared, and, owing to the very defective organisation of the Saxons and the conditions of the period, they achieved a fuller realisation of their desires than any of those who have emulated their proficiency—and there have been many.

Ivar "the Boneless" was a warrior of command and guile. He was the master-mind behind the Scandinavian invasion of England in the last quarter of the ninth century. In the spring of 866 his powerful army, organised on the basis of ships' companies, but now all mounted not for fighting but for locomotion, rode north along the old Roman road and was ferried across the Humber. He laid siege to York. And now—too late—the Northumbrians, who had been divided in their loyalties between two rival kings, forgot their feuds and united in one final effort. They attacked the Danish army before York. The defenders sallied out, and in the confusion the Vikings defeated them all with grievous slaughter, killing both their kings and destroying completely their power of resistance. This was the end of Northumbria.

But Ivar's object was nothing less than the conquest of Mercia, which, as all men knew, had for nearly a hundred years represented the strength of England. The King of Mercia called for help from Wessex. The old King of Wessex was dead, but his two sons, Ethelred and Alfred, answered the appeal. They marched to his aid, but the Mercians flinched and preferred a parley. Ivar warred with policy as well as arms. While the Danes in their formidable attempt at conquest spread out from East Anglia, subdued Mercia, and ravaged Northumbria, the King of Wessex and his brother Alfred quietly built up their strength.

The Danish raiders now stayed longer every year. Thus again behind piracy and rapine there grew the process of settlement. But these settlements of the Danes differed from those of the Saxons; they were the encampment of armies, and their boundaries were the fighting fronts sustained by a series of fortified towns. Stamford, Nottingham, Lincoln, Derby, Leicester were the bases of the new invading force. The Saxons, now for four centuries entitled to be deemed the owners of the soil, very nearly succumbed completely to the Danish inroads. That they did not was due—as almost every critical turn of historic fortune has been due—to the sudden apparition in an era of confusion and decay of one of the great figures of history.

When the dynasties of Kent, Northumbria, and Mercia had disappeared all eyes turned to Wessex, where there was a royal House going back without a break to the first years of the Saxon settlement. The Danes had occupied London, not then the English capital, but a town in the kingdom of Mercia, and their army had fortified itself at Reading. Moving forward, they met the forces of the West Saxons on the Berkshire Downs, and here, in January 871, was fought the Battle of Ashdown. The fight was long and hard. At last the Danes gave way, and, hotly pursued, fled back to Reading. This was the first time the invaders had been beaten in the field. The last of the Saxon kingdoms had withstood the assault upon it.

All through the year 871 the two armies waged deadly war. At twenty-four Alfred became King, and entered upon a desperate inheritance. Seven or eight battles were fought, and we are told the Danes usually held the field. At Wilton, in the summer, about a month after Alfred had assumed the Crown, he sustained a definite defeat in the heart of his own country. On the morrow of this misfortune Alfred thought it best to come to terms while he still had an army. We do not know the conditions, but there is no doubt that a heavy payment was among them. By this inglorious treaty and stubborn campaign Alfred secured five years in which to consolidate his power. Still maintaining

King Alfred (849–900)

their grip on London, the Danes moved back to the Midlands, which were now in complete submission.

Alfred and the men of Wessex had proved

too stubborn a foe for easy subjugation. Some of the Danes wished to settle on the lands they already held. Henceforward they began to till the ground for a livelihood. From Yorkshire to Norfolk this sturdy, upstanding stock took root. As time passed they forgot the sea; they forgot the army; they thought only of the land—their own land. Although they were sufficiently skilful agriculturists, there was nothing they could teach the older inhabitants; they brought no new implements or methods, but they were resolved to learn. Thus the Danish differs in many ways from the Saxon settlement four hundred years earlier. There was no idea of exterminating the older population. The two languages were not very different; the way of life, the methods of cultivation, very much the same. The blood-stream of these vigorous individualists, proud and successful men of the sword, mingled henceforward in the Island race. They had a different view of social justice from that entertained by the manorialised Saxons. Their customary laws as they gradually took shape were an undoubted improvement upon the Saxon theme. Scandinavian England reared a free peasant population which the burdens of taxation and defence had made difficult in Wessex and English Mercia. It remained only for conversion to Christianity to mingle these races inextricably in the soul and body of a nation.

Alfred's dear-bought truce was over, and in January 878 occurred the most surprising reversal of his fortunes. His headquarters and Court lay at Chippenham, in Wiltshire. It was Twelfth Night, and the Saxons, who in these days of torment refreshed and fortified themselves by celebrating the feasts of the Church, were off their guard, engaged in pious exercises, or perhaps even drunk. Down swept the ravaging foe. The whole army of Wessex, sole guarantee of England south of the Thames, was dashed into confusion. A handful of officers and personal attendants hid themselves with Alfred in the marshes and forests of Somerset and the Isle of Athelney which rose from the quags. We see the warrior-king disguised as a minstrel harping in the Danish camps. We see him acting as kitchen-boy to a Saxon housewife in the celebrated story of Alfred and the cakes. Low were the fortunes of the once ruthless English.

The leaders of the Danish army felt sure at this time that mastery was in their hands. To the people of Wessex it seemed that all was over. Their forces were dispersed, the country overrun; their King, if alive, was a fugitive in hiding. It is the supreme proof of Alfred's quality that he was able in such a plight to exercise his full authority and keep contact with his subjects.

Towards the end of Lent the Danes suffered an unexpected misfortune in an attack on one of Alfred's strongholds on Exmoor.

The Christians . . . judged it to be better either to suffer death or to gain the victory. Accordingly at daybreak they suddenly rushed forth against the heathen, and at the first attack they laid low most of the enemy, including their king. A few only by flight escaped to their ships.[1]

Eight hundred Danes were killed. Alfred, cheered by this news and striving to take the field again, continued a brigand warfare against the enemy while sending his messengers to summon the "fyrd", or local militia, for the end of May. All the fighting men came back. Battle must be sought before they lost interest. Alfred advanced to Ethandun—now Edington—and on the bare downs was fought the largest and culminating battle of Alfred's wars. All was staked. But the heathen had lost the favour of God through their violated oath, and eventually from this or other causes they fled from the cruel and clanging field. This time Alfred's pursuit was fruitful. Guthrum, King of the Viking army, so lately master of the one unconquered English kingdom, found himself penned in his camp. Bishop Asser says, "the heathen, terrified by hunger, cold, and fear, and at the last full of despair, begged for peace".

[1] Quoted in Hodgkin, vol. ii, pp. 565–6.

They offered to give without return as many hostages as Alfred should care to pick and to depart forthwith. But Alfred had had longer ends in view. He could have starved them into surrender and slaughtered them to a man. He wished instead to divide the land with them, and that the two races, in spite of fearful injuries given and received, should dwell together in amity. He received Guthrum with thirty prominent buccaneers in his camp. He stood godfather to Guthrum; he raised him from the font; he entertained him for twelve days; he presented him and his warriors with costly gifts; he called him his son. This sublime power to rise above the whole force of circumstances, to remain unbiased by the extremes of victory or defeat, to persevere in the teeth of disaster, to greet returning fortune with a cool eye, to have faith in men after repeated betrayals, raises Alfred far above the turmoil of barbaric wars to his pinnacle of deathless glory.

Fourteen years intervened between the victory of Ethandun and any serious Danish attack. Alfred worked ceaselessly to strengthen his realm. He reorganised the "fyrd", dividing it into two classes which practised a rotation of service. He saw too the vision of English sea-power. He made great departures in ship design, and hoped to beat the Viking numbers by fewer ships of much larger size. These conclusions have only recently become antiquated. In spite of the disorders a definite treaty was achieved after the reconquest of London in 886. The treaty defined a political boundary running up the Thames, up the Lea, along the Lea to its source, then straight to Bedford, and after by the Ouse to Watling Street, beyond which no agreement was made. This line followed no natural frontiers. It recognised a war front.

King Alfred's Book of Laws, or Dooms, as set out in the existing laws of Kent, Wessex, and Mercia, attempted to blend the Mosaic code with Christian principles and old Germanic customs. The Laws of Alfred, continually amplified by his successors, grew into that body of customary law administered by the shire and hundred courts which, under

A page from the Saxon Chronicle, set on foot by King Alfred. BRITISH MUSEUM

the name of the Laws of St Edward (the Confessor), the Norman kings undertook to respect, and out of which, with much manipulation by feudal lawyers, the Common Law was founded. He sought to reform the monastic life, which in the general confusion had grossly degenerated. He it was who set on foot the compiling of the Saxon Chronicle. The Christian culture of his Court sharply contrasted with the feckless barbarism of Viking life. The older race was to tame the warriors and teach them the arts of peace, and show them the value of a settled common existence. We are watching the birth of a nation. The result of Alfred's work was the future mingling of Saxon and Dane in a common Christian England.

One final war awaited Alfred. It was a crisis in the Viking story. Guthrum died in 891, and the pact which he had sworn with Alfred, and loosely kept, ended. Suddenly in the autumn of 892 a hostile armada of two hundred and fifty ships appeared off Lympne, carrying to the invasion of England "the Great Heathen Army" that had ravaged France. Unlike Charlemagne, Alfred had a valiant son. The King, in ill-health, is not often seen in this phase at the head of armies; we have glimpses of him, but the great episodes of the war were centred, as they should be, upon the young leaders. The English beat the Vikings. In 896 this third war petered out, and the Vikings, whose strength seemed at this time to be in decline, dispersed, some settling in the Danelaw, some going back to France.

Alfred died in 899, but the struggle with the Vikings had yet to pass through strangely contrasted phases. In his son Edward, who was immediately acclaimed King, the armies had already found a redoubtable leader. Edward the Elder, as he was afterwards called, and his sister Ethelfleda, "the Lady of the Mercians", conducted the national war in common, and carried its success to heights which Alfred never knew. In 917 the whole resistance of East Anglia collapsed, and all the Danish leaders submitted to Edward as their protector and lord. In this hour of success Ethelfleda died, and Edward, hastening to Tamworth, was invited by the nobles of Mercia to occupy the vacant throne. Alfred's son was now undisputed King of all England south of the Humber, and the British princes of North and South Wales hastened to offer their perpetual allegiance. Edward the Elder reigned five years more in triumphant peace, and when he died in 924 his authority and his gifts passed to a third remarkable sovereign.

Athelstan, the third of the great West Saxon kings, sought at first, in accordance with the traditions of his House, peaceful relations with the unconquered parts of the Danelaw; but upon disputes arising he marched into Yorkshire in 926, and there established himself. Northumbria submitted; the Kings of the Scots and of Strathclyde acknowledged him as their "father and lord", and the Welsh princes agreed to pay tribute. There was an uneasy interlude; then in 933

came a campaign against the Scots, and in 937 a general rebellion and renewed war, organised by all the hitherto defeated characters in the drama. The victory of the English was overwhelming. Thus did King Alfred's grandson, the valiant Athelstan, become one of the first sovereigns of Western Europe. He styled himself on coin and charter *Rex totius Britanniæ*.

For eighty years five warrior-kings—Alfred, Edward, Athelstan, Edmund, and Edred—defeated the invaders. The English rule was now restored, though in a form changed by the passage of time, over the whole country. Yet underneath it there had grown up, deeply rooted in the soil, a Danish settlement covering the great Eastern plain, in which Danish blood and Danish customs survived under the authority of the English king. Finally, with this military and political revival marched a great rebirth of monastic life and learning and the beginning of our native English literature. From whatever point of view we regard it, the tenth century is a decisive step forward in the destinies of

King Athelstan (895-939)

Above, right: *King Edward the Elder (d. 924)*

King Edgar (944-75)

England. In the brilliant and peaceful reign of Edgar all this long building had reached its culmination. It must have seemed to contemporaries that with the magnificent Coronation at Bath in 973 the seal was set on the unity of the realm. Everywhere the courts are sitting regularly, in shire

25

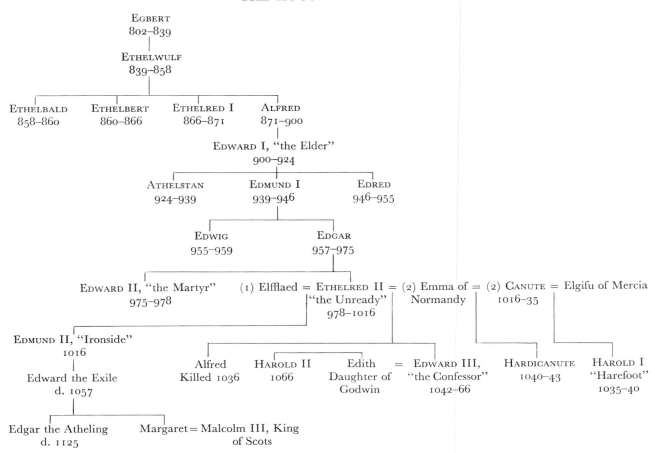

EGBERT
802–839

ETHELWULF
839–858

ETHELBALD   ETHELBERT   ETHELRED I   ALFRED
858–860   860–866   866–871   871–900

EDWARD I, "the Elder"
900–924

ATHELSTAN   EDMUND I   EDRED
924–939   939–946   946–955

EDWIG   EDGAR
955–959   957–975

EDWARD II, "the Martyr"   (1) Elfflaed = ETHELRED II = (2) Emma of = (2) CANUTE = Elgifu of Mercia
975–978   "the Unready"   Normandy   1016–35
                                         978–1016

EDMUND II, "Ironside"
1016
                        Alfred   HAROLD II   Edith   = EDWARD III,   HARDICANUTE   HAROLD I
Edward the Exile   Killed 1036 1066   Daughter of   "the Confessor" 1040–43   "Harefoot"
d. 1057   Godwin   1042–66   1035–40

Edgar the Atheling   Margaret = Malcolm III, King
d. 1125   of Scots

and borough and hundred; there is one coinage, and one system of weights and measures. The arts of building and decoration are reviving; learning begins to flourish again in the Church; there is a literary language, a King's English, which all educated men write. Civilisation had been restored to the Island.

But now the political fabric which nurtured it was about to be overthrown. Now a child, a weakling, a vacillator, a faithless, feckless creature, succeeded to the warrior throne. We have reached the days of Ethelred the Unready. In 980 serious raids began again. We have an epic poem upon "The Battle of Maldon", fought in 991. No sooner had it begun than the English were worsted. Then followed the most shameful period of Danegeld. We have seen that Alfred in his day had never hesitated to use money as well as arms. Ethelred used money instead of arms. Panic-stricken, he planned the slaughter

of all Danes in the South of England, whether in his pay or living peaceably on the land. This atrocious design was executed in 1002 on St Brice's Day. Among the victims was Gunnhild, the wife of one of the principal Vikings, and sister of Sweyn, King of Denmark. Sweyn swore implacable revenge, and for two years executed it upon the wretched Islanders. The fury of the avenger was not slaked by blood. A desperate effort was now made to build a fleet. Its leaders quarrelled. Some ships were sunk in the fighting; others were lost in a storm, and the rest were shamefully abandoned by the naval commanders. It is vain to recount further the catalogue of miseries. It suffices to note that in 1013 Sweyn, accompanied by his younger son, Canute, though repulsed from London, was proclaimed King of England, while Ethelred fled for refuge to the Duke of Normandy, whose sister he had married. On these triumphs Sweyn died at the beginning of

King Ethelred the Unready (968–1016)

26

King Canute (995–1035) and Queen Elgifu at the dedication of Newminster Abbey, Winchester. From the eleventh-century Hyde Abbey Register. BRITISH MUSEUM

to rally his forces for the renewal of the struggle; but in 1016, at twenty-two years of age, Edmund Ironside died, and the whole realm abandoned itself to despair. All resistance, moral and military, collapsed before the Dane.

Canute became the ruling sovereign of the North, and was reckoned as having five or six kingdoms under him. But of all his realms Canute chose England for his home and capital. He married Emma of Normandy, the widow of Ethelred, and so forestalled any action by the Duke of Normandy on behalf of her descendants by Ethelred. He ruled according to the laws, and he made it known that these were to be administered in austere detachment from his executive authority. He built churches, he professed high devotion to the Christian faith and to the Papal diadem. His daughter was married to the Emperor Conrad's eldest son, who ultimately carried his empire across Schleswig to the banks of the Eider. Here again we see the power of a great man to bring order out of ceaseless broils and command harmony and unity to be his servants, and how the lack of such men has to be paid for by the inestimable suffering of the many.

Meanwhile, across the waters of the English Channel, a new military power was growing up. The Viking settlement founded in Normandy in the early years of the tenth century had become the most vigorous military State in France. In Normandy a class of knights and nobles arose who held their lands in return for military service, and sublet to inferior tenants upon the same basis. The Normans, with their craving for legality and logic, framed a general scheme of society, from which there soon emerged an excellent army. The dukes of Normandy created relations with the Church which became a model for medieval Europe. It was from this virile and well-organised land that the future rulers of England were to come.

In 1035 Canute died, and his empire with him. He left three sons, two by a former wife and one, Hardicanute, by Emma. Sweyn reigned in Norway for a spell, but his two

1014. But soon the young Danish prince, Canute, set forth to claim the English Crown.

At this moment the flame of Alfred's line rose again in Ethelred's son, Edmund—Edmund Ironside, as he soon was called. He gained battles, he relieved London, he contended with every form of treachery; the hearts of all men went out to him. Ethelred died, and Edmund, last hope of the English, was acclaimed King. In spite of all odds and a heavy defeat he was strong enough to make a partition of the realm, and then set himself

The residence of a Saxon nobleman. A tenth-century manuscript illustration. BRITISH MUSEUM

brothers who ruled England were short-lived, and within seven years the throne of England was again vacant. There was still living in exile in Normandy Edward, the remaining son of Ethelred and Emma. The West Saxon line was the oldest in Europe. A Wessex earl, Godwin, was the leader of the Danish party in England. Godwin saw that he could consolidate his power and combine both English and Danish support by making Edward King.

Edward was a quiet, pious person, without liking for war or much aptitude for administration. His Norman upbringing made him the willing though gentle agent of Norman influence, so far as Earl Godwin would allow.

King Edward the Confessor (d. 1066) and his Abbey Church of Westminster, from the Bayeux Tapestry. BRITISH MUSEUM

For some years a bitter intrigue was carried on between Norman and Anglo-Danish influences at the English Court. A crisis came in the year 1051, when the Norman party at Court succeeded in driving Godwin into exile. But in the following year Godwin returned, backed by a force raised in Flanders, and with the active help of his son Harold. Many of the principal Norman agents in the country were expelled, and the authority of the Godwin family was felt again throughout the land.

The political condition of England at the close of the reign of Edward the Confessor was one of widespread weakness. Illuminated manuscripts, sculpture, metalwork, and architecture of much artistic merit were still produced, religious life flourished, and a basis of sound law and administration remained, but the virtues and vigour of Alfred's posterity were exhausted and the Saxon monarchy itself was in decline. The Island had come to count for little on the Continent, and had lost the thread of its own progress. The defences, both of the coast and of the towns, were neglected. To the coming conquerors the whole system, social, moral, political, and military, seemed effete.

The figure of Edward the Confessor comes down to us faint, misty, frail. The medieval legend, carefully fostered by the Church, whose devoted servant he was, surpassed the man. Canonised in 1161, he lived for centuries in the memories of the Saxon folk. The Normans also had an interest in his fame. For them he was the King by whose wisdom the Crown had been left, or so they claimed, to their Duke. Hence both sides blessed his memory, and until England appropriated St George during the Hundred Years War St Edward the Confessor was the kingdom's patron saint. St George proved undoubtedly more suitable to the Islanders' needs, moods, and character.

CHAPTER TWO

The Making of the Nation

WILLIAM of Normandy had a virile origin and a hard career. The Normans claimed that their Duke held his cousin Edward's promise of the throne. He and his knights looked out upon the world with fearless and adventurous eyes. William was in close touch with the Saxon Court, and had watched every move on the part of the supporters of the Anglo-Danish party, headed by Godwin and his son Harold.

Fate played startlingly into the hands of the Norman Duke. On some visit of inspection, probably in 1064, Harold was driven by the winds on to the French coast. The Count of Ponthieu reluctantly relinquished his windfall and conducted Harold to the Norman Court. All this story is told with irresistible charm in the tapestry chronicle of the reign commonly attributed to William's wife, Queen Matilda, but actually designed by English artists under the guidance of his half-brother, Odo, Bishop of Bayeux. It is probable that Harold swore a solemn oath to William to renounce all rights or designs upon the English Crown, and it is likely that if he had not done so he might never have seen either crown or England again.

At length, in January 1066, Edward the Confessor died, absolved, we trust, from such worldly sins as he had been tempted to commit. With his dying breath, in spite of his alleged promise to William, he is supposed to have commended Harold, his young, valiant counsellor and guide, as the best choice for the Crown which the Witan, or Council, could make. At any rate, Harold, at the beginning of the fateful year 1066, was blithely accepted by London, the Midlands, and the South, and crowned King with all solemnity in Westminster Abbey. This event opened again the gates of war. Every aspiring thane who heard the news of Harold's

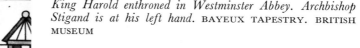
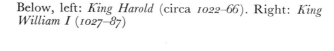

King Harold enthroned in Westminster Abbey. Archbishop Stigand is at his left hand. BAYEUX TAPESTRY. BRITISH MUSEUM

Below, left: *King Harold* (circa *1022–66*). Right: *King William I* (*1027–87*)

King Harold, standing with his bodyguard by the royal standard of the Dragon of Wessex, is struck in the eye by a Norman arrow. BAYEUX TAPESTRY

elevation was conscious of an affront, and also of the wide ranges open to ability and the sword. Moreover, the entire structure of the feudal world rested upon the sanctity of oaths. Against the breakers of oaths the censures both of chivalry and the Church were combined with blasting force. Two rival projects of invasion were speedily prepared. The successors of Canute in Norway determined to revive their traditions of English sovereignty. An expedition was already being organised when Tostig, Harold's exiled and revengeful half-brother, ousted from his Earldom of Northumbria, arrived with full accounts of the crisis in the Island and of the weak state of its defences. King Harold Hardrada set forth to conquer the English Crown.

Harold of England was thus faced with a double invasion from the North-East and from the South. In September 1066 he heard that a Norwegian fleet, with Hardrada and Tostig on board, had sailed up the Humber, beaten the local levies under Earls Edwin and Morcar, and encamped near York at Stamford Bridge. He now showed the fighting qualities he possessed. Within five days of the defeat of Edwin and Morcar Harold reached York, and the same day marched to confront the Norwegian army ten miles from the city. Hardrada was hit by an arrow in the throat, and Tostig, assuming the command, paid for his restless malice with his life. Though the Battle of Stamford Bridge has been overshadowed by Hastings it has a claim to be regarded as one of the decisive contests of English history. Never again was a Scandinavian army able seriously to threaten the power of an English king or the unity of the realm.

William the Conqueror's invasion of England was planned like a business enterprise.

31

A Saxon axe-man. BIBLIOTHÈQUE MUNICIPALE, ANGERS

The resources of Normandy were obviously unequal to the task; but the Duke's name was famous throughout the feudal world, and the idea of seizing and dividing England commended itself to the martial nobility of many lands. During the summer of 1066 this great gathering of audacious buccaneers, land-hungry, war-hungry, assembled in a merry company around St Valery, at the mouth of the Somme. But the winds were contrary. For six whole weeks there was no day when the south wind blew. The bones of St Edmund were brought from the Church of St Valery and carried with military and religious pomp along the sea-shore. This proved effective, for the very next day the wind changed, not indeed to the south, but to the south-west. William thought this sufficient, and gave the signal. On September 28 the fleet hove in sight, and all came safely to anchor in Pevensey Bay.

Meanwhile, Harold and his house-carls, sadly depleted by the slaughter of Stamford Bridge, jingled down Ermine Street on their ponies. Remaining only five days in London, Harold marched out towards Pevensey, and in the evening of October 13 took up his position upon the slope of a hill which barred the direct march upon the capital. The military opinion of those as of these days has criticised his staking all upon an immediate battle. Some have suggested that he should have used the tactics which eleven hundred years before Cassivellaunus had employed against Cæsar. But these critics overlook the fact that whereas the Roman army consisted only of infantry, and the British only of charioteers and horsemen, Duke William's was essentially a cavalry force assisted by archers, while Harold had nothing but foot-soldiers who used horses only as transport. King Harold had great confidence in his redoubtable axe-men, and it was in good heart that he formed his shield-wall on the morning of October 14. There is a great dispute about the numbers engaged. Some modern authorities suppose the battle was fought by five or six thousand Norman knights and men-at-arms, with a few thousand archers, against eight to ten thousand axe- and spear-men, and the numbers on both sides may have been fewer. However it may be, at the first streak of dawn William set out from his camp at Pevensey, resolved to put all to the test; and Harold, eight miles away, awaited him in resolute array.

The cavalry charges of William's mail-clad knights, cumbersome in manœuvre, beat in vain upon the dense, ordered masses of the English. Neither the arrow hail nor the assaults of the horsemen could prevail against them. Never, it was said, had the Norman knights met foot-soldiers of this stubbornness. The autumn afternoon was far spent before any result had been achieved, and it was then that William adopted the time-honoured ruse of a feigned retreat. The house-carls around Harold preserved their discipline and kept their ranks, but the sense of relief to the less trained forces after these hours of combat was such that seeing their enemy in flight proved irresistible. They surged forward on the impulse of victory, and when half-way down the hill were savagely slaughtered by William's horsemen. There remained, as the dusk grew, only the valiant bodyguard who fought round the King and his standard. His brothers, Gyrth and Leofwine, had already been killed. William now directed his archers to shoot high into the air, so that the arrows would fall behind the shield-wall, and one of these pierced Harold in the right eye, inflicting a mortal wound. He fell at the foot of the royal standard, unconquerable except by death, which does not count in honour. The hard-fought battle was now decided.

Duke William knew that his work was but begun. He was a prime exponent of the doctrine, so well known in this civilised age as "frightfulness"[1]—of mass terrorism through the spectacle of bloody and merciless examples. When William arrived near London he marched round the city by a circuitous route, isolating it by a belt of cruel desolation. On Christmas Day Aldred, Archbishop of York, crowned him King of England at Westminster. He rapidly established his power over all England south of the Humber.

The North still remained under its Saxon lords, Edwin and Morcar, unsubdued and defiant. From coast to coast the whole region was laid desolate, and hunted men took refuge in the wooded valleys of Yorkshire, to die of famine and exposure, or to sell themselves into slavery for food. The Saxon resistance died hard. Legends and chroniclers have painted for us the last stand of Hereward the Wake in the broad wastes of the fens round Ely. Not until five years after Hastings, in 1071, was Hereward put down. For at least twenty years after the invasion the Normans were an army camped in a hostile country, holding the population down by the castles at key points.

Here were the Normans entrenched on English soil, masters of the land and the fullness thereof. An armed warrior from Anjou or Maine or Brittany, or even from beyond the Alps and the Pyrenees, took possession of manor and county, according to his rank and prowess, and set to work to make himself secure. Everywhere castles arose. These were not at first the massive stone structures of a later century; they were simply fortified military posts consisting of an earthen rampart and a stockade, and a central keep made of logs. In their early days the Normans borrowed no manners and few customs from the Islanders. The only culture was French.

[1] Written early in 1939.

The Domesday Book. PUBLIC RECORD OFFICE

E dimence vin. jour du mois d'octobre ensieu uant lan de gra ce mil.lxvi. Le duc guillame fut a tresgrant solempnite par les prelatz z hault barons dangleterre couronne oinct et sacre a roy a westmonstier emprez londres. Aprez son couronnement il demoura sur le pais enquerat

de lestre des jens qui parauant auoient fait serment de le tenir a roy aprez le trespas du bon roy edouard et sen estoient pariurez mais par sa misericorde le pardo na atous. Aprez ceulx qui en cel le sa conqueste lauoient seru aux aucuns donna denfert. Aux autres il fist auoir en ma riage aucunes nobles dames Ou pais heritiere de trans ter res a cause de leurs marie qui

Surviving Saxon notables sent their sons to the monasteries of France for education. The English repeated the experience of the ancient Britons; all who could learnt French, as formerly the contemporaries of Boadicea had learnt Latin. At first the conquerors, who despised the uncouth English as louts and boors, ruled by the force of sharpened steel. But very soon in true Norman fashion they intermarried with the free population and identified themselves with their English past.

William's work in England is the more remarkable from the fact that all the time as Duke of Normandy he was involved in endless intrigues and conflicts with the King of France. Queen Matilda was a capable regent at Rouen, but plagued by the turbulence of her sons. Matilda died, and with increasing years William became fiercer in mood. When death drew near, his sons William and Henry came to him. William, whose one virtue had been filial fidelity, was named to succeed the Conqueror in England. The graceless Robert would rule in Normandy at last. For the youngest, Henry, there was nothing but five thousand pounds of silver, and the prophecy that he would one day reign over a united Anglo-Norman nation. On Thursday, September 9, 1087, as the early bells of Rouen Cathedral echoed over the hills, William and his authority died.

The Normans introduced into England their system of land tenure based upon military service. A military caste was imposed from above. The essence of Norman feudalism was that the land remained under the lord, whatever the man might do. Thus the landed pyramid rose up tier by tier to the King, until every acre in the country could be registered as held of somebody by some form of service. But the mass of the inhabitants were only indirectly affected by the change, and the feudal superstructure was for many years as unsure as it was impressive. The history of many an English village begins with an entry in Domesday Book. The result

of this famous survey showed that the underlying structure of England and its peasant life were little changed by the shock of the invasion.

The Normans were administrators and lawyers rather than legislators. Their centre of government was the royal Curia, the final court of appeal and the instrument of supervision; here were preserved and developed the financial and secretarial methods of the Anglo-Saxon kingdom. Not only the courts, but also the dues and taxes such as Danegeld, were preserved for the sake of the Norman revenues. Thus in the future government of England both Norman and Saxon institutions were unconsciously but profoundly blended. This survival of the hundred, the county court, and the sheriff makes the great difference between English and Continental feudalism.

In the Norman settlement lay the germ of a constitutional Opposition, with the effect if not the design of controlling the Government, not breaking it up. The seat of this potential Opposition was found in the counties, among the smaller nobility and their untitled descendants, Justices of the Peace and knights of the shire. This is the class—people of some consideration in the neighbourhood, with leisure to go to the sheriff's court and thereafter to Westminster. Out of this process in time the Pyms and Hampdens arose.

The Conquest was the supreme achievement of the Norman race. It linked the history of England anew to Europe, and prevented for ever a drift into the narrower orbit of a Scandinavian empire. Henceforward English history marched with that of races and lands south of the Channel.

Once the secular conquest had been made secure William turned to the religious sphere. The key appointment was the Archbishopric of Canterbury. In 1070 the Saxon Stigand was deposed and succeeded by Lanfranc. In a series of councils such as had not been held in England since the days of Theodore

35

THE NORMAN AND PLANTAGENET DYNASTIES

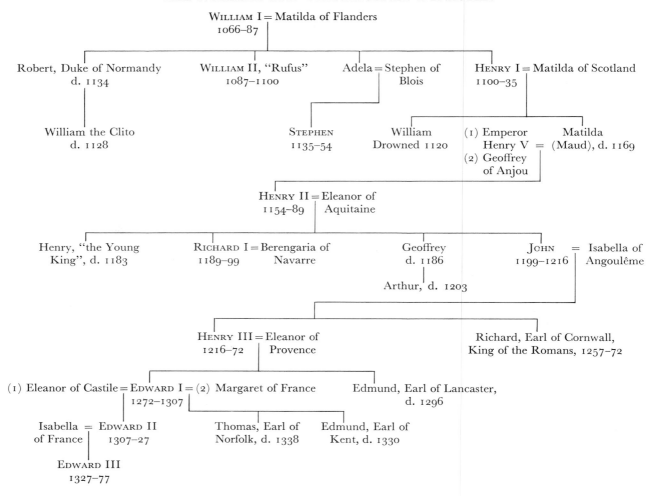

WILLIAM I = Matilda of Flanders
1066–87

Robert, Duke of Normandy
d. 1134

WILLIAM II, "Rufus"
1087–1100

Adela = Stephen of Blois

HENRY I = Matilda of Scotland
1100–35

William the Clito
d. 1128

STEPHEN
1135–54

William
Drowned 1120

(1) Emperor Henry V = Matilda (Maud), d. 1169
(2) Geoffrey of Anjou

HENRY II = Eleanor of Aquitaine
1154–89

Henry, "the Young King", d. 1183

RICHARD I = Berengaria of Navarre
1189–99

Geoffrey
d. 1186

JOHN = Isabella of Angoulême
1199–1216

Arthur, d. 1203

HENRY III = Eleanor of Provence
1216–72

Richard, Earl of Cornwall, King of the Romans, 1257–72

(1) Eleanor of Castile = EDWARD I = (2) Margaret of France
1272–1307

Edmund, Earl of Lancaster, d. 1296

Isabella of France = EDWARD II
1307–27

Thomas, Earl of Norfolk, d. 1338

Edmund, Earl of Kent, d. 1330

EDWARD III
1327–77

organisation and discipline were reformed. Older sees were transplanted from villages to towns—Crediton to Exeter, and Selsey to Chichester. New episcopal seats were established, and by 1087 the masons were at work on seven new cathedrals. At the same time the monastic movement, which had sprung from the Abbey of Cluny, began to spread in England. The English Church was rescued by the Conquest from the backwater in which it had languished. Under Lanfranc and his successor, Anselm, it came once again into contact with the wider European life of the Christian Church and its heritage of learning.

During the thirteen years of the reign of William Rufus the Anglo-Norman realms were vexed by fratricidal strife and successive baronial revolts. The Saxon inhabitants of England, fearful of a relapse into the chaos of pre-Conquest days, stood by the King against all rebels. In August 1100 he was mysteriously shot through the head by an arrow while hunting in the New Forest, leaving a memory of shameless exactions and infamous morals, but also a submissive realm to his successor.

Prince Henry, the youngest of the royal brothers, made straight for the royal Treasury at Winchester, and gained possession of it after sharp argument with its custodians. He set the precedent, which his successor followed, of proclaiming a charter upon his accession. Henry's desire to base himself in part at least upon the Saxon population of England led him, much to the suspicion of the Norman barons, to make a marriage with Matilda, niece of the last surviving Saxon claimant to the English throne and descendant of the old English line of kings. He knew that the friction caused by the separation of Normandy from England was by no means soothed. In September 1106 the most

The seal of Henry I. BRITISH MUSEUM

important battle since Hastings was fought at Tinchebrai. King Henry's victory was complete. Duke Robert was carried to his perpetual prison in England. There was now no challenged succession. The King of England's authority was established on both sides of the Channel.

There survived in medieval Europe a tradition of kingship more exalted than that of feudal overlord. The king was not merely the apex of the feudal pyramid, but the anointed Vicegerent of God upon earth. The collapse of the Roman Empire had not entirely destroyed this Roman conception of sovereignty, and Henry now set himself to inject this idea of kingship into the Anglo-Norman State. The chroniclers spoke well of Henry I. We must regard his reign as a period when the central Government, by adroit and sharp accountancy and clerking, established in a more precise form the structure and resources of the State. In the process the feudatory chiefs upon whom the local government of the land depended were angered. We see therefore the beginning of an attachment to the King or central Government on the part of the people, which invested the Crown with a new source of strength, sometimes forthcoming and sometimes estranged, but always to be gathered, especially after periods of weakness and disorder, by a strong and righteous ruler.

The King had a son, his heir apparent, successor indisputable. In the winter of 1120 he was coming back from a visit to France in the royal yacht called the *White Ship*. Off

the coast of Normandy the vessel struck a rock and all but one were drowned. The King had a daughter, Matilda, or Maud as the English called her, but although there was no Salic Law in the Norman code this clanking, jangling aristocracy, mailed and spurred, did not take kindly to the idea of a woman's rule. Against her stood the claim of Stephen, son of the Conqueror's daughter Adela. At the age of thirteen Maud had been married to the Holy Roman Emperor. In 1125, five years after the *White Ship* sank, he died, and at twenty-two she was a widow and an Empress. Fierce, proud, hard, cynical, living for politics above all other passions, however turbulent, she was fitted to bear her part in any war and be the mother of one of the greatest English kings. Upon this daughter, after mature consideration, Henry founded all his hopes. In order to enhance her unifying authority, and to protect Normandy from the claims of Anjou after his death, he married her to the Count of Anjou, thus linking the interests of the most powerful State in Northern France with the family and natural succession in England.

After giving the Island thirty years of peace and order and largely reconciling the Saxon population to Norman rule, Henry I expired on December 1, 1135, in the confident hope that his daughter Maud would carry on his work. But she was with her husband in Anjou and Stephen was the first on the spot. Swiftly returning from Blois, he made his way to London and claimed the Crown. A succession established on such

King Henry I
(1068–1135)

disputable grounds could only be maintained unchallenged by skilful sovereignty. There were grievous discontents among the high, the middle, and the low. In 1139 Maud, freed from entanglements that had kept her in France, entered the kingdom to claim her rights. The civil war developed into the first successful baronial reaction against the centralising policy of the kings. Over large parts of England fighting was sporadic and local in character. It was the Central Southern counties that bore the brunt of civil war. But these commotions bit deep into the consciousness of the people. It was realised how vital an institution a strong monarchy was for the security of life and property. No better reasons for monarchy could have been found than were forced upon all minds by the events of Stephen's reign.

In 1147 Robert of Gloucester died and the leadership of Maud's party devolved upon her son. To contemporaries he was best known as Henry Fitz-Empress; but he carried into English history the emblem of his House, the broom, the *Planta Genesta*, which later generations were to make the name of this great dynasty, the Plantagenets. In his high feudal capacity Henry repaired to Paris to render homage to his lord the King of France, of which country he already possessed, by the accepted law of the age, a large part. Louis VII was a French Edward the Confessor; he practised with faithful simplicity the law of Christ. These pious and exemplary habits did not endear him to his Queen. Eleanor of Aquitaine was in her own right a reigning princess, with the warmth of the South in her veins. The Papacy bowed to strong will in the high feudal chiefs, and Eleanor obtained a divorce from Louis VII in 1152 on the nominal grounds of consanguinity. But what staggered the French Court and opened the eyes of its prayerful King was the sudden marriage of Eleanor to Henry two months later. Thus half of France passed out of royal control into the hands of Henry. From all sides the potentates confronted the upstart. A month after the marriage these foes converged upon Normandy. But the youthful Duke Henry beat them back,

Louis VII of France and Eleanor of Aquitaine. CHARTRES CATHEDRAL. CLICHÉ ARCHIVES PHOTOGRAPHIQUES

Right: *The martyrdom of Thomas Becket, Archbishop of Canterbury, in Canterbury Cathedral on December 29, 1170. From an English Psalter,* circa *1200.* BRITISH MUSEUM

ruptured and broken. He turned forthwith to England.

It was a valiant figure that landed in January 1153, and from all over England, distracted by civil war, hearts and eyes turned towards him. Merlin had prophesied a deliverer; had he not in his veins blood that ran back to William the Conqueror, and beyond him, through his grandmother Matilda, wife of Henry I, to Cerdic and the long-vanished Anglo-Saxon line? Glamour, terror, success, attended this youthful, puissant warrior, who had not only his sword, but his title-deeds. A treaty was concluded at Winchester in 1153 whereby Stephen made Henry his adopted son and his appointed heir. On this Henry did homage and made all the formal submissions, and when a year later Stephen died he was acclaimed and crowned King of England with more general hope and rejoicing than had ever uplifted any monarch in England since the days of Alfred the Great.

The accession of Henry II began one of the most pregnant and decisive reigns in English history. The new sovereign ruled an empire, and, as his subjects boasted, his warrant ran "from the Arctic Ocean to the Pyrenees". A vivid picture is painted of this gifted and, for a while, enviable man: square, thick-set, bull-necked, with powerful arms and coarse, rough hands; his legs bandy from endless riding; a large, round head and closely cropped red hair; a freckled face; a voice harsh and cracked. Intense love of the chase; other loves, which the Church deplored and Queen Eleanor resented; frugality in food and dress; days entirely concerned with public business; travel unceasing; moods various. Everything was stirred and moulded by him in England, as also in his other much greater estates, which he patrolled with tireless attention.

England has had greater soldier-kings and subtler diplomatists than Henry II, but no man has left a deeper mark upon our laws and institutions. Fastening upon the elastic Saxon concept of the King's Peace, Henry used it to draw all criminal cases into his

THE POSSESSION OF HENRY II

Boundary of lands under direct rule of Henry II

Lands owing him Suzerainty

Boundary of lands inherited from his father

MILES
0   50   100   150   200

courts. Civil cases he attracted by straining a different principle, the old right of the King's court to hear appeals in cases where justice had been refused and to protect men in possession of their lands.

A bait was needed with which to draw litigants to the royal courts; the King must offer them better justice than they could have at the hands of their lords. Henry accordingly threw open to litigants in the royal courts a new procedure for them—trial by jury. Henry did not invent the jury; he put it to a new purpose. The idea of the jury is the one great contribution of the Franks to the English legal system, for, unknown in this country before the Conquest, the germ of it lies far back in the practice of the Carolingian kings. It was through this early form of jury that William the Conqueror had determined the Crown rights in the great Domesday survey. The genius of Henry II, perceiving new possibilities in such a procedure, turned to regular use in the courts an instrument which so far had only been used for administrative purposes. It was an astute move. Until this time both civil and criminal cases had been decided through the oath, the ordeal, or the duel. The jury of Henry II was not the jury that we know. Good men and true were picked, not yet for their impartiality, but because they were the men most likely to know the truth. In time the jurors with local knowledge would cease to be jurors at all and become witnesses, giving their evidence in open court to a jury entirely composed of bystanders. Very gradually, as the laws of evidence developed, the change came.

These methods gave good justice. Trial by jury became popular. Professional judges, removed from local prejudice, secured swifter decisions, and a strong authority to enforce them. Henry accordingly had to build up almost from nothing a complete system of royal courts, capable of absorbing a great rush of new work. The instrument to which he turned was the royal Council, the organ through which all manner of governmental business was already regularly carried out. It was to be the common parent of Chancery and Exchequer, of Parliament, of the Common Law courts, and those Courts of Prerogative on which the Tudors and Stuarts relied.

Henry also had to provide means whereby the litigant, eager for royal justice, could remove his case out of the court of his lord into the King's court. The device which Henry used was the royal writ. It was not until de Montfort's revolt against the third Henry in the thirteenth century that the multiplication of writs was checked and the number fixed at something under two hundred. This system then endured for six hundred years.

It was in these fateful and formative years that the English-speaking peoples began to devise methods of determining legal disputes

Thomas Becket, from a thirteenth-century stained-glass window in Canterbury Cathedral. PHOTO: JOHN R. FREE-MAN. COURTESY: THE DEAN AND CHAPTER

which survive in substance to this day. A man can only be accused of a civil or criminal offence which is clearly defined and known to the law. The judge is an umpire. Witnesses must testify in public and on oath. The truth of their testimony is weighed not by the judge but by twelve "good men and true". Under Roman law, and systems derived from it, a trial in those turbulent centuries, and in some countries even today, is often an inquisition. The judge makes his own investigation into the civil wrong or the public crime, and such investigation is largely uncontrolled. The suspect can be interrogated in private. And only when these processes have been accomplished is the accusation or charge against him formulated and published. Thus often arise secret intimidation, enforced confessions, torture, and blackmailed pleas of guilty. These sinister dangers were extinguished from the Common Law of England more than six centuries ago. By the time Henry II's great-grandson, Edward I, had died English criminal and civil procedure had settled into a mould and a tradition which in the mass govern the English-speaking peoples today. In all claims and disputes, whether they concerned the grazing lands of the Middle West, the oil-fields of California, the sheep-runs and gold-mines of Australia, or the territorial rights of the Maoris, these rules have obtained, at any rate in theory, according to the procedure and mode of trial evolved by the English Common Law.

The military State in feudal Christendom bowed to the Church in things spiritual; it never accepted the idea of the transference of secular power to priestly authority. But the Church, enriched continually by the bequests of hardy barons, anxious in the death agony about their life beyond the grave, became the greatest landlord and capitalist in the community. The power of the State was held in constant challenge by this potent interest.

The Church in England, like the baronage, had gained greatly in power since the days of William the Conqueror and his faithful Archbishop Lanfranc. Stephen in his straits had made sweeping concessions to the Church, whose political influence then reached its zenith. These concessions, Henry felt, compromised his royal rights. He schemed to regain what had been lost, and as the first step in 1162 appointed his trusted servant Becket to be Archbishop of Canterbury, believing he would thus secure the acquiescence of the Episcopacy. In fact he provided the Church with a leader of unequalled vigour and obstinacy. He ignored or missed the ominous signs of the change in Becket's attitude, and proceeded to his second step, the publication in 1164 of the Constitutions of Clarendon. But Becket resis-

ted. He regarded Stephen's yieldings as irrevocable gains by the Church. Stiff in defiance, Becket took refuge on the Continent, where the same conflict was already distracting both Germany and Italy. Only in 1170 was an apparent reconciliation brought about between him and the King at Fréteval, in Touraine. After the Fréteval agreement Henry supposed that bygones were to be bygones. But Becket had other views. His welcome home after the years of exile was astonishing. Henry Plantagenet was transported with passion. "What a pack of fools and cowards," he cried, "I have nourished in my house, that not one of them will avenge me of this turbulent priest!" Another version says "of this upstart clerk". A council was immediately summoned to devise measures for reasserting the royal authority. But meanwhile another train of action was in process. Four knights had heard the King's bitter words spoken in the full circle. They crossed the Channel. They called for horses and rode to Canterbury. There on December 29, 1170, they found the Archbishop in the cathedral. The scene and the tragedy are famous. After haggard parleys they fell upon him, cut him down with their swords, and left him bleeding like Julius Cæsar, with a score of wounds to cry for vengeance.

This tragedy was fatal to the King. The immediately following years were spent in trying to recover what he had lost by a great parade of atonement for his guilt. By the Compromise of Avranches in 1172 he made his peace with the Papacy on comparatively easy terms. But Becket's sombre sacrifice had not been in vain. Until the Reformation the Church retained the system of ecclesiastical courts independent of the royal authority, and the right of appeal to Rome, two of the major points upon which Becket had defied the King.

All Europe marvelled at the extent of Henry's domains, to which in 1171 he had added the lordship of Ireland. Yet Henry knew well that his splendour was personal in origin, tenuous and transient in quality; and he had also deep-clouding family sorrows. During these years he was

꜀ Deuise les ordomancet dufa
e au roy richard dantleterre ·

et autres en chappes de draps de
brodees de verles deuant les…

The Coronation procession of Richard I in 1189, as depicted in the fifteenth-century Les Anciennes et Nouvelles Chroniques d'Angleterre. BRITISH MUSEUM

King Henry II (1133–89), from his tomb at Fontevrault. CLICHÉ ARCHIVES PHOTOGRAPHIQUES

confronted with no fewer than four rebellions by his sons. On each occasion they could count on the active support of the watchful King of France. These boys were typical sprigs of the Angevin stock. They wanted power as well as titles, and they bore their father no respect. In 1188 Richard, his eldest surviving son, after the death of young Henry, was making war upon him in conjunction with King Philip of France. Already desperately ill, Henry was defeated at Le Mans and recoiled into Touraine. When he saw in the list of conspirators against him the name of his son John, upon whom his affection had strangely rested, he abandoned the struggle with life. "Let things go as they will," he gasped. "Shame, shame on a conquered King." So saying, this hard, violent, brilliant, and lonely man expired at Chinon on July 6, 1189.

The new King affected little grief at the death of a father against whom he was in arms. Richard, with all his characteristic virtues and faults cast in a heroic mould, is one of the most fascinating medieval figures. When Richard's contemporaries called him "Cœur de Lion" they paid a lasting compliment to the king of beasts. Little did the English people owe him for his services, and heavily did they pay for his adventures. He was in England only twice for a few short months in his ten years' reign; yet his memory has always stirred English hearts, and seems to present throughout the centuries the pattern of the fighting man. Although a man of blood and violence, Richard was too impetuous to be either treacherous or habitually cruel. He was as ready to forgive as he was hasty to offend; he was open-handed and munificent to profusion; in war circumspect in design and skilful in execution; in politics a child, lacking in subtlety and experience. His political alliances were formed upon his likes and dislikes; his political schemes had neither unity nor clearness of purpose. The advantages gained for him by military genius were flung away through diplomatic ineptitude. His life was one magnificent parade, which, when ended, left only an empty plain.

The King's heart was set upon the new Crusade. Richard was crowned with peculiar State, by a ceremonial which, elaborating the most ancient forms and traditions of the Island monarchy, is still in all essentials observed today. Thereafter the King, for the sake of Christ's Sepulchre, virtually put the realm up for sale. Confiding the government to two Justiciars, William Longchamp, Bishop of Ely, and Hugh de Puiset, Bishop of Durham, under the supervision of the one trustworthy member of his family, his mother, the old Queen, Eleanor of Aquitaine, he started for the wars in the winter of 1189. The glamours of chivalry illumine the tale of the Third Crusade. King Richard dominated the scene. By the time Acre fell King Richard's glory as a warrior and also his skill as a general were the talk of all nations. But the quarrels of the allies paralysed the campaign. The Crusading army, ably led by Richard, in spite of the victory at Arsuf, where many thousand infidels were slain, could do no more than reach an eminence which commanded a distant view of the Holy City. In the next year, 1192, he captured Jaffa. Once again the distant prospect of Jerusalem alone rewarded the achievements of the Crusaders. By now the news from England was so alarming that the King felt it imperative to return home. A peace or truce for three years was at length effected, by which the coastal towns were divided and the Holy Sepulchre opened as a place of pilgrimage to small parties of Crusaders. Late in 1192 the King set out for home. Wrecked in the Adriatic, he sought to make his way through Germany in disguise, but his enemy the Duke of Austria was soon upon his track. He was arrested, and held prisoner in a castle. So valuable a prize was not suffered to remain in the Duke's hands. The Emperor himself demanded the famous captive. For many months his prison was a secret, but, as a pretty legend tells us, Blondel, Richard's faithful minstrel, went from castle to castle striking the chords which the King loved best, and at last was rewarded by an answer from Richard's own harp.

William Longchamp, Bishop of Ely, and, with magnificent pluralism, Papal Legate, Chancellor, and Justiciar, had addressed himself with fidelity and zeal to the task of governing England, entrusted to him by Richard in 1189. As the King's faithful servant he saw that the chief danger lay in the over-mighty position of Prince John. In the summer of 1191 there was open conflict between the two parties, and Longchamp marched against a revolt of John's adherents in the North Midlands. The French King saw in Richard's absence the chance of breaking up the Angevin power and driving the English out of France. In John he found a willing partner. Early in 1193, at a moment already full of peril, the grave news reached England that the King was prisoner "somewhere in Germany". John declared that Richard was dead, appeared in arms, and claimed the Crown. That England was held for Richard in his long absence against all these powerful and subtle forces is a proof of the loyalties of the Feudal Age. John's forces melted. The Holy Roman Emperor demanded the prodigious ransom of a hundred and fifty thousand marks, twice the annual revenue of the English Crown. At the end of 1193 the stipulated first instalment was paid, and at the beginning of February 1194 Richard Cœur de Lion was released from bondage. The King was re-crowned in London with even more elaborate ceremony than before. These processes well started, he crossed the Channel to defend his French possessions. He never set foot in England again.

The five remaining years of Richard's reign were spent in defending his French domains and raising money for that purpose from England. Once again the country was ruled by a deputy, this time Hubert Walter, a man bred in the traditions of Henry II's official Household, Archbishop of Canterbury, and Richard's Justiciar. With determination, knowledge, and deft touch he

The Canterbury Pilgrims of Chaucer's Canterbury Tales (*written circa 1387*) *by William Blake.* THE SIR JOHN STIRLING MAXWELL COLLECTION, POLLOCK HOUSE, GLASGOW

developed the system of strong centralised government devised by Henry II. Hubert Walter stands out as one of the great medieval administrators.

In France the war with Philip proceeded in a curious fashion. The negotiations were unceasing. Every year there was a truce, which every year was broken as the weather and general convenience permitted. In 1199, when the difficulties of raising revenue for the endless war were at their height, good news was brought to King Richard. It was said there had been dug up near the Castle of Chaluz, on the lands of one of his vassals, a treasure of wonderful quality. The King claimed this treasure as lord paramount. The lord of Chaluz resisted the demand, and the

King laid siege to his small, weak castle. On the third day, as he rode daringly near the wall, confident in his hard-tried luck, a bolt from a crossbow struck him in the left shoulder by the neck. For seven years he had not confessed for fear of being compelled to be reconciled to Philip, but now he received the offices of the Church with sincere and exemplary piety, and died in the forty-second year of his age on April 6, 1199, worthy, by the consent of all men, to sit with King Arthur and Roland and other heroes of martial romance at some Eternal Round Table.

There is no animal in nature that combines the contradictory qualities of John. He

united the ruthlessness of a hardened warrior with the craft and subtlety of a Machiavellian. Although from time to time he gave way to furious rages, in which "his eyes darted fire and his countenance became livid", his cruelties were conceived and executed with a cold, inhuman intelligence. Monkish chroniclers have emphasised his violence, greed, malice, treachery, and lust. But other records show that he was often judicious, always extremely capable, and on occasions even generous. He possessed an original and inquiring mind, and to the end of his life treasured his library of books. In him the restless energy of the Plantagenet race was raised to a furious pitch of instability. Although Richard had declared John to

be King there were two views upon the succession. Geoffrey, his elder brother, had left behind him a son, Arthur, Prince of Brittany. It was already possible to hold that this grandson of Henry II of an elder branch had a prior right against John, and that is now the law of primogeniture. John was accepted without demur in England. In the French provinces however the opposite view prevailed. Brittany in particular adopted Arthur. The King of France and all French interests thought themselves well served by a disputed succession and the espousal of a minor's cause. John felt that he would never be safe so long as Arthur lived. The havoc of disunity that was being wrought throughout the French provinces by the French King

The statue of King Richard I, Cœur de Lion (1157–99) outside the Houses of Parliament. JOHN R. FREEMAN

using Arthur as a pawn might well have weighed with a better man than John. Arthur, caught in open fight besieging his own grandmother, was a prisoner of war. No one knows what happened to Arthur. Hubert de Burgh, of whom more and better hereafter, gave out that upon the King's order he had delivered his prisoner at Easter 1203 to the hands of agents sent by John to castrate him, and that Arthur had died of the shock. That he was murdered by John's orders was not disputed at the time nor afterwards, though the question whether or not he was mutilated or blinded beforehand remains unanswered.

With the accession of John there emerges plainly in the Northern French provinces a sense of unity with one another and with the kingdom of France; at the same time on this side of the Channel the English baronage became ever more inclined to insular and even nationalistic ideas. Ties with the Continent were weakening through the gradual

division of honours and appanages in England and Normandy between different branches of Anglo-Norman families. Moreover, the growing brilliance of the French Court and royal power in the late twelfth century was a powerful magnet which drew Continental loyalties to Paris. King John found himself compelled to fight at greater odds than his predecessors for his possessions on the Continent. He was also opposed by an increasing resistance to taxation for that purpose in England.

Arthur had been removed, but John failed to profit by his crime. Brittany and the central provinces of the Angevin Empire revolted. Having encircled Normandy, Philip prepared to strike at the stronghold of the Angevin power. In March 1204 King Richard's "fair child", the frowning Château Gaillard, fell, and the road to Rouen lay open. Three months later the capital itself was taken, and Normandy finally became French. No English tears need have been shed over this loss. The Angevin Empire at its peak had no real unity. Time and geography lay on the side of the French. The separation proved as much in the interest of England as of France. It rid the Island of a dangerous, costly distraction and entanglement, turned its thought and energies to its own affairs, and above all left a ruling class of alien origin with no interest henceforth that was not English or at least insular.

John, like William Rufus, pressed to logical limits the tendencies of his father's system. By systematic abuse of his feudal prerogatives John drove the baronage to violent resistance. The year 1205 brought a crisis. It also reopened the thorny question of who should elect the Primate of England. The Papal throne at this time was occupied by Innocent III; setting aside the candidates both of the Crown and of the Canterbury clergy, he caused Stephen Langton to be selected with great pomp and solemnity at Rome in December 1206. In his wrath, and without measuring the strength of his opponents, the King proceeded to levy a bloodless war upon the Church. When John began to persecute the clergy and seize Church lands the Pope retaliated by laying all England under an interdict. When John hardened his heart to the interdict and redoubled the attacks upon Church property, the Pope, in 1209, took the supreme step of excommunication. But John was stubborn and unabashed. The royal administration, never more efficient, found little difficulty in coping with the fiscal and legal problems presented to it or in maintaining order. But for the combination of the Church quarrel with stresses of mundane politics, the Crown might have established a position not reached till the days of Henry VIII.

After the loss of Normandy John had embarked upon a series of grandiose schemes for a Continental alliance against Philip Augustus; but his breach with the Church hastened a far more formidable league between the King of France and the Papacy, and in 1213 he had to choose between submission and a French invasion, backed by all the military and spiritual resources which Innocent III could set in motion. John, however, was not at the end of his devices, and by a stroke of cunning choice enough to be called political genius he turned defeat into something very like triumph. He offered to make England a fief of the Papacy, and to do homage to the Pope as his feudal lord. Innocent leapt at this addition to his worldly dignities. He accepted the sovereignty of England from the hands of John, and returned it to him as his vassal with his blessing.

This turned the tables upon John's secular enemies. Stephen Langton himself, the Pope's elect, was as good an Englishman as he was a Churchman. He foresaw the unbridled exploitation by Rome of the patronage of the English Church and the wholesale engrossment of its benefices by Italian nominees. Both John and Innocent persevered in their new partnership, and the disaffected barons drew together under the leadership of Stephen Langton. In 1214 an English

expedition which John had led to Poitou failed. In Northern France the army commanded by his nephew, Otto of Saxony, and by the Earl of Salisbury, was defeated by King Philip at Bouvines. Here again was the opportunity of the King's domestic enemies. But John had still one final resource. Encouraged by the Pope, he took the vows of a Crusader and invoked sentence of excommunication upon his opponents. This was not denied him. But this agile use of the Papal thunders had robbed them of some of their virtues as a deterrent. The barons, encouraged by the King's defeat abroad, persisted in their demands in spite of the Papal Bull. Armed revolt seemed the only solution.

Although in the final scene of the struggle the Archbishop showed himself unwilling to go to the extreme of civil war, it was he who persuaded the barons to base their demands upon respect for ancient custom and law, and who gave them some principle to fight for besides their own class interests. The leaders of the barons in 1215 groped in the dim light towards a fundamental principle. Government must henceforward mean something more than the arbitrary rule of any man, and custom and the law must stand even above the King. It was this idea, perhaps only half understood, that gave unity and force to the barons' opposition and made the Charter which they now demanded imperishable. On a Monday morning in June, between Staines and Windsor, the barons and Churchmen began to collect on the great meadow at Runnymede. An uneasy hush fell on them from time to time. Many had failed to keep their tryst; and the bold few who had come knew that the King would never forgive this humiliation. He would hunt them down when he could, and the laymen at least were staking their lives in the cause they served. They had arranged a little throne for the King and a tent. The handful of resolute men had drawn up, it seems, a short document on parchment. Their retainers and the groups and squadrons of horsemen in sullen steel kept at some distance and well in the background. For was not armed rebellion

In die mandauit dominus milen
cordiam suam:t nocte canticū eius.
pud me oracio deo uite mee: di
cam deo susceptor meus es.

Richard I's foremost opponent in the Third Crusade was Saladin, Sultan of Egypt. This fanciful manuscript illustration shows the English King (left) unhorsing the great Saracen. BRITISH MUSEUM

against the Crown the supreme feudal crime? Then events followed rapidly. A small cavalcade appeared from the direction of Windsor. Gradually men made out the faces of the King, the Papal Legate, the Archbishop of Canterbury, and several bishops. They dismounted without ceremony. Someone, probably the Archbishop, stated briefly the terms that were suggested. The King declared at once that he agreed. He said the details should be arranged immediately in his Chancery. The original "Articles of the Barons" on which Magna Carta is based exist today in the British Museum. They

were sealed in a quiet, short scene, which has become one of the most famous in our history, on June 15, 1215.

If we set aside the rhetorical praise which has been so freely lavished upon the Charter and study the document itself we may find it rather surprising reading. It is entirely lacking in any spacious statement of the principles of democratic government or the rights of man. It is not a declaration of constitutional doctrine, but a practical document to remedy current abuses in the feudal system. Magna Carta must not, however, be dismissed lightly, in the words of a modern writer, as "a monument of class selfishness". In securing themselves the barons of Runnymede were in fact establishing the rights of the whole landed class, great and small—the simple knight with two hundred acres, the farmer or small yeoman with sixty. And there is evidence that their action was so understood throughout the country. If the thirteenth-century magnates understood little and cared less for popular liberties or Parliamentary democracy, they had all the same laid hold of a principle which was to be of prime importance for the future development of English society and English institutions. Throughout the document it is implied that here is a law which is above the King and which even he must not break. This reaffirmation of a supreme law and its expression in a general charter is the great work of Magna Carta; and this alone justifies the respect in which men have held it. The underlying idea of the sovereignty of law, long existent in feudal custom, was raised by it into a doctrine for the national State. And when in subsequent ages the State, swollen with its own authority, has attempted to ride roughshod over the rights or liberties of the subject it is to this doctrine that appeal has again and again been made, and never, as yet, without success.

King John died in the toils; but he died at bay. He was at war with the English barons who had forced him to grant the Charter. They had invited Louis, son of the implacable Philip, King of France, into the country to be their liege lord, and with him came foreign troops and hardy adventurers. Everything threatened a long, stubborn civil war and a return to the anarchy of Stephen and Maud. Shakespeare has limned John's final agony:

And none of you will bid the winter come
To thrust his icy fingers in my maw. . . .
I beg cold comfort, and you are so strait
And so ungrateful, you deny me that.

Yet the sole reason and justification for revolt died with John.

Henry, a child of nine, was the undoubted heir to all the rights and loyalties of his grandfather's wide empire. The boy-King was crowned at Gloucester, and began his reign of fifty-six years on October 28, 1216. William the Marshal, aged seventy, reluctantly undertook what we should now call the Regency. He joined to himself the Earl of Chester, who might well have been his rival but did not press his claims, and Hubert de Burgh, John's faithful servant. The rebellion of the barons was quelled by fights on land and sea. After a year of fighting Louis of France was compelled to leave the country in 1217, his hopes utterly dashed. In 1219

Part of the "Articles of the Barons", on which Magna Carta is based. BRITISH MUSEUM

the old victorious Marshal died, and Hubert ruled the land for twelve years. In 1225, as a sign of pacification, the Great Charter was again reissued in what was substantially its final form. Thus it became an unchallenged part of English law and tradition. But for the turbulent years of Henry III's minority, it might have mouldered in the archives of history as a merely partisan document.

No long administration is immune from mistakes, and every statesman must from time to time make concessions to wrong-headed superior powers. But Hubert throughout his tenure stood for the policy of doing the least possible to recover the King's French domains. He resisted the Papacy in its efforts to draw money at all costs out of England for its large European schemes. He maintained order, and as the King grew up he restrained the Court party which was forming about him from making inroads upon the Charter. His was entirely the English point of view. In 1232 he was driven from power by a small palace clique. The leader of this intrigue was his former rival Peter des Roches, the Bishop of Winchester. De Burgh was the last of the great Justiciars who had wielded plenary and at times almost sovereign power. Henceforward the Household offices like the Wardrobe, largely dependent upon the royal will and favour, began to overshadow the great "national" offices, like the Justiciarship, filled by the baronial magnates. Des Roches himself kept in the background, but at the Christmas Council of 1232 nearly every post of consequence in the administration was conferred upon his friends, most of them, like him, men of Poitou. Under the leadership of Richard the Marshal, a second son of the faithful William, the barons began to growl against the foreigners. In alliance with Prince Llewellyn the young Marshal drove the King among the Welsh Marches, sacked Shrewsbury, and harried des Roches's lands. In the spring of 1234 Henry was forced to accept terms.

The Poitevins were the first of the long succession of foreign favourites whom Henry III gathered round him in the middle years of his reign. In 1236 he married Eleanor, the daughter of Raymond of Provence. A new wave of foreigners descended upon the profitable wardships, marriages, escheats, and benefices, which the disgusted baronage regarded as their own. An even more copious source of discontent in England was the influence of the Papacy over the grateful and pious King. Robert Grosseteste, scholar, scientist, and saint, a former Master of the Oxford Schools and since 1235 Bishop of Lincoln, led the English clergy in evasion or refusal of Papal demands. The Church, writhing under Papal exactions, and the baronage, offended by Court encroachments, were united in hatred of foreigners. The final stroke was the King's complete failure to check the successes of Llewellyn, who in 1256 had swept the English out of Wales and intrigued to overthrow the English faction in Scotland. Despised, discredited, and frightened, without money or men, the King faced an angered and powerful opposition.

Effigy of King John (circa *1167–1216*) *from his tomb in Worcester Cathedral.* PHOTO: A. F. KERSTING. COURTESY: THE DEAN AND CHAPTER

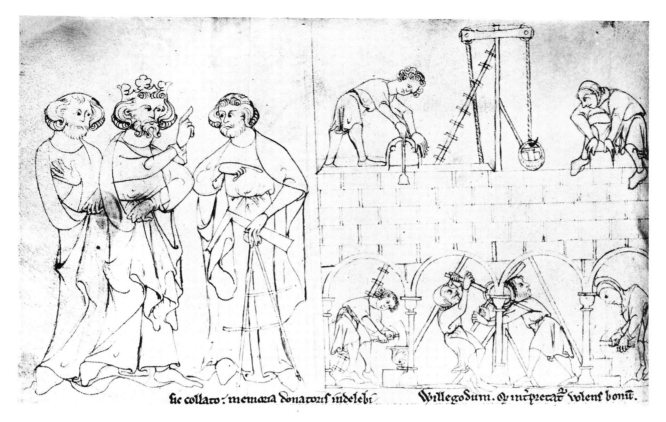

fic collato: memoria donatorus indelebit   Willegodum. Qy interpretat volent bonu.

Henry III and his masons. BRITISH MUSEUM

A letter of a Court official, written in July 1258, has been preserved. The King, so it says, had yielded to what he felt was overwhelming pressure. A commission for reform of government was set up.

The later years of Henry III's troubled reign were momentous in their consequences for the growth of English institutions. The commission for reform set about its work seriously, and in 1258 its proposals were embodied in the Provisions of Oxford, supplemented and extended in 1259 by the Provisions of Westminster. The staple of the barons' demand was that the King in future should govern by a Council of Fifteen, to be elected by four persons, two from the baronial and two from the royal party. It is significant that the King's proclamation accepting the arrangement in English as well as French is the first public document to be issued in both languages since the time of William the Conqueror. For a spell this Council, animated and controlled by Simon de Montfort, governed the land.

It is about this time that the word "Parle-ment"—Parliament—began to be current. In 1086 William the Conqueror had "deep speech" with his wise men before launching the Domesday inquiry. In Latin this would have appeared as *colloquium*; and "colloquy" is the common name in the twelfth century for the consultations between the King and his magnates. The occasional colloquy "on great affairs of the Kingdom" can at this point be called a Parliament. But more often the word means the permanent Council of officials and judges which sat at Westminster to receive petitions, redress grievances, and generally regulate the course of the law. By the thirteenth century Parliament establishes itself as the name of two quite different, though united, institutions. If we translate their functions into modern terms we may say that the first of these assemblies deals with policy, the second with legislation and administration. In the reign of Henry III, and even of Edward I, it was by no means a foregone conclusion that the two assemblies would be amalgamated. Rather did it look as if the English Constitution would develop as did the French Constitution, with a King

The shield and seal of Simon de Montfort.
COURTESY: DEAN AND CHAPTER OF WEST-
MINSTER ABBEY; SOCIETY OF ANTIQUARIES

in Council as the real Government, with the magnates reduced to a mere nobility, and "Parlement" only a clearing-house for legal business. Our history did not take this course. In the first place the magnates during the century that followed succeeded in mastering the Council and identifying their interests with it. Secondly, the English counties had a life of their own, and their representatives at Westminster were to exercise increasing influence. But without the powerful impulse of Simon de Montfort these forces might not have combined to shape a durable legislative assembly.

The King, the Court party, and the immense foreign interests associated therewith had no intention of submitting indefinitely to the thraldom of the Provisions. His son Edward was already the rising star of all who wished to see a strong monarchy. Supporters of this cause appeared among the poor and turbulent elements in London and the towns. It is the merit of Simon de Montfort that he did not rest content with a victory by the barons over the Crown. The "apprentice" or bachelor knights, who may be taken as voicing the wishes of the country gentry, formed a virile association of their own entitled "the Community of the Bachelors

of England". Simon de Montfort became their champion. Very soon he began to rebuke great lords for abuse of their privileges. At Easter in 1261 Henry, freed by the Pope from his oath to accept the Provisions of Oxford and Westminster, deposed the officials and Ministers appointed by the barons. Both parties competed for popular support. In the civil war that followed the feudal party more or less supported the King. The people, especially the towns, and the party of ecclesiastical reform, especially the Franciscans, rallied to de Montfort.

At Lewes a fierce battle was fought. In some ways it was a forerunner of Edgehill. Edward, like Rupert four hundred years later, conquered all before him, pursued incontinently, and returned to the battlefield only to find that all was lost. The King and all his Court and principal supporters were taken prisoner by de Montfort, and the energetic Prince returned only to share their plight. Simon made a treaty with the captive King and the beaten party, whereby the rights of the Crown were in theory respected, though in practice the King and his son were to be subjected to strict controls. For the moment de Montfort was content that the necessary steps should be taken by a Council

Edward I in Parliament, an illustration circa *1523 from the Wriothesley MS in Windsor Castle. On the King's right sit the Archbishop of Canterbury and King Alexander III of Scotland (the Master of the Rolls behind). On his left are the Welsh prince, Llywelyn ab Gruffydd, and the Archbishop of York. The principal officers of the Crown sit on the Woolsacks, while the benches are occupied by the Clergy and Nobility. The crowned figure seated on a bench is thought to represent the Prince of Wales, later Edward II.* REPRODUCED BY GRACIOUS PERMISSION OF HER MAJESTY THE QUEEN

longtain voiage: quil souffrira de porter seulement vng
las de soye a vng ymage de samct george pendat a icellui.
Aussi se ledit colier dor auoit besomg de reparacion il pora
estre mis en la mam de louurier iusques a ce quil soit
repare. Lequel colier aussi ne pourra estre enrichy de
pierres ou daultres choses reserue les ymage qui pourra
estre garmy au plaisir du cheualier. Et aussi ne pourra
estre ledit colier vendu engaige donne ne aliene pour
necessite ou cause quelconque que ce soit

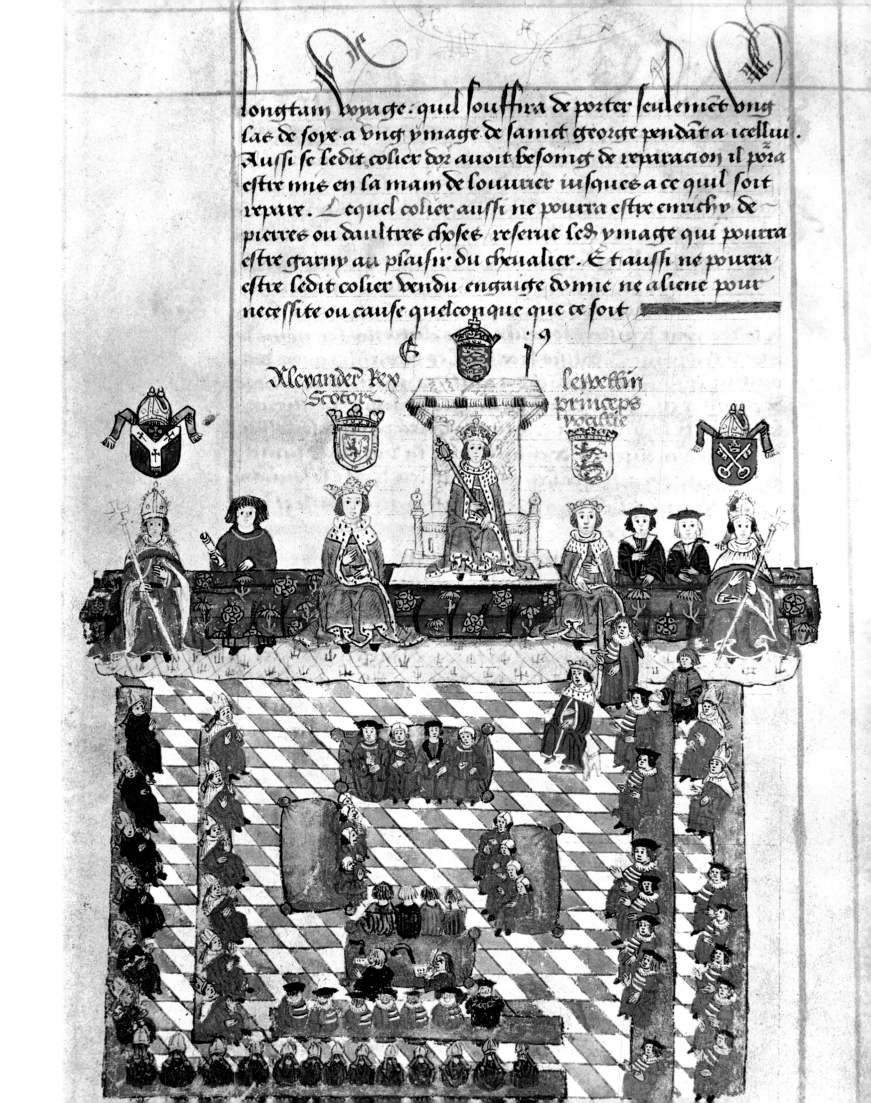

of nine who controlled expenditure and appointed officials. In January 1265 a Parliament met in London to which Simon summoned representatives both from the shires and from the towns. Its purpose was to give an appearance of legality to the revolutionary settlement, and this, under the guidance of de Montfort, it proceeded to do. Its importance lay, however, more in its character as a representative assembly than in its work. The practical reason for summoning the strong popular element was de Montfort's desire to weight the Parliament with his own supporters: among the magnates only five earls and eighteen barons received writs of summons. Again he fell back upon the support of the country gentry and the burgesses against the hostility or indifference of the magnates. In this lay his message and his tactics.

Throughout these struggles of lasting significance the English barons never deviated from their own self-interest. At Runnymede they had served national freedom when they thought they were defending their own privilege. They had now no doubt that Simon was its enemy. He was certainly a despot, with a king in his wallet and the forces of social revolution at his back. The barons formed a hard confederacy among themselves, and with all the forces of the Court not in Simon's hands schemed night and day to overthrow him. By promising to uphold the Charters, to remedy grievances, and to expel the foreigners Edward succeeded in uniting the baronial party and in cutting away the ground from under de Montfort's feet. Out-manœuvred politically by Edward, he also placed himself at a serious military disadvantage. The Earl was caught in turn at Evesham; and here on August 4 the final battle took place. De Montfort died a hero on the field.

In the last years of his life, with de Montfort dead and Edward away on Crusade, the feeble King enjoyed comparative peace; he could turn back to the things of beauty that interested him far more than political struggles. The new Abbey of Westminster, a masterpiece of Gothic architecture, was now dedicated; its consecration had long been the dearest object of Henry III's life. And here in the last weeks of 1272 he was buried. The quiet of these last few years should not lead us to suppose that de Montfort's struggle and the civil war had been in vain. Among the common people he was for many years worshipped as a saint, and miracles were worked at his tomb. Though a prince among administrators, he suffered as a politician from over-confidence and impatience. He trampled upon vested interests, broke with all traditions, did violence to all forms, and needlessly created suspicion and distrust. Yet de Montfort had lighted a fire never to be quenched in English history. Already in 1267 the Statute of Marlborough had re-enacted the chief of the Provisions of Westminster. Not less important was his influence upon his nephew, Edward, the new King, who was to draw deeply upon the ideas of the man he had slain. In this way de Montfort's purposes survived both the field of Evesham and the reaction which succeeded it, and in Edward I the great Earl found his true heir.

Few princes had received so thorough an education in the art of rulership as Edward I when at the age of thirty-three his father's death brought him to the Crown. He was of elegant build and lofty stature, a head and shoulders above the height of the ordinary man. He was an experienced leader and a skilful general. He presents us with qualities which are a mixture of the administrative capacity of Henry II and the personal prowess and magnanimity of Cœur de Lion. No English king more fully lived up to the maxim he chose for himself: "To each his own." He was animated by a passionate regard for justice and law, as he interpreted them, and for the rights of all groups within the community. Injuries and hostility roused, even to his last breath, a passionate torrent of resistance. But submission, or a generous act, on many occasions earned a swift response and laid the foundation of future friendship.

Proportion is the keynote of his greatest

King Edward I
(1239–1307)

56

years. He saw in the proud, turbulent baronage and a rapacious Church checks upon the royal authority; but he also recognised them as oppressors of the mass of his subjects; and it was by taking into account to a larger extent than had occurred before the interests of the middle class, and the needs of the people as a whole, that he succeeded in producing a broad, well-ordered foundation upon which an active monarchy could function in the general interest. Here was a time of setting in order. In this period we see a knightly and *bourgeois* stage of society increasingly replacing pure feudalism. The organs of government, land tenure, the military and financial systems, the relations of Church and State, all reach definitions which last nearly till the Tudors.

The first eighteen years of the reign witnessed an outburst of legislative activity for which there was to be no parallel for centuries. Nearly every year was marked by an important statute. Few of these were original, most were conservative in tone, but their cumulative effect was revolutionary. The First Statute of Westminster in the Parliament of 1275 dealt with administrative abuses. The Statute of Gloucester in 1278 directed the justices to inquire by writs of *Quo Warranto* into the rights of feudal magnates to administer the law by their own courts and officials within their demesnes, and ordained that those rights should be strictly defined. In 1279 the Statute of Mortmain, *De Religiosis*, forbade gifts of land to be made to the Church, though the practice was allowed to continue under royal licence. In 1285 the Statute of Winchester attacked local disorder, and in the same year was issued the Second Statute of Westminster, *De Donis Conditionalibus*, which strengthened the system of entailed estates. The Third Statute of Westminster, *Quia Emptores*, dealt with land held, not upon condition, but in fee simple.

In those days, when the greatest princes were pitifully starved in cash, there was already in England one spring of credit bubbling feebly. The Jews had unseen and noiselessly lodged themselves in the social fabric of that fierce age. Land began to pass into the hand of Israel, either by direct sale or more often by mortgage. For some time past there had been growing a wrathful reaction. Edward saw himself able to conciliate powerful elements and escape from awkward debts, by the simple and well-trodden path of anti-Semitism. The Jews, held up to universal hatred, were pillaged, maltreated, and finally expelled the realm. Not until four centuries had elapsed was Oliver Cromwell by contracts with a moneyed Israelite to open again the coasts of England to the enterprise of the Jewish race. It was left to a Calvinist dictator to remove the ban which a Catholic king had imposed.

Edward I was remarkable among medieval kings for the seriousness with which he regarded the work of administration and good government. By the end of the thirteenth century three departments of specialised administration were already at work. One was the Exchequer, established at Westminster, where most of the revenue was received and the accounts kept. The second was the Chancery, a general secretariat responsible for the writing and drafting of innumerable royal charters, writs, and letters. The third was the Wardrobe, with its separate secretariat, the Privy Seal, attached to the ever-moving royal Household, and combining financial and secretarial functions, which might range from financing a Continental war to buying a pennyworth of pepper for the royal cook.

Though the most orthodox of Churchmen, Edward I did not escape conflict with the Church. Anxious though he was to pay his dues to God, he had a far livelier sense than his father of what was due to Cæsar, and circumstances more than once forced him to protest. The leader of the Church party was John Pecham, a Franciscan friar, Archbishop of Canterbury from 1279 to 1292. With great courage and skill Pecham defended what he regarded as the just rights of the Church and its independence against the Crown. Yet moderation was observed, and in 1286 by a famous writ Edward wisely ordered his itinerant justices to act circumspectly in

matters of ecclesiastical jurisdiction, and listed the kinds of case which should be left to Church courts.

At the beginning of the reign relations between England and France were governed by the Treaty of Paris, which the baronial party had concluded in 1259. For more than thirty years peace reigned between the two countries, though often with an undercurrent of hostility. Finally however the Parlement of Paris declared the Duchy of Gascony forfeit. Edward now realised that he must either fight, or lose his French possessions. The war itself had no important features. Any enthusiasm which had been expressed at the outset wore off speedily under the inevitable increases of taxation. In the winter of 1294 the Welsh revolted, and when the King had suppressed them he returned to find that Scotland had allied itself with France. From 1296 onward war with Scotland was either smouldering or flaring. After October 1297 the French War degenerated into a series of truces which lasted until 1303. Such conditions involved expense little less than actual fighting. The position of the clergy was made more difficult by the publication in 1296 of the Papal Bull *Clericis Laicos*, which forbade the payment of extraordinary taxation without Papal authority. For a time passion ran high, but eventually a calmer mood prevailed. Edward was the more prepared to come to terms with the Church because opposition had already broken out in another quarter. He proposed to the barons at Salisbury that a number of them should serve in Gascony while he conducted a campaign in Flanders. This was ill received. Humphrey de Bohun, Earl of Hereford and Constable of England, together with the Marshal, Roger Bigod, Earl of Norfolk, voiced the resentment felt by a large number of the barons who for the past twenty years had steadily seen the authority of the Crown increased to their own detriment. The time was ripe for a revival of the baronial opposition which a generation before had defied Edward's father.

For the moment the King ignored the challenge. The opposition saw their long-awaited opportunity. They demanded the confirmation of those two instruments, Magna Carta and its extension, the Charter of the Forest, which were the final version of the terms extorted from John, together with six additional articles. The Regency, unable to resist, submitted. The articles were confirmed, and in November at Ghent the King ratified them, reserving however certain financial rights of the Crown. By this crisis and its manner of resolution two principles had been established from which important consequences flowed. One was that the King had no right to dispatch the feudal host wherever he might choose. This limitation sounded the death-knell of the feudal levy, and inexorably led in the following century to the rise of indentured armies serving for pay. The second point of principle now recognised was that the King could not plead "urgent necessity" as a reason for imposing taxation without consent. Other English monarchs as late as the seventeenth century were to make the attempt. But by Edward's failure a precedent had been set up, and a long stride had been taken towards the dependence of the Crown upon Parliamentary grants.

Edward I was the first of the English kings to put the whole weight of the Crown's resources behind the effort of national expansion in the West and North, and to him is due the conquest of the independent areas of Wales and the securing of the Western frontier. He took the first great step towards the unification of the Island. All assertions of Welsh independence were a vexation to Edward; but scarcely less obnoxious was a system of guarding the frontiers of England by a confederacy of robber barons who had more than once presumed to challenge the authority of the Crown. Edward I, utilising all the local resources which the barons of the Welsh Marches had developed in the chronic strife of many generations, conquered Wales in several years of persistent warfare, coldly and carefully devised, by land and sea. The land of Llewellyn's Wales was transferred to the King's dominions and organised into the shires of Anglesey, Carnarvon,

The seal of Robert Bruce. BRITISH MUSEUM

Edward I returning from Gascony. An illustration from
a fifteenth-century Flemish manuscript. BRITISH MUSEUM

Merioneth, Cardigan, and Carmarthen. The King's son Edward, born in Carnarvon, was proclaimed the first English Prince of Wales.

The Welsh wars of Edward reveal to us the process by which the military system of England was transformed from the age-long Saxon and feudal basis of occasional service to that of paid regular troops. Instead of liege service Governments now required trustworthy mercenaries, and for this purpose money was the solvent. At the same time a counter-revolution in the balance of warfare was afoot. The mailed cavalry which from the fifth century had eclipsed the ordered ranks of the legion were wearing out their long day. A new type of infantry raised from the common people began to prove its dominating quality. This infantry operated, not by club or sword or spear, or even by hand-flung missiles, but by an archery which, after a long development, concealed from Europe, was very soon to make an astonishing entrance upon the military scene and gain a dramatic ascendancy upon the battlefields of the Continent. Here was a prize taken by the conquerors from their victims. In South Wales the practice of drawing the long-bow had already attained an astonishing efficiency. This was a new fact in the history of war, which is also a part of the history of civilisation, deserving to be mentioned with the triumph of bronze over flint, or iron over bronze. Thus the Welsh wars, from two separate points of departure, destroyed the physical basis of feudalism, which had already, in its moral aspect, been outsped and outclassed by the extension and refinement of administration.

The great quarrel of Edward's reign was with Scotland. Since the days of Henry II the English monarchy had intermittently claimed an overlordship of Scotland, based on the still earlier acknowledgment of Saxon overlordship by Scottish kings. King Edward now imposed himself with considerable acceptance as arbitrator in the Scottish succession. But the national feeling of Scotland was pent up behind these barriers of legal affirmation. To resist Edward the Scots allied themselves with the French. Since Edward was at war with France he regarded this as an act of hostility. Edward struck with ruthless severity. He advanced on Berwick. The city, then the great emporium of Northern trade, was unprepared, after a hundred years of peace, to resist attack, and sank in a few hours from one of the active centres of European commerce to the minor seaport which exists today. This act of terror quelled the resistance of the ruling classes in Scotland. But, as in Wales, the conqueror introduced not only an alien rule, but law and order, all of which were equally unpopular. It has often been said that Joan of Arc first raised the standard of nationalism in the Western World. But over a century before she appeared an outlaw knight, William Wallace, arising from the recesses of South-West Scotland which had been his refuge, embodied, commanded, and led to victory the Scottish nation. He had few cavalry and few archers; but his confidence lay in the solid "schiltrons" (or circles) of spearmen, who were invincible except by actual physical destruction. It was not until 1305 that Wallace was captured, tried with full ceremonial in Westminster Hall, and hanged, drawn, and quartered at Tyburn. But the Scottish War was one in which, as a chronicler said, "every winter undid every summer's work". Wallace was to pass the torch to Robert Bruce.

King Edward was old, but his will-power was unbroken. He launched a campaign in the summer of 1306 in which Bruce was defeated and driven to take refuge on Rathlin Island, off the coast of Antrim. Here, according to the tale, Bruce was heartened by the persistent efforts of the most celebrated spider known to history. Next spring he returned to Scotland. Edward was now too ill to march or ride. Like the Emperor Severus a thousand years before, he was carried in a litter against this stern people, and like him he died upon the road.

Edward I was the last great figure in the formative period of English law. His statutes, which settled questions of public order, assigned limits to the powers of the seigneurial courts, and restrained the sprawling and luxurious growth of judge-made law, laid down principles that remained fundamental to the law of property until the mid nineteenth century. In the constitutional sphere the work of Edward I was not less durable. He had made Parliament—that is to say, certain selected magnates and representatives of the shires and boroughs—the associate of the Crown, in place of the old Court of Tenants-in-Chief. By the end of his reign this conception had been established. Dark constitutional problems loomed in the future. Idle weaklings, dreamers, and adventurous boys disrupted the nascent unity of the Island. Long years of civil war, and despotism in reaction from anarchy, marred and delayed the development of its institutions. But when the traveller gazes upon the plain marble tomb at Westminster on which is inscribed, "Here lies Edward I, the Hammer of the Scots. Keep troth", he stands before the resting-place of a master-builder of British life, character, and fame.

Edward II's reign may fairly be regarded as a melancholy appendix to his father's and the prelude to his son's. A strong, capable King had with difficulty upborne the load. He was succeeded by a perverted weakling, of whom some amiable traits are recorded. He was addicted to rowing, swimming, and baths. He carried his friendship for his advisers beyond dignity and decency.

In default of a dominating Parliamentary institution, the Curia Regis seemed to be the centre from which the business of Government could be controlled. On the death of Edward I the barons succeeded in gaining control of this mixed body of powerful magnates and competent Household officials. They set up a committee called "the Lords Ordainers". Piers Gaveston, a young, handsome Gascon, enjoyed the King's fullest confidence. His decisions made or marred. The barons' party attacked Piers Gaveston. Edward and his favourite tried to stave off opposition by harrying the Scots. They failed, and in 1311 Gaveston was exiled to Flanders. Thence he was so imprudent as to return, in defiance of the Lords Ordainers. Besieged in

The tomb of Edward II, the first Prince of Wales, in Gloucester Cathedral. COURTESY: THE DEAN AND CHAPTER

the Castle of Scarborough, Gaveston made terms with his foes. His life was to be spared; and on this they took him under guard. But other nobles overpowered the escort, seized the favourite at Deddington in Oxfordshire, and hewed off his head on Blacklow Hill, near Warwick.

Edward was still in control of Government, although he was under restraint. To wipe out his setbacks at home he resolved upon the conquest of the Northern kingdom. A great army crossed the Tweed in the summer of 1314. Twenty-five thousand men, hard to gather, harder still to feed in those days, with at least three thousand armoured knights and men-at-arms, moved against the champion of Scotland, Robert Bruce. The Scottish army, of perhaps ten thousand men, was composed mainly of the hard, unyielding spearmen. Bruce, who had pondered deeply upon the impotence of pikemen, however faithful, with a foresight and skill which proves his military quality, took three precautions. First, he chose a position where his flanks were secured by impenetrable woods; secondly, he dug upon his front a large number of small round holes and covered them with branches and turfs as a trap for charging cavalry; thirdly, he kept in his own hand his small but highly trained force of mounted knights to break up any attempt at planting archers upon his flank. These dispositions made, he awaited the English onslaught. On the morning of June 24 the English advanced, and a dense wave of steel-clad horsemen descended the slope, splashed and scrambled through the Bannock Burn, and charged uphill upon the schiltrons. No more grievous slaughter of English chivalry ever took place in a single day. Even Towton in the Wars of the Roses was less destructive. The Scots claimed to have slain or captured thirty thousand men, more than the whole English army, but their feat in virtually destroying an army of cavalry and archers mainly by the agency of spearmen must nevertheless be deemed a prodigy of war.

The feudal baronage had striven successfully against kings. They now saw in the royal officials agents who stood in their way, yet at the same time were obviously indispensable to the widening aspects of national life. The whole tendency of their movement was therefore in this generation to acquire control of an invaluable machine. One of the main charges brought against Edward II at his deposition was that he had failed in his task of government. From early in his reign he left too much to his Household officials. Outside this select, secluded circle the rugged, arrogant, virile barons prowled morosely. It is the nature of supreme executive power to withdraw itself into the smallest compass; and without such contraction there is no executive power. But when this exclusionary process was tainted by unnatural vice and stained by shameful defeat in the field it was clear that those who beat upon the doors had found a prosperous occasion. The forces were not unequally balanced. The barons might have a blasting case against the King at Westminster, but if he appeared in Shrop-

shire or Westmorland with his handful of guards and the royal insignia he could tell his own tale, and men, both knight and archer, would rally to him. Thus we see in this ill-starred reign both sides operating in and through Parliament, and in this process enhancing its power. Parliament was called together no fewer than twenty-five times under King Edward II. In the long story of a nation we often see that capable rulers by their very virtues sow the seeds of future evil and weak or degenerate princes open the pathway of progress.

Thomas of Lancaster, nephew to Edward I, was the forefront of the baronial opposition. Little is known to his credit. Into the hands of Thomas and his fellow Ordainers Edward was now thrown by the disaster of Bannockburn, and Thomas for a while became the most important man in the land. Within a few years however the moderates among the Ordainers became so disgusted with Lancaster's incompetence and with the weakness into which the process of government had sunk that they joined with the royalists to edge him from power. Edward, for his part, began to build up a royalist party, at the head of which were the Despensers, father and son, both named Hugh. They were especially unpopular among the Marcher lords, who were disturbed by their restless ambitions in South Wales. In 1321 the Welsh Marcher lords and the Lancastrian party joined hands with intent to procure the exile of the Despensers. Edward soon recalled them, and for once showed energy and resolution. By speed of movement he defeated first the Marcher lords and then in the next year the Northern barons under Lancaster at Boroughbridge in Yorkshire. Lancaster was beheaded by the King.

But a tragedy with every feature of classical ruthlessness was to follow. One of the chief Marcher lords, Roger Mortimer, though captured by the King, contrived to escape to France. In 1324 Charles IV of France took advantage of a dispute in Gascony to seize the Duchy, except for a coastal strip. Edward's wife, Isabella, "the she-wolf of France", who was disgusted by his passion

Soldiers pillaging and looting a house. An illustration by Matthew Paris, thirteenth century. BRITISH MUSEUM

for Hugh Despenser, suggested that she should go over to France to negotiate with her brother Charles about the restoration of Gascony. As soon as the fourteen-year-old Prince Edward, who as heir to the throne could be used to legitimatise opposition to King Edward, was in her possession she and Mortimer staged an invasion of England at the head of a large band of exiles. So unpopular and precarious was Edward's government that Isabella's triumph was swift and complete, and she and Mortimer were emboldened to depose him. The end was a holocaust. In the furious rage which in those days led all who swayed the government of England to a bloody fate the Despensers were seized and hanged. For the King a more terrible death was reserved. He was imprisoned in Berkeley Castle, and there by hideous methods, which left no mark upon his skin, was slaughtered. His screams as his bowels were burnt out by red-hot irons

passed into his body were heard outside the prison walls, and awoke grim echoes which were long unstilled.

The failures of the reign of Edward II had permanent effects on the unity of the British Isles. Bannockburn ended the possibility of uniting the English and Scottish Crowns by force. Hatred of the English was the mark of a good Scot. Though discontented nobles might accept English help and English pay, the common people were resolute in their refusal to bow to English rule in any form. The memory of Bannockburn kept a series of notable defeats at the hands of the English from breeding despair or thought of surrender.

The disunity of the kingdom, fostered by English policy and perpetuated by the tragedies that befell the Scottish sovereigns, was not the only source of Scotland's weakness. The land was divided in race, in speech, and in culture. The rift between Highlands and Lowlands was more than a geographical

63

distinction. The Lowlands formed part of the feudal world, and, except in the South-West, in Galloway, English was spoken. The Highlands preserved a social order much older than feudalism. In the Lowlands the King of Scots was a feudal magnate; in the Highlands he was the chief of a loose federation of clans. Meanwhile, the Scots peasant farmer and the thrifty burgess, throughout these two hundred years of political strife, pursued their ways and built up the country's real strength in spite of the numerous disputes among their lords and masters. The Church devoted itself to its healing mission, and many good bishops and divines adorn the annals of medieval Scotland. In the fifteenth century three Scottish universities were founded, St Andrew's, Glasgow, and Aberdeen—one more than England had until the nineteenth century.

When the long, sorrowful story began of English intervention in Ireland the country had already endured the shock and torment of Scandinavian invasion. In 1169 there arrived in the country the first progenitors of the Anglo-Norman ascendancy, but there was no organised colonisation and settlement. English authority was accepted in the Norse towns on the southern and eastern coasts, and the King's writ ran over a varying area of country surrounding Dublin. Immediately outside lay the big feudal lordships, and beyond these were the "wild" unconquered Irish of the West. Within a few generations of the coming of the Anglo-Normans the Irish chieftains began to recover from the shock of new methods of warfare. They regained for the Gaelic-speaking peoples wide regions of Ireland, and might have won more, had they not incessantly quarrelled among themselves. Meanwhile, a change of spirit had overtaken many of the Anglo-Norman Irish barons. Their stock was seldom reinforced from England, except by English lords who wedded Irish heiresses, and then became absentee landlords. Gradually a group of Anglo-Irish nobles grew up, largely assimilated to their adopted land, and as impatient as their Gaelic peasants of rule from London.

If English kings had regularly visited Ireland, or regularly appointed royal princes as resident lieutenants, the ties between the two countries might have been closely and honourably woven together. As it was, when the English king was strong English laws generally made headway; otherwise a loose Celtic anarchy prevailed. King John, in his furious fitful energy, twice went to Ireland, and twice brought the quarrelsome Norman barons and Irish chiefs under his suzerainty. Although Edward I never landed in Ireland English authority was then in the ascendant. Thereafter the Gaels revived.

It seemed that the strong blood of Edward I had but slumbered in his degenerate son, for in Edward III England once more found leadership equal to her steadily growing strength. Beneath the squalid surface of Edward II's reign there had none the less proceeded in England a marked growth of national power and prosperity. The English people stood at this time possessed of a commanding weapon, the qualities of which were utterly unsuspected abroad. The long-bow, handled by the well-trained archer class, brought into the field a yeoman type of soldier with whom there was nothing on the Continent to compare. The power of the long-bow and the skill of the bowmen had developed to a point where at two hundred and fifty yards the arrow hail produced effects never reached again by infantry missiles at such a range until the American Civil War. The skilled archer was a professional soldier, earning and deserving high pay. The protracted wars of the two Edwards in the mountains of Wales and Scotland had taught the English many hard lessons, and although European warriors had from time to time shared in them they had neither measured nor imparted the secret of the new army. It was with a sense of unmeasured superiority that the English looked out upon Europe at the end of the first quarter of the fourteenth century.

The reign of King Edward III passed through several distinct phases. In the first he was a minor, and the land was ruled by his mother and her lover, Roger Mortimer.

King Edward III
(1312-77)

64

This government, founded upon unnatural murder and representing only a faction in the nobility, was condemned to weakness at home and abroad. Its rule of nearly four years was marked by concession and surrender both in France and in Scotland. In May 1328 the "Shameful Treaty of Northampton", as it was called at the time, recognised Bruce as King north of the Tweed, and implied the abandonment of all the claims of Edward I in Scotland. All eyes were therefore turned to the young King. When fifteen, in 1328, he had been married to Philippa of Hainault. In June 1330 a son was born to him; he felt himself now a grown man who must do his duty by the realm. In October Parliament sat at Nottingham. Mortimer and Isabella, guarded by ample force, were lodged in the castle. An underground passage led into its heart. Through this on an October night a small band of resolute men entered, surprised Mortimer in his chamber, which as usual was next to the Queen's, and, dragging them both along the subterranean way, delivered them to the King's officers. Mortimer, conducted to London, was brought before the peers, accused of the murder in Berkeley Castle and other crimes, and, after condemnation by the lords, hanged on November 29. Isabella was consigned by her son to perpetual captivity.

The guiding spirit of the new King was to revive the policy, assert the claims, and restore the glories of his grandfather. The quarrel with Scotland was resumed. The contacts between Scotland and France and the constant aid given by the French Court to the Scottish enemies of England roused a deep antagonism. Thus the war in Scotland pointed the path to Flanders. Here a new set of grievances formed a substantial basis for a conflict. The loss of all the French possessions, except Gascony, and the constant bickering on the Gascon frontiers, had been endured perforce since the days of John. But in 1328 the death of Charles IV without a direct heir opened a further issue. Philip of Valois assumed the royal power and demanded homage from Edward, who made

Edward III with his prisoner, King David II of Scotland, captured at the Battle of Neville's Cross in 1346. BRITISH MUSEUM

difficulties. King Edward III, in his mother's right—if indeed the female line was valid—had a remote claim to the throne of France. This claim, by and with the assent and advice of the Lords Spiritual and Temporal, and of the Commons of England, he was later to advance in support of his campaigns. He was conscious moreover from the first of the advantage to be gained by diverting the restless energies of his nobles from internal intrigues and rivalries to the unifying purpose of a foreign war. This was also in harmony with the temper of his people. Now we see the picture of the Estates of the Realm becoming themselves ardently desirous of foreign conquests.

The wool trade with the Low Countries was the staple of English exports, and almost the sole form of wealth which rose above the resources of agriculture. Repeated obstructions were placed by the counts of Flanders upon the wool trade, and each aroused the anger of those concerned on both sides of the Narrow Sea. In 1336 Edward was moved to retaliate in a decisive manner. He decreed an embargo on all exports of English wool, thus producing a furious crisis in the

65

Spinning and weaving, a scene from the fourteenth-century Luttrell Psalter. BRITISH MUSEUM

Netherlands. The townspeople rose against the feudal aristocracy, and under Jacques Van Arteveldt, a warlike merchant of Ghent, gained control, after a struggle of much severity, over a large part of the country. The victorious burghers, threatened by aristocratic and French revenge, looked to England for aid, and their appeals met with a hearty and deeply interested response.

Thus all streams of profit and ambition flowed into a common channel at a moment when the flood-waters of conscious military strength ran high, and in 1337, when Edward repudiated his grudging homage to Philip VI, the Hundred Years War began. It was never to be concluded; no general peace treaty was signed, and not until the Peace of Amiens in 1802, when France was a republic and the French royal heir a refugee within these isles, did the English sovereign formally renounce his claims to the throne of the Valois and the Bourbons.

Edward slowly assembled the expeditionary army of England. This was not a feudal levy, but a paid force of picked men. Philip VI looked first to the sea. But Edward had not neglected the sea-power. His interest in the Navy won him from Parliament early in his reign the title of "King of the Sea". In the summer of 1340 the hostile navies met off Sluys, and a struggle of nine hours ensued. The French admirals had been ordered, under pain of death, to prevent the invasion, and both sides fought well; but the French fleet was decisively beaten and the command of the Channel passed into the hands of the invading Power. Joined with the revolted Flemings, Edward's numbers were greatly augmented, and this combined force, which may have exceeded twenty thousand, undertook the first Anglo-Flemish siege of Tournai. But the capture of this fortress was beyond Edward's resources in money and supplies; the first campaign of what was a great

66

European war yielded no results, and a prolonged truce supervened. The French wreaked their vengeance on the burghers of the Netherlands, whom they crushed utterly, and Van Arteveldt met his death in a popular tumult at Ghent. The English retaliated as best they could. There was a disputed succession in Brittany, which they fomented with substantial aids. The chronic warfare on the frontiers of Gascony continued.

By the spring of 1346 Parliament had at length brought itself to the point of facing the taxation necessary to finance a new invasion. In one wave two thousand four hundred cavalry, twelve thousand archers, and other infantry sailed, and landed unopposed at St Vaast in Normandy on July 12, 1346. Their object this time was no less than the capture of Paris by a sudden dash. A huge force which comprised all the chivalry of France and was probably three times as big as Edward's army assembled in the neighbourhood of St Denis. Against such opposition, added to the walls of a fortified city, Edward's resources could not attempt to prevail. The thrust had failed and retreat imposed itself upon the army. They must now make for the Somme, and hope to cross between Amiens and the sea.

Philip, at the head of a host between thirty and forty thousand strong, was hard upon the track. He had every hope of bringing the insolent Islanders to bay with their backs to the river, or catching them in transit. When he learned that they were already over he called a council of war. His generals advised that, since the tide was now in, there was no choice but to ascend to Abbeville and cross by the bridge which the French held there. To Abbeville they accordingly moved, and lay there for the night. Edward gathered his chiefs to supper and afterwards to prayer. It was certain that they could not gain the coast without a battle. No other resolve was open than to fight at enormous odds. The King and the Prince of Wales, afterwards famous as the Black Prince, received all the offices of religion, and Edward prayed that the impending battle should at least leave him unstripped of honour.

King Philip at sunrise on Saturday, August 26, 1346, heard Mass in the Monastery of Abbeville, and his whole army, gigantic for those times, rolled forward in their long pursuit. About midday the King, having arrived with large masses on the farther bank of the Somme, received their reports. The English were in battle array and meant to fight. He gave the sage counsel to halt for the day, bring up the rear, form the battle-line, and attack on the morrow. While many great bodies halted obediently, still larger masses poured forward, forcing their way through the stationary or withdrawing troops, and at about five in the afternoon came face to face with the English army lying in full view on the broad slopes of Crécy. King Philip, arriving on the scene, was carried away by the ardour of the throng around him. The sun was already low; nevertheless, all were determined to engage.

There was a corps of six thousand Genoese crossbowmen in the van of the army. These were ordered to make their way through the masses of horsemen, and with their missiles break up the hostile array in preparation for the cavalry attacks. At this moment, while the crossbowmen were threading their way to the front, dark clouds swept across the sun and a short, drenching storm beat upon the hosts. After wetting the bow-strings of the Genoese, it passed as quickly as it had come, and the setting sun shone brightly in their eyes and on the backs of the English. The Genoese, drawing out their array, gave a loud shout, advanced a few steps, shouted again, and a third time advanced, "hooted", and discharged their bolts. Unbroken silence had wrapped the English lines, but at this the archers, six or seven thousand strong, ranged on both flanks in "portcullis" formation, who had hitherto stood motionless, advanced one step, drew their bows to the ear, and came into action. They "shot their arrows with such force and quickness", says Froissart, "that it seemed as if it snowed". The effect upon the Genoese was annihilating; at a range which their own weapons could not attain they were in a few minutes killed by thousands. The front line of the French cavalry rode among the retreating

67

Genoese, cutting them down with their swords. In doing so they came within the deadly distance. The arrow snow-storm beat upon them, piercing their mail and smiting horse and man. Valiant squadrons from behind rode forward into the welter, and the main attack of the French now developed. Evading the archers as far as possible, they sought the men-at-arms, and French, German, and Savoyard squadrons actually reached the Prince of Wales's division. The enemy's numbers were so great that those who fought about the Prince sent to the windmill, whence King Edward directed the battle, for reinforcements. But the King would not part with his reserves, saying, "Let the boy win his spurs"—which in fact he did. Continuous cavalry charges were launched upon the English front, until utter darkness fell upon the field. And all through the night fresh troops of brave men, resolved not to quit the field without striking their blow, struggled forward, groping their way. All these were slain, for "No quarter" was the mood of the English, though by no means the wish of their King. "When on this Saturday night the English heard no more

An incident at the Battle of Poitiers, from the Holisham MS Chronicle of the Counts of Flanders. MANSELL COLLECTION

hooting or shouting, nor any more crying out to particular lords, or their banners, they looked upon the field as their own and their enemies as beaten." On the Sunday morning fog enshrouded the battlefield, and the King sent a strong force of five hundred lancers and two thousand archers to learn what lay upon his front. "It has been assured to me for fact", says Froissart, "that of foot-soldiers, sent from the cities, towns, and municipalities, there were slain, this Sunday morning, four times as many as in the battle of the Saturday." This astounding victory of Crécy ranks with Blenheim, Waterloo, and the final advance in the last summer of the Great War as one of the four supreme achievements of the British Army.[1]

Edward marched through Montreuil and Etaples to Boulogne, passed through the Forest of Hardelot, and opened the siege of Calais. Calais presented itself to English eyes as the hive of that swarm of privateers who were the endless curse of the Channel. Calais held out for eleven months, and yet this did not suffice. Famine at length left no choice to the besieged. They sued for terms. Calais, then, was the fruit, and the sole territorial fruit so far, of the exertions, prodigious in quality, of the whole power of England in the war with France. But Crécy had a longer tale to tell.

Christendom has no catastrophe equal to the Black Death. We read of lawsuits where all parties died before the cases could be heard; of monasteries where half the inmates perished; of dioceses where the surviving clergy could scarcely perform the last offices for their flocks and for their brethren; of the Goldsmiths' Company, which had four Masters in a year. These are detailed indications. But far more convincing is the gap which opens in all the local annals of the nation. A whole generation is slashed through by a hideous severance.

Philosophers might suggest that there was no need for the use of the destructive mechanism of plague to procure the changes deemed necessary among men. The early fifteenth century was to see the end of the

[1] Written in 1939.

rule of the armoured men. Gunpowder, which we have seen used in the puny bombards which, according to some authorities, Edward had fired at Crécy and against Calais, was soon decisively to establish itself as a practical factor in war and in human affairs based on war. If cannon had not been invented the English mastery of the longbow might have carried them even farther in their Continental domination.

The war between England and France continued in a broken fashion, and the Black Prince, the most renowned warrior in Europe, became a freebooter. In 1355 King Edward obtained from Parliament substantial grants for the renewal of active war. The Black Prince would advance northward from the English territories of Gascony and Aquitaine towards the Loire. His younger brother, John of Gaunt, Duke of Lancaster, struck in from Brittany. But all this miscarried, and the Black Prince found himself, with forces shrunk to about four thousand men, of whom however nearly a half were the dreaded archers, forced to retire with growing urgency before the advance of a French royal army twenty thousand strong. Terms were rejected by the French, who once again saw their deeply hated foe in their grasp. At Poitiers the Prince was brought to bay. But King John of France was resolved to avenge Crécy and finish the war at a stroke.

Ten years had passed since Crécy, and French chivalry and high command alike had brooded upon the tyranny of that event. They had been forced to accept the fact that horses could not face the arrow storm. King John was certain that all must attack on foot, and he trusted to overwhelming numbers. But the great merit of the Black Prince is that he did not rest upon the lessons of the past or prepare himself to repeat the triumphs of a former battle. The French nobility left their horses in the rear. The Black Prince had all his knights mounted. The French chivalry, encumbered by their mail, plodded ponderously forward amid vineyards and scrub. Many fell before the arrows, but the arrows would not have been enough at the crisis. It was the English spear-

Funeral achievements of the Black Prince, in Canterbury Cathedral. From left to right the great helm and crest, the jupon *or coat of arms, and the shield.* PHOTO: JOHN R. FREEMAN. COURTESY: THE DEAN AND CHAPTER

and axe-men who charged in the old style upon ranks disordered by their fatigue of movement and the accidents of the ground. At the same time, in admirable concert, a strong detachment of mounted knights, riding round the French left flank, struck in upon the harassed and already disordered attack. The result was a slaughter as large and a victory as complete as Crécy, but with even greater gains. The whole French army was driven into ruin. King John and the flower of his nobility were captured or slain.

King John was carried to London. In May 1360, the Treaty of Brétigny was concluded. By this England acquired, in addition to her old possession of Gascony, the whole of Henry II's possessions in Aquitaine in full sovereignty, Edward I's inheritance of Ponthieu, and the famous port and city of Calais, which last was held for nearly two hundred years. A ransom was fixed for King John at three million gold crowns, the equivalent of £500,000 sterling. This was eight times the annual revenue of the English Crown in time of peace. The triumph and the exhaustion of England were simultaneously complete. A great French hero appeared in Bertrand du Guesclin, who, like Fabius Cunctator against Hannibal, by refusing battle and acting through sieges and surprises, rallied the factor of time to the home side. It was proved that the French army could not beat the English, and at the same time that England could not conquer France. The main effort of Edward III, though crowned with all the military laurels, had failed.

The years of the war with France are important in the history of Parliament. The need for money drove the Crown and its officials to summoning it frequently. Under Edward I the Commons were not an essential element in a Parliament, but under Edward III they assumed a position distinct, vital, and permanent. They had their own clerk, who drafted their petitions and their rejoinders to the Crown's replies. The separation of the Houses now appears. The concessions made by Edward III to the Commons mark a decisive stage. He consented that all aids should be granted only in Parliament. He accepted the formal drafts of the Commons' collective petitions as the preliminary bases for future statutes, and by the time of his death it was recognised that the Commons had assumed a leading part in the granting of taxes and the presentation of petitions.

Against Papal agents feeling was strong. The war with France had stimulated and embittered national sentiment, which resented the influence of an external institution whose great days were already passing. Moreover, this declining power had perforce abandoned its sacred traditional seat in Rome, and was now installed under French influence in enemy territory at Avignon. The renewal in 1369 of serious fighting in Aquitaine found England exhausted and disillusioned. Churchmen were ousting the nobility from public office and anti-clerical feeling grew in Parliament. The King was old and failing and a resurgence of baronial power was due. John of Gaunt set himself to redress

Sir Thomas Hungerford, the first recorded Speaker of the House of Commons, 1377. FROM A WINDOW IN FARLEIGH HUNGERFORD CHURCH

70

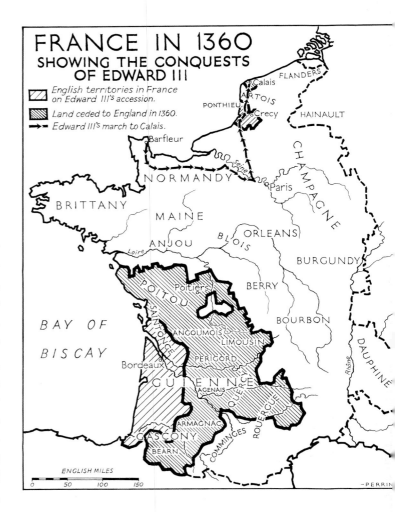

FRANCE IN 1360
SHOWING THE CONQUESTS OF EDWARD III

English territories in France on Edward III's accession.

Land ceded to England in 1360.

Edward III's march to Calais.

Sir Geoffrey Luttrell, armed and mounted. From the fourteenth-century Luttrell Psalter. BRITISH MUSEUM

the balance in favour of the Lords by a carefully planned political campaign against the Church. The arguments for reform set forth by a distinguished Oxford scholar named Wyclif attracted attention. Wyclif's doctrine could not remain the speculation of a harmless schoolman. It involved reducing the powers of the Church temporal in order to purify the Church spiritual. John of Gaunt was interested in the first, Wyclif in the second. They entered into alliance. Both suffered from their union. The bishops, recognising in Wyclif Gaunt's most dangerous supporter, arraigned him on charges of heresy at St Paul's. Gaunt, coming to his aid, encountered the hostility of the London mob. The ill-matched partnership fell to pieces and Wyclif ceased to count in high politics.

It was at this same point that his enduring influence began. He resolved to appeal to the people. Church abuses and his own reforming doctrines had attracted many young students around him. He wrote English tracts, of which the most famous was *The Wicket*, which were passed from hand to hand. Finally, with his students he took the tremendous step of having the Bible translated into English.

The long reign had reached its dusk. The

glories of Crécy and Poitiers had faded. A few coastal towns alone attested the splendour of victories long to be cherished in the memories of the Island race. The old King had fallen under the consoling thrall of Alice Perrers, a lady of indifferent extraction, but of remarkable wit and capacity, untrammelled by scruple or by prudence. In 1376 the Black Prince expired, leaving a son not ten years old as heir apparent to the throne. King Edward III's large share of life narrowed sharply at its end. Mortally stricken, he retired to Sheen Lodge, where Alice, after the modern fashion, encouraged him to dwell on tournaments, the chase, and wide plans when he should recover. But hostile chroniclers have it that when the stupor preceding death engulfed the King she took the rings from his fingers and other movable property in the house and departed for some time to extreme privacy. The Black Prince's son was recognised as King by general assent on the very day his grandfather died, no question of election being raised, and the Crown of England passed to a minor, Richard II.

Left: *The first page of the Acts of the Apostles, from Wyclif's Bible.* MANSELL COLLECTION

Chepstow Castle, Monmouthshire, built by John of Gaunt in the fourteenth century. AEROFILMS

CHAPTER THREE

The End of the Feudal Age

JOHN OF GAUNT, Duke of Lancaster, younger brother of the Black Prince, uncle of the King, was head of the Council of Regency and ruled the land. Both the impact and the shadow of the Black Death dominated the scene. In the economic and social sphere there arose a vast tumult. Nearly one-third of the population being suddenly dead, a large part of the land passed out of cultivation. The survivors turned their ploughs to the richest soils and quartered their flocks and herds on the fairest pastures. Many landowners abandoned ploughs and enclosed, often by encroachment, the best grazing. Ploughmen and labourers found themselves in high demand, and were competed for on all sides. They in their turn sought to better themselves, or at least to keep their living equal with the rising prices. But their masters saw matters differently. They repulsed fiercely demands for increased wages; they revived ancient claims to forced or tied labour. Assertions of long-lapsed authority, however good in law, were violently resisted by the country folk. They formed unions of labourers to guard their interests. There were escapes of villeins from the estates, like those of the slaves from the Southern States of America in the 1850's. On some manors the serfs were enfranchised in a body and a class of free tenants came into being. But this feature was rare. The turmoil through which all England passed affected the daily life of the mass of the people in a manner not seen again in our social history till the Industrial Revolution of the nineteenth century. Many vehement agitators, among whom John Ball is the best known, gave forth a stream of subversive doctrine. The country was full of broken soldiers, disbanded from the war, and all knew about the long-bow and its power to kill nobles, however exalted and well armed. The preaching of revolutionary ideas was widespread, and a popular ballad expressed the response of the masses:

> When Adam delved, and Eve span,
> Who was then a gentleman?

King Richard II (1367–1400), from the portrait by Beauneven of Valenciennes (1398) in Westminster Abbey. COURTESY: THE DEAN AND CHAPTER

This was a novel question for the fourteenth century, and awkward at any time. The rigid, time-enforced framework of medieval England trembled to its foundations.

Throughout the summer of 1381 there was a general ferment. Beneath it all lay organisation. The royal Council was bewildered and inactive. Early in June the main body of rebels from Essex and Kent moved on London. Here they found support. For three days the city was in confusion. Foreigners were murdered; two members of the Council, Simon Sudbury, the Archbishop of Canterbury and Chancellor, and Sir Robert Hales, the Treasurer, were dragged from the Tower and beheaded on Tower Hill; the Savoy Palace of John of Gaunt was burnt; Lambeth and Southwark were sacked. But the loyal citizen body rallied round the Mayor, and at Smithfield the young King faced the rebel leaders. Wat Tyler, a military adventurer with gifts and experience of leadership, was first wounded by Mayor Walworth and then smitten to death by one of the King's esquires. As the rebel leader rolled off his horse, dead in the sight of the great assembly, the King met the crisis by riding forward alone with the cry, "I will be your leader. You shall have from me all you seek. Only follow me to the fields outside." But the death of Tyler proved a signal for the wave of reaction. The leaderless bands wandered home and spread a vulgar lawlessness through their counties. They were pursued by reconstructed authority. Vengeance was wreaked. The rising had spread throughout the South-West. In Hertfordshire the peasants rose against the powerful and hated Abbey of St Albans, and marched on London under Jack Straw. There was a general revolt in Cambridgeshire, accompanied by burning of rolls and attacks on episcopal manors. In Norfolk and Suffolk, where the peasants were richer and more independent, the irritation against legal villeinage was stronger. Waves of revolt rippled on as far North as Yorkshire and Cheshire, and to the West in Wiltshire and Somerset.

But after Tyler's death the resistance of the ruling classes was organised. Letters were sent out from Chancery to the royal officials commanding the restoration of order, and justices under Chief Justice Tresilian gave swift judgment upon insurgents. Nevertheless, the reaction was, according to modern examples, very restrained. Not more than a hundred and fifty executions are recorded in the rolls. Even in this furious class reaction no men were hanged except after trial by jury. Yet for generations the upper classes lived in fear of a popular rising and the labourers continued to combine. Servile labour ceased to be the basis of the system. The legal aspect of serfdom became of little importance, and the development of commutation went on, speaking broadly, at an accelerated pace after 1349.

In the charged, sullen atmosphere of the England of the 1380's Wyclif's doctrines gathered wide momentum. But, faced by social revolution, English society was in no mood for Church reform. The landed classes gave silent assent to the ultimate suppression of the preacher by the Church. Cruel days lay

King Richard II and his Queen, Anne of Bohemia, from the fourteenth-century Coronation Order of Service, the Liber Regalis.
It is thought that this manuscript was written and illuminated for Queen Anne's Coronation in 1382; it was probably used by all subsequent sovereigns up to Queen Elizabeth I. COURTESY: THE DEAN AND CHAPTER OF WESTMINSTER

ahead. The political tradition was to be burned out in the misery of Sir John Oldcastle's rebellion under Henry V. But a vital element of resistance to the formation of a militant and triumphant Church survived in the English people.

It was not till he was twenty that Richard determined to be complete master of his Council, and in particular to escape from the control of his uncles. A group of younger nobles threw in their fortunes with the Court. Of these the head was Robert de Vere, Earl of Oxford, who now played a part resembling that of Gaveston under Edward II. The accumulation of Household and Government offices by the clique around the King and his effeminate favourite affronted the feudal party, and to some extent the national spirit. As so often happens, the opposition found in foreign affairs a vehicle of attack. Parliament was led to appoint a Commission of five Ministers and nine lords, of whom the former Councillors of Regency were the chiefs. When the Commissioners presently compelled the King to dismiss his personal friends Richard in deep distress withdrew from London. He sought to marshal his forces for civil war at the very same spot where Charles I would one day unfurl the royal standard. Upon this basis of force Tresilian and four other royal judges

pronounced that the pressure put upon him by the Lords Appellant, as they were now styled, and the Parliament was contrary to the laws and Constitution of England. The King's uncle, Gloucester, together with other heads of the baronial oligarchy, denounced the Chief Justice and those who had acted with him, including de Vere and the other royal advisers, as traitors to the realm. Gloucester, with an armed power, approached London. In Westminster Hall the three principal Lords Appellant, Gloucester, Arundel, and Warwick, with an escort outside of three hundred horsemen, bullied the King into submission. De Vere retired to Chester and raised an armed force to secure the royal rights. But now appeared in arms the Lords Appellant, and also Gaunt's son Henry. At Radcot Bridge, in Oxfordshire, Henry and they defeated and broke de Vere. The favourite fled overseas. The King was now at the mercy of the proud faction which had usurped the rights of the monarchy. "The Merciless Parliament" opened its session. Only the person of the King was respected, and that by the narrowest of margins. Richard, forced not only to submit but to assent to the slaughter of his friends, buried himself as low as he could in retirement. He laid his plans for revenge and for his own rights with far more craft than before.

On May 3, 1389, Richard took action which none of them had foreseen. Taking his seat at the Council, he asked blandly to be told how old he was. On being answered that he was three-and-twenty he declared that he had certainly come of age, and that he would no longer submit to restrictions upon his rights. He would manage the realm himself; he would choose his own advisers; he would be King indeed. Richard used his victory with prudence and mercy. The terrible combination of 1388 had dissolved. The machinery of royal government, triumphant over faction, resumed its sway, and for the next eight years Richard governed England in the guise of a constitutional and popular King. The patience and skill with which Richard accomplished his revenge are most striking. While the lords were at variance the King sought to strengthen himself by gathering Irish resources. In 1394 he went with all the formality of a royal Progress to Ireland, and for this purpose created an army dependent upon himself, which was to be useful later in overawing opposition in England. To free himself from the burden of war, which would make him directly dependent upon the favours of Parliament, he made a settlement with France. He wished beyond doubt to gain absolute power over the nobility and Parliament. Whether he also purposed to use this dictatorship in the interests of the humble masses of his subjects is one of the mysteries, but also the legend, long linked with his name. The King next devoted himself to the construction of a compact, efficient Court party. Both Gaunt and his son and Mowbray, Earl of Norfolk, one of the former Appellants, were now rallied to his side, partly in loyalty to him and partly in hostility to Arundel and Gloucester.

In January 1397 the Estates were summoned to Westminster, where under deft and at the same time resolute management they showed all due submission. Thus assured, Richard decided at last to strike. Arundel and some others of his associates were declared traitors and accorded only the courtesy of decapitation. Warwick was exiled to the Isle of Man. Gloucester, arrested and taken to Calais, was there murdered by Richard's agents; and this deed, not being covered by constitutional forms, bred in its turn new retributions. Parliament was called only to legalise these events. Never has there been such a Parliament. With ardour pushed to suicidal lengths, it suspended almost every constitutional right and privilege gained in the preceding century. The relations between Gaunt's son, Henry, the King's cousin and contemporary, passed through drama into tragedy. A quarrel arose between Henry and Thomas Mowbray, now Duke of Norfolk. Henry accused Mowbray of treasonable language. Trial by battle appeared the correct solution. The famous scene took place in September 1398. The lists were drawn; the

John of Gaunt, "time-honoured Lancaster", from a painting on glass in All Souls, Oxford. MANSELL COLLECTION

English world assembled; the champions presented themselves; but the King, exasperating the spectators of all classes who had gathered in high expectation to see the sport, cast down his wardour, forbade the combat, and exiled Mowbray for life and Henry for a decade. During 1398 there were many in the nation who awoke to the fact that a servile Parliament had in a few weeks suspended many of the fundamental rights and liberties of the realm. Not only the old nobility, who in the former crisis had been defeated, but all the gentry and merchant classes were aghast at the triumph of absolute rule.

In February of 1399 died old John of Gaunt, "time-honoured Lancaster". Richard, pressed for money, could not refrain from a

77

technically legal seizure of the Lancaster estates in spite of his promises. He declared his cousin disinherited. This challenged the position of every property-holder. And forthwith, by a fatal misjudgment of his strength and of what was stirring in the land, the King set forth in May upon a punitive expedition, which was long overdue, to assert the royal authority in Ireland. In July Henry of Lancaster, as he had now become, landed in Yorkshire, declaring that he had only come to claim his lawful rights as heir to his venerated father. The course of his revolt followed exactly that of Isabella and Mortimer against Edward II seventy-two years before. It took some time for the news of Henry's apparition and all that followed so swiftly from it to reach King Richard in the depths of Ireland. Having landed in England on July 27, he made a rapid three weeks' march through North Wales in an attempt to gather forces. The Welsh, who would have stood by him, could not face the advancing power of what was now all England. At Flint Castle he submitted to Henry, into whose hands the whole administration had now passed. His abdication was extorted; his death had become inevitable. The last of all English kings whose hereditary right was indisputable disappeared for ever beneath the portcullis of Pontefract Castle. Henry, by and with the consent of the Estates of the Realm and the Lords Spiritual and Temporal, ascended the throne as Henry IV.

From the outset Henry depended upon Parliament to make good by its weight the defects in his title, and rested on the theory of the elective, limited kingship rather than on that of absolute monarchy. He was therefore alike by mood and need a constitutional King. During this time therefore Parliamentary power over finance was greatly strengthened. Not only did the Estates supply the money by voting the taxes, but they began to follow its expenditure, and to require and to receive accounts from the high officers of the State. Nothing like this had been tolerated by any of the Kings before.

On one issue indeed, half social, half religious, King and Parliament were heartily agreed. The Lollards' advocacy of a Church purified by being relieved of all worldly goods did not command the assent of the clergy. The lords saw that their own estates stood on no better title than those of the Church. They therefore joined with the clergy in defence of their property. Thus did orthodoxy and property make common cause and march together.

The Welsh, already discontented, under the leadership of Owen Glendower, presently espoused Richard's cause. Armed risings appeared in several parts of the country, but the conspiracy received no genuine support and was fatal to the former King. Richard's death was announced in February 1400. But far and wide throughout England spread the tale that he had escaped, and that in concealment he awaited his hour to bring the common people of the time to the enjoyment of their own. All this welled up against Henry Bolingbroke. The trouble with the Welsh deepened into a national insurrection. Owen Glendower, who was a remarkable man, of considerable education, carried on a war which was the constant background of English affairs till 1409. The King was also forced to fight continually against the

Richard II (standing, centre) submits to Henry Bolingbroke later Henry IV (left), at Flint Castle. From an early fifteenth-century French manuscript. BRITISH MUSEUM

The siege of a town, from a manuscript of 1480. BRITISH MUSEUM

Scots. After six years of this harassment we are told that his natural magnanimity was worn out, and that he yielded himself to the temper of his supporters and of his Parliament in cruel deeds.

His most serious conflict was with the Percys. These lords of the Northern Marches, the old Earl of Northumberland and his fiery son Hotspur, had for nearly three years carried on the defence of England against the Scots unaided and almost entirely at their own expense. The Percys had played a great part in placing Henry on the throne. They held a great independent power, and an antagonism was perhaps inevitable. Hotspur raised the standard of revolt. But at Shrewsbury on July 21, 1403, Henry overcame and slew him in a small, fierce battle. The old Earl, who was marching to his aid, was forced to submit, and pardon was freely extended to him. But two years later, with his son's death at heart, he rebelled again, and this time the conspiracy was far-reaching. Once again Henry marched north, and once again he was successful. At the same

time the King's health failed. He still managed to triumph in the Welsh War, and Owen Glendower was forced back into his mountains. But Parliament took all advantages from the King's necessities. Henry saw safety only in surrender. A Council must be nominated by the King which included the Parliamentary leaders. The accounts of Government expenses were subjected to a Parliamentary audit. By these submissions Henry became the least of kings.

Henry's eldest son, the Prince of Wales, showed already an extraordinary force and quality. As his father's health declined he was everywhere drawn into State business. But there can be no doubt that the dying sovereign still gripped convulsively the reins of power. In 1412, when the King could no longer walk and scarcely ride, he was with difficulty dissuaded by his Council from attempting to command the troops in Aquitaine. He lingered through the winter, talked of a Crusade, summoned Parliament in February, but could do no business with it. In March, when praying in Westminster Abbey,

79

he had a prolonged fit, from which he rallied only to die in the Jerusalem Chamber on March 20, 1413. Thus the life and reign of King Henry IV exhibit to us another instance of the vanities of ambition and the harsh guerdon which rewards its success.

Henry V was King at twenty-five. His face, we are told, was oval, with a long, straight nose, ruddy complexion, dark, smooth hair, and bright eyes, mild as a dove's when unprovoked, but lion-like in wrath; his frame was slender, yet well-knit, strong, and active. His disposition was orthodox, chivalrous, and just. The romantic stories of his riotous youth and sudden conversion to gravity and virtue when charged with the supreme responsibility must not be pressed too far. He led the nation away from internal discord to foreign conquest; and he had the dream, and perhaps the prospect, of leading all Western Europe into the high championship of a Crusade. The Commons were thereupon liberal with supply. A wave of reconciliation swept the land. The King declared a general pardon. He sought to assuage the past.

At Henry V's accession the Orleanists had gained the preponderance in France, and unfurled the Oriflamme against the Duke of Burgundy. Henry naturally allied himself with the weaker party, the Burgundians, who, in their distress, were prepared to acknowledge him as King of France.

During the whole of 1414 Henry V was absorbed in warlike preparations by land and sea. He reorganised the Fleet. Instead of mainly taking over and arming private ships, as was the custom, he, like Alfred, built many vessels for the Royal Navy. The English army of about ten thousand fighting men sailed to France on August 11, 1415, in a fleet of small ships, and landed without opposition at the mouth of the Seine. Harfleur was besieged and taken by the middle

of September. The King was foremost in prowess:

> Once more unto the breach, dear friends, once more;
> Or close the wall up with our English dead.

Leaving a garrison in Harfleur, and sending home several thousand sick and wounded, the King resolved, with about a thousand knights and men-at-arms and four thousand archers, to traverse the French coast in a hundred-mile march to his fortress at Calais, where his ships were to await him. All the circumstances of this decision show that his design was to tempt the enemy to battle. This was not denied him. He had to ascend the Somme to above Amiens by Boves and Corbie, and could only cross at the ford of Béthencourt. All these names are well known to our generation. On October 20 he camped near Péronne. The French heralds came to the English camp and inquired, for mutual convenience, by which route His Majesty would desire to proceed. "Our path lies straight to Calais", was Henry's answer. This was not telling them much, for he had no other choice. The French army, which was already interposing itself, by a right-handed movement across his front fell back before his advance-guard behind the Canche River. Henry, moving by Albert, Frévent, and Blangy, learned that they were before him in apparently overwhelming numbers. He must now cut his way through, perish, or surrender. When one of his officers, Sir Walter Hungerford, deplored the fact "that they had not but one ten thousand of those men in England that do no work today", the King rebuked him and revived his spirits in a speech to which Shakespeare has given an immortal form:

> If we are marked to die, we are enough
> To do our country loss; and if to live,
> The fewer men, the greater share of honour.

"Wot you not," he actually said, "that the Lord with these few can overthrow the pride of the French?" He and the "few" lay for the night at the village of Maisoncelles, maintaining utter silence and the strictest discipline. The French headquarters were at Agincourt, and it is said that they kept high revel and diced for the captives they should take.

The English victory of Crécy was gained against great odds upon the defensive. Poitiers was a counter-stroke. Agincourt ranks as the most heroic of all the land battles England has ever fought. It was a vehement assault. The French, whose numbers have been estimated at about twenty thousand, were drawn up in three lines of battle, of which a proportion remained mounted. With justifiable confidence they awaited the attack of less than a third their number, who, far from home and many marches from the sea, must win or die. The whole English army, even the King himself, dismounted and sent their horses to the rear; and shortly after eleven o'clock on St Crispin's Day, October 25, he gave the order, "In the name of Almighty God and of Saint George, Avaunt Banner in the best time of the year, and Saint George this day be thine help." The archers kissed the soil in reconciliation to God, and, crying loudly, "Hurrah! Hurrah! Saint George and Merrie England!" advanced to within three hundred yards of the heavy masses in their front. They planted their stakes and loosed their arrows. The

Long-bowmen at the Battle of Agincourt, St Crispin's Day, October 25, 1415, imaginatively depicted in this fifteenth-century manuscript illustration. BIBLIOTHÈQUE NATIONALE: FALQUET

French were once again unduly crowded upon the field. They stood in three dense lines, and neither their crossbowmen nor their battery of cannon could fire effectively. Under the arrow storm they in their turn moved forward down the slope, plodding heavily through a ploughed field already trampled into a quagmire. But once again the long-bow destroyed all before it. Horse and foot alike went down; a long heap of armoured dead and wounded lay upon the ground, over which the reinforcements struggled bravely, but in vain. Now occurred a terrible episode. The King, believing himself attacked from behind, while a superior force still remained unbroken on his front, issued the dread order to slaughter the prisoners. Then perished the flower of the French nobility, many of whom had yielded themselves to easy hopes of ransom. The alarm in the rear was soon relieved; but not before the massacre was almost finished. The French third line quitted the field without attempting to renew the battle in any serious manner. Henry, who had declared at daybreak, "For me this day shall never England ransom pay", now saw his path to Calais clear before him. But far more than that: the victory of Agincourt made him the supreme figure in Europe. When in 1416 the Holy Roman Emperor Sigismund visited London in an effort to effect a peace he recognised Henry as King of France. But there followed long, costly campaigns and sieges which outran the financial resources of the Island and gradually cooled its martial ardour. After hideous massacres in Paris, led by the Burgundians, hot-headed supporters of the Dauphin murdered the Duke of Burgundy at Montereau in 1419, and by this deed sealed the alliance of Burgundy with England. In May 1420, by the Treaty of Troyes, Charles VI recognised Henry as heir to the French kingdom upon his death and as Regent during his life. To implement and consolidate these triumphs Henry married Charles's daughter Catherine, a comely princess, who bore him a son long to reign over impending English miseries.

This was the boldest bid the Island ever

King Henry V (1387–1422), by an unknown artist. NATIONAL PORTRAIT GALLERY

Henry V in battle, a detail from his tomb in Westminster Abbey. PHOTO: JOHN R. FREEMAN. COURTESY: THE DEAN AND CHAPTER

made in Europe. Henry V was no feudal sovereign of the old type with a class interest which overrode social and territorial barriers. He was entirely national in his outlook: he was the first King to use the English language in his letters and his messages home from the Front; his triumphs were gained by English troops; his policy was sustained by a Parliament that could claim to speak for the English people. For it was the union of the country gentry and the rising middle class of the towns, working with the Common Lawyers, that gave the English Parliament thus early a character and a destiny that the States-General of France and the Cortes of Castile were not to know. Henry stood, and with him his country, at the summit of the world.

But glory was, as always, dearly bought. When Henry V revived the English claims to France he opened the greatest tragedy in our medieval history. Agincourt was a glittering victory, but the wasteful and useless campaigns that followed more than outweighed its military and moral value, and the miserable, destroying century that ensued casts its black shadow upon Henry's heroic triumph. If Henry V united the nation against France he set it also upon the Lollards. This degradation lies about him and his times, and our contacts with his personal nobleness and prowess, though imperishable, are marred. Fortune, which had bestowed upon the King all that could be dreamed of, could not afford to risk her handiwork in a long life. In the full tide of power and success he died at the end of August 1422 of a malady contracted in the field, probably dysentery, against which the medicine of those times could not make head. He was more deeply loved by his subjects of all classes than any King has been in England.

At the time of the great King's death the ascendancy of the English arms in France

The medieval concept of chivalry and knightly tournament, shown in the "Jousts of Ingleuerch", from Froissart's Chronicles. BRITISH MUSEUM

83

Henry V's siege of Rouen, 1418–19, from the fifteenth-century The Life and Acts of Richard Beauchamp, Earl of Warwick. *The King, wearing his crown, is on the left; Warwick is on the right.* BRITISH MUSEUM

The helm on the left, the sword, shield, and saddle, are relics of Henry V. The helm on the right belonged to Henry VII. COURTESY: THE DEAN AND CHAPTER OF WESTMINSTER ABBEY

was established. In 1421 the French and their Scottish allies under the Earl of Buchan defeated the English at Baugé, but three other considerable actions ended in English victories. At Cravant, in August 1423, the French were again aided by a strong Scots contingent. But the English archers, with their Burgundian allies, shot most of them down. At Verneuil a year later this decision was repeated. The English attempt to conquer all vast France with a few thousand archers led by warrior-nobles, with hardly any money from home, and little food to be found in the ruined regions, reached its climax in the triumph of Verneuil. There seemed to the French to be no discoverable way to contend against these rugged, lusty, violent Islanders, with their archery, their flexible tactics, and their audacity. At this time the loves and the acquisitiveness of the Duke of Gloucester, who in Bedford's absence in France became Protector of the English child-King, drove a wedge between England and Burgundy. Jacqueline, Princess of Hainault, Holland, and Zeeland, and heir to these provinces, had been married for reasons of Burgundian policy to the Duke of Brabant, a sickly lout fifteen years of age. She revolted from this infliction, took refuge in England, and appealed to Gloucester for protection. This was accorded in full measure. Gloucester resolved to marry her, enjoy her company, and acquire her inheritance. This questionable romance gave deep offence to the Duke of Burgundy, whose major interests in the Low Countries were injured. Although both Bedford in France and the English Council at home completely disclaimed Gloucester's action, and were prodigal in their efforts to repair the damage, the rift between England and Burgundy dates from this event.

There now appeared upon the ravaged scene an Angel of Deliverance, the noblest patriot of France, the most splendid of her heroes, the most beloved of her saints, the most inspiring of all her memories, the peasant Maid, the ever-shining, ever-glorious Joan of Arc. In the poor, remote hamlet of Domrémy, on the fringe of the Vosges Forest, she served at the inn. She rode the horses of travellers, bareback, to water. She wandered on Sundays into the woods, where there were shrines, and a legend that some day from these oaks would arise one to save France. In the fields where she tended her sheep the saints of God, who grieved for France, rose before her in visions. St Michael himself appointed her, by right divine, to command the armies of liberation. Joan shrank at first from the awful duty, but when he returned attended by St Margaret and St Catherine, patronesses of the village church, she obeyed their command. She convinced Baudricourt, Governor of the neighbouring town, that she was inspired. He recommended her to a Court ready to clutch at straws. There, among the nobles and courtiers, she at once picked out the King, who had purposely mingled with the crowd. "Most noble Lord Dauphin," she said, "I am Joan the Maid, sent on the part of God to aid you and the kingdom, and by His order I announce that you will be crowned in the city of Rheims."

Orleans in 1429 lay under the extremities of siege. The Maid now claimed to lead a convoy to the rescue. Upon her invocation the spirit of victory changed sides, and the French began an offensive which never rested till the English invaders were driven out of France. The siege was broken, Orleans saved and the Earl of Suffolk later captured.

Joan told Charles he must march on Rheims to be crowned upon the throne of his ancestors. The idea seemed fantastic: Rheims lay deep in enemy country. But under her spell he obeyed, and everywhere the towns opened their gates before them and the people crowded to his aid. With all the pomp of victory and faith, with the most sacred ceremonies of ancient days, Charles was crowned at Rheims.

When in May 1430 the town of Compiègne revolted against the decision of the King that it should yield to the English, Joan with only six hundred men attempted its succour. The enemy, at first surprised, rallied, and a panic among the French ensued. Flavy, the Governor, whose duty it was to save the town, felt obliged to pull up the drawbridge in her face and leave her to the Burgundians. She was

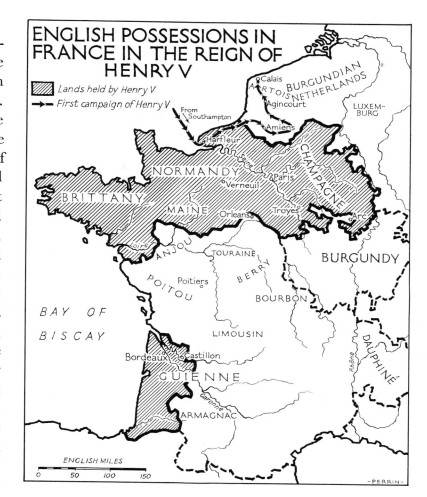

ENGLISH POSSESSIONS IN FRANCE IN THE REIGN OF HENRY V

sold to the rejoicing English for a moderate sum.

Joan of Arc perished on May 30, 1431. Amid an immense concourse she was dragged to the stake in the market-place of Rouen. High upon the pyramid of faggots the flames rose towards her, and the smoke of doom wreathed and curled. She raised a cross made of firewood, and her last word was "Jesus!" History has recorded the comment of an English soldier who witnessed the scene. "We are lost," he said. "We have burnt a saint." All this proved true. The tides of war flowed remorselessly against the English. The boy Henry was crowned in Paris in December amid chilly throngs. Burgundy became definitely hostile in 1435. The French gained a series of battles. Their artillery now became the finest in the world. All Northern France, except Calais, was reconquered. Even Guienne, dowry of Eleanor of Aquitaine, for three hundred years a loyal, contented fief of the English Crown, was overrun.

A baby was King of England, and two months later, on the death of Charles VI, was proclaimed without dispute the King of France. Bedford and Gloucester, his uncles, became Protectors, and with a Council comprising the heads of the most powerful families attempted to sustain the work of Henry V. As Henry VI grew up his virtues and simpleness became equally apparent. At the hour when a strong king alone could re-create the balance between the nation and the nobility, when all demanded the restraint of faction at home and the waging of victorious war without undue expense abroad, the throne was known to be occupied by a devout simpleton suited alike by his qualities and defects to be a puppet.

The princes of the House of Lancaster disputed among themselves. After Bedford's death in 1435 the tension grew between Gloucester and the Beauforts. At twenty-three it was high time that King Henry should marry. Each of the Lancastrian factions was anxious to provide him with a queen; but Cardinal Beaufort and his brothers, with their ally, Suffolk, whose ancestors, the de la Poles of Hull, had founded their fortunes upon trade, prevailed over the Duke of Gloucester, weakened as he was by maladministration and ill-success. Suffolk was sent to France to arrange a further truce, and it was implied in his mission that he should treat for a marriage between the King of England and Margaret of Anjou, niece of the King of France. This remarkable woman added to rare beauty and charm a masterly intellect and a dauntless spirit. Like Joan the Maid, though without her inspiration or her cause, she knew how to make men fight. Even from the seclusion of her family her qualities became well known. Was she not then the mate for this feeble-minded King? Would she not give him the force that he lacked? And would not those who placed her at his side secure a large and sure future for themselves? Suffolk was enthralled by Margaret. He made the match; and in his eagerness, by a secret article, agreed without formal authority that Maine should be the reward of France. The marriage was solemnised in 1445 with such splendour as the age could afford.

Joan of Arc, in the only known contemporary likeness, sketched by the Notary of the Paris Parlement in the margin of the official history of the siege of Orleans. ARCHIVES NATIONAUX

It soon appeared that immense forces of retribution were on foot. It was generally believed, though wrongly, that Gloucester, arrested when he came to a Parliament summoned at St Edmondsbury, had been murdered by the express direction of Suffolk and Edmund Beaufort. It has, however, been suggested that his death was induced by choler and amazement at the ruin of his fortunes. When in 1448 the secret article for the cession of Maine became public through its occupation by the French anger was expressed on all sides. Suffolk was impeached. Straining his Prerogative, Henry burked the proceedings by sending him in 1450 into a five years' exile. When the banished Duke was crossing the Channel with his attendants and treasure in two small vessels, the *Nicholas of the Tower*, the largest warship in the Royal Navy, bore down upon him and carried him on board.

The Court of the King's Bench, during the reign of Henry VI. The prisoner stands at the bar, the jury to his left. Other prisoners awaiting trial are in the foreground.

It is a revealing sign of the times that a royal ship should seize and execute a royal Minister who was travelling under the King's special protection. In June and July a rising took place in Kent, which the Lancastrians claimed to bear the marks of Yorkist support. Jack Cade, a soldier of capacity and bad character, home from the wars, gathered several thousand men, all summoned in due form by the constables of the districts, and marched on London. He was admitted to the City, but on his executing Lord Say, the Treasurer, in Cheapside, after a mob trial, the magistrates and citizens turned against him, his followers dispersed under terms of pardon, and he himself was pursued and killed.

As the process of expelling the English from France continued fortresses fell, towns and districts were lost, and their garrisons for the most part came home. The nobles, in the increasing disorder, were glad to gather these hardened fighters to their local defence. They gave them pay or land, or both, and uniforms or liveries bearing the family crest. Cash and ambition ruled and the land sank rapidly towards anarchy. The celebrated Paston Letters show that England, enormously advanced as it was in comprehension, character, and civilisation, was relapsing from peace and security into barbaric confusion. A statute of 1429 had fixed the county franchise at the forty-shilling freeholder. It is hard to realise that this arbitrarily contracted franchise ruled in England for four hundred years, and that all the wars and quarrels, the decision of the greatest causes, the grandest events at home and abroad, proceeded upon this basis until the Reform Bill of 1832.

The claims and hopes of the opposition to the House of Lancaster were embodied in Richard, Duke of York. He was a virtuous, law-respecting, slow-moving, and highly competent prince. He had given good service. He had accepted the government of Ireland and won the goodwill of the Irish people. According to established usage he had a prior right to the Crown. York was the son of Richard, Earl of Cambridge, and grandson of Edmund, Duke of York, a younger brother of John of Gaunt. As the great-grandson of Edward III he was the only other person besides Henry VI with an unbroken male descent from Edward III, but in the female line he had also a superior claim through his descent from Gaunt's elder brother, Lionel of Clarence. By the Act of 1407 the Beauforts—Gaunt's legitimatised bastards—had been barred from the succession. If Henry VI should succeed in annulling the Act of 1407 then Edmund Beaufort (Somerset) would have a better male claim with York. It was this that York feared. York had taken Gloucester's place as first Prince of the Blood. Around York and beneath him there gathered an immense party of discontent, which drove him hesitantly to demand a place in the government, and eventually, through Queen Margaret's increasing hostility, the throne itself.

Although the Yorkists predominated in the rich South, and the Lancastrians were supreme in the warlike North, there were

THE HOUSES OF YORK AND LANCASTER

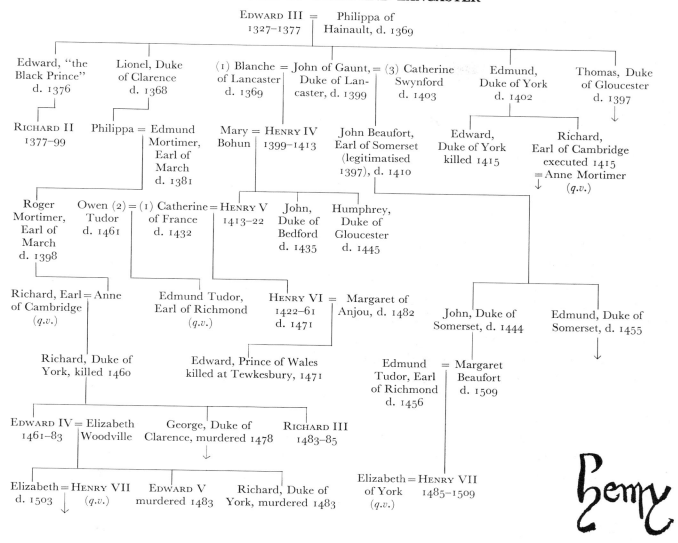

Edward III = Philippa of
1327–1377 | Hainault, d. 1369

Edward, "the Black Prince" d. 1376 — Lionel, Duke of Clarence d. 1368 — (1) Blanche of Lancaster d. 1369 = John of Gaunt, Duke of Lancaster, d. 1399 = (3) Catherine Swynford d. 1403 — Edmund, Duke of York d. 1402 — Thomas, Duke of Gloucester d. 1397

Richard II 1377–99 — Philippa = Edmund Mortimer, Earl of March d. 1381 — Mary Bohun = Henry IV 1399–1413 — John Beaufort, Earl of Somerset (legitimatised 1397), d. 1410 — Edward, Duke of York killed 1415 — Richard, Earl of Cambridge executed 1415 = Anne Mortimer (q.v.)

Roger Mortimer, Earl of March d. 1398 — Owen (2) = (1) Catherine Tudor of France d. 1461 d. 1432 = Henry V 1413–22 — John, Duke of Bedford d. 1435 — Humphrey, Duke of Gloucester d. 1445

Richard, Earl of Cambridge (q.v.) = Anne — Edmund Tudor, Earl of Richmond (q.v.) — Henry VI 1422–61 d. 1471 = Margaret of Anjou, d. 1482 — John, Duke of Somerset, d. 1444 — Edmund, Duke of Somerset, d. 1455

Richard, Duke of York, killed 1460 — Edward, Prince of Wales killed at Tewkesbury, 1471 — Edmund Tudor, Earl of Richmond d. 1456 = Margaret Beaufort d. 1509

Edward IV = Elizabeth 1461–83 Woodville — George, Duke of Clarence, murdered 1478 — Richard III 1483–85

Elizabeth = Henry VII d. 1503 (q.v.) — Edward V murdered 1483 — Richard, Duke of York, murdered 1483 — Elizabeth of York = Henry VII 1485–1509 (q.v.)

many interlacements and overlaps. We are, however, in the presence of the most ferocious and implacable quarrel of which there is factual record. The individual actors were bred by generations of privilege and war, into which the feudal theme had brought its peculiar sense of honour, and to which the Papacy contributed such spiritual sanction as emerged from its rivalries and intrigues. It was a conflict in which personal hatreds reached their maximum, and from which mass effects were happily excluded. The attitude and feeling of the public, in all parts and at all times, weighed heavily with both contending factions. Thus Europe witnessed the amazing spectacle of nearly thirty years of ferocious war, conducted with hardly the sack of a single town, and with the mass of

King Henry VI (1421–71), by an unknown artist.
NATIONAL PORTRAIT GALLERY

the common people little affected and the functions of local government very largely maintained.

In 1450 the ferment of discontent and rivalries drew the Duke of York into his first overt act. He quitted his government in Ireland and landed unbidden in Wales. Prayers and protests had failed; there remained the resort to arms. Accordingly, on February 3, 1452, York sent an address to the citizens of Shrewsbury, accusing Somerset of the disgrace in France and of "labouring continually about the King's Highness for my undoing". Civil war seemed about to begin. In the event York dispersed his forces and presented himself unarmed and bareheaded before King Henry, protesting his loyalty, but demanding redress. Since he was supported by the Commons and evidently at the head of a great party, the King promised that "a sad and substantial Council" should be formed, of which he should be a member. The Court had still to choose between Somerset and York. The Queen, always working with Somerset, decided the issue in his favour.

The disasters culminated in France. Somerset, the chief commander, bore the burden of defeat. In this situation the King went mad. He recognised no one, not even the Queen. He could eat and drink, but his speech was childish or incoherent. He could not walk. For another fifteen months he remained entirely without comprehension. The pious Henry had been withdrawn from the worry of existence to an island of merciful oblivion. When these terrible facts became known Queen Margaret aspired to be Protector. On October 13 she gave birth to a son. How far this event was expected is not clear, but, as long afterwards with James II, it inevitably hardened the hearts of all men. It seemed to shut out for ever the Yorkist claim.

But the insanity of the King defeated Somerset: he could no longer withstand York. The strength of York's position bore him to the Protectorate. His party was astounded at his tolerance. When the Government was in his hands, when his future was marred by the new heir to the Crown, when his power or his life might be destroyed at any moment by the King's recovery, he kept absolute faith with right and justice. Here then is his monument and justification.

Surprises continued. When it was generally believed that Henry's line was extinct he had produced an heir. At Christmas 1454 he regained all his faculties. York ceased legally to be Protector from the moment that the King's mental recovery was known; he made no effort to retain the power. Queen Margaret took the helm. Somerset was not only released but restored to his key position.

York's lords agreed upon a resort to arms. St Albans was the first shedding of blood in strife. The Yorkist triumph was complete. They gained possession of the King. Somerset was dead. Margaret and her child had taken sanctuary. But soon we see the inherent power of Lancaster. They had the majority of the nobles on their side, and the majesty of the Crown. The four years from 1456 to 1459 were a period of uneasy truce. There were intense efforts at reconciliation. The spectacle was displayed to the Londoners of the King being escorted to Westminster by a procession in which the Duke of York and Queen Margaret walked side by side, followed by the Yorkist and Lancastrian lords, the most opposed in pairs. In 1459 fighting broke out again.

War began in earnest in July 1460. York was still in Ireland; but the Yorkist lords under Warwick, holding bases in Wales and at Calais, with all their connections and partisans, supported by the Papal Legate and some of the bishops, and, on the whole, by the Commons, confronted the Lancastrians and the Crown at Northampton. The royal forces fled in panic. The so-called compromise in which all the Estates of the Realm concurred was then attempted. Henry was to be King for life; York was to conduct the government and succeed him at his death. The Queen fought on. At Wakefield on December 30, 1460, the first considerable battle of the war was fought. The Lancastrians, with superior forces, caught the Yorkists by surprise, when many were foraging, and a frightful rout and massacre ensued. No quarter was given. The Duke of York was killed; his son, the Earl of Rutland, seventeen years old, was flying, but the new Lord Clifford, remembering St Albans, slaughtered him with joy, exclaiming, "By God's blood, thy father slew mine; and so will I do thee, and all thy kin." The old Earl of Salisbury, caught during the night, was beheaded immediately by Lord Exeter, a natural son of the Duke of Buckingham. The

ENGLAND & WALES
DURING THE
WARS OF THE ROSES

Battlefields marked �

heads of the three Yorkist nobles were exposed over the gates and walls of York. The great Duke's head, with a paper crown, grinned upon the landscape, summoning the avengers.

Now a new generation took charge. There was a new Lord Clifford, a new Duke of Somerset, above all a new Duke of York, all in their twenties, sword in hand, with fathers to avenge and England as the prize. When York's son, hitherto Earl of March, learned that his father's cause had devolved upon him he did not shrink. He fell upon the Earl of Wiltshire and the Welsh Lancastrians, and on February 2, 1461, at the Battle of Mortimer's Cross, near Hereford, he beat and broke them up. He made haste to repay the cruelties of Wakefield. The victorious Yorkists under their young Duke now marched to help the Earl of Warwick, who had returned from Calais and was being hard pressed in London; but Queen Margaret forestalled him, and on February 17, at the Second Battle of St Albans, she inflicted upon Warwick a bloody defeat. Margaret now had her husband safe back in her hands and with him the full authority of the Crown. The road to London was open, but she did not choose to advance upon it. This was the turning-point in the struggle. Nine days after the Second Battle of St Albans Edward of York entered London. He declared himself King, and on March 4, 1461, was proclaimed at Westminster with such formalities as were possible.

King Edward IV marched north to settle once and for all with King Henry VI. Near York the Queen, with the whole power of Lancaster, confronted him not far from Tadcaster, by the villages of Saxton and Towton. On March 28 the Yorkist advance-guard was beaten back at Ferry Bridge by the young Lord Clifford, and Warwick himself was wounded; but as heavier forces arrived the bridge was carried. The next day one of the most ruthless battles on English soil began in a blinding snowstorm, which drove in the faces of the Lancastrians. For six hours the two sides grappled furiously, with varying success. But all hung in the balance until late in the afternoon, when the arrival of the Duke of Norfolk's corps upon the exposed flank of the Lancastrians drove the whole mass into retreat, which soon became a rout. Margaret and her son escaped to York, where King Henry had been observing the rites of Palm Sunday. Gathering him up, the imperious Queen set out with her child and

King Edward IV (1442–83), by an unknown artist. REPRODUCED BY GRACIOUS PERMISSION OF HER MAJESTY THE QUEEN.

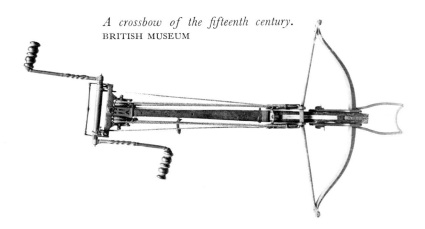

A crossbow of the fifteenth century. BRITISH MUSEUM

a cluster of spears for the Scottish border. The bodies of thousands of Englishmen and the flower of the Lancastrian nobility and knighthood fell upon the field. When Edward reached the town of York his first task was to remove the heads of his father and others of Margaret's victims and to replace them with those of his noblest captives. Three months later, on June 28, he was crowned King at Westminster, and the Yorkist triumph seemed complete. It was followed by wholesale proscriptions and confiscations. Not only the throne but one-third of the estates in England changed hands.

After Towton the Lancastrian cause was sustained by the unconquerable will of Queen Margaret. Never has her tenacity and rarely have her vicissitudes been surpassed in any woman. In 1462 Margaret, after much personal appeal to the Courts of France, Burgundy, and Scotland, found herself able to land with a power, and whether by treachery or weakness the three strongest Northern castles, Bamburgh, Alnwick, and Dunstanburgh, opened their gates to her. In the winter of 1462 therefore King Edward gathered his Yorkist powers, and, carrying his new train of artillery by sea to Newcastle, began the sieges of these lost strongholds. All three fortresses fell in a month.

The behaviour of Edward at this moment constitutes a solid defence for his character. This voluptuous young King, sure of his position, now showed a clemency unheard of in the Wars of the Roses. His magnanimity and forgiveness were ill repaid by Somerset and Percy. When Margaret returned with fresh succours from France and Scotland in 1463 Percy opened the gates of Bamburgh to the Scots, and Alnwick was betrayed about the same time by a soured Yorkist officer, Sir Ralph Grey. Once again Edward and the Yorkists took the field, and the redoubtable new artillery, at that time esteemed as much among the leading nations as atomic weapons are today, was carried to the North. Margaret fled to France, while Henry buried himself amid the valleys and the pious foundations of Cumberland.

At Christmas 1463 Somerset deserted Edward and returned to the Lancastrian side. Again the banner of Lancaster was raised. Somerset joined King Henry. Alnwick and Bamburgh still held out. Norham and Skipton had been captured, but now Warwick's brother Montagu with a substantial army was in the field. On April 25, 1464, at Hedgeley Moor, near Alnwick, he broke and destroyed the Lancastrian revolt. Edward's experiment of mercy in this quarrel was now at an end, and the former rigours were renewed in their extreme degree. Somerset, defeated with a small following at Hexham on May 15, 1464, was beheaded

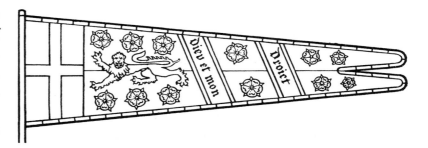

The standard of Edward IV. AFTER C. W. SCOTT-GILES

the next morning. Before the month was out in every Yorkist camp Lancastrian nobles and knights by dozens and half-dozens were put to death. Poor King Henry was at length tracked down near Clitheroe, in Lancashire, and conveyed to London. This time there was no ceremonial entry. With his feet tied by leather thongs to the stirrups, and with a straw hat on his head, the futile but saintly figure around whom such storms had beaten was led three times round the pillory, and finally hustled to the Tower, whose gates closed on him—yet not, this time, for ever.

The Castle of Harlech, on the Western sea, alone flaunted the Red Rose. When it surrendered in 1468 there were found to be but fifty effective men in the garrison. Among them was a child of twelve, who had survived the rigours of the long blockade. His name was Richmond, later to become King Henry VII.

The successes of these difficult years had been gained for King Edward by the Neville family. Warwick, and Montagu, now Earl

A pikeman's helmet. BRITISH MUSEUM

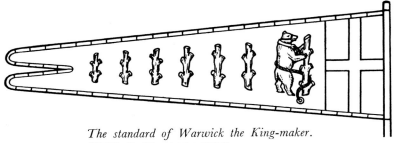

The standard of Warwick the King-maker.
AFTER C. W. SCOTT-GILES

of Northumberland, with George Neville, Archbishop of York, had the whole machinery of government in their hands. Thus some years slipped by, while the King, although gripping from time to time the reins of authority, led in the main his life of ease. His marriage in 1464 with Elizabeth Woodville was a secret guarded in deadly earnest. The statesmen at the head of the Government, while they smiled at what seemed an amorous frolic, never dreamed it was a solemn union, which must shake the land to its depths. Here was the occasion which sundered him from the valiant King-maker, fourteen years older, but also in the prime of life. Eight new peerages came into existence in the Queen's family: her father, five brothers-in-law, her son, and her brother Anthony. This was generally thought excessive. The arrival of a new nobility who had done nothing notable in the war and now surrounded the indolent King was not merely offensive, but politically dangerous to Warwick and his proud associates. But the clash came over foreign policy. Margaret with her retinue of shadows was welcomed in her pauper stateliness both in Burgundy and in France. It was the policy of Warwick and his connection to make friends with France, by far the stronger Power, and thus obtain effectual security. Edward took the opposite line. With the instinct which afterwards ruled our Island for so many centuries, he sought to base English policy upon the second strongest State in Western Europe. The King therefore, to Warwick's chagrin and alarm, in 1468 married his sister Margaret to Charles the Bold, who had in 1467 succeeded as Duke of Burgundy.

The offended chiefs took deep counsel together. Warwick's plan was singular in its skill. He had gained the King's brother, Clarence, to his side by whispering that but for this upstart brood of the Woodvilles he might succeed Edward as King. When all was ready Warwick struck. A rising took place in the North. At the same time in London the House of Commons petitioned against lax and profuse administration. As soon as the King had been enticed northwards by the rebellion Warwick and Clarence, who had hitherto crouched at Calais, came to England with the Calais garrison. But before he and Clarence could bring their forces against the King's rear the event was decided. The Northern rebels, under "Robin of Redesdale", intercepted Pembroke and Devon, and at Edgcott, near Banbury, defeated them with a merciless slaughter. The King, trying to rally his scattered forces at Olney, in Buckinghamshire, found himself in the power of his great nobles. At this moment therefore Warwick the King-maker had actually the two rival Kings, Henry VI and Edward IV, both his prisoners, one in the Tower and the other at Middleham. This was a remarkable achievement for any subject. The King found it convenient in his turn to dissemble. Thus was a settlement reached between Warwick and the Crown. But all this was on the surface.

In March 1470, under the pretence of suppressing a Lancastrian rebellion in Lincolnshire, the King called his forces to arms. At Losecoat Field he defeated the insurgents, who fled; and in the series of executions which had now become customary after every engagement he obtained a confession from Sir Robert Welles which accused both Warwick and Clarence of treason. The King, with troops fresh from victory, turned on them all of a sudden. The King-maker found himself by one sharp twist of fortune deprived of almost every resource he had counted upon as sure. He in his turn presented himself at the French Court as a suppliant.

This was the best luck Louis XI had ever

Harlech Castle. BRITISH TRAVEL AND HOLIDAYS ASSOCIATION

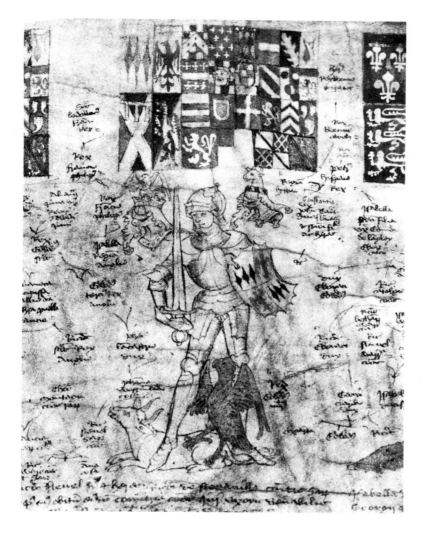

known. At Angers he confronted Margaret and her son, now a fine youth of seventeen, with Warwick and Clarence, and proposed brutally to them that they should join together with his support to overthrow Edward. They agreed to forgive and unite. The confederacy was sealed by the betrothal of Margaret's son, the Prince of Wales, to Warwick's youngest daughter, Anne. A son born of this union would have had a great hope of uniting torn, tormented England. But Clarence had been swayed in his desertion of his brother by thoughts of the Crown, and although he was now named as the next in succession after Margaret's son the value of his chance was no longer high. He must have been a great dissembler; for Warwick was no more able to forecast his actions in the future than his brother had been in the past.

Warwick and Clarence landed at Dartmouth in September 1470. Kent and other Southern counties rose in his behalf. He brought the miserable Henry VI from his prison in the Tower, placed a crown on his head, paraded him through the capital, and seated him upon the throne. At Nottingham Edward received alarming news. Suddenly he learned that while the Northern rebels were moving down upon him and cutting him from his Welsh succours, and while Warwick was moving northward with strong forces, the Marquis of Montagu, Warwick's brother, hitherto faithful, had made his men throw up their caps for King Henry. He had but one refuge—the Court of Burgundy; and with a handful of followers he cast himself upon his brother-in-law. Meanwhile, the King-maker ruled England, and it seemed that he might long continue to do so. He had King Henry VI a puppet in his hand. Statutes were passed in his name which annihilated all the disinheritances and attainders of the Yorkist Parliament. A third of the land of England returned to its old possessors.

In March 1471 Edward landed with his small expedition at Ravenspur, a port in Yorkshire now washed away by the North Sea, but then still famous for the descent of Henry of Bolingbroke in 1399. The King, fighting for his life, was, as usual, at his best. Montagu, with four times his numbers, approached to intercept him. Edward, by extraordinary marches, manœuvred past him. At Warwick he was strong enough to proclaim himself King again.

Edward had a resource unsuspected by Warwick. He knew Clarence was his man. Edward entered London, and was cordially received by the bewildered citizens. Henry VI, who had actually been made to ride about the streets at the head of six hundred horsemen, was relieved from these exertions and taken back to his prison in the Tower.

The decisive battle impended on the North Road, and at Barnet on April 14, 1471, Edward and the Yorkists faced Warwick and the House of Neville, with the new Duke of Somerset, second son of Edmund Beaufort, and important Lancastrian allies.

Throughout England no one could see clearly what was happening, and the Battle of Barnet, which resolved their doubts, was itself fought in a fog. The lines of battle overlapped; Warwick's right turned Edward's left flank, and vice versa. The King-maker, stung perhaps by imputations upon his physical courage, fought on foot. The badge of a star and rays on Lord Oxford's banners was mistaken by Warwick's troops for the sun and rays of King Edward. The cry of treason ran through Warwick's hosts. North of the town near which the main struggle was fought the King-maker, just as he was about to reach the necessary horse, was overtaken by the Yorkists and battered to death. By his depraved abandonment of all the causes for which he had sent so many men to their doom he had deserved death; and for his virtues, which were distinguished, it was fitting that it should come to him in honourable guise.

On the very day of Barnet Margaret at last landed in England. On learning that Warwick was slain and his army beaten and dispersed the hitherto indomitable Queen had her hour of despair. Her only hope was to reach the Welsh border, where strong traditional Lancastrian forces were already in arms. Edward, near London, strove to cut Margaret off from Wales. Both armies marched incessantly. The Lancastrians succeeded in reaching the goal first, but only with their troops in a state of extreme exhaustion. Edward, close behind, pressed on, and on the 4th of May brought them to battle at Tewkesbury. The Lancastrians were scattered or destroyed. Margaret was captured. The Prince of Wales, fighting valiantly, was slain on the field, according to one chronicler, crying in vain for succour to his brother-in-law, the treacherous Clarence. Margaret was kept for a show, and also because women, especially when they happened to be queens, were not slaughtered in this fierce age. Eleven years after Tewkesbury she died in poverty in her father's Anjou.

After the battle Richard of Gloucester, known to legend as "Crookback" because of his alleged deformity, had hastened to London. He had a task to do at the Tower. As long as the Prince of Wales lived King Henry's life had been safe, but with the death of the last hope of Lancaster his fate was sealed. On the night of May 21 the Duke of Gloucester visited the Tower with full authority from the King, where he probably supervised the murder of the melancholy spectator who had been the centre of fifty years of cruel contention.

The King was now supreme. He was now a matured and disillusioned statesman. Edward was resolved to have as little to do with Parliament as possible, and even as a boy of twenty in the stress of war he had tried hard and faithfully to "live of his own". He had a new source of revenue in the estates of the attainted Lancastrians. Thus so long as there was peace the King could pay his way. But the nobility and the nation sought more. They wanted to reconquer France. He had never liked war, and had had enough of it. Nevertheless, he obtained from the Parliament considerable grants for a war in alliance with Burgundy against France. In 1475 he invaded France, but advanced only as far as Picquigny, near Amiens. Louis XI shared his outlook. He too saw that kings might grow strong and safe in peace, and would be the prey and tool of their subjects in war. Louis XI offered Edward IV a lump sum of seventy-five thousand crowns, and a yearly tribute of fifty thousand. Edward closed on the bargain, and signed the Treaty of Picquigny. He went back home and drew for seven successive years this substantial payment for not harrying France, and at the same time he pocketed most of the moneys which Parliament had voted for harrying her. At this date the interest of these transactions centres mainly upon the character of Edward IV, and we can see that though he had to strive through fierce deeds and slaughter to his throne he was at heart a Little-Englander and a lover of ease. It by no means follows that his policy was injurious to the realm. He made his administration live thriftily, and on his death he was the first King since Henry II to leave not debts but a fortune.

Memoire de saint george. ã.

eorgi martir inclite te decet laus

et gloria. pre dotatum milicia p quẽ

St George killing the Dragon, a
illustration from a Book of Hour.
prepared in Normandy circa 1430-4
BODLEIAN LIBRARY, OXFORD

There came a day when he had to call Parliament together. Nothing could burn out from his mind the sense that Clarence was a traitor who had betrayed his cause and his family at one decisive moment and had been rebought at another. Clarence for his part knew that the wound although skinned over was unhealed; but he was a magnificent prince, and he sprawled buoyantly over the land. When in January 1478 Edward's patience was exhausted he called the Parliament with no other business but to condemn Clarence. Clarence was already in the Tower. How he died is much disputed. According to Shakespeare the Duke was drowned in a butt of Malmsey wine. This was certainly the popular legend believed by the sixteenth century. Why should it not be true? At any rate no one has attempted to prove any different tale.

Queen Elizabeth over the course of years had produced not only five daughters, but two fine boys, who were growing up. The King himself was only forty. His main thought was set on securing the Crown to his son, the unfledged Edward V; but in April 1483 death came so suddenly upon him that he had no time to take the necessary precautions.

All were caught by surprise. The King's eldest son, Edward, dwelt at Ludlow, on the Welsh border, under the care of his uncle, the second Lord Rivers. A Protectorate was inevitable. Richard of Gloucester, the King's faithful brother renowned in war, grave and competent in administration, enriched by Warwick's inheritance and many other great estates, in possession of all the chief military offices, stood forth without compare, and had been nominated by the late King himself. Around him gathered most of the old nobility. One thing at least they would not brook: Queen Elizabeth and her low-born relations should no longer have the ascendancy. For three weeks both parties eyed one another and parleyed.

It was agreed in April that the King should be crowned at the earliest moment, but that he should come to London attended by not more than two thousand horsemen. Accordingly this cavalcade, headed by Lord Rivers and his nephew, Grey, rode through Shrewsbury and Northampton. They had reached Stony Stratford when they learned that Gloucester and his ally, the Duke of Buckingham, coming to London from Yorkshire, were only ten miles behind them. Richard received them amicably; they

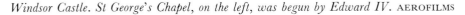

Windsor Castle. St George's Chapel, on the left, was begun by Edward IV. AEROFILMS

dined together. But with the morning there was a change. When he awoke Rivers found the doors of the inn locked. Gloucester and Buckingham met him with scowling gaze and accused him of "trying to set distance" between the King and them. He and Grey were immediately made prisoners. Richard then rode with his power to Stony Stratford, forced his way to the young King, and told him he had discovered a design on the part of Lord Rivers and others to seize the Government and oppress the old nobility. On this declaration Edward V took the only positive action recorded of his reign. He wept. Well he might. The next morning Duke Richard presented himself again to Edward. He embraced him as an uncle; he bowed to him as a subject. He announced himself as Protector. He dismissed the two thousand horsemen to their homes; their services would not be needed. To London then! To the Coronation! Thus this melancholy procession set out.

The Queen, who was already in London, had no illusions. She took sanctuary at once with her other children at Westminster, making a hole through the wall between the church and the palace to transport such personal belongings as she could gather. The report that the King was in duress caused a commotion in the capital. But Lord Hastings reassured the Council that all was well and that any disturbance would only delay the Coronation, upon which the peace of the realm depended. The King arrived in London only on May 4, and the Coronation, which had been fixed for that date, was necessarily postponed. He was lodged at the Bishop of London's palace, but Richard argued that it would be more fitting to the royal dignity to dwell in one of his own castles and on his own ground. With much ceremony and protestations of devotion the child of twelve was conducted to the Tower, and its gates closed behind him. The next step in the tragedy concerned Lord Hastings. He had played a leading part in the closing years of Edward IV. After the King's death he had been strong against the Woodvilles; but he was the first to detach himself from Richard's proceedings. Of what happened next all we really know is that Hastings was abruptly arrested in council at the Tower on June 13 and beheaded without trial on the

The Tower of London, on the north bank of the Thames. The Bloody Tower, where the uncrowned Edward V and his brother were said to have been murdered by their uncle, Richard III, is the square tower on the inner wall, to the left of the great central keep, William I's White Tower. The site of the scaffold is at the northern end of Tower Green, the tree-surrounded ground to the west of the White Tower. AEROFILMS

same day. Meanwhile, the Queen and her remaining son still sheltered in sanctuary. Richard felt that it would be more natural that the two brothers should be together under his care. Having no choice, the Queen submitted, and the little prince of nine was handed over in Westminster Hall to the Protector, who embraced him affectionately and conducted him to the Tower, which neither he nor his brother was ever to leave again.

The Coronation of Edward V had been postponed several times. Now a preacher named Shaw, brother of the Lord Mayor of London, one of Richard's partisans, was engaged to preach a sermon at St Paul's Cross. He argued that Edward's children were illegitimate and that the Crown rightly belonged to Richard. On June 25 Parliament met, and after receiving a roll declaring that the late King's marriage with Elizabeth was no marriage at all and that Edward's children were bastard it petitioned Richard to assume the Crown. With becoming modesty Richard persistently refused; but when Buckingham assured him that if he would not serve the country they would be forced to choose some other noble, he overcame his conscientious scruples at the call of public duty.

The Coronation of King Richard III was fixed for July 6, and pageants and processions diverted the uneasy public. Yet from this very moment there began that marked distrust and hostility of all classes towards King Richard III which all his arts and competence could not allay. It is contended by the defenders of King Richard that the Tudor version of these events has prevailed. But the English people who lived at the time and learned of the events day by day formed their convictions two years before the Tudors gained power, or were indeed a prominent factor. Richard III held the authority of Government. He told his own story with what facilities were available, and he was spontaneously and almost universally disbelieved.

No man had done more to place Richard upon the throne than the Duke of Buckingham, and upon no one had the King bestowed greater gifts and favours. Yet during these first three months of Richard's reign Buckingham from being his chief supporter became his mortal foe. Meanwhile, King Richard began a Progress from Oxford through the Midlands. At every city he laboured to make the best impression, righting wrongs, settling disputes, granting favours, and courting popularity. Yet he could not escape the sense that behind the displays of gratitude and loyalty which naturally surrounded him there lay an unspoken challenge to his Kingship. In London, Kent, Essex, and throughout the Home Counties feeling already ran high against him, and on all men's lips was the demand that the princes should be liberated. So we

King Richard III (1452–85), by an unknown artist.
REPRODUCED BY GRACIOUS PERMISSION OF HER MAJESTY THE QUEEN

come to the principal crime ever afterwards associated with Richard's name. It is certain that the helpless children in the Tower were not seen again after the month of July 1483. Yet we are invited by some to believe that they languished in captivity, unnoticed and unrecorded, for another two years, only to be done to death by Henry Tudor.

Buckingham had now become the centre of a conspiracy throughout the West and South of England against the King. He met at this time Margaret, Countess of Richmond, survivor of the Beaufort line, and recognised that even if the House of York were altogether set aside both she and her son Henry Tudor, Earl of Richmond, stood between him and the Crown. The Countess of Richmond, presuming him to be still Richard's right-hand man, asked him to win the King's consent to a marriage between her son Henry of Richmond and one of King Edward's daughters, Elizabeth, still in sanctuary with their mother at Westminster. All Buckingham's preparations were for a general rising on October 18. But the anger of the people at the rumoured murder of the princes deranged this elaborate plan. King Richard acted with the utmost vigour. He had an army and he marched against rebellion. The sporadic risings in the South were suppressed. Buckingham, with a high price on his head, was betrayed to Richard, who lost not an hour in having him slaughtered. The usual crop of executions followed. Order was restored throughout the land, and the King seemed to have established himself securely upon his throne.

He proceeded in the new year to inaugurate a series of enlightened reforms in every sphere of Government. He revived the power of Parliament, which it had been the policy of Edward IV to reduce to nullity. He declared the practice of raising revenue by "benevolences" illegal. Parliament again legislated copiously after a long interval. But all counted for nothing. The hatred which Richard's crime had roused against him throughout the land remained sullen and

The arms, crown, and supporters of Richard III. AFTER C. W. SCOTT-GILES

quenchless, and no benefits bestowed, no sagacious measures adopted, no administrative successes achieved could avail the guilty monarch. In April 1484 his only son, the Prince of Wales, died at Middleham, and his wife, Anne, the daughter of the King-maker, whose health was broken, could bear no more children. Henry Tudor, Earl of Richmond, now became obviously the rival claimant and successor to the throne.

All hopes in England were now turned towards Richmond, and it was apparent that the marriage which had been projected between him and Edward IV's eldest daughter Elizabeth offered a prospect of ending for ever the cruel dynastic strife of which the land was unutterably weary. In March 1485 Queen Anne died, probably from natural causes. Rumours were circulating that Richard intended to marry his niece himself, in order to keep her out of Richmond's way. All through the summer Richmond's expedition was preparing at the mouth of the Seine, and the exodus from England of substantial people to join him was unceasing. The suspense was wearing to Richard. He felt he was surrounded by hatred and distrust, and that none served him but from fear or hope of favour. His dogged, indomitable nature had determined him to make for his Crown the greatest of all his fights. He fixed his headquarters in a good central position at Nottingham. He set forth his

The Tower of London, a manuscript illustration from the Poems of Charles, Duke of Orleans. *Charles d'Orléans was imprisoned in the Tower after his capture at Agincourt.* BRITISH MUSEUM

and shouting "Treason! Treason!" hurled himself into the thickest of the fray in the desperate purpose of striking down Richmond with his own hand. Richmond was preserved, and the King, refusing to fly, was borne down and slaughtered as he deserved.

> One foot I will never flee, while the breath is my breast within.
> As he said, so did it he—if he lost his life he died a king.

Richard's crown, which he wore to the last, was picked out of a bush and placed upon the victor's head. His corpse, naked, and torn by wounds, was bound across a horse, with his head and long hair hanging down, bloody and hideous, and in this condition borne into Leicester for all men to see.

Bosworth Field may be taken as closing a long chapter in English history. Richard's death also ended the Plantagenet line. For over three hundred years this strong race of warrior- and statesmen-kings, whose gifts and vices were upon the highest scale, whose sense of authority and Empire had been persistently maintained, now vanished from the fortunes of the Island. The Plantagenets and the proud, exclusive nobility which their system evolved had torn themselves to pieces. As Cœur de Lion said of his House, "From the Devil we sprang and to the Devil we shall go."

cause in a vehement proclamation, denouncing ". . . one, Henry Tydder, son of Edmund Tydder, son of Owen Tydder". But this fell cold.

On August 1 Richmond embarked at Harfleur with his Englishmen, Yorkist as well as Lancastrian, and a body of French troops. He evaded the squadrons of "Lovell our dogge", doubled Land's End, and landed at Milford Haven on the 7th. The Welsh were gratified by the prospect of one of their race succeeding to the Crown of mighty England. Appearances favoured the King. He had ten thousand disciplined men under the royal authority against Richmond's hastily gathered five thousand rebels. And when on Sunday, the 21st, this whole array came out of Leicester to meet Richmond near the village of Market Bosworth it was certain that a decisive battle impended on the morrow. At some distance from the flanks of the main army, on opposite hill-tops, stood the respective forces, mainly from Lancashire and Cheshire, of Sir William Stanley and Lord Stanley, the whole situation resembling, as has been said, four players in a game of cards. But even now Richmond was not sure what part Lord Stanley and his forces would play. When, after archery and cannonade, the lines were locked in battle all doubts were removed. The Earl of Northumberland, commanding Richard's left, stood idle at a distance. Lord Stanley's force joined Richmond. The King saw that all was lost,

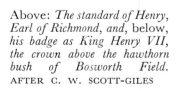

Above: *The standard of Henry, Earl of Richmond, and, below, his badge as King Henry VII, the crown above the hawthorn bush of Bosworth Field.*
AFTER C. W. SCOTT-GILES

CHAPTER FOUR

Renaissance and Reformation

For two hundred years or more the Renaissance had been stirring the thought and spirit of Italy, and now came forth in the vivid revival of the traditions of ancient Greece and Rome, in so far as these did not affect the foundations of the Christian faith.

The urge to inquire, to debate, and seek new explanations spread from the field of classical learning into that of religious studies. Greek and even Hebrew texts, as well as Latin, were scrutinised afresh. Inevitably this led to the questioning of accepted religious beliefs. The Renaissance bred the Reformation.

While the forces of Renaissance and Reformation were gathering strength in Europe the world beyond was yielding its secrets to European explorers, traders, and missionaries. From the days of the ancient Greeks some men had known in theory that the world was round and global. Now in the sixteenth century navigations were to prove it so. The scattered civilisations of the world were being drawn together, and the new discoveries were to give the little kingdom in the Northern sea a fresh importance. Here was to be the successor both of Portugal and Spain, though the time for entering into the inheritance was not yet. The whole course of trade was shifted and revolutionised. The primacy of the Italian cities was eclipsed by North-West Europe; and the future lay not in the Mediterranean, but on the shores of the Atlantic, where the new Powers, England, France, and Holland, had ports and harbours which gave easy access to the oceans.

Henry VII's first task was to induce magnates, Church, and gentry to accept the decision of Bosworth and to establish himself upon the throne. He was careful to be crowned before facing the representatives of the nation, thus resting his title first upon conquest, and only secondly on the approbation of Parliament. Then he married, as had long been planned, the heiress of the rival House, Elizabeth of York. Lack of money had long weakened the English throne, but military victory now restored to Henry most of the Crown lands alienated during the fifteenth century by confiscation and attainder, and many other great estates besides. Henry was thus assured of a settled income. Legislation was passed stating that all who gave their allegiance to the King for the time being—that is, to the King upon the throne—should be secure in

Christopher Columbus, by an unknown artist. R. GALLERIA UFFIZI, FLORENCE. PHOTO: MANSELL COLLECTION

Portuguese Carracks. A painting on a panel, attributed to Cornelius Athoniszoon (d. circa 1553). NATIONAL MARITIME MUSEUM

Early Tudor ship, from a window in King's College Chapel, Cambridge (showing St Paul leaving Troas). BY KIND PERMISSION OF THE PROVOST. PHOTO: FRANK A. NEWENS

their lives and property. This idea of an actual King as distinct from a rightful King was characteristic of the new ruler.

Henry had to keep ceaseless watch for the invasion of pretenders supported by foreign aid. The first was Lambert Simnel, who finished ingloriously as a scullion in the royal kitchens. The second and more formidable was Perkin Warbeck, the son of a boatman and collector of taxes at Tournai, put forward as the younger of the princes murdered in the Tower. But the classes who had backed the King since Bosworth were staunch.

Throughout the history of medieval England there runs a deep division between North and South. In the South a more fully advanced society dwelt in a rich countryside, with well-developed towns and a prosperous wool trade with Flanders and Italy. The Wars of the Roses had been a serious threat to this organised life, and it was in the South that Henry found his chief support. The North was very different. Great feudal Houses like the Percys dominated the scene. Councils were accordingly established to administer the Northern parts and Welsh Marches. The Wars of the Roses had weakened English authority in Wales, but it was in Ireland that their effects were most manifest. Lords Deputy from England found it profitless to assert their legal powers in face of the dominating local position and island-wide alliances of Kildare, who was called "Garret More", or Great Earl. Sir Edward Poynings, appointed Lord Deputy of Ireland in 1494, tried to limit his powers of mischief. He persuaded the Irish Parliament at Drogheda to pass the celebrated Poynings' Law, subordinating the Irish Parliament to the English, which was not repealed for three hundred years and remained a grievance till the twentieth century.

Henry's dealings with Scotland are characteristic of his shrewd judgment. Although not obviously a man of imagination, he had his dreams. At any rate, Henry took the first steps to unite England and Scotland by marrying his daughter Margaret to James IV in 1502, and there was peace in the North until after his death. Like the other princes of his age, his main interest, apart from an absorbing passion for administration, was foreign policy. He maintained the first permanent English envoys abroad. He realised that more could be gained by the threat of war than by war itself. Like Edward IV, he pocketed not only a considerable subsidy from France, which was punctually paid, but also the taxes collected in England for war.

Henry VII as a statesman was imbued with the new, ruthless political ideas of Renaissance Europe. He strove to establish a strong monarchy in England, moulded out of native institutions. The King's Council was strengthened. It was given Parliamentary authority to examine persons with or without oath, and condemn them, on written evidence alone, in a manner foreign to the practice of the Common Law. The Court of Star Chamber met regularly at Westminster, with the two Chief Justices in attendance. It was originally a judicial committee of the King's Council, trying cases which needed special treatment because of the excessive might of one of the parties or the novelty or enormity of the offence. But the main function of the King's Council was to govern rather than to judge. A small inner committee conducted foreign affairs. Another managed the finances, hacking a new path through the cumbrous practices of the medieval Exchequer; treasurers were now appointed who were answerable personally to the King.

Henry VII was probably the best business man to sit upon the English throne. He was also a remarkably shrewd picker of men. How far he was a conscious innovator, turning his back on ancient ways, is in dispute among historians, but his skill and wisdom in transmuting medieval institutions into the organs of modern rule has not been questioned. His achievement was indeed massive and durable. He built his power amid the ruins and ashes of his predecessors. He thriftily and carefully gathered what seemed in those days a vast reserve of liquid wealth. He trained a body of efficient servants. He magnified the Crown without losing the co-operation of the Com-

King Henry VII (1457–1509). A portrait painted in 1505 by an unknown Flemish artist. NATIONAL PORTRAIT GALLERY

mons. He identified prosperity with monarchy. Among the princes of Renaissance Europe he is not surpassed in achievement and fame by Louis XI of France or Ferdinand of Spain. Such was the architect of the Tudor monarchy, which was to lead England out of medieval disorder into greater strength and broader times.

Until the death of his elder brother, Prince Arthur, Henry VIII had been intended for the Church. He had therefore been brought up by his father in an atmosphere of learning. Henry in his maturity was a tall, red-headed man who preserved the vigour and energy of ancestors accustomed for centuries to the warfare of the Welsh Marches. Bursts of restless energy and ferocity were combined with extraordinary patience and diligence. Although Henry appeared to strangers open, jovial, and trustworthy, with a bluff good-humour which appealed at once to the crowd, even those who knew him most intimately seldom penetrated the inward secrecy and reserve which allowed him to confide freely in no one. As time passed his wilfulness

THE TUDOR AND STUART DYNASTIES

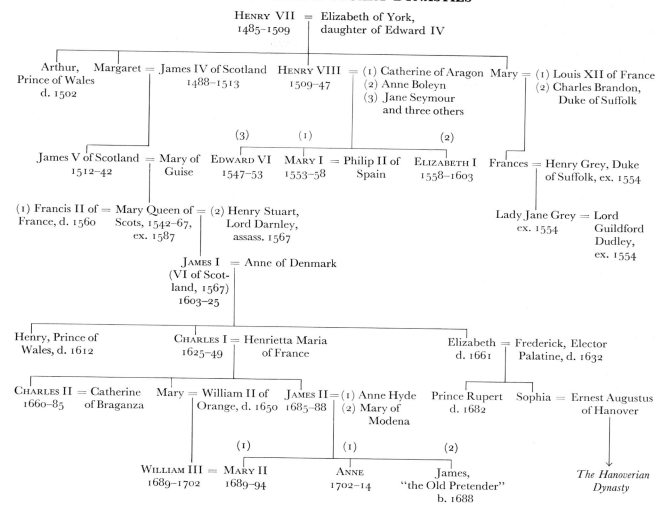

HENRY VII = Elizabeth of York,
1485–1509 | daughter of Edward IV

Arthur, Prince of Wales d. 1502   Margaret = James IV of Scotland 1488–1513   HENRY VIII 1509–47 = (1) Catherine of Aragon / (2) Anne Boleyn / (3) Jane Seymour and three others   Mary = (1) Louis XII of France / (2) Charles Brandon, Duke of Suffolk

James V of Scotland 1512–42 = Mary of Guise   (3) EDWARD VI 1547–53   (1) MARY I 1553–58 = Philip II of Spain   (2) ELIZABETH I 1558–1603   Frances = Henry Grey, Duke of Suffolk, ex. 1554

(1) Francis II of France, d. 1560 = Mary Queen of Scots, 1542–67, ex. 1587 = (2) Henry Stuart, Lord Darnley, assass. 1567   Lady Jane Grey ex. 1554 = Lord Guildford Dudley, ex. 1554

JAMES I (VI of Scotland, 1567) 1603–25 = Anne of Denmark

Henry, Prince of Wales, d. 1612   CHARLES I 1625–49 = Henrietta Maria of France   Elizabeth d. 1661 = Frederick, Elector Palatine, d. 1632

CHARLES II 1660–85 = Catherine of Braganza   Mary = William II of Orange, d. 1650   JAMES II 1685–88 = (1) Anne Hyde / (2) Mary of Modena   Prince Rupert d. 1682   Sophia = Ernest Augustus of Hanover

WILLIAM III 1689–1702 = MARY II (1) 1689–94   ANNE (1) 1702–14   James, "the Old Pretender" (2) b. 1688   *The Hanoverian Dynasty*

---

hardened and his temper worsened. The only secret of managing him, both Wolsey and Cromwell disclosed after they had fallen, was to see that dangerous ideas were not permitted to reach him. Almost his first act, six weeks after the death of his father in 1509, was to marry his brother Arthur's widow, Princess Catherine of Aragon. Catherine was at Henry's side during the first twenty-two years of his reign, while England was becoming a force in European affairs, perilous for foreign rulers to ignore.

Henry VII had only once sent English levies abroad, preferring to hire mercenaries who fought alongside foreign armies. Henry VIII now determined that this policy should be reversed. France was preoccupied with Italian adventures, and Henry planned to reconquer Bordeaux, lost sixty years before, while King Ferdinand invaded Navarre, an independent kingdom lying athwart the Pyrenees, and the Pope and the republic of Venice operated against the French armies in Italy. The year was 1512, and this was the first time since the Hundred Years War that an English army had campaigned in Europe.

The English expedition to Gascony failed. After negotiations lasting throughout the winter of 1512–13 Ferdinand and the Venetians deserted Henry and the Pope and made peace with France. In England the responsibility for these failures was cast on Henry's adviser, Thomas Wolsey. In fact it was in the hard work of administration necessitated by the war that he had first shown his abilities and immense energy. But Henry VIII and the Pope never wavered. Under Henry's command, the English, with Austrian mercenaries, routed the French in August 1513 at the Battle of the Spurs, so called because

King Henry VIII (1491–1547). A painting on copper after Holbein. NATIONAL PORTRAIT GALLERY

of the rapidity of the French retreat. To aid their French ally the Scots in the King's absence had crossed the Tweed in September and invaded England with an army of fifty thousand men. At Flodden Field a bloody battle was fought on September 9, 1513. The whole of Scotland, Highland and Lowland alike, drew out with their retainers in the traditional schiltrons, or circles of spearmen, and around the standard of their King. The English archers once again directed upon these redoubtable masses a long, intense, and murderous arrow storm. When night fell the flower of the Scottish chivalry lay in their ranks where they had fought, and among them King James IV. This was the last great victory gained by the long-bow.

Henry had every intention of renewing his campaign in France in 1514, but his successes had not been to the liking of Ferdinand of Spain. Faced with the defection of his allies, Henry was quick to launch a counter-stroke. The crowning event of the peace was the marriage between Henry's young sister, Mary, and Louis XII himself.

For fourteen years Wolsey in the King's name was the effective ruler of the realm. He owed his position not only to his great capacity for business, but to his considerable personal charm. In the King's company he was brilliant, convivial, and "a gay seeker out of new pastimes". Other would-be counsellors of Henry's saw a different side of the Cardinal's character. They resented being scornfully overborne by him in debate; they detested his arrogance, and envied his ever-growing wealth and extensive patronage. He kept a thousand servants, and his palaces surpassed the King's in splendour. Successes abroad enabled Wolsey to develop Henry VII's principles of centralised government. During the twelve years that he was Lord Chancellor Parliament met only once, for two sessions spreading over three months in all. The Court of Star Chamber grew more active. It evolved new and simple methods copied from Roman law, by which the Common Law rules of evidence were dispensed with, and persons who could give evidence were simply brought in for interrogation,

Catherine of Aragon (1485–1536). A portrait by Michael Sittow, circa *1502, attributed to Catherine on strong, but circumstantial grounds.* KUNSTHISTORISCHES MUSEUM, VIENNA

Anne Boleyn (1507–36), a drawing by Holbein. REPRODUCED BY GRACIOUS PERMISSION OF HER MAJESTY THE QUEEN

Jane Seymour (d. 1537), a drawing by Holbein. REPRODUCED BY GRACIOUS PERMISSION OF HER MAJESTY THE QUEEN

one by one, often without even the formality of an oath. This system of arbitrary government, however despotic in theory, however contrary to the principles believed to lie behind Magna Carta, in fact rested tacitly on the real will of the people. Henry VIII, like his father, found an institution ready to his hand in the unpaid Justice of the Peace, the local squire or landlord, and taught him to govern.

Within a few years of his accession Henry embarked upon a programme of naval expansion, while Wolsey concerned himself with diplomatic manœuvre. For some years at least Wolsey was a powerful factor and balancing weight in Europe. The zenith of this brilliant period was reached at the Field of the Cloth of Gold in June 1520, when Henry crossed the Channel to meet his rival, Francis I of France, for the first time. It was the last display of medieval chivalry. Many noblemen, it was said, carried on their shoulders their mills, their forests, and their meadows. But Henry and Francis failed to become personal friends. Henry, indeed, was already negotiating with Francis's enemy,

the new Emperor Charles V, who had lately succeeded his grandfather, Maximilian. When the Emperor declared war on Francis English wealth was squandered feverishly on an expedition to Boulogne and subsidies to mercenary contingents serving with the Emperor. Wolsey had to find the money. The Government had to beat a retreat, the campaign was abandoned, and Wolsey got the King's consent to make secret overtures for peace to Francis. These overtures were Wolsey's fatal miscalculation; only six weeks later the Imperial armies won an overwhelming victory over the French at Pavia, in Northern Italy. Henry could no longer turn the scales in Europe.

Then there was Queen Catherine. A typical Spanish princess, she had matured and aged rapidly; it was clear that she would bear Henry no male heir. Either the King's illegitimate son, the Duke of Richmond, now aged six, would have to be appointed by Act of Parliament, or perhaps England might accept Catherine's child, Mary, now aged nine, as the first Queen of England in her own right since Matilda. Would England tolerate being ruled by a woman? The first

Anne of Cleves (1515–57). This Holbein painting in the Louvre is generally accepted as the portrait of Anne painted for Henry VIII before their marriage. PHOTO: HACHETTE

Catherine Howard (d. 1542), from a miniature by Holbein. (The identity of the subject has been questioned.) REPRODUCED BY GRACIOUS PERMISSION OF HER MAJESTY THE QUEEN

Catherine Parr (1512–48), an engraving after the Holbein painting

Thomas Wolsey (1472/3–1530). Drawing by an unknown artist, in the Arras Library. PHOTO: NATIONAL PORTRAIT GALLERY

step, clearly, was to get rid of Catherine. We first hear of Anne Boleyn at Court in a dispatch of the Imperial Ambassador dated August 16, 1527, four months after Henry had begun proceedings for the annulment of his marriage.

The Papal Legate, Cardinal Campeggio, who was sent to England to hear the case, used all possible pretexts to postpone a decision. The Pope was now practically a prisoner of Charles V, who was determined that Henry should not divorce his aunt. This broke Wolsey. New counsellors were called in. At the same time the King had the writs sent out for a Parliament, the first for six years, to strengthen his hand in the great changes he was planning. Wolsey's high offices of State were conferred on a new administration: Gardiner secured the Bishopric of Winchester, the richest see in England; Norfolk became President of the Council, and Suffolk the Vice-President. During the few days that elapsed until Wolsey was replaced by Sir Thomas More as Lord Chancellor the King applied the Great Seal himself to documents of State. With the death of the Cardinal political interests hitherto submerged made their bid for power.

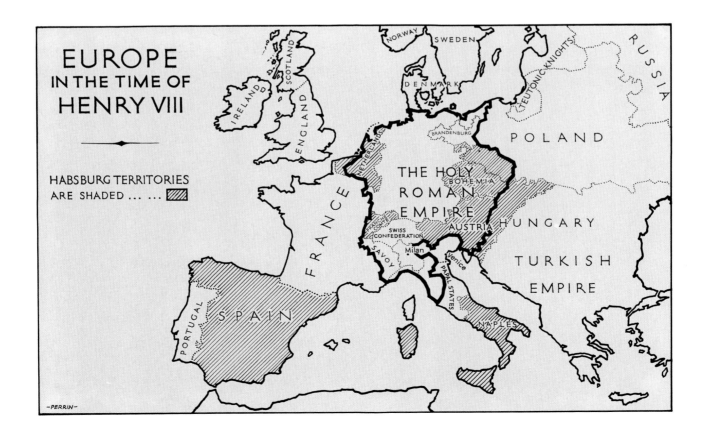

EUROPE IN THE TIME OF HENRY VIII

HABSBURG TERRITORIES ARE SHADED ... ...

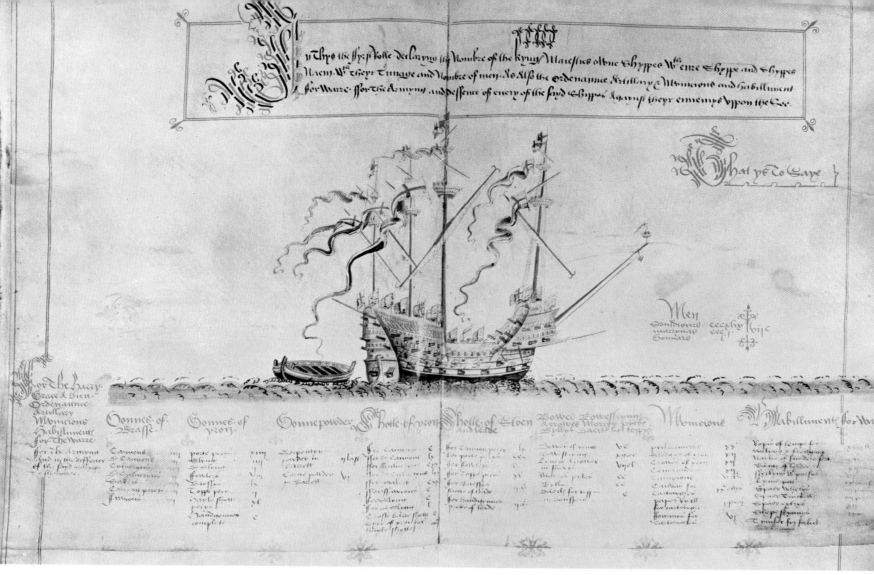

The Henry Grace à Dieu (Great Harry), *from Anthony Anthony's Roll of the Navy, 1546. Built as a 1,500-ton ship of 186 guns in 1514 as part of Henry VIII's programme of naval expansion, she was rebuilt in 1539–40 as a 1,000-ton ship of 122 guns. In 1553 she was destroyed by fire at Woolwich.* PEPYSIAN LIBRARY, MAGDALENE COLLEGE, CAMBRIDGE

Thomas Cranmer's idea of an appeal to the universities about Henry's marriage to Catherine proved a great success, and the young lecturer was rewarded with an appointment as Ambassador to the Emperor. The King had known all along that he was right, and here, it seemed, was final proof. He determined to mark his displeasure with the Pope by some striking measure against the power of the Church of England. The House of Lords, where the bishops and abbots still had more votes than the lay peers, agreed to the Bills reforming sanctuaries and abolishing mortuary fees, which affected the lower clergy only, but when the Probate Bill came up to the Lords the Archbishop of Canterbury "in especial", and all the other bishops in general, both frowned and grunted. Thus from the outset the

Reformation House of Commons acquired a corporate spirit, and during its long life, longer than any previous Parliament, eagerly pursued any measure which promised revenge against the bishops for what it deemed their evasion and duplicity over the Probate Bill. Hostility to the Episcopate smouldered, and marked the Commons for more than a hundred years.

During December 1530 the Attorney-General charged the whole body of the clergy with breaking the fourteenth-century Statutes of Præmunire and Provisors which had been passed to limit the powers of the Pope. This they had done by acquiescing in Wolsey's many high-handed actions in his role as Papal Legate. In return for a pardon the King extracted large sums from Convocation, £100,000 from the province of Canterbury

115

and £19,000 from York, which was much more than at first they were prepared to pay. After further negotiation he also obtained a new title. On February 7, 1531, the clergy acknowledged that the King was "their especial Protector, one and supreme lord, and, as far as the law of Christ allows, even supreme head". Parliament, which had been prorogued from month to month since the great doings about probate in 1529, was now recalled to hear and disseminate the royal view on the divorce.

The winter of 1531–2 was marked by the tensest crisis of Henry's reign. The Annates Bill armed the King for a greater struggle with the Papacy than had preceded Magna Carta. If the Court of Rome, its preamble ran, endeavoured to wield excommunication, interdict, or process compulsory in England, then all manner of sacraments and divine service should continue to be administered, and the interdict should not by any prelate or minister be executed or divulged. If any one named by the King to a bishopric were restrained by Bulls from Rome from accepting office he should be consecrated by the Archbishop, or any one named to an archbishopric. And the Annates, a mainstay of the Papal finances, were limited to five per cent of their former amount. This was the most difficult Bill which Henry ever had to steer through Parliament. The next step was to make the clergy submit to the royal supremacy. Henry got the Commons to prepare a document called the Supplication against the Ordinaries, directed against the authority of Church courts. On the very afternoon these articles were submitted for the royal consent, May 16, 1532, Sir Thomas More resigned the Lord Chancellorship as a protest against royal supremacy in spiritual affairs. Thus the English Reformation was a slow process. An opportunist King measured his steps as he went, until England was wholly independent of administration from Rome.

The death in August of old William Warham, Archbishop of Canterbury and principal opponent of the King's divorce, opened further possibilities and problems. Cranmer took leave of the Emperor at

Sir Thomas More (1478–1535). A Holbein drawing.
REPRODUCED BY GRACIOUS PERMISSION OF HER MAJESTY THE QUEEN

Mantua on November 1, 1532, and left the following day, arriving in London in the middle of December. A week later he was offered the Archbishopric of Canterbury. He accepted. A month later Henry secretly married Anne Boleyn. Cranmer became Archbishop in the traditional manner. At the King's request Bulls had been obtained from Rome by threatening the Papacy with a rigorous application of the Act of Annates. This was important: the man who was to carry through the ecclesiastical revolution had thus been accepted by the Pope and endowed with full authority. Two days afterwards, however, a Bill was introduced into Parliament vesting in the Archbishop of Canterbury the power, formerly possessed by the Pope, to hear and determine all appeals from the ecclesiastical courts in England. This momentous Bill, the work of Thomas Cromwell, which abolished what still remained of Papal authority in England, passed through Parliament in due course, and became known as the Act of Appeals. The following month Henry himself wrote a letter describing his position as "King and Sovereign, recognising no superior in earth but only God, and not subject to the laws of any earthly creature". The breach between England and Rome was complete.

The Duke of Norfolk with royal commissioners waited on Queen Catherine at Ampthill. She refused to resign. A fortnight later Cranmer opened a court at Dunstable, and sent a Proctor to Ampthill citing Catherine to appear. She refused. In her absence the Archbishop pronounced judgment. Catherine's marriage with Henry had existed in fact but not in law; it was void from the beginning; and five days afterwards the marriage with Anne was declared valid. Queen Anne Boleyn was crowned on June 1 in Westminster Abbey.

The following month it became clear that the new Queen was expecting a child. A magnificent and valuable bed, which had lain in the Treasury since it had formed part of a French nobleman's ransom, was brought forth, and in it on September 7, 1533, the future Queen Elizabeth was born. Although bonfires were lighted there was no rejoicing in Henry's heart. A male heir had been his desire. An Act was passed vesting the succession in Elizabeth. In March 1534 every person of legal age, male or female, throughout the kingdom was forced to swear allegiance to this Act and renounce allegiance to all foreign authority in England. Bishop Fisher and Sir Thomas More, who both refused the oath, were confined in the Tower for many months. Fisher was executed in June 1535 and More in July.

Sir John Seymour, a worthy old courtier, had a pretty daughter, a former Maid of Honour to Queen Catherine. Jane Seymour was about twenty-five, and although she was attractive no one considered her a great beauty. But she was gay, and generally liked, and Henry fell in love with her. The King was still paying court to Jane when it became known that Anne was expecting another baby. But this time Henry refused to have anything to do with her. Soon afterwards her uncle, the Duke of Norfolk, strode into the room and told her that Henry had had a serious accident out hunting. In her grief and alarm she nearly fainted. Five days later she miscarried.

In January 1536 Queen Catherine died. If the King was minded to marry again he could now repudiate Queen Anne without raising awkward questions about his earlier union. The Queen had accordingly been watched, and one Sunday two young courtiers, Henry Norris and Sir Francis Weston, were seen to enter the Queen's room, and were, it was said, overheard making love to her. The following Sunday a certain Smeaton, a gentleman of the King's Chamber, who played with great skill on the lute, was arrested as the Queen's lover. On Monday Norris was among the challengers at the May Day tournament at Greenwich, and as the King rode to London after the jousting he called Norris to his side

Thomas Cranmer (d. 1556). A portrait by Gerlach Flicke, 1546. NATIONAL PORTRAIT GALLERY

The Field of the Cloth of Gold, 1520. Painting by an unknown artist, now in Hampton Court Palace. REPRODUCED
BY GRACIOUS PERMISSION OF HER MAJESTY THE QUEEN

and told him what was suspected. That night Anne learned that Smeaton and Norris were in the Tower. The following morning she was requested to come before the Council. At the conclusion of the proceedings she was placed under arrest, and kept under guard until the tide turned to take her up-river to the Tower. On Friday morning the special commissioners of treason appointed the previous week, including Anne Boleyn's father, the Earl of Wiltshire, and the entire bench of judges except one, formed the court for the trial of Anne's lovers. They were sentenced to be hanged, drawn, and quartered, but execution was deferred until after the trial of the Queen. This opened the following Monday in the Great Hall of the Tower. The Queen denied the charges vigorously, and replied to each one in detail. The peers retired, and soon returned with a verdict of guilty. Norfolk pronounced sentence: the Queen was to be burnt or beheaded, at the King's pleasure.

On May 19, 1536, the headsman was already waiting, leaning on his heavy two-handed sword, when the Constable of the Tower appeared, followed by Anne in a beautiful night robe of heavy grey damask trimmed with fur, showing a crimson kirtle beneath. "Pray for me," she said, and knelt down while one of the ladies-in-waiting bandaged her eyes. "God have pity on my soul." "God have mercy on my soul," she repeated, as the executioner stepped forward and slowly took his aim. Then the great blade hissed through the air, and with a single stroke his work was done.

As soon as the execution was known Henry appeared in yellow, with a feather in his cap, and ten days later was privately married to Jane Seymour at York Place. She was the only Queen whom Henry regretted and mourned, and when she died, still aged only twenty-seven, immediately after the birth of her first child, the future Edward VI, Henry had her buried with royal honours in St George's Chapel at Windsor. He himself lies near her.

The King had now a new chief adviser. Thomas Cromwell, in turn mercenary soldier in Italy, cloth agent, and money-lender, had served his apprenticeship in Statecraft under Wolsey, but he had also learned the lessons of his master's downfall. Ruthless, cynical, Machiavellian, Cromwell was a man of the New Age. Before his day Government policy had for centuries been both made and implemented in the royal Household. Though Henry VII had improved the system he had remained in a sense a medieval king. Thomas Cromwell thoroughly reformed it during his ten years of power, and when he fell in 1540 policy was already carried out by Government departments, operating outside the Household.

The religious Orders had for some time been in decline, and parents were becoming more and more averse to handing over their sons to the cloisters. The idea of suppression was not altogether new: Wolsey had suppressed several small houses to finance his college at Oxford, and the King had since suppressed over twenty more for his own benefit. During the summer of 1536 royal commissioners toured the country, completing the dissolution as swiftly as possible. As First Minister Cromwell handled the

Thomas Cromwell (d. 1540) by Hans Holbein the Younger.
THE FRICK COLLECTION, NEW YORK

dissolution of the monasteries with conspicuous, cold-blooded efficiency. It was a step which appealed to the well-to-do. The high nobility and country gentry acquired on favourable terms all kinds of fine estates. The main result of this transaction was in effect, if not in intention, to commit the landed and mercantile classes to the Reformation settlement and the Tudor dynasty. The immediate impact on the masses is more difficult to judge. In the North, where the old traditions died hard, the new order aroused stiffer resistance than in the South, and the new lay landlord could be harsher than his clerical predecessor.

The older generation considered that Holy Writ was dangerous in the hands of the unlearned and should only be read by priests. But complete printed Bibles, translated into English by Tyndale and Coverdale, had appeared for the first time late in the autumn of 1535, and were now running through several editions. In the autumn of 1536, when the new taxes came to be assessed after Michaelmas, farmers and yokels collected in large numbers throughout the North of England and Lincolnshire, swearing to resist the taxes and maintain the old order in the Church. The revolt, which took the name of "the Pilgrimage of Grace", was spontaneous. Its leader, a lawyer named Robert Aske, had his position thrust upon him. The nobles and higher clergy took no part. In early 1537 the rebellion collapsed as quickly as it had arisen, but Henry determined to make examples of the ringleaders. Altogether some two hundred and fifty of the insurgents were put to death.

Up to this point Thomas Cromwell had consistently walked with success. But he now began to encounter the conservatism of the older nobility. The Duke of Norfolk headed the reaction, and the King, who was rigidly orthodox, except where his lusts or interests were stirred, agreed with it. Stephen Gardiner, Bishop of Winchester and later Queen Mary's adviser, was the brain behind the Norfolk party.

An alliance with the princes of Northern Germany against the two Catholic monarchs now seemed imperative, and negotiations for a marriage between Henry and Anne, the eldest Princess of Cleves, were hurried on. Anne spent Christmas at Calais, waiting for storms to abate, and on the last day of the year 1539 arrived at Rochester. Henry had sailed down in his private barge, in disguise, bearing a fine sable fur among the presents. On New Year's Day he hurried to visit her. But on seeing her he was astonished and abashed. Privately he dubbed her "the Flanders Mare". But the threat from abroad compelled the King to fulfil his contract. Since he now knew as much about the Canon Law on marriage as anyone in Europe, he turned himself into the perfect legal example of a man whose marriage might be annulled. Norfolk and Gardiner now saw their chance to break Cromwell, as Wolsey had been broken, with the help of a new lady. Yet another of Norfolk's nieces, Catherine Howard, was presented to Henry at Gardiner's house, and captured his affections at first sight. In June 1540 the King was persuaded to get rid of Cromwell and Anne together. Cromwell was condemned under a Bill of Attainder charging him principally with heresy and "broadcasting" erroneous books and implicitly with treason. Anne agreed to have her marriage annulled, and Convocation pronounced it invalid. She lived on in England, pensioned and in retirement, for another seventeen years.

A few days after Cromwell was executed on July 28 Henry was privately married to his fifth wife, Catherine Howard. Aged about twenty-two, with auburn hair and hazel eyes, she was the prettiest of Henry's wives. But wild, tempestuous Catherine was not long content with a husband nearly thirty years older than herself. Her reckless love for her cousin, Thomas Culpeper, was discovered, and she was executed in the Tower in February 1542 on the same spot as Anne Boleyn.

Henry's sixth wife, Catherine Parr, was a serious little widow from the Lake District, thirty-one years of age, learned, and interested in theological questions, who had had two husbands before the King. She married Henry at Hampton Court on July

The frontispiece to the Great Bible, 1539–41, showing Henry VIII presenting it to Cromwell, his Vicar-General, and to Archbishop Cranmer. BRITISH MUSEUM

war into the enemy's country. Their decision proved disastrous. Badly led and imperfectly organised, they lost more than half their army of ten thousand men in Solway Moss and were utterly routed. The news of this second Flodden killed James V, who died leaving the kingdom to an infant of one week, Mary, the famous Queen of Scots.

Once again England and the Holy Roman Empire made common cause against the French, and in May 1543 a secret treaty was ratified between Charles V and Henry. While Scotland was left to Edward Seymour, brother of Queen Jane, and now Earl of Hertford, the King himself was to cross the Channel and lead an army against Francis in co-operation with an Imperial force from the north-east. The plan was excellent, but the execution failed. Meanwhile, the English in Scotland, after burning Edinburgh and laying waste much country, ceased to make headway, and in February 1545 were defeated at Ancrum Moor. Without a single ally, the nation faced the possibility of invasion from both France and Scotland. The crisis called for unexampled sacrifices from the English people; never had they been called upon to pay so many loans, subsidies, and benevolences. Next year a peace treaty was signed, which left Boulogne in English hands for eight years, at the end of which time France was to buy it back at a heavy price. Henry completely failed in Scotland. He would make no generous settlement with his neighbours, yet he lacked the force to coerce them.

In these last few months one question dominated all minds: the heir to the kingdom was known, a child of nine, but who would be the power behind the throne? Norfolk or Hertford? The party of reaction or the party of reform? The King remembered that years before Norfolk had been put forward as a possible heir to the throne, and his son Surrey had been suggested as a husband for Princess Mary. His suspicions aroused, he acted swiftly; in mid-January Surrey was executed. Parliament assembled to pass a Bill of Attainder against Norfolk. On Thursday the 27th the royal assent was given and Norfolk was condemned to death.

12, 1543, and until his death three years later made him an admirable wife, nursing his ulcerated leg, which grew steadily worse and in the end killed him.

The brilliant young Renaissance prince had grown old and wrathful. Reviving the obsolete claim to suzerainty, Henry denounced the Scots as rebels, and pressed them to relinquish their alliance with France. The Scots successfully defeated an English raid at Halidon Rig. Then in the autumn of 1542 an expedition under Norfolk had to turn back at Kelso, principally through the failure of the commissariat, which, besides its other shortcomings, left the English army without its beer, and the Scots proceeded to carry the

The Siege of Boulogne, 1544. This engraving by James Basire after a contemporary painting shows the high and low town and castle, the English camps of Henry VIII (centre, in armour and holding a baton), Lord Admiral Lisle, and Sir Anthony Browne. BRITISH MUSEUM

But that same evening the King himself was dying.

The English Reformation under Henry VIII had received its guiding impulse from the King's passions and his desire for power. He still deemed himself a good Catholic. With the new reign a deeper and more powerful tide began to flow. The guardian and chief counsellor of the child-king was his uncle, Edward Seymour, now Duke of Somerset. He and Cranmer proceeded to transform the political reformation of Henry VIII into a religious revolution. The Book of Common Prayer, in shining English prose, was drawn up by Cranmer and accepted by Parliament in 1549. Then followed, after Somerset's fall, the Forty-two Articles of Religion, and a second Prayer Book, until, on paper at least, England became a Protestant State.

Somerset himself was merely one of the regents appointed under Henry's will, and his position as Protector, at once dazzling and dangerous, had little foundation in law or precedent. His brother, Thomas Seymour, Lord High Admiral, had his own ambitions.

Proofs were discovered of Thomas Seymour's plots against his brother, and the Protector was forced in January 1549 to dispose of him by Act of Attainder and the block on Tower Hill.

The life and economy of medieval England were fast dissolving. Landlords saw that vast fortunes could be made from wool, and the village communal strips barred their profits. Common land was seized, enclosed, and turned to pasture for flocks. In some counties as much as one-third of the arable land was turned over to grass, and the people looked in anger upon the new nobility, fat with sacrilegious spoil, but greedy still. Somerset had thus to face one of the worst economic crises that England has endured. The popular preachers were loud in denunciation. The Sermon of the Plough, preached by Hugh Latimer at Paul's Cross in 1548, is a notable piece of Tudor invective. Somerset himself sympathised with the yeomen and peasantry, and appointed commissions to inquire into the enclosures. But this increased the discontent, and encouraged the oppressed to

123

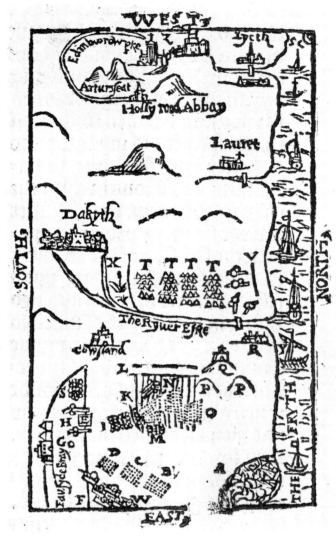

The Battle of Pinkie, September 10, 1547, from Patten's The Expedicione into Scotlande . . . *of Edward Duke of Somerset:* A B C D *the English army;* M N O *the Scots army;* T *the Scots' tents;* Y *"our galley";* Z *Edinburgh Castle.* BRITISH MUSEUM

take matters into their own hands. The Catholic peasantry in the South-West rose against the Prayer Book, and the yokels of the Eastern Counties against the enclosing landlords. Foreign mercenaries suppressed the Western rebellion. But in Norfolk the trouble was more serious. A tannery-owner named Robert Ket took the lead. The disorders spread to Yorkshire, and presently reverberated in the Midlands. John Dudley, Earl of Warwick, son of the man who had been Henry VII's agent, now seized his opportunity. Warwick's best troops were German mercenaries, whose precise fire-drill shattered the peasant array. Three thousand five hundred were killed.

Somerset's enemies claimed the credit for restoring order. Warwick became the leader of the Opposition. "The Lords in London", as Warwick's party were called, met to take

measures against the Protector. They quietly took over the Government. After a spell in the Tower, Somerset, now powerless, was for some months allowed to sit in the Council, but as conditions got worse so the danger grew of a reaction in his favour. In January 1552, splendidly garbed as for a State banquet, he was executed on Tower Hill. This handsome, well-meaning man had failed completely to heal the dislocation of Henry's reign and fell a victim to the fierce interests he had offended. Nevertheless, the people of England remembered him for years as "the Good Duke". The nominal King of England, Edward VI, was a cold, priggish invalid of fifteen. In his diary he noted his uncle's death without a comment.

The Government of Warwick, now become Duke of Northumberland, was held together by class resistance to social unrest. His three years of power displayed to the full the rapacity of the ruling classes. Doctrinal reformation was a pretence for confiscating yet more Church lands, and new bishops paid for their consecration with portions of the episcopal estates. One gleam of enterprise distinguishes this period. It saw the opening of relations between England and a growing new Power in Eastern Europe, hitherto known as Muscovy, but soon to be called Russia.

Under the Succession Act of 1543 the next heir to the throne was Princess Mary, the Catholic daughter of Catherine of Aragon. Northumberland might well tremble for the future. A desperate scheme was evolved. The younger daughter of Henry VII had married the Duke of Suffolk, and their heirs had been named in Henry VIII's will as next in line of succession after his own children. The eldest grandchild in this Suffolk line was Lady Jane Grey, a girl of sixteen. Northumberland married this girl to his son, Guildford Dudley. Nothing remained but to effect a military *coup* when the young King died. On July 6, 1553, Edward VI expired, and Lady Jane Grey was proclaimed Queen in London. The common people flocked to Mary's support. The Privy Counsellors and the City authorities swam with the tide.

Northumberland was left without an ally. He asserted that he had always been a Catholic, with shattering effect on the Protestant party. But nothing could save him from an ignominious death.

The woman who now became Queen was probably the most unhappy and unsuccessful of England's sovereigns. Her accession portended a renewal of the Roman connection and a political alliance with the Empire. The religious legislation of the Reformation Parliament was repealed. But one thing Mary could not do. She could not restore to the Church the lands parcelled out among the nobility.

The most urgent question was whom Mary should marry. The Commons supported an English candidate, Edward Courtenay, Earl of Devon, a descendant of the House of York. But Mary's eyes were fixed overseas. Renard, envoy of the Emperor Charles V, worked fast, and she promised to wed the Emperor's son, the future Philip II of Spain. In the West Courtenay precipitated a rising. Sir Thomas Wyatt raised his standard in Kent and marched slowly towards London, gathering men as he came. Mary, bitter and disappointed with her people, and knowing she had failed to win their hearts, showed she was not afraid. In a stirring speech at Guildhall she summoned the Londoners to her defence. There was division among the rebels. Wyatt was disappointed by Courtenay, whose rising was a pitiable failure.

Straggled fighting took place in the streets, and the Queen's men cut up the intruders. Wyatt was executed. This sealed the fate of Lady Jane Grey and her husband. In February 1554 the two walked calmly to their death on Tower Green. Elizabeth's life was now in great danger. But Mary had shed blood enough and Renard could not persuade her to sign away the life of her half-sister.

Mary journeyed to Winchester to greet her bridegroom. With all the pomp of sixteenth-century royalty the marriage was solemnised in July 1554 according to the rites of the Catholic Church. Gardiner was now dead; but a successor was found in the English cardinal Reginald Pole. Pole had been in exile throughout the reign of Henry VIII, his family having been lopped and shorn in Henry's judicial murders. Mary has been for ever odious in the minds of a Protestant nation as the Bloody Queen who martyred her noblest subjects. Generations of Englishmen in childhood learnt the sombre tale of their sacrifice from Foxe's *Book of Martyrs*, with its gruesome illustrations. These stories have become part of the common memory of the people—the famous scenes at Oxford in 1555, the faggots which consumed the Protestant bishops, Latimer and Ridley, the pitiful recantation and final heroic end in March 1556 of the frail, aged Archbishop, Cranmer. Their martyrdom rallied to the Protestant faith many who till now had

The Coronation procession of Edward VI, from the Tower of London to Westminster Abbey, February 19, 1547. James Basire's engraving after a contemporary painting shows the young King beneath the canopy, preceded by the Archbishop of Canterbury, the Lord Mayor of London, and the Imperial Ambassador. BRITISH MUSEUM

Queen Elizabeth I (1533–1603), by an unknown artist. NATIONAL PORTRAIT GALLERY

The martyrdom of Bishops Latimer and Ridley at Oxford on October 16th, 1555

shown indifference. These martyrs saw in vision that their deaths were not in vain, and, standing at the stake, pronounced immortal words. "Be of good comfort, Master Ridley," Latimer cried at the crackling of the flames. "Play the man. We shall this day light such a candle, by God's grace, in England as I trust shall never be put out."

In vain the Queen strove to join English interests to those of the Spanish State. As the wife of the King of Spain, against the interests of her kingdom, and against the advice of prudent counsellors, among them Cardinal Pole, she allowed herself to be dragged into war with France, and Calais, the last possession of the English upon the Continent, fell without resistance. Hope of a child to secure the Catholic succession was unfulfilled. Philip retired to the Netherlands and then to Spain, aloof and disappointed at the barrenness of the whole political scheme. Surrounded by disloyalty and discontent,

Mary's health gave way. In November 1558 she died, and a few hours later, in Lambeth Palace, her coadjutor, Cardinal Pole, followed her. The tragic interlude of her reign was over. It had sealed the conversion of the English people to the Reformed faith. Until the reign of Henry VIII there lay beneath the quarrels of the nobility, the conflicts between King and Church, between the ruling classes and the people, a certain broad unity of acceptance. The evils and sorrows of the medieval ages had lasted so long that they seemed to be the inseparable conditions of existence in a world of woe. With the Reformation there came a new influence cutting to the very roots of English life. The old framework, which, in spite of its many jars, had held together for centuries, was now torn by a division in which all other antagonisms of class and interest were henceforward to be ranged and ruled.

Elizabeth was twenty-five years old when, untried in the affairs of State, she succeeded

127

her half-sister on November 17, 1558. A commanding carriage, auburn hair, eloquence of speech, and natural dignity proclaimed her King Henry's daughter. Other similarities were soon observed: high courage in moments of crisis, a fiery and imperious resolution when defied, and an almost inexhaustible fund of physical energy. She could speak six languages, and was well read in Latin and Greek. Always subtle of intellect, she was often brazen and even coarse in manners and expression. Nevertheless, she had a capacity for inspiring devotion that is perhaps unparalleled among British sovereigns.

The times demanded a politic, calculating, devious spirit at the head of the State, and this Elizabeth possessed. She had, too, a high gift for picking able men to do the country's work. She was a paragon of the New Learning. Around her had gathered some of the ablest Protestant minds: Matthew Parker, who was to be her Archbishop of Canterbury; Nicholas Bacon, whom she appointed Lord Keeper of the Great Seal; Roger Ascham, the foremost scholar of the day; and, most important of all, William Cecil, the adaptable civil servant who had already held office

as Secretary under Somerset and Northumberland. Of sixteenth-century English statesmen Cecil was undoubtedly the greatest.

England became Protestant by law, Queen Mary's Catholic legislation was repealed, and the sovereign was declared supreme Governor of the English Church. But this was not the end of Elizabeth's difficulties. With the Reformation the notion that it might be a duty to disobey the established order on the grounds of private conviction became for the first time since the conversion to Christianity of the Roman Empire the belief of great numbers. It is at this point that the party known as the Puritans, who were to play so great a role in the next hundred years, first enter English history. Democratic in theory and organisation, intolerant in practice of all who differed from their views, the Puritans challenged the Queen's authority in Church and State. The gentry in Parliament were themselves divided. It was the future distinction of Cavalier and Puritan, Churchman and Dissenter, Tory and Whig.

The security of the English State depended in the last resort on an assured succession. In vain the Houses of Parliament begged their Virgin Queen to marry and produce an heir. Elizabeth was angry. She would admit no discussion. Her policy was to spend her life in saving her people from such a commitment, and using her potential value as a match to divide a European combination against her.

French troops supported the French Queen Mother in Scotland. A powerful Puritan party among the Scottish nobility were in arms against them, while John Knox raised his harsh voice from exile in Geneva. Arms and supplies were smuggled across the Border to the Protestant party. Knox was permitted to return to his native land and his preachings had a powerful effect. By the Treaty of Leith in 1560 the Protestant cause in Scotland was assured for ever. Meanwhile, there was Mary Stuart, Queen of Scots. Her young husband, King Francis II,

Westmorland led a rising in the North. In the South the Catholic lords made no move. There seems to have been no common plan of action, and the rebel force scattered into small parties in the Northern hills. After twelve years of very patient rule Elizabeth was unchallenged Queen of all England.

In February 1570 Pope Pius V, a former Inquisitor-General, issued a Bull of excommunication against Elizabeth. She entered into negotiations with Catherine de Médicis, and a political alliance was concluded at Blois in April 1572. By a sudden massacre of the Huguenots on the eve of the Feast of St Bartholomew, August 23, 1572, the Guises, pro-Spanish and ultra-Catholic, recaptured the political power they had lost ten years earlier. Elizabeth's alliance with the French Court had clearly failed, and she was now driven to giving secret subsidies and support to the French Huguenots and the Dutch. Francis Walsingham, Cecil's assistant and later his rival in the Government, tracked down Spanish agents and English traitors. Exile in Mary's reign and service as Ambassador in Paris had convinced him that Protestantism would only survive in Europe if England gave it unlimited encouragement and aid. Opposed to all this was Cecil, now Lord Burghley. Aware of the slender resources of the State, deeply concerned for the loss of trade with Spain and the Netherlands, he maintained that Walsingham's policy would founder in bankruptcy and disaster. Elizabeth was inclined to agree.

Most of the Puritans had at first been willing to conform to Elizabeth's Church Settlement in the hope of transforming it from within, but they now strove to drive the Government into an aggressive Protestant foreign policy, and at the same time secure their own freedom of religious organisation. Their aim and object was nothing less than the establishment of a theocratic despotism. The Lutheran Church fitted well enough with monarchy, even with absolutism, but Calvinism, as it spread out over

had died shortly after his accession, and in December 1560 she returned to her own kingdom. Her presence in Scotland disturbed the delicate balance which Elizabeth had achieved by the Treaty of Leith. The Catholic English nobility, particularly in the North, were not indifferent to Mary's claims. But Elizabeth knew her rival. The Queen of Scots lacked the vigilant self-control which Elizabeth had learnt in the bitter years of childhood. Mary's power melted slowly and steadily away. Defeat and imprisonment followed, and in 1568 she escaped into England and threw herself upon the mercy of the waiting Elizabeth.

Mary in England proved even more dangerous than Mary in Scotland. She became the focus of plots and conspiracies against Elizabeth's life. The whole force of the Counter-Reformation was unloosed against the one united Protestant country in Europe. The idea was now advanced that Mary should marry the Duke of Norfolk, senior of the pre-Tudor nobility, and his somewhat feeble head was turned at the prospect of gambling for a throne. He repented in time. But in 1569 the Earls of Northumberland and

On following pages: *Queen Elizabeth's progress to Blackfriars to the wedding of Anne Russell and Lord Herbert. Artist unknown.* BY PERMISSION OF SIMON WINGFIELD DIGBY, M.P.

Europe, was a dissolving agency, and a violent interruption of historic continuity. Elizabeth's Council therefore struck back. The censorship of the Press was entrusted to a body of ecclesiastical commissioners, known as the Court of High Commission, which had been constituted in 1559 to deal with offences against the Church Settlement. This combining of the functions of bishop and censor infuriated the Puritan party. They set up a secret, itinerant Press which poured forth over the years a stream of virulent and anonymous pamphlets, culminating in 1588 with those issued under the name of "Martin Marprelate", attacking the persons and office of "the wainscot-faced bishops". Their sturdy and youthful invective shows a robust and relishing consciousness of the possibilities of English prose.

Elizabeth was slow to believe that any of her Catholic subjects were traitors, and the failure of the 1569 rising had strengthened her confidence in their loyalty. But about the year 1579 missionaries of a new and formidable type began to slip into the country. These were the Jesuits, the heralds and missionaries of the Counter-Reformation. By their enemies they were accused of using assassination to achieve their aims. Queen Mary had burnt some three hundred Protestant martyrs in the last three years of her reign. In the last thirty years of Elizabeth's reign about the same number of Catholics were executed for treason. The conspiracies naturally focused upon the person of Mary Queen of Scots, long captive. A voluntary association of Protestant gentry was formed in 1585 for the defence of Elizabeth's life. In the following year evidence of a conspiracy, engineered by one Anthony Babington, an English Catholic, was laid before the Council by Walsingham. Mary's connivance was undeniable. Elizabeth was at last persuaded that her death was a political necessity. Within twenty-four hours she regretted it and tried, too late, to stop the execution.

The scene of Mary's death has caught the imagination of history. In the early morning of February 8, 1587, she was summoned to the great hall of Fotheringay Castle. Accompanied by six of her attendants, Mary appeared at the appointed hour soberly clad in black satin. In the quietness of the hall she walked with stately movements to the cloth-covered scaffold erected by the fireplace. As she disrobed for the headsman's act, her garments of black satin, removed by the weeping handmaids, revealed a bodice and petticoat of crimson velvet. One of her ladies handed her a pair of crimson sleeves, which she put on. Thus the unhappy Queen halted, for one last moment, standing blood-red from head to foot against the black background of the scaffold. There was a deathly hush throughout the hall. She knelt, and at the second stroke the fatal blow was delivered. In death the majestic illusion was shattered. The head of an ageing woman with false hair was held

The execution of Mary Queen of Scots, at Fotheringay Castle, February 8, 1587. The drawing, and the key, are from the papers of Robert Beale, Clerk of the Council, who witnessed the execution. BRITISH MUSEUM

up by the executioner. A lapdog crept out from beneath the clothes of the bleeding trunk.

As the news reached London, Elizabeth sat alone in her room, weeping more for the fate of a Queen than a woman.

In the hope of strengthening her own finances and harassing the enemy's preparations against the Netherlands and ultimately against herself, Elizabeth had sanctioned a number of unofficial expeditions against the Spanish coasts and colonies in South America. Gradually these expeditions had assumed an official character, and the Royal Navy surviving from the days of Henry VIII was rebuilt and reorganised by John Hawkins, son of a Plymouth merchant, who had formerly traded with the Portuguese possessions in Brazil. In 1573 he was appointed Treasurer and Controller of the Navy. He had moreover educated an apt pupil, a young adventurer from Devon, Francis Drake. This "Master Thief of the unknown world", as his Spanish contemporaries called Drake, became the terror of their ports and crews.

Spain was deliberately blocking the commercial enterprise of other nations in the New World so far as it was then known. A Devon gentleman, Humphrey Gilbert, began to look elsewhere, and was the first to interest the Queen in finding a route to China, or Cathay, as it was called, by the North-West. He was the first Englishman who realised that the value of these voyages did not lie only in finding precious metals. The idea of planting colonies in America now began to take hold of men's imaginations. In 1583 Gilbert took possession of Newfoundland in the Queen's name, but no permanent settlement was made. Walter Raleigh tried to continue Gilbert's work. In 1585 a small colony was established on Roanoke Island, off the American continent, and christened Virginia in honour of the Queen. This venture also foundered, as did a second attempt two years later. Colonial efforts were postponed for another twenty years by the Spanish War.

The Spaniards had long contemplated an enterprise against England. Preparations were delayed for a year by Drake's famous

Above: *Sir John Hawkins. From a portrait painted in 1591 by an unknown artist.* BY PERMISSION OF THE CURATOR, CITY MUSEUM AND ART GALLERY, PLYMOUTH

Below: *Sir Francis Drake. From a portrait painted in 1591 by an unknown artist.* NATIONAL MARITIME MUSEUM

raid on Cadiz in 1587, "singeing of the King of Spain's beard". Nevertheless, in May 1588 the Armada was ready. A hundred and thirty ships were assembled, carrying twenty-five hundred guns and more than thirty thousand men, two-thirds of them soldiers. The renowned Spanish Admiral Santa Cruz was now dead, and the command was entrusted

On following pages: *Queen Elizabeth and Robert Dudley, Earl of Leicester, dancing the volta. Artist unknown.*
BY PERMISSION OF THE RT. HON. VISCOUNT DE L'ISLE, FROM HIS COLLECTION AT PENSHURST PLACE, KENT

to the Duke of Medina-Sidonia, who had many misgivings about the enterprise.

The nation was united in the face of the Spanish preparations. An army was assembled at Tilbury which reached twenty thousand men, under the command of Lord Leicester. This, with the muster in the adjacent counties, constituted a force which should not be underrated. While the Armada was still off the coasts of England Queen Elizabeth reviewed the army at Tilbury and addressed them in these stirring words:

My loving people, we have been persuaded by some that are careful for our safety to take heed how we commit ourselves to armed multitudes, for fear of treachery. But I assure you I do not desire to live to distrust my faithful and loving people. Let tyrants fear. I have always so behaved myself that, under God, I have placed my chiefest strength and safeguard in the loyal hearts and goodwill of my subjects; and therefore I am come amongst you, as you see, resolved, in the midst and heat of the battle, to live or die amongst you all, to lay down for my God, and for my kingdom, and for my people, my honour and my blood, even in the dust. I know I have the body of a weak and feeble woman, but I have the heart and stomach of a king, and of a king of England too, and think foul scorn that Parma or Spain or any prince of Europe should dare to invade the borders of my realm; to which, rather than any dishonour shall grow by

me, I myself will take up arms, I myself will be your general, judge and rewarder of every one of your virtues in the field. I know already for your forwardness you have deserved rewards and crowns; and we do assure you, in the word of a prince, they shall be duly paid you.

Hawkins's work for the Navy was now to be tested. He had begun over the years to revise the design of English ships from his experience of buccaneering raids in colonial waters. The castles which towered above the galleon decks had been cut down; keels were deepened, and design was concentrated on sea-worthiness and speed. Most notable of all, heavier long-range guns were mounted. In spite of Hawkins's efforts only thirty-four of the Queen's ships, carrying six thousand men, could put to sea in 1588. As was the custom, however, all available privately owned vessels were hastily collected and armed for the service of the Government, and a total of a hundred and ninety-seven ships was mustered; but at least half of them were too small to be of much service.

The Armada left the Tagus on May 20, but smitten by storms, put in to refit at Corunna, and did not set sail again until July 12. News of their approach off the Lizard was brought into Plymouth harbour

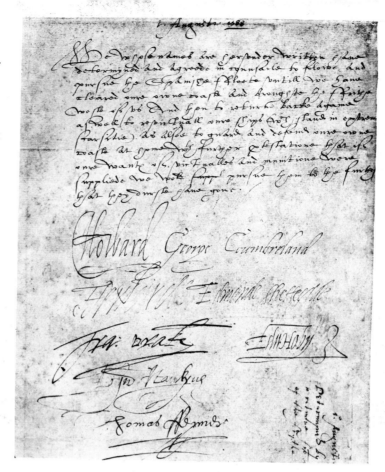

The Armada Resolution of eight English commanders, August 1, 1588, to follow the Armada past the Firth of Forth "with further protestation that if our wants of victuals and munitions were supplied we would pursue them to the furthest they durst have gone".

on the evening of July 19. The English fleet had to put out of the Sound the same night against light adverse winds which freshened the following day. If Medina-Sidonia had attacked the English vessels to leeward of his ships as they struggled to clear the land on the Saturday there would have been a disaster. But his instructions bound him to sail up the Channel, unite with Parma, and help transport to England the veteran troops assembled near Dunkirk. His report to Madrid shows how little he realised his opportunity. By difficult, patient, precarious tacking the English fleet got to windward of him, and for nine days hung upon the Armada as it ran before the westerly wind up the Channel, pounding away with their long-range guns at the lumbering galleons. On July 23 the wind sank and both fleets lay becalmed off Portland Bill. A further engagement followed on the 25th off the Isle of Wight. The Channel passage was a torment to the Spaniards. Medina then made a fatal mistake. He anchored in Calais Roads. The Queen's ships which had been stationed in the eastern end of the Channel joined the main fleet in the Straits, and the whole sea-power of England was now combined. The decisive engagement opened. After darkness had fallen eight ships from the eastern squadron which had been filled with explosives and prepared as fire-ships—the torpedoes of those days—were sent against the crowded Spanish fleet at anchor in the Roads. The Spanish captains cut their cables and made for the open sea. Collisions without number followed. The rest of the fleet, with a south-south-west wind behind it, made eastwards to Gravelines. The army and the transports were not at their rendezvous. The Spaniards turned to face their pursuers. A long and desperate fight raged for eight hours, a confused conflict of ships engaging at close quarters. The English had completely exhausted their ammunition, and but for this hardly a Spanish ship would have got away.

The tormented Armada now sailed northwards out of the fight. The horrors of the long voyage round the north of Scotland began. Sailing southwards, they were forced to make for the western coast of Ireland to replenish their supplies of water. The search for water cost more than five thousand Spanish lives. Nevertheless, over sixty-five ships, about half of the fleet that had put to sea, reached Spanish ports during the month of October.

The English had not lost a single ship, and scarcely a hundred men. But their captains were disappointed; half the enemy's fleet had got away. For the last thirty years they had believed themselves superior to their opponents. But to the English people as a whole the defeat of the Armada came as a miracle. One of the medals struck to commemorate the victory bears the inscription *Flavit Deus et dissipati sunt*" — "God blew

The Armada Medal struck at Middelburg by order of Prince Maurice. BRITISH MUSEUM

The Chariott drawne by foure Horses vpon which Charret stood the Coffin couered wth purple Veluett and vpon that the representation, The Canapy borne by six Knights.

Queen Elizabeth's funeral cortège. From a manuscript prepared shortly after the Queen's death. BRITISH MUSEUM

and they were scattered." Elizabeth and her seamen knew how true this was. Yet the event was decisive. The nation was transported with relief and pride. Shakespeare was writing *King John* a few years later. His words struck into the hearts of his audiences:

Come the three corners of the world in arms,
And we shall shock them. Nought shall make us rue
If England to itself do rest but true.

England had emerged from the Armada year as a first-class Power. Poets and courtiers alike paid their homage to the sovereign who symbolised the great achievement. Hakluyt speaks for the thrusting spirit of the age when he proclaims that the English nation, "in searching the most opposite corners and quarters of the world, and, to speak plainly, in compassing the vast globe of the earth

footemen.

Gentlemen Pensioners   Gentlemen Pensioners

more than once, have excelled all the nations and peoples of the earth". Before the reign came to a close another significant enterprise took its beginning. The British Empire in India, which was to be painfully built up in the course of the next three centuries, owes its origins to the Charter granted by Queen Elizabeth to a group of London merchants and financiers in the year 1600. The coming years resound with attacks upon the forces and allies of Spain throughout the world—expeditions to Cadiz, to the Azores, into the Caribbean Sea, to the Low Countries, and, in support of the Huguenots, to the northern coasts of France. But there was no way of delivering a decisive stroke against Spain. The English Government had no money for further efforts. The lights of enthusiasm slowly faded out.

One epic moment has survived in the

annals of the English race—the last fight of the *Revenge* at Flores, in the Azores. "In the year 1591", says Bacon, "was that memorable fight of an English ship called the *Revenge*, under the command of Sir Richard Grenville . . . for the space of fifteen hours, sate like a stag amongst hounds at bay, and was sieged and fought with, in turn, by fifteen great ships of Spain . . . . This brave ship the *Revenge*, being manned only with two hundred soldiers and marines, whereof eighty lay sick, yet nevertheless after a fight maintained (as was said) of fifteen hours, and two ships of the enemy sunk by her side, besides many more torn and battered and great slaughter of men, never came to be entered, but was taken by composition; the enemies themselves having in admiration the virtue of the commander and the whole tragedy of that ship." It is well to remember the ordinary seamen. These men faced death in many forms—death by disease, death by drowning, death from Spanish pikes and guns, death by starvation and cold on uninhabited coasts, death in the Spanish prisons. The Admiral of the English fleet, Lord Howard of Effingham, spoke their epitaph: "God send us to sea in such a company together again, when need is."

Sir Richard Grenville, from a portrait by an unknown artist, 1571. NATIONAL PORTRAIT GALLERY

Victory over Spain was the most shining achievement of Elizabeth's reign, but by no means the only one. The repulse of the Armada had subdued religious dissension at home. The Church she had nursed to strength was a very different body from the half-hearted and distracted community of her early years: more confident, more learned, far less inclined to compromise with dissidents

Robert Adams's chart of 1588, showing the course of the Armada and the pursuing English fleet. BRITISH MUSEUM

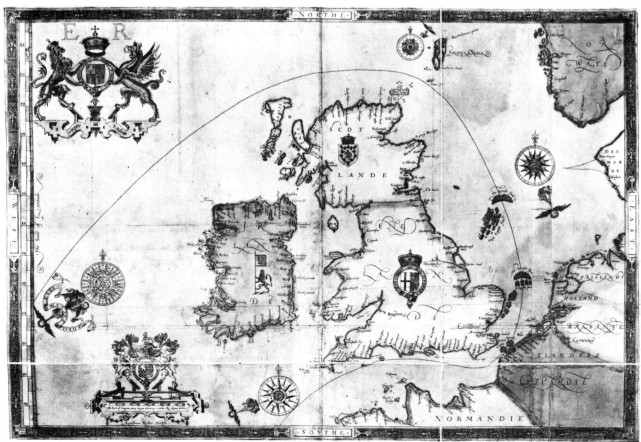

within or separatists without; strong in the attachment of thousands to whom its liturgy had become dear by habit and who thought of it as the Church into which they had been baptised.

War with Spain had set a premium on martial virtues. Young and eager men like Walter Raleigh and Robert Devereux, Earl of Essex, quarrelled for permission to lead enterprises against the Spaniards. Essex was Leicester's stepson, and Leicester brought him into the circle of the Court. He found the Government in the hands of the cautious Cecils, William, Lord Burghley, and his son Robert. Essex soon headed the war party in the Council. In 1596 an expedition was sent against Cadiz under the joint command of Essex and Raleigh. The fleet returned home triumphant, but, to Elizabeth's regret, little the richer. Essex was made Master of the Ordnance. He was given command of an expedition to intercept a further Armada now gathering in the ports of western Spain. The English ships headed south-west and made for the Azores; the Spanish Treasure Fleet eluded them; the Armada put out into the Bay of Biscay with the seas clear of defending ships to the north. Once again the winds saved the Island. The muddle and quarrelling which had marred the Azores expedition enraged Elizabeth. Essex retired from Court, and thunderous days followed.

Henry VIII had assumed the title of King of Ireland, but this involved no real extension of his authority. The Counter-Reformation revived and reanimated opposition to Protestant England. In April 1599 Essex was allowed to go to Ireland, at the head of the largest army that England had ever sent there. He accomplished nothing and was on the verge of ruin. Disobeying the express orders of the Queen, he deserted his command and rode in haste to London unannounced. Weeks dragged by, and a desperate plot was made by Essex and his younger companions, including Shakespeare's patron, the Earl of Southampton. The scheme failed, and the end came in February 1601 with Essex's

Sir Robert Cecil (1563–1612), afterwards 1st Earl of Salisbury. A portrait of 1602, attributed to Jean de Critz. NATIONAL PORTRAIT GALLERY

death within the Tower. The spoils of office, power, and influence were at stake, and victorious Essex would have dispensed appointments throughout England, and perhaps even have dictated terms to the Queen. She struck back; and in destroying Essex she saved England from the consumption of civil war.

Throughout the reign the weight and authority of Parliament had been steadily growing. Now the issue turned on monopolies. In 1601 grievances flared up into a full-dress debate in the House of Commons. The

The successful assault on Cadiz in 1596, led by Raleigh afloat and Essex ashore. NATIONAL MARITIME MUSEUM

uproar in the House brought a stinging rebuke from Mr Secretary Cecil. But the Queen preferred subtler methods. Some monopolies were abolished forthwith. All, she promised, would be investigated. It was to be her last appearance in their midst. The immense vitality displayed by the Queen throughout the troublous years of her rule in England ebbed slowly and relentlessly away. She lay for days upon a heap of cushions in her room. For hours the soundless agony was prolonged. At last Robert Cecil dared to speak. "Your Majesty, to content the people you must go to bed." "Little man," came the answer, "is 'must' a word to use to princes?" In the early hours of the morning of March 24, 1603, Queen Elizabeth died.

Thus ended the Tudor dynasty. For over a hundred years, with a handful of bodyguards, it had maintained its sovereignty, kept the peace, baffled the diplomacy and on-slaughts of Europe, and guided the country through changes which might well have wrecked it.

Robert Dudley, Earl of Leicester. BY PERMISSION OF THE TRUSTEES, THE WALLACE COLLECTION

Ireland, in a map of 1567. The ruling families in each district are shown, and the archbishoprics and bishoprics by double and single crosses on the churches. The notes written on the map are in the hand of William Cecil, Lord Burghley. PUBLIC RECORD OFFICE

Queen Elizabeth I, by an unknown artist, circa 1593. This portrait is said to have been painted to commemorate the Queen's visit to Sir Henry Lee at Ditchley, Oxfordshire, September 1592. NATIONAL PORTRAIT GALLERY

my Lord out of the loue i beare to some of youere frendz
i haue acare of youer preseruacion therfor i would
aduyse yowe as yowe tender youer lyf to deuys some
exscuse to shift of youer attendance at this parleament
for god and man hathe concurred to punishe the wickednes
of this tyme and thinke not slightlye of this aduertisment
but retyere youre self into youre contri wheare yowe
maye expect the euent in safti for thowghe theare be no
apparance of anni stir yet i saye they shall receyue a terrible
blowe this parleament and yet they shall not seie who
hurts them this councel is not to be contemned becausse
it maye do yowe good and can do yowe no harme for the
dangere is passed as soon as yowe haue burnt the letter
and i hope god will giue yowe the grace to mak good
use of it to whose holy protecion i commend yowe

The letter from Francis Tresham to his brother-in-law, Lord Monteagle, which led to the discovery of the Gunpowder Plot. PUBLIC RECORD OFFICE

Below: *The conspirators in the Gunpowder Plot are hanged, drawn, and quartered.* MANSELL COLLECTION

Iustitia

Fama

SUPPLICIUM
De octo coniuratis sumtum in Britannia, diebus 30. et 31 Jan. Styl. vet. Anno CIↃ.IↃ.CVI. Sumtum quidem separatim de quaternis, Sed tamen propter eandem omnino Supplicii rationem, hac tabella coniunctim expressum.

CHAPTER FIVE

The Civil War

KING JAMES VI of Scotland was the only son of Mary Queen of Scots. He had fixed ideas about kingship and the divine right of monarchs to rule. He was a scholar with pretensions to being a philosopher, and in the course of his life published numerous tracts and treatises, ranging from denunciations of witchcraft and tobacco to abstract political theory. He came to England with a closed mind, and a weakness for lecturing.

England was secure, free to attend to her own concerns, and a powerful class was now eager to take a hand in their management. Who was to have the last word in the matter of taxation? Was the King beneath the law or was he not? And who was to say what the law was? The greater part of the seventeenth century was to be spent in trying to find answers, historical, legal, theoretical, and practical, to such questions. Over these deep-cutting issues there loomed a fiscal crisis of the first magnitude. To his surprise James very soon found himself pressed for money. This meant frequent Parliaments. Frequent Parliaments gave Members the opportunity to organise themselves, and James neglected to control Parliamentary sessions through his Privy Counsellors, as Elizabeth had done. It was an ancient and obstinate belief that the King should "live of his own", and that the traditional revenues from the Crown lands and from the customs should suffice for the upkeep of the public services. Parliament normally voted customs duties to each monarch for life, and did not expect to have to provide more money except in emergencies. Fortunately, the judges ruled that the ports. were under the King's exclusive jurisdiction and that he could issue a "book of rates"—that is, impose extra customs duties—as he thought fit. Here, but only for a time, the matter rested.

The King had decided views on religion. He realised that Calvinism and monarchy would quarrel in the long run and that if men could decide for themselves about religion they could also decide for themselves on politics. James made it clear there would be no changes in the Elizabethan Church Settlement. His slogan was "No Bishop, no King."

The Catholics were also anxious and hopeful. But the Pope would not yield. He forbade allegiance to a heretical sovereign. James, although inclined to toleration, was forced to act. Disappointment and despair led a small group of Catholic gentry to an infernal design for blowing up James and his whole Parliament by gunpowder while they were in session at Westminster. One of their followers warned a relative who was a Catholic peer. The story reached Robert Cecil, Earl of Salisbury, and the cellars of Parliament were searched. Guy Fawkes, a veteran of the Spanish Wars against the Dutch, was taken on the spot, and there was a storm of excitement in the City. So novel and so wholesale a treason exposed the Catholic community to immediate and severe persecution and a more persistent and widespread detestation.

At this time a splendid and lasting monument was created to the genius of the English-speaking peoples. In 1611 the Authorised Version of the Bible was produced by the King's Printer. This may be deemed James's greatest achievement, for

and the powers of an Act of Parliament. Chief Justice Coke, one of the most learned of English judges, gave a blunt answer to these controversies. He declared that conflicts between Prerogative and statute should be resolved not by the Crown but by the judges. James had a very different view of the function of judges. Their business, as Bacon put it, was to be "lions under the throne". James first tried to muzzle Coke by promoting him from the Court of Common Pleas to the King's Bench. Unsuccessful in this, he dismissed him in 1616. Five years later Coke entered the House of Commons and found that the most active lawyers of the day were in agreement with him. Learned in the law, and not always too scrupulous in the interpretations they twisted from it, they gradually built up a case on which Parliament could claim with conviction that it was fighting, not for something new, but for the traditional and lawful heritage of the English people.

James's foreign policy perhaps met the needs of the age for peace, but often clashed with its temper. When he came to the throne England was still technically at war with Spain. With Cecil's support hostilities were concluded and diplomatic relations renewed. The Princess Elizabeth had married one of the Protestant champions of Europe, Frederick, the Elector Palatine of the Rhine, and Frederick was soon projected into violent revolt against the Habsburg Emperor Ferdinand. The Elector Frederick was soon driven out of Bohemia, and his ·hereditary lands were occupied by Habsburg troops. The House of Commons clamoured for war. James contented himself with academic discussions upon Bohemian rights with the Spanish Ambassador. To pose as Protestant champion in the great war now begun might gain a fleeting popularity with his subjects, but would also deliver him into the hands of the House of Commons.

In the midst of these turmoils Sir Walter Raleigh was executed in Palace Yard to please the Spanish Government. Raleigh had been imprisoned at the beginning of the reign for conspiring to supplant James by his cousin. This charge was probably unjust,

the impulse was largely his. The Scottish pedant built better than he knew. The scholars who produced this masterpiece are mostly unknown and unremembered. But they forged an enduring link, literary and religious, between the English-speaking peoples of the world.

The Tudors had been discreet in their use of the Royal Prerogative and had never put forward any general theory of government, but James saw himself as the schoolmaster of the whole Island. He found a brilliant supporter in the person of Francis Bacon, the ambitious lawyer who had dabbled in politics with Essex, and crept back to obedience when his patron fell. The subsequent conflict centred on the nature of the Royal Prerogative

Their rype corne

Their greene corne

Corne newly sprong

Their sitting at meate

The place of solemne prayer

The house wherin the Tombe of their Herounds standeth.

SECOTON

A Ceremony in their prayers strange testurs and songs dansi abowt posts carued on the topp lyke mens faces.

John White's watercolour of the Indian village of Secoton, in Virginia, made by him in 1585, when he accompanied Sir Richard Grenville's expedition to the colony. BRITISH MUSEUM

and the trial was certainly so. Raleigh's last expedition, for which he was specially released from the Tower, had merely affronted the Spanish Governors of South America. His death on October 29, 1618, was intended to mark the new policy of appeasement and prepare the way for good relations with Spain. This deed of shame sets a barrier for ever between King James and the English people. There are others.

James was much addicted to favourites, and his attention to handsome young men resulted in a noticeable loss of respect for the monarchy. One of his favourites, Robert Carr, created Earl of Somerset by the King's caprice, was implicated in a murder by poison, of which his wife was undoubtedly guilty. Carr was succeeded in the King's regard by a good-looking, quick-witted, extravagant youth, George Villiers, soon ennobled as Duke of Buckingham. This young man quickly became all-powerful at Court, and in the affections of James. He formed a deep and honourable friendship with Charles, Prince of Wales. He accepted unhesitatingly the royal policy of a Spanish marriage, and in 1623 staged a romantic journey to Madrid for the Prince and himself to view the bride.

Chief Justice Coke. Detail from a portrait by an unknown artist. COURTESY: THE EARL OF LEICESTER

George Villiers, Duke of Buckingham. Detail from the family group by Honthorst. NATIONAL PORTRAIT GALLERY

The negotiations with Spain foundered. In this sharp pinch Buckingham with remarkable agility turned himself from a royal favourite into a national, if short-lived, statesman. Whereas all interference by Parliament in foreign affairs had been repelled by the Tudors, and hitherto by James, the Minister-Favourite now invited Lords and Commons to give their opinion. The answer of both Houses was prompt and plain. It was contrary, they said, to the honour of the King, to the welfare of his people, to the interest of his children, and to the terms of his former alliances to continue the negotiations with Spain. But now came the question of raising funds for the war that was to follow. Parliament urged a purely naval war with Spain, in which great profits from the Indies might be won. Suspicious of the King's intentions, the Commons voted less than half the sum for which he asked, and laid down stringent conditions as to how it should be spent.

No sooner was the Spanish match broken off than Buckingham turned to France for a bride for Charles. The old King wanted to see his son married. He ratified the marriage treaty in December 1624. Three months later the first King of Great Britain was dead.

For a while little was heard of the New World. The change came in 1604, when James I made his treaty of peace with Spain. Raleigh's attempts had demonstrated the ill-success of individual effort, but a new method of financing large-scale trading enterprises was evolving in the shape of the joint stock company. In 1606 a group of speculators acquired a royal Charter creating the Virginia Company. The objects of the directors were mixed and ill-defined. A settlement was made at Jamestown, in the Chesapeake Bay, on the Virginian coast, in May 1607. By chance a crop of tobacco was planted, and the soil proved benevolent. Small-holders were bought out, big estates were formed, and the colony began to stand on its own feet.

The Elizabethan bishops had driven the nobler and tougher Puritan spirits out of the Established Church. A congregation at Scrooby, in Nottinghamshire, led by one of their pastors, John Robinson, and by William Brewster, the Puritan bailiff of the manor of the Archbishop of York, resolved to seek freedom of worship abroad. In 1607 they left England and settled at Leyden, hoping to find asylum among the tolerant and industrious Dutch. They were persistent and persevering, but a bleak future faced them in Holland. Emigration to the New World presented itself as an escape from a sinful generation. Their first plan was to settle in Guiana, but then they realised it was impossible to venture out upon their own. They accordingly sent agents to London to negotiate with the only body interested in emigration, the Virginia Company. Thirty-five members of the Leyden congregation left Holland and joined sixty-six West Country adventurers at Plymouth, and in September 1620 they set sail in the *Mayflower*, a vessel of 180 tons.

After two and a half months of voyaging across the winter ocean they reached the shores of Cape Cod, and thus, by an accident, landed outside the jurisdiction of the Virginia Company. This invalidated their patent from London. Before they landed there was trouble among the group about who was to enforce discipline. Those who had joined the ship at Plymouth were no picked band of saints, and had no intention of submitting to the Leyden set. There was no possibility of appealing to England. Yet, if they were not all to starve, some agreement must be reached. Forty-one of the more responsible members thereupon drew up a solemn compact which is one of the remarkable documents in history, a spontaneous covenant for political organisation. "In the name of God, Amen. We whose names are under-written, the loyal subjects of our dread sovereign Lord, King James, by the grace of God, of Great Britain, France, and Ireland King, Defender of the Faith, etc. Having undertaken, for the glory of God, and advancement of the Christian faith, and honour of our King and country, a voyage to plant the first colony in the northern parts of Virginia, do by these presents solemnly and mutually in the presence of God, and one of another, covenant and combine ourselves together into a civil body politic, for our better ordering and preservation and

Plymouth Rock, the granite boulder on the shoreline at Plymouth, Massachusetts, where traditionally the May-flower emigrants came ashore on December 21, 1620.
UNITED STATES INFORMATION SERVICE

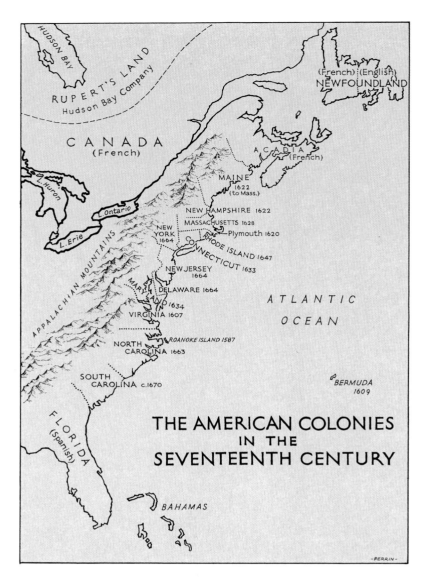

THE AMERICAN COLONIES
IN THE
SEVENTEENTH CENTURY

Company, John Winthrop, followed with a thousand settlers. Some of the Puritan stockholders realised that there was no obstacle to transferring the Company, directors and all, to New England. From the joint stock company was born the self-governing colony of Massachusetts.

The leaders and ministers who ruled in Massachusetts, however, had views of their own about freedom. By no means all were rigid Calvinists, and recalcitrant bodies split off from the parent colony when quarrels became strident. In 1635 and 1636 some of them moved to the valley of the Connecticut River, and founded the town of Hartford near its banks. Religious strife drove others beyond the bounds of the parent colony. A scholar from Cambridge, Roger Williams, had been forced to leave the University by Archbishop Laud. He followed the now known way to the New World, and settled in Massachusetts. The magistrates considered him a promoter of disorder, and resolved to send him back to England. Warned in time, he fled beyond their reach, and, followed at intervals by others, founded the town of Providence, to the south of Massachusetts. Other exiles from Massachusetts, some of them forcibly banished, joined his settlement in 1636, which became the colony of Rhode Island.

Two other ventures, both essentially commercial, established the English-speaking peoples in the New World. By the 1640's Barbados, St Christopher, Nevis, Montserrat, and Antigua were in English hands and several thousand colonists had arrived. Sugar assured their prosperity, and the Spanish grip on the West Indies was shaken. There was much competition and warfare in the succeeding years, but for a long time these island settlements were commercially much more valuable to England than the colonies in North America. In 1632 George Calvert, Lord Baltimore, a Roman Catholic courtier who had long been interested in colonisation, applied for a patent for settling in the neighbourhood of Virginia. Courtiers and merchants subscribed to the venture, and the new colony was named Maryland in honour of Charles's Queen, Henrietta Maria.

furtherance of the ends aforesaid; and by virtue hereof to enact, constitute, and frame such just and equal laws, ordinances, acts, constitutions, and offices, from time to time, as shall be thought most meet and convenient for the general good of the colony, unto which we promise all due submission and obedience." In December on the American coast in Cape Cod Bay these men founded the town of Plymouth. The financial supporters in London reaped no profits. In 1627 they sold out and the Plymouth colony was left to its own resources. Such was the founding of New England.

After the precedent of Virginia a chartered company was formed, eventually named "The Company of the Massachusetts Bay in New England". An advance-party founded the settlement of Salem, to the north of Plymouth. In 1630 the Governor of the

In these first decades of the great emigration over eighty thousand English-speaking people crossed the Atlantic. Never since the days of the Germanic invasions of Britain had such a national movement been seen. Saxon and Viking had colonised England. Now, one thousand years later, their descendants were taking possession of America. Many different streams of migrants were to make their confluence in the New World and contribute to the manifold character of the future United States. But the British stream flowed first and remained foremost.

A great political and religious crisis was overhanging England. Already in King James's time Parliament had begun to take the lead, not only in levying taxes but increasingly in the conduct of affairs, and especially in foreign policy. An intense desire for England to lead and champion the Protestant cause wherever it was assailed drove forward the Parliamentary movement with a force far greater than would ever have sprung merely from the issues which were now opening at home. The secular issues were nevertheless themselves of enormous

The Americas, from the Mercator Atlas of 1633. BRITISH MUSEUM

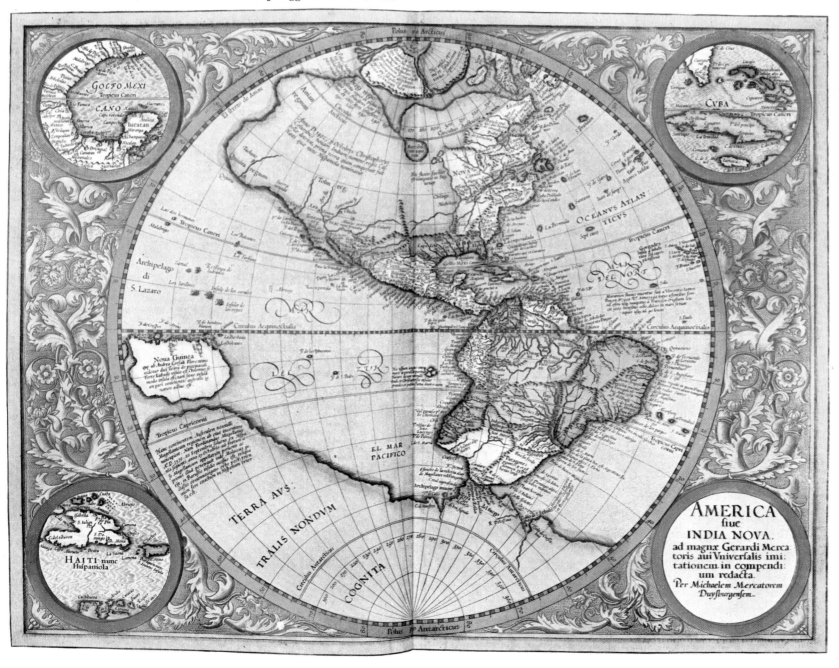

weight. Tudor authority had been accepted as a relief from the anarchy of the Wars of the Roses, and had now ceased to fit either the needs or the temper of a continually growing society. Coke had taught the later Parliaments of James I the arguments upon which they could rest and the methods by which they might prevail. Two country gentlemen stand with him; one from the West, Sir John Eliot, a Cornishman; the other, Thomas Wentworth, a Yorkshire squire. Behind them, lacking nothing in grit, were leaders of the Puritan gentry, Denzil Holles, Arthur Hazelrigg, John Pym. Pym was eventually to go far and to carry the cause still farther. Here was a man who understood every move in the political game, and would play it out remorselessly.

The King was affronted by the manner in which his father's overtures for a Spanish match, and he himself, had been slighted in Madrid. He at once carried through his marriage with the French Princess, Henrietta Maria. The new Parliament granted supplies against Spain; but their purpose to review the whole question of indirect taxation was plain when they resolved that the customs duties of tonnage and poundage without which the King could not live, even in peace, should for the first time for many reigns be voted, not for the King's life, but only for one year. The war with Spain went badly. Buckingham was impeached, and to save his friend the King hastily dissolved Parliament. A new complication was now added to the scene. The new, powerful French Minister, Cardinal Richelieu, was determined to curb the independence of the Huguenots in France, and in particular to reduce their maritime stronghold of La Rochelle. In 1627 a considerable force was dispatched under Buckingham to help the Rochelais. It landed off the coast in the Île de Ré, failed to storm the citadel, and withdrew in disorder. Forced loans could not suffice to replenish the Treasury, and having secured a promise that the impeachment of Buckingham would not be pursued the King agreed to summon Parliament. They offered no fewer than five subsidies, amounting to £300,000, all to be

Cardinal Richelieu, by Champaigne. PHOTO: GIRANDOT. MANSELL COLLECTION

paid within twelve months; but before they would confirm this in a Bill they demanded their price.

The following four Resolutions were passed unanimously: that no freeman ought to be restrained or imprisoned unless some lawful cause was expressed; that the writ of *habeas corpus* ought to be granted to every man imprisoned or restrained, even though it might be at the command of the King or of the Privy Council; that if no legal cause for imprisonment were shown the party ought to be set free or bailed; that it was the ancient and undoubted right of every freeman to have a full and absolute property in his goods and estate, and that no tax, loan, or benevolence ought to be levied by the King or his Ministers without common consent by Act of Parliament. At Coke's prompting the Commons now went on to frame the Petition of Right. Its object was to curtail the King's Prerogative. The Petition complained against forced loans, imprisonment without trial, billeting, and martial law. Charles, resorting to manœuvre, secretly consulted the judges, who assured him that even his consent to these liberties would not affect his ultimate Prerogative. We reach here, amid much confusion, the main foundation of English freedom.

Both sides pressed farther along their paths. The Commons came forward with further complaints against the growth of Popery. The King and Buckingham hoped that a second and successful expedition would relieve the Huguenots in La Rochelle and present a military or diplomatic result in which all could rejoice. Far better to rescue Protestants abroad than to persecute Catholics at home. This was not a discreditable position to take up; but Fate moved differently.

The death of Buckingham was a devastating blow to the young King. The murderer, John Felton, seems to have been impaled by nature upon all those prongs of dark resolve which make such deeds possible. He had the private sting of being passed over for promotion. But the documents which he left behind him proved him a slave of larger thoughts. Parliament's remonstrations to the King against Buckingham's lush splendour and corrupt methods had sunk into his soul.

Though the Commons had granted the five subsidies, they held tonnage and poundage in reserve. When the year lapsed for which this had been voted the Parliamentary party throughout the country were angered to find that the King continued to collect the tax by his officers, as had been the custom for so many reigns. The expedition to La Rochelle, which had sailed under another commander, miscarried. Thus when Parliament met again at the beginning of 1629 there was no lack of grievances both in foreign and domestic policy. Yet it was upon questions of religion that the attack began. All was embodied in a single Remonstrance. The Speaker, who had been gained to the King's side, announced on March 2 that the King adjourned the House till the 10th, thus frustrating the carrying of the Remonstrance. When the Speaker rose to leave he was forced back and held down on his chair by two resolute and muscular Members, Holles and Valentine. The doors were barred against Black Rod, and the Remonstrance, recited from memory by Holles, was declared carried by acclamation. It had become plain to all that King and Commons could not work together on any terms.

The Personal Rule of King Charles was not set up covertly or by degrees. First, there must be peace with France and Spain. Without the support of Parliament Charles had not the strength to carry on foreign wars. The second condition was the gaining of some at least of the Parliamentary leaders. Wentworth was more than willing. He knew he judged better than most other men; he was a born administrator; all he wanted was scope for his endeavours. In December 1628 he became Lord President of the Council of the North and a member of the Privy Council. From this moment he not only abandoned all the ideas of which he had been the ablest exponent, but all the friends who had fought at his side. He was "the Satan of the Apostasy", "the lost Archangel", "the suborned traitor to the cause of Parliament". But the third and least sentimental condition of the Personal Rule was dominant —money. The Crown had to make shift with what it could scrape from old taxes. No large question could be stirred. The King, with his elegant, dignified Court, whose figures are portrayed by the pencil of Van Dyck, whose manners and whose morals were an example to all, reigned on the smallest scale. He was a despot, but an unarmed despot. The Prerogative of the Crown offered a wide and vaguely defined field within which taxes could be raised. The King, supported by his judges, strained all expedients to the limit. Hungry forces still lay in shadow. All the ideas which they cherished and championed stirred in their minds, but they had no focus, no expression. The Poor Law was administered with exceptional humanity. Ordinary gentlefolk might have no share in national

et liberatonum per multos Annos sum

government, but they were still lords on their own estates. The malcontents looked about for points which would inflame the inert forces of the nation.

Meanwhile, Wentworth, now Lord-Lieutenant of Ireland, had, by a combination of tact and authority, reduced that kingdom to a greater submission to the British Crown than ever before or since. His repute in history must rest upon his Irish administration.

According to the immemorial laws of England, perhaps of Alfred the Great, the whole land should pay for the upkeep of the Fleet. Why should not all pay where all benefited? The project commended itself to the King. In August 1635 he levied "Ship Money" upon the whole country. Forthwith a Buckinghamshire gentleman, a former Member of Parliament, solidly active against the Crown, stood forth among many others and refused to pay upon the principle that even the best of taxes could be levied only with the consent of Parliament. John Hampden's refusal was selected by both sides as a test case. The Crown prevailed. But the grievance ran far and wide.

Here emerges the figure of the man who of all others was Charles's evil genius— William Laud, Archbishop of Canterbury. The Elizabethan Settlement was dependent on the State. By itself the Church had not the strength to bear the strain. An informal compact therefore grew up between the secular and spiritual aspects of government, whereby the State sustained the Church in its property and the Church preached the duty of obedience and the Divine Right of Kings. Laud by no means initiated this compact, but he set himself with untimely vigour to enforce it. Among his innovations was the railing off of the altar, and a new emphasis on ceremony and the dignity of the clergy. Laud now found a new source of revenue for the Crown. All over England men and women found themselves haled before the justices for not attending church, and fined one shilling a time. Here indeed

was something that ordinary men and women could understand. The Parliamentary agitation which had been conducted during all these years with so much difficulty gained a widespread accession of strength at a time when the King's difficulties had already massed themselves into a stack.

It was in Scotland, the home of the Stuarts and Charles's birthplace, that the torch was lighted which began the vast conflagration. The Scots must adopt the English Prayer Book, and enter broadly into communion with their English brethren. Charles and his advisers had no thought of challenging doctrine, still less of taking any step towards Popery. They desired to assert the Protestant High Church view. The Scottish people believed, and were told by their native leaders to believe, that they were to be forced by the royal authority to take the first fatal steps towards Roman Catholicism. When in July 1637 the dignitaries of Scottish Church and State were gathered in St Giles's Church in Edinburgh for the first solemn

William Laud, Archbishop of Canterbury. Studio of Van Dyck. NATIONAL PORTRAIT GALLERY

reading of the new Prayer Book, an outburst of fury and insult overwhelmed the Dean when he sought to read the new dispensation. Edinburgh defied the Crown. A surge of passion swept the ancient capital before which the episcopal and royal authorities trembled. At length the whole original policy of the King was withdrawn.

Meanwhile, the Scottish nation was forming a union which challenged existing conditions both in Church and State. On February 28, 1638, the Covenant was read in Greyfriars churchyard in Edinburgh. It embodied the unalterable resolve of a whole people to perish rather than submit to Popery.

Force was now to be invoked. The Covenanters had resources overseas. The famous part played by the Scots brigades and by Scottish generals under Gustavus Adolphus in Germany had left Scotland with an incomparable military reserve. Alexander Leslie had risen in the Thirty Years War to the rank of Field-Marshal. In a few months, and long before any effective preparations could be made in the South, Scotland had the strongest armed force in the Island. Wentworth was now summoned from Ireland to strengthen the Council. "Thorough" was his maxim; and we have no means of judging how far he would have pushed on in success. He dreamed of a new Flodden; and he was fully prepared to use his Irish army in Scotland whenever it might be necessary.

At this decisive moment England's monarchy might well have conformed to the absolutism which was becoming general throughout Europe. Wentworth saw clearly enough that the royal revenues were not sufficient to support the cost of the campaign. He concluded therefore that Parliament must be summoned. In his over-confidence he thought that the Commons would prove manageable. Parliament met on April 13, 1640. Only a quarter of the former Members reappeared. Eliot was dead in the Tower; Wentworth was now Earl of Strafford, and the King's First Minister. Charles and his chief counsellors, Strafford and Laud, found no comfort from the new assembly. On the contrary, they were met by such a temper that by an act of extreme imprudence it was dissolved on May 5 after a few days.

Strafford wished to bring over his Irish troops, but fear of the reactions which this step might provoke paralysed the Council. Presently the Scots crossed the Tweed in good order. They met with no opposition until they reached the Tyne. Then, as once before, the two hosts faced one another. Someone pulled a trigger; the shot went home; all the Scots cannon fired and all the English army fled. A contemporary wrote that "Never so many ran from so few with less ado." The King could not defend the country himself. He had plumbed the depths of personal failure.

The Privy Council addressed itself to making a truce with the Scots, who demanded £40,000 a month to maintain their army on English soil until their claims should be met. By haggling this was reduced to £850 a day. The so-called "Bishops' War" was over; the real war had yet to begin. There now arose from all quarters a cry that Parliament should be summoned. Thus on November 3, 1640, was installed the

Thomas Wentworth, Earl of Strafford. Studio of Van Dyck. NATIONAL PORTRAIT GALLERY

second longest and most memorable Parliament that ever sat in England. It derived its force from a blending of political and religious ideas. It was upborne by the need of a growing society to base itself upon a wider foundation than Tudor paternal rule. All the rage of the Parliamentary party, all the rancour of old comradeship forsworn, all that self-preservation dictated, concentrated upon "the wicked Earl", Strafford, a blast of fury such as was never recorded in England before or since. Such a downfall recalls, in its swiftness at least, the fate of Sejanus, the hated Minister of Tiberius. The proscription extended to all the Ministers, as they would now be called, of the King. Respect for law and for human life nevertheless prevailed. In this mortal struggle physical violence was long held in check, and even when it broke into civil war all those conventions were observed which protect even the sternest exercise of the human will from the animal barbarism of earlier and of later times.

The aggressive tendencies of the majority in the Commons shaped themselves into a demand for the abolition of Episcopacy. The Scots, now so influential in London and masters in the North, sought to establish the Presbyterian system of Church government. But now for the first time effective counter-forces appeared. A second petition proposed the restriction of the bishops' power to spiritual matters. It was known that the King regarded the Episcopate, based upon the Apostolic Succession, as inseparable from the Christian faith, but whereas in politics the opposition to Personal Rule was at this moment overwhelming, on the Church question the balance was far more even. Pym realised this and decided to delay a full debate.

Meanwhile, the trial of Strafford had begun. Proceeding as they did upon admittedly rival interpretations of law and justice, the Commons at once found difficulty in establishing a case against the hated Minister. They would dispense with a trial and have him declared guilty by Act of Parliament. The cry for "Justice!" rang through London streets. This was the agony of Charles's life,

Charles I's letter to the House of Lords, begging that the sentence of death passed upon Strafford be commuted to one of perpetual imprisonment. HOUSE OF LORDS RECORD OFFICE

to which none of his other sufferings compared. The question was not whether he could save Strafford, but whether the royal authority would perish with him. He gave his assent to the Bill of Attainder. Strafford died with fortitude and dignity. The circumstances of his trial and of the Attainder threw odium upon his pursuers. They slaughtered a man they could not convict. But that man, if given his full career, would have closed perhaps for generations the windows of civic freedom upon the English people.

The Triennial Bill providing for the summoning of Parliament at least once in three years, if necessary in spite of the Crown, put a final end to the system of Personal Rule over which Charles had so far presided. The grant of tonnage and poundage for one year only was accompanied by a censure upon the exaction of Ship Money, and reparation to all who had suffered for their resistance to

Charles I seeking the five Members, in the painting by Copley. The Speaker, William Lenthall, kneels before the King.

it. The King perforce subscribed to all this. But he must have been completely broken for the moment when he assented to a measure designed "to prevent inconvenience that may happen by the untimely prorogation or dissolving of this present Parliament" except by its own consent. The judges, whose tenure had hitherto been dependent upon the pleasure of the Crown, now held office on good behaviour. The Court of Star Chamber, which, as we have seen, Henry VII had used to curb the baronage, but which had in the lapse of time become oppressive to the people, was abolished. So was the Court of High Commission, which had striven to impose religious uniformity. The whole Tudor system which the Stuarts had inherited was shaken from its base.

Charles now felt that his hope lay in a reconciliation with Scotland. But all was in vain. The Scots were confirmed in their obduracy, and the King returned to England crestfallen. Upon this melancholy scene a hideous apparition now appeared. The execution

of Strafford liberated all the elemental forces in Ireland which his system had so successfully held in restraint. The passions of the original inhabitants and of the hungry, downtrodden masses, bursting from all control, were directed upon the gentry, the landowners, and the Protestants, both within and without the Pale. The mere fact of his absence from London, which had left the Parliamentary forces to their full play, had served the King's interests better than the closest attention to English affairs. Englishmen, irrespective of religious and constitutional convictions, were ill disposed to be taxed for the upkeep of invading Scottish troops. The House of Commons at the end of 1641 had travelled far. From being the servants of the national cause the Puritans had became an aggressive faction. It was in this stormy weather that Pym and Hampden sought to rally their forces by bringing forward what was called the "Grand Remonstrance". It was intended to advertise all that had so far been accomplished by Parliament

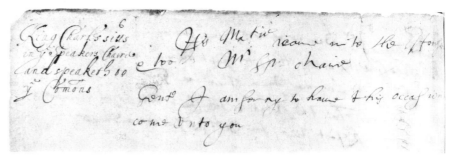

in remedying old grievances, and to proclaim the future policy of the Parliamentary leaders. Nevertheless, the growing body of Conservatives, or "Episcopalian Party", as they were sometimes named, were affronted by the Remonstrance and determined to oppose it. When Parliament had met a year earlier the King's party could not count on a third of its Members. Now the Grand Remonstrance was carried only by eleven votes.

The King, who, in spite of his failure in Scotland and the Irish catastrophe, had been conscious of ever-gathering support, was now drawn into various contradictory blunders. Still seeking desperately for a foothold, he invited Pym himself to become Chancellor of the Exchequer. Such a plan had no contact with reality. Colepeper took the post instead, and Falkland became Secretary of State. Next, in violent revulsion, Charles resolved to prosecute five of his principal opponents in the Commons for high treason. He certainly convinced himself that Pym meant to impeach the Queen. Thus goaded, Charles, accompanied by three or four hundred swordsmen—"Cavaliers" we may now call them—went down to the House of Commons. It was January 4, 1642. Never before had a king set foot in the Chamber. But a treacherous message from a lady of the Queen's Bedchamber had given Pym a timely warning. The accused Members had already embarked at Westminster Steps and

were safe amid the train-bands and magistrates of the City. Speaker Lenthall could give no information. "I have neither eyes to see, nor tongue to speak in this place, but as the House is pleased to direct me, whose servant I am here," he pleaded. The King, already conscious of his mistake, cast his eyes around the quivering assembly. "I see that the birds are flown," he said lamely, and after some civil reassurances he departed at the head of his disappointed, growling

ENGLAND DURING THE CIVIL WAR

COUNTRY HELD BY THE ROYALISTS AT THE END OF 1643
✕ BATTLES

Sir Ralph Hopton. Detail from a portrait by an unknown artist. NATIONAL PORTRAIT GALLERY

adherents. But as he left the Chamber a low, long murmur of "Privilege" pursued him. Henceforth London was irretrievably lost to the King. By stages he withdrew to Newmarket, to Nottingham, and to York. There were now two centres of government.

Sir Thomas Fairfax, 1647

The negotiations between King and Parliament which occupied the early months of 1642 served only to emphasise their differences while both were gathering their forces. On June 1, 1642, Parliament presented nineteen Propositions to the King. In brief, the King was invited to surrender his whole effective sovereignty over Church and State.

The arrogant tone and ever-growing demands of the Parliamentary party shaped the lines of the struggle and recruited the forces of the King. The greater part of the nobility gradually rallied to the Royalist cause; the tradesmen and merchants generally inclined to the Parliament; but a substantial section of the aristocracy were behind Pym, and many boroughs were devotedly Royalist. The gentry and yeomen in the counties were deeply divided. Those nearer London generally inclined to Parliament, while the North and West remained largely Royalist. Both sides fought in the name of the King, and both upheld the Parliamentary institution. Behind all class and political issues the religious quarrel was the driving power. At Nottingham, where town and county alike had proclaimed devotion, Charles set up his standard on August 22 and called his loyal subjects to his aid. This was the ancient signal for feudal duty, and its message awoke ancestral memories throughout the land.

At Nottingham the King had only eight hundred horse and three hundred foot, and at first it seemed doubtful whether any royal army could be raised. But the violence of Parliament served him well. By the end of September he had with him two thousand horse and six thousand foot. A few weeks later their numbers were more than doubled, and other forces were raised for him all over the country. Meanwhile, the Roundheads, sustained by ample funds from the wealth and regular taxation of London, levied and trained an army of twenty-five thousand men under Essex. As on the Royalist side, most of the regiments were raised personally by prominent people. But whereas the King could give only a commission to raise a regiment or a troop Parliament could provide the equipment as well.

The King, skilfully avoiding Essex's army, now moved west to join his Welsh reinforcements, and then struck south for the Thames valley and London. At Edgehill, in Warwickshire, on October 23 the royal army turned on its pursuers and attacked them before their rearguard, which was approaching the village of Kineton, had come in. The battle was marked by abundant ignorance and zeal on both sides. Edgehill, which might so easily have ended the war in the King's favour, was judged a drawn battle. At least five thousand Englishmen lay upon the field; twelve hundred were buried by the vicar of Kineton. It has often been asked whether Charles could have reached London before Essex, and what would have happened when he got there. But now the advance was made from Oxford and the King contented himself with disarming and dispersing the local forces that stood in the way. A few days later, at Turnham Green, a few miles west of London, the King found himself confronted with the combined forces of Essex's field army and the London garrison. After a cannonade he withdrew towards Oxford, being, as some held, lucky in getting clear. Thus closed the fighting of the year 1642.

From the beginning of 1643 the war became general. The ports and towns, the manufacturing centres, mostly adhered to the Parliament; what might be called Old England rallied to Charles. At first the decisive action was not in the North. Parliament was already in some doubts about the capacity of Essex as a general. The peace party favoured him, but the fancy of those who wanted all-out war was Sir William Waller, now sent to command the Parliamentary army in the West. Here also the most sagacious and skilful of the Royalist generals, Sir Ralph Hopton, commanded. Three fierce battles on a small scale were fought by Hopton and Waller. King Charles was master in the West. His cause had also prevailed in Yorkshire. Here Lord Fairfax and his son, Sir Thomas, led the Parliamentary forces. Sir Thomas besieged York; but

the Marquis of Newcastle, a man of no military aptitude, rich, corpulent, proud, but entirely devoted, led his territorial retainers, the valiant "white-coats", to its relief, and later in the summer overwhelmed the Fairfaxes at Adwalton Moor.

Charles possessed a certain strategic comprehension. From the beginning of 1643 his design was for a general advance on London. On the other hand, Gloucester was the sole stronghold remaining to the Parliament between Bristol and York. Its fall would open the Severn to the Royalist flotillas and supply-barges, as well as uniting Oxford and the West to Royalist Wales. Accordingly on August 10 the city was invested. The Earl of Essex had fallen into just disrepute as a general, and was suspected of political lukewarmness. Now, however, he was ordered and conjured to relieve Gloucester. He entered the city in triumph, but found himself immediately short of supplies and food, with a formidable enemy between him and home. Both armies headed for London, and on September 20 they clashed at Newbury, in Berkshire. A third of the troops were casualties, and on the Royalist side many nobles fell. The battle was undecided when darkness fell. Essex had no choice but to renew it at dawn; but the King withdrew, stricken by the loss of so many personal friends, and short of powder, and the London road lay open to the Roundheads.

The King's large plan for 1643 had failed. Nevertheless, the campaign had been very favourable to him. His troops were still, on the whole, better fighting men than the Roundheads. Then on December 8 Pym died, uncheered by success, but unwearied by misfortune. He remains the most famous of the old Parliamentarians, and the man who more than any other saved England from absolute monarchy and set her upon the path she has since pursued.

There was a lull during the winter. Declaring that the Parliament at Westminster was no longer a free Parliament, Charles summoned all who had been expelled or who had fled from it to a Counter-Assembly. The response was remarkable.

Eighty-three peers and a hundred and seventy-five Members met in Oxford on January 22, 1644. But these advantages were overwhelmed by the arrival in England of a Scottish army of eighteen thousand foot and three thousand horse, who crossed the Tweed in January. For this succour the London Parliament paid £31,000 a month and the cost of equipment. But the Scots, though in a sense hired, had other objects besides money. They now aspired to outroot the Episcopacy and impose by armed force the Presbyterian system of Church government upon England.

It was now that Oliver Cromwell came into prominence. The Member for Cambridge was deemed the best officer on the Parliamentary side, though he had not yet held a supreme command. The rise of Cromwell to the first rank of power during 1644 sprang both from his triumphs on the battlefield and his resistance to the Presbyterians and the Scots at Westminster. All the obscurer Protestant sects saw in him their champion.

In the North the Marquis of Newcastle had now to contend with the Scottish army on one side and the two Fairfaxes on the other. The loss of York would ruin the King's cause in the North. Charles therefore sent Prince Rupert with a strong cavalry force, which gathered strength as it marched, to relieve the city and sustain the harassed and faithful Marquis. The Scots and Roundheads withdrew together westwards, covering Leeds and joining the forces from East Anglia under Lord Manchester and Cromwell. The three Puritan armies were thus combined, and numbered twenty thousand foot and seven thousand horse. Their outposts lay upon a ridge at Marston Moor. Rupert met the Marquis of Newcastle, and their united forces reached eleven thousand foot and seven thousand horse. Accordingly the Royalist army followed the enemy to Marston Moor, and on July 2 found themselves near their encampments. Marston Moor was the largest

and also the bloodiest battle of the war. For the first time the heroic, dreaded Cavaliers met their match, and their master. "We drove the entire cavalry of the Prince off the field," wrote Cromwell. "God made them as stubble to our swords. Then we took their regiments of foot with our cavalry, and overthrew all that we encountered." Newcastle's "white-coats" fought to the death, and fell where they stood. The prestige of Rupert's cavalry was broken. A disaster of the first magnitude had smitten the King's cause.

The success of the King's campaign in the South veiled, at least for a time, the disaster at Marston Moor. It was expected, not only by the Parliament, but in his own circles, that the King would be caught in Oxford and compelled to surrender. However, after providing for the defence of the city, Charles, with great skill, eluded both of the converging armies and reached Worcester. Waller manœuvred against the King, who gradually moved northwards, while Essex broke into the Royalist West. Then, turning east, the King inflicted a severe check on Waller at Cropredy Bridge, in Oxfordshire, on June 6, capturing all his artillery. Outmarching and outwitting Waller, he suddenly during August began to march westward, with the intention of taking Essex in the rear. Essex was outnumbered, his supplies were cut off,

King Charles I (1600–49). Triple portrait by Van Dyck, now in Windsor Castle.
REPRODUCED BY GRACIOUS PERMISSION OF HER MAJESTY THE QUEEN

Charles R

and after rejecting a proposal for surrender he sailed with his officers to Plymouth, ordered his cavalry to cut their way out of the trap, and left the rest of his army to its fate. All the infantry and artillery, to the number of eight thousand men, surrendered at Lostwithiel, in Cornwall, on September 2.

The main forces of the Parliament were now thrown against the King. Once again, on October 27, the armies met at Newbury and once again there was a drawn battle, followed by a Royalist retirement. It was late in November before active warfare paused. Charles re-entered Oxford in triumph. In the teeth of adversity he had maintained himself with little money or supplies

163

against odds of two or three to one.

Cromwell rode in from the Army to his duties as a Member of Parliament. He made a vehement and organised attack on the conduct of the war, and its mismanagement by luke-warm generals of noble rank, namely Essex and Manchester. While he urged the complete reconstitution of the Parlia-mentary army, his friends in the House of Commons proposed a so-called "Self-denying Ordi-nance", which would exclude Members of either House from military employment. The handful of lords who still remained at West-minster realised well enough that this was an attack on their prominence in the conduct of the war, if not on their social order. During the winter months the Army was reconstituted in accordance with Cromwell's ideas. The old personally raised regiments of the Parliamentary nobles were broken up and their officers and men incorporated in entirely new formations. These, the New Model, comprised eleven regiments of horse, each six hundred strong, twelve regiments of foot, twelve hundred strong, and a thousand dragoons, in all twenty-two thousand men. Compulsion was freely used to fill the ranks. Sir Thomas Fairfax was appointed Com-mander-in-Chief. Cromwell, as Member for Cambridge, was at first debarred from serv-ing. However, it soon appeared that his Self-denying Ordinance applied only to his rivals. In June 1645 he was appointed General of the Horse, and was thus the only man who combined high military command with an outstanding Parliamentary position. From this moment he became the domi-nant figure in both spheres. Amid these

The Battle of Naseby, by Shore

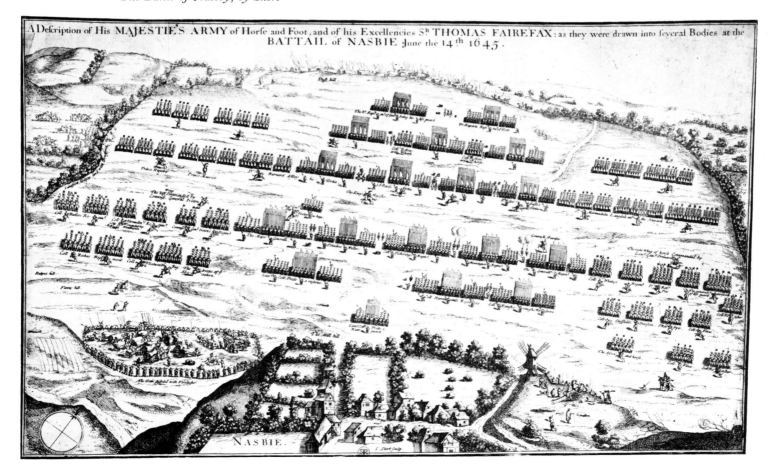

stresses Archbishop Laud, who languished ailing in the Tower, was brought to the scaffold.

Largely to please the Scots, a parley for a peace settlement was set on foot at Uxbridge, near London, and on this many hopes were reposed, though not by the die-hards in Parliament. But neither King Charles nor the Roundhead executive had the slightest intention of giving way upon the two main points—Episcopacy and the control of the armed forces. At the same time the Marquis of Montrose sprang upon the scene. He wrote to Charles assuring him that he would bring all Scotland to his rescue if he could hold out. But a decisive battle impended in the South. On June 14, 1645, the last trial of strength was made. Charles, having taken Leicester, which was sacked, met Fairfax and Cromwell in the fine hunting country about Naseby. Rupert shattered the Parliamentary left, and though, as at Edgehill, his troopers were attracted by the Parliamentary baggage column, he returned to strike heavily at the central Roundhead infantry. But Cromwell on the other flank drove all before him, and also took control of the Roundhead reserves. The Royalist foot, beset on all sides by overwhelming numbers, were killed or captured. Naseby was the expiring effort of the Cavaliers in the open field. There still remained many sieges, with reliefs and manœuvrings, but the final military decision of the Civil War had been given.

By the spring of 1646 all armed resistance to the Parliamentary army was beaten down. In the main the middle class, being more solid for Parliament, had beaten the aristocracy and gentry, who were divided. Montrose had been defeated in the autumn of 1645 at Philiphaugh, near the Border, by detachments from the regular Scottish army in England. Yet it was to the Scots government that Charles thought of turning. Kept at Newcastle in hard circumstances, he entered upon nearly a year's tenacious bargainings on the national issues at stake. The King naturally hoped to profit by the differences between Parliament and the Army

General Ireton, after S. Cooper. NATIONAL PORTRAIT GALLERY

and between the English and Scottish governments. He delayed so long that the Governments came to terms without him. In February 1647 the Scots, having been paid an instalment of half the sum due to them for their services in England, handed over Charles under guarantee for his safety to Parliamentary Commissioners and returned to their own country. This transaction, though highly practical, wore and still wears a sorry look.

Now that the war was won most Members of Parliament and their leaders had no more need of the Army. But here a matter very awkward on such occasions obtruded itself. The pay of the Army was in arrear. In the first phase of the dispute Parliament assumed it had the power to give orders. Cromwell, as Member for Cambridge, assured them in the name of Almighty God that the Army would disband when ordered. The reply of the Army was to concentrate at Newmarket. The Presbyterians in Parliament looked to the Scots and the Army leaders looked to the King. Even after Marston Moor and Naseby the victorious Ironsides did not feel sure that

165

anything counted without the royal authority. Here is the salient fact which distinguishes the English Revolution from all others: that those who wielded irresistible physical force were throughout convinced that it could give them no security. Nothing is more characteristic of the English people than their instinctive reverence even in rebellion for law and tradition.

Cromwell and Ireton felt that if they could get hold of the King physically, and before Parliament did so, it would be much. If they could gain him morally it would be all. Ireton was already secretly in touch with the King. Now in early June on his and Cromwell's orders Cornet Joyce, with near four hundred Ironside troopers, rode to Holmby House, where the King, surrounded by his Household and attended by the Parliamentary Commissioners, was agreeably residing. In the morning Cornet Joyce intimated with due respect that he had come to remove the King. Charles made no protest. Off they all rode together, a jingling and not unhappy company, feeling they had English history in their hands. At this moment there was at

finger-tips a settlement in the power of the English people and near to their hearts' desire. But of course it was too good to be true. Charles was never wholly sincere in his dealings with the Army leaders; he still pinned his hopes on help from the Scots. Parliament for their part rejected the military and royal proposals. Here were checks. But another came from the Army itself.

The soldiers were deep in the Old Testament. They particularly admired the conduct of Samuel when before the Lord he hewed to pieces Agag, delicately though he walked. The only chance for the arrangement between Charles and Cromwell was that it should be carried swiftly into effect. Instead there was delay. The mood of the soldiers became increasingly morose; and the generals saw themselves in danger of losing their control over them. On August 6, the Army marched on London, occupied Westminster, entered the City, and everything except their problems fell prostrate before them.

At Putney in the autumn of 1647 the

Carisbrooke Castle, Isle of Wight. AEROFILMS

Army held keen debate. The regiments had elected their delegates. These were called by them the "agents", or "agitators". Their ideas were soon abreast of those of the Chartists in the nineteenth century—manhood suffrage at twenty-one, equal electoral districts, biennial Parliaments, and much more in prospect. Cromwell heard all this and brooded over it. Clearly this was dangerous nonsense. He replaced the General Council of the Army by a General Council of his officers.

Late in this autumn of 1647 Cromwell and Ireton came to the conclusion that even with the pay and indemnity settled they could not unite King and Army. In November the King, convinced that he would be murdered by the soldiery, whom their officers could no longer restrain, rode off in the night, and by easy stages made his way to Carisbrooke Castle, in the Isle of Wight. There remained the Scots. With them he signed a secret Engagement by which Royalism and Presbyterianism were to be allied. From this conjunction there shortly sprang the Second Civil War. The King and his Prerogative were now seen, not as obstacles to Parliamentary right, but as the repository of ordinary English freedom. Prisoner at Carisbrooke, Charles was now more truly King than he had ever been in the palmiest days of the Personal Rule.

The story of the Second Civil War is short and simple. King, Lords and Commons, landlords and merchants, the City and the countryside, bishops and presbyters, the Scottish army, the Welsh people, and the English Fleet, all now turned against the New Model Army. The Army beat the lot. And at their head was Cromwell. By the end of 1648 all was over. Cromwell was Dictator.

Plainly the fruit of the victory that could most easily be gathered was the head of the King. The Army meant to have his blood in the manner which would most effectively vindicate their power and their faith. London lay locked under the guard and countersign of the Army. Some Parliamentary time-server had stood by Colonel Pride, when the Members sought to take their seats in the House of Commons, and had ticked off all those not likely to obey the Army's will. Forty-five Members who tried to enter were arrested, and out of a total of over five hundred three hundred did not take their seats again. This was "Pride's Purge". The great trial of "the Man of Blood" was to be presented to the nation and to the world. No English jurist could be found to frame

The Death Warrant of Charles I signed between January 26 and 29, 1649, by the Commissioners who tried the King.
HOUSE OF LORDS RECORD OFFICE

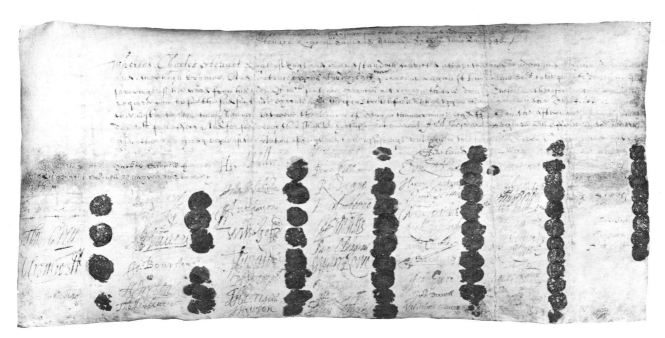

the indictment or invent the tribunal. An Ordinance passed by the docile remnant of the Commons created a court of a hundred and thirty-five Commissioners, of whom barely sixty would serve, to try the King. The carpenters fitted Westminster Hall for its most memorable scene. The King, basing himself upon the law and Constitution he had strained and exploited in his years of prosperity, confronted his enemies with an unbreakable defence. He refused to acknowledge the tribunal. Cromwell and the Army could however cut off the King's head, and this at all costs they meant to do. On the morning of January 30, 1649, Charles was conducted from St James's, whither he had been removed from his comfortable lodgings by the river, to Whitehall. At one o'clock in the afternoon Charles was informed that his hour had come. He walked through a window of the Banqueting House on to the scaffold. Masses of soldiers, many ranks deep, held an immense multitude afar. He resigned himself to death, and assisted the executioner in arranging his hair under a small white satin cap. He laid himself upon the block, and upon his own signal his head was struck off at a single stroke.

A strange destiny had engulfed this King of England. None had resisted with more untimely stubbornness the movement of his age. He was not a martyr in the sense of one who dies for a spiritual ideal. His own kingly interests were mingled at every stage with the larger issues. Some have sought to represent him as the champion of the small or humble man against the rising money-power. This is fanciful. He cannot be claimed as the defender of English liberties, nor wholly of the English Church, but none the less he died for them, and by his death preserved them not only to his son and heir, but to our own day.

The seal of Oliver Cromwell. <small>MANSELL COLLECTION</small>

CHAPTER SIX

The Restoration

THE English Republic had come into existence even before the execution of the King. On February 5 it was declared that the House of Lords "is useless and dangerous and ought to be abolished". The country was now to be governed by a Council of State chosen annually by Parliament. The highly conservative elements at the head of the Army held firmly to the maintenance of the Common Law and the unbroken administration of justice in all non-political issues. Mutinies broke out. Many hundreds of veteran soldiers appeared in bands in support of "the sovereignty of the people", manhood suffrage, and annual Parliaments. This mood was not confined to the soldiers. Behind these broad principles the idea of equal rights in property as well as in citizenship was boldly announced by a group led by Gerard Winstanley, which came to be known as "the Diggers". It was essential to divide and disperse the Army, and Cromwell was willing to lead the larger part of it to a war of retribution in the name of the Lord Jehovah against the idolatrous and blood-stained Papists of Ireland.

The spirit and peril of the Irish race might have prompted them to unite upon Catholic toleration and monarchy, and on this they could have made a firm alliance with the Protestant Royalists, who, under the Marquess of Ormonde, had an organised army of twelve thousand men. Ormonde would have done better to have kept the open field with his regulars and allowed the severities of the Puritan invaders to rally the Irish nation behind him, but he had occupied the towns of Drogheda and Wexford and was resolved to defend them. He hoped that Cromwell would break his teeth upon a long siege of Drogheda, in which he placed a garrison of three thousand men, comprising the flower of the Irish Royalists, and English volunteers. Cromwell saw that the destruction of these men would not only ruin Ormonde's military power, but spread a helpful terror throughout the island. Having unsuccessfully summoned the garrison to surrender, he breached the ramparts with his

Oliver Cromwell, after Cooper.
NATIONAL PORTRAIT GALLERY

Cromwell's army at Dunbar, "confidently appealing to Jehovah". From the painting by Gow. MANSELL COLLECTION

cannon, and at the third assault, which he led himself, stormed the town. There followed a massacre so all-effacing as to startle even the opinion of those fierce times. A similar atrocity was perpetrated a few weeks later at the storm of Wexford. "I am persuaded," Cromwell wrote, "that this is a righteous judgment of God upon these barbarous wretches, who have imbrued their hands in so much innocent blood."[1]

In the safe and comfortable days of Queen Victoria, when Liberals and Conservatives, Gladstone and Disraeli, contended about the past, and when Irish Nationalists and Radical Nonconformists championed their old causes, a school grew up to gape in awe and some in furtive admiration at these savage crimes. The twentieth century has sharply recalled its intellectuals from such vain indulgences. We have seen the technique of "frightfulness" applied in our own time with Cromwellian brutality and upon a far larger scale. It is necessary to recur to the simpler principle that the wholesale slaughter of unarmed or disarmed men marks with a mordant and eternal brand the memory of conquerors, however they may have prospered. In Oliver's smoky soul there were evident misgivings. He writes of the "remorse and regret" which are inseparable from such crimes. The consequences of Cromwell's rule

in Ireland have distressed and at times distracted English politics down even to the present day. They became for a time a potent obstacle to the harmony of the English-speaking peoples throughout the world.

At the moment when the axe severed the head of Charles the First from his body his eldest son became, in the opinion of most of his subjects and of Europe, King Charles the Second. Montrose, when his army fell to pieces, had on the advice of the late King quitted Scotland, believing at first that the Whitehall execution robbed his life of all purpose. His spirit was revived by a priest who preached to him a duty of revenge. With a handful of followers he landed in Caithness, was defeated by the Government forces and betrayed for a paltry bribe into their power. He was dragged through many Scottish towns, and hanged at Edinburgh on a specially high gallows amid an immense agitated concourse. Yet at the same time that Argyll and the Covenanters inflicted this savage punishment upon an unorthodox Royalist they themselves prepared for war with England in the cause of monarchy and entered into urgent treaty with the young King.

Charles II must bind himself to destroy the Episcopacy and enforce upon England a

[1] Thomas Carlyle, *Oliver Cromwell's Letters and Speeches* (1846), vol. ii, pp. 59–62.

Boscobel, Charles II's refuge after the Battle of Worcester, 1651. RADIO TIMES HULTON PICTURE LIBRARY

religious system odious to all who had fought for his father. He hesitated long before taking the grim decision of selling his soul to the Devil, as he conceived it, for the interest of the Crown and betraying the cause to save its life. Still there was again an army to fight for the Crown, and both Cardinal Mazarin in France and Prince William of Orange in Holland lent their aid to Scotland.

The menace in the North brought Cromwell back from Ireland. The armies manœuvred against each other. Cromwell was forced back upon Dunbar, dependent on wind and weather for his daily bread. The pious Scottish army descended from their blockading heights and closed down upon Cromwell and his Saints to prevent their embarkation. Both sides confidently appealed to Jehovah; and the Most High, finding so little to choose between them in faith and zeal, must have allowed purely military factors to prevail. Once the battle was joined among these politico-religious warriors the end was speedy. The Scots fled, leaving three thousand dead on the field. Nine thousand were prisoners in Oliver's hungry camp, and the Army of the Presbyters was broken. A Scottish army now invaded England in 1651 upon a Royalist rather than a Presbyterian enterprise. It is proof of Cromwell's political and military sagacity that he allowed them to pass. On his day of fate, September 3, sixteen thousand Scots were brought to battle at Worcester, not only by the twenty thousand veterans of the New Model, but by the English militia, who rallied in large numbers against this fresh inroad of the hated and interfering Scots. The struggle was one of the stiffest contests of the civil wars, but it was forlorn, and the Scots and their Royalist comrades were destroyed as a military force.

To Cromwell this was "the crowning mercy". To Charles II it afforded the most romantic adventure of his life. He escaped with difficulty from the stricken field. The land was scoured for him. He hid for a whole day in the famous oak tree at Boscobel, while his pursuers passed by. On every side were

men who would have rejoiced to win the price of catching him. But also on every side were friends, if they could be found, secret, silent, unflinching. Nearly fifty persons recognised him, and thus became privy to his escape and liable to grave penalties. The magic of the words "the King, our master", cast its spell upon all classes. "The King of England, my master, your master, and the master of all good Englishmen, is near you and in great distress: can you help us to a boat?" "Is he well? Is he safe?" "Yes." "God be blessed." This was the temper of all who were trusted with or discovered the secret. Thus after six weeks of desperate peril did the King find himself again in exile. This was the end of the Civil War or Great Rebellion.

The three kingdoms were united under a government in London which wielded autocratic power.

The monarchy had gone; the Lords had gone; the Church of England was prostrate; of the Commons there remained nothing but the few survivors contemptuously named the Rump. It was a nationalistic Rump, at once protectionist and bellicose. While Cromwell was fighting in Ireland and Scotland these Puritan grandees through their chosen Council of State ruled with efficiency. When he returned victorious he was struck by their unpopularity. The Lord General's outlook was clear and his language plain. "These men," Oliver had said, "will never leave till the Army pull them down by the ears." He called in his musketeers to clear the House and lock the doors. While the indignant politicians, most of whom were men of force and fire, were being hustled into the street the General's eye fell on the Mace, symbol of the Speaker's authority. "What shall we do with this bauble?" he asked. "Take it away!" Here sank for the moment all the constitutional safeguards and processes built and treasured across the centuries, from Simon de Montfort to the Petition of Right.

Cromwell's successes and failures in foreign policy bore consequences throughout the reign of Charles II. In 1654 he ended the

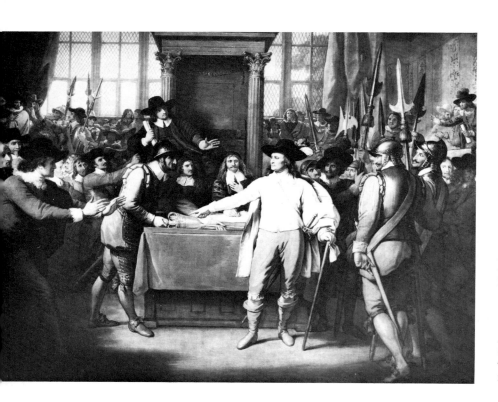

Benjamin West's painting of the expulsion of the Rump by Cromwell, April 20, 1653. PHOTO: JEAN LANGE. COURTESY: PERMANENT COLLECTION, MONTCLAIR ART MUSEUM, MONTCLAIR, NEW JERSEY

sea war against the Dutch which had begun two years earlier. In spite of grave arguments to the contrary urged by the Council, he sent a naval expedition to the West Indies in September 1654 and Jamaica was occupied. This act of aggression led slowly but inevitably to war between England and Spain, and a consequent alliance between England and France.

Cromwell sought the right kind of Parliament to limit his own dictatorship without crossing his will, and he boxed the compass in his search. He had expelled the Rump in the cause of an overdue popular election. He replaced it not by an elected but by a handpicked body of Puritan notables, who became known to history as "Barebone's Parliament", after one of their 'members, Praise-God Barebone. The political behaviour of the Saints was a sad disappointment to their convoker. With breath-taking speed they proceeded to sweep the board clear of encumbrances in order to create a new Heaven and earth. With a temerity justified only by spiritual promptings, they reformed taxation in a manner which seemed to weaken the security for the soldiers' pay. The Army leaders, wishing to avoid the scandal of another forcible ejection, persuaded or compelled the more moderate Saints to get up very early one morning before the others were awake and pass a resolution yielding back their power to the Lord General from whom it had come.

Ireton had died in Ireland, but Lambert and other Army leaders of various ranks drew up an "Instrument of Government", which was in fact the first and last written English Constitution. The executive office of Lord Protector conferred upon Cromwell was checked and balanced by a Council of State, nominated for life, consisting of seven Army leaders and eight civilians. A single Chamber was also set up, elected upon a new property qualification in the country. It was probably not a narrower franchise, but all those who had fought against Parliament were disqualified from voting. Cromwell gratefully accepted the Instrument and assumed the title of Lord Protector. But

The frigate Assistance, *built* circa 1650, *from a manuscript illustration of the time.* BRITISH MUSEUM

once again all went wrong with the Parliament. It no sooner met in September 1654 than it was seen to contain a fierce and lively Republican group, which, without the slightest gratitude to the Army leaders or to the Protector for their apparent deference to Republican ideas, set themselves to tear the new Constitution to pieces. At the earliest moment allowed by the Instrument Cromwell dissolved the Commons.

Cromwell's expulsion of the Rump was recorded in the House of Commons Journal. On January 7, 1659, the entry was expunged by order of the exhumed Parliament. HOUSE OF LORDS RECORD OFFICE

Military dictatorship supervened, naked if not wholly unashamed. Cromwell now proceeded to divide England and Wales into eleven districts, over each of which a Major-General was placed, with the command of a troop of horse and a reorganised militia. The Major-Generals assured him of their ability to pack a compliant House. But Levellers, Republicans, and Royalists were able to exploit the discontent against the military dictatorship, and a large number of Members who were known enemies of the Protector were returned. It was at this stage that a group of lawyers and gentry decided to offer Cromwell the Crown. The "Humble Petition and Advice" in 1657 which embodied the proposed Constitution provided not only for the restoration of kingship, but also for the firm re-establishment of Parliament, including a nominated Upper House and a substantial reduction in the powers of the Council of State. But the Army leaders and still more the soldiers showed at once their inveterate hostility to the trappings of monarchy, and Cromwell had to content himself with the right to nominate his successor to the Protectoral throne. In May 1657 he accepted the main provisions of the new Constitution without the title of King. Cromwell, in the exaggerated belief that a hostile design was on foot against him, suddenly, in January 1658, dissolved the most friendly Parliament which he had ever had. He ended his speech of dissolution with the words, "Let God judge between you and me." "Amen," answered the unrepentant Republicans.

The maintenance of all privilege and authority in their own hands at home and a policy of aggression and conquest abroad absorbed the main energies of Cromwell and his Council. They were singularly barren in

General John Lambert, after Walker. NATIONAL PORTRAIT GALLERY

social legislation. The English Puritans, like their brethren in Massachusetts, concerned themselves actively with the repression of vice. The feast days of the Church, regarded as superstitious indulgences, were replaced by a monthly fast day. Christmas excited the most fervent hostility of these fanatics. Parliament was deeply concerned at the liberty which it gave to carnal and sensual delights. Soldiers were sent round London on Christmas Day before dinner-time to enter private houses without warrants and seize meat cooking in all kitchens and ovens. Everywhere was prying and spying. To the mass of the nation the rule of Cromwell manifested itself in the form of numberless and miserable petty tyrannies, and thus became hated as no government has ever been hated in England before or since. For the first time the English people felt themselves governed from a centre in the control of which they had no say.

The repulsive features fade from the picture and are replaced by colour and even charm as the summit of power is reached. We see the Lord Protector in his glory, the champion of Protestantism, the arbiter of Europe, the patron of learning and the arts. We feel the dignity of his bearing to all men, and his tenderness toward young people. We feel his passion for England, as fervent as Chatham's and in some ways more intimate and emotional. Cromwell, although crafty and ruthless as occasion claimed, was at all times a reluctant and apologetic dictator. Liberty of conscience as conceived by Cromwell did not extend to the public profession of Roman Catholicism, Prelacy, or Quakerism. Believing the Jews to be a useful element in the civil community, he opened again to them the gates of England, which Edward I had closed nearly four hundred years before. There was in practice comparatively little persecution on purely religious grounds, and even Roman Catholics were not seriously molested. Religious toleration challenged all the beliefs of Cromwell's day and found its best friend in the Lord Protector himself.

On September 3, 1658, the anniversary of the Battles of Dunbar and Worcester and of the siege of Drogheda, in the crash and howling of a mighty storm, death came to the Lord Protector. If in a tremendous crisis Cromwell's sword had saved the cause of Parliament, he must stand before history as a representative of dictatorship and military rule who, with all his qualities as a soldier and a statesman, is in lasting discord with the genius of the English race.

In his last hours Cromwell had in terms "very dark and imperfect" nominated his eldest son, Richard, to succeed him. He was at first accepted by the Army and duly installed in his father's seat; but when he attempted to exercise authority he found he had but the form. Within four months of succeeding to his august office Richard Cromwell found himself deserted even by his personal guard. The Army was master, with Fleetwood and Lambert rivals at its head. Even in this hour of bloodless and absolute triumph the soldiery felt the need of some civil sanction for their acts. Thus was the Rump of the Long Parliament exhumed and exhibited to a bewildered land. In the summer of 1659 Cavaliers, strangely consorting with Presbyterian allies, appeared in arms in several counties. The revolt was so swiftly crushed that Charles II, fortunately for himself, had no chance of putting himself at its head. At this moment Lambert became the most prominent figure. He seems to have believed that he could satisfy the Army, both in politics and religion, better under a restored monarchy than under either the Rump or a Protectorate. His course was secret, tortuous, and full of danger. At Christmas the Army resolved to be reconciled with Parliament. But obviously this could not last. Someone must set in train the movement which would produce in England a government which stood for something old or new.

The Cromwellian commander in Scotland, though very different in temperament from Lambert, was also a man of mark. He ranged himself from the first against the violence of the Army in London. Monk was one of those Englishmen who understand to perfection

General George Monk, Duke of Albemarle. Studio of Lely.

the use of time and circumstance. It is a type which has thriven in our Island. The General received the emissaries of every interest and party in his camp. He listened patiently, as every great Englishman should, to all they had to urge, and with that simple honesty of character on which we flatter ourselves as a race he kept them all guessing for a long time what he would do. Informed of events in London, he crossed the Tweed from Coldstream on the cold, clear New Year's Day of 1660. At York he received what he had long hoped for, the invitation of the House of Commons, the desperate Rump, to come to London. He marched south through towns and counties in which there was but one cry—"A free Parliament!" When Monk and his troops reached London he was soon angered by the peremptory orders given him by the Rump. Unlike Cromwell and Lambert, Monk decided to tame the Rump by diluting, not by dissolving, it. In February he recalled the Members who had been excluded by Pride's Purge. They declared Monk Commander-in-Chief of all the forces. The Rump of the Long Parliament was dissolved by its own consent. Monk was satisfied that a free Parliament should be summoned, and that such a Parliament would certainly recall Charles II.

175

The King might "enjoy his own again", but not all the Cavaliers. There must be a full recognition that men should keep what they had got or still had left. There must be no reprisals. Monk's advice was accepted by Charles's faithful Chancellor, Hyde, who had shared his master's exile and was soon to be rewarded with the Earldom of Clarendon. The Lords and Commons were restored. It remained only to complete the three Estates of the Realm by the recall of the King. The Fleet, once so hostile, was sent to conduct him to his native shores. Immense crowds awaited him at Dover. There on May 25, 1660, General Monk received him with profound reverence as he landed. The journey to London was triumphal.

The wheel had not however swung a full circle, as many might have thought. Indeed, it was the greatest hour in Parliamentary history. All the laws of the Long Parliament since Charles I quitted London at the beginning of 1642, all the statutes of the Commonwealth or of the Protectorate, now fell to the ground. But there remained the potent limitations of the Prerogative to which Charles I had agreed. The King relinquished his feudal dues from wardships, knight service, and other medieval survivals. Parliament granted him instead revenues for life which, with his hereditary property, were calculated to yield about £1,200,000. For all extra-ordinary expenditure the King was dependent upon Parliament, and both he and Clarendon accepted this. The Crown was not to be free of Parliament. The Cavaliers were mortified that the vindication of their cause brought them no relief from the mulctings of which they had been the victims. Everyone however, except the soldiers, was agreed about getting rid of the Army; and that this could be done, and done without bloodshed, seemed a miracle. The Ironside soldiers were abashed by public opinion. They were paid their dues. They returned to their homes and their former callings, and within a few months this omnipotent, invincible machine, which might at any moment have devoured the whole realm and society of

Edward Hyde, Earl of Clarendon. Portrait after Hanneman. NATIONAL PORTRAIT GALLERY

Britain, vanished in the civil population, leaving scarcely a trace behind.

In all, through Charles's exertions, and at some expense to his popularity, less than a dozen persons were put to death in this intense Counter-Revolution. Leading figures of the Parliamentary party, peers and commoners, high officers under the Republic or Cromwell, made ready shift to sit upon the tribunals which slaughtered the regicides; and it is upon these that history may justly cast whatever odium belongs to these melancholy but limited reprisals.

The Parliament which recalled the King was a balanced assembly, and represented both sides of the nation. The House could not claim to be a Parliament, but only a Convention. At the end of 1660 it was thought necessary to dissolve it. The longest Parliament in English history now began. It lasted eighteen years. It has been called the Cavalier Parliament—or, more significantly, the Pension Parliament. From the moment when it first met it showed itself more Royalist in theory than in practice. It did not mean to part with any of the Parliamentary rights which had been gained in the struggle. It was ready to make provision for the defence of the country by means of militia; but the militia must be controlled by the Lord-Lieutenants of the counties. The repository of force had now become the county families and gentry.

Since Clarendon as Lord Chancellor was the chief Minister, and preponderant in the government, his name is identified with the group of Acts which re-established the Anglican Church and drove the Protestant sects into enduring opposition. In so doing it consolidated Nonconformity as a political force with clear objectives: first, toleration, which was secured at the Revolution of 1688; and thereafter the abolition of the privileged status of the Church. The Clarendon Code of 1662 went some way beyond the ideas of Clarendon himself. Neither did Charles will this great separation. He walked by the easy path of indifference to the uplands of toleration. The Cavalier Parliament sternly corrected this deplorable laxity. The Code embodied the triumph of those who had been beaten in the field and who had played little part in the Restoration. Its echoes divide the present-day religious life of England. It potently assisted the foundation of parties. Thus from the Restoration there emerged no national settlement, but rather two Englands, each with its different background, interests, culture, and outlook. As Macaulay wrote, and later writers have confirmed his view, "there was a great line which separated the official men and their friends and dependants, who were sometimes called the Court party, from those who were sometimes honoured with the appellation of the Country party". We enter the era of conflict between broad party groups which shaped the destinies of the British Empire till all was melted in the fires of the Great War of 1914.

For these far-reaching fissures Charles II had no responsibility. Throughout his reign he consistently strove for toleration. But Charles II had need of an Act of Indulgence for himself. Court life was one unceasing flagrant and brazen scandal. The King's example spread its demoralisation far and wide, and the sense of relief from the tyranny of the Puritans spurred forward every amorous adventure. Nature, affronted, reclaimed her rights with usury. The people of England did not wish to be the people of God in the sense of the Puritan God. They descended with thankfulness from the superhuman levels to which they had been painfully hoisted.

Two personalities of force and capacity, vividly contrasted in character, Clarendon

Catherine of Braganza, Charles II's Queen. Portrait by Stoop. NATIONAL PORTRAIT GALLERY

Lord Ashley, Earl of Shaftesbury, after Greenhill. NATIONAL PORTRAIT GALLERY

and Ashley, afterwards Earl of Shaftesbury, swayed the Privy Council. Shaftesbury was the most powerful representative of the vanished domination. Throughout the reign he stood by the City of London, and the City stood by him. For the first seven years of the reign Clarendon continued First Minister. This wise, venerable statesman wrestled stoutly with the licentiousness of the King and Court, with the intrigues of the royal mistresses, with the inadequacy of the revenue, and with the intolerance of the House of Commons. The Chief Minister was now father-in-law to the King's brother. His grandchildren might succeed to the throne.

The acquisition of Tangier as part of the

The Restoration of King Charles II. The scene in Whitehall, in a painting attributed to I. Fuller. COURTESY: J. Y. SANGSTER, ESQ.

dowry of Catherine of Braganza turned the eyes of the Government to Mediterranean and Oriental trade. Cromwell's capture of Dunkirk imposed upon the royal Exchequer an annual cost of no less than £120,000 a year, or one-tenth of the normal revenue. The Tory policy already looked to "trade and plantations" in the outer seas rather than to action in Europe. Charles, on Clarendon's advice, sold Dunkirk to the

French for £400,000. The rivalry of England and Holland upon the seas in fishery and in trade had become intense, and the strength of the Dutch had revived since Cromwell's war. The King was roused to patriotic ardour, the Duke of York thirsted for naval glory. The great sum of over two and a half millions was voted. More than a hundred new ships were built, armed with new and heavier cannon. Former Cavalier and Cromwellian officers joined hands and received commissions from the King. Rupert and Monk commanded divisions of the Fleet. War at sea began off the West African coast in

1664, and spread to home waters in the following year. In June the English fleet of more than one hundred and fifty ships, manned by twenty-five thousand men and mounting five thousand guns, met the Dutch in equal strength off Lowestoft, and a long, fierce battle was fought, in which many of the leaders on both sides perished. The English artillery was markedly superior in weight and skill, and the Dutch withdrew worsted though undismayed. The return of Admiral De Ruyter from the West Indies restored the fortunes of the Republic. An even greater battle than Lowestoft was fought in June 1666. For four days the English and Dutch fleets battled off the North Foreland. At the close of the second day's cannonading the English were outmatched; then Rupert, arriving on the third day, restored the balance. But the fourth day was adverse, and Monk and Rupert, with heavy losses, retired into the Thames. De Ruyter had triumphed.

Both sides bent beneath the financial strain. But other calamities drained the strength of the Island. From the spring of 1665 the Great Plague had raged in London. Never since the Black Death in 1348 had pestilence spread such ravages. In London at the climax about seven thousand people died in a single week. The worst of the plague was over when in September 1666 the Great Fire engulfed the tormented capital. It broke out near London Bridge, in a narrow street of wooden houses, and, driven by a strong east wind, the flames spread with resistless fury for four whole days. When the fire was at length stopped outside the City walls by blowing up whole streets more than thirteen thousand dwelling-houses, eighty-nine churches, and St Paul's Cathedral had been devoured.

Want of money prevented the English battle fleet from keeping the sea, and while the negotiations lingered the Dutch, to spur

them, sailed up the Medway under Admiral De Witt, brother of the famous John, Grand Pensionary of Holland, broke the boom which guarded Chatham harbour, burnt four ships of the line, and towed away the battleship *Royal Charles*, which had destroyed Admiral Opdam in the Battle of Lowestoft. Peace, of which both sides had equal need, was made on indifferent terms. England's chief gain in the war was New Amsterdam, now renamed New York.

Clarendon, expostulating with all sides,

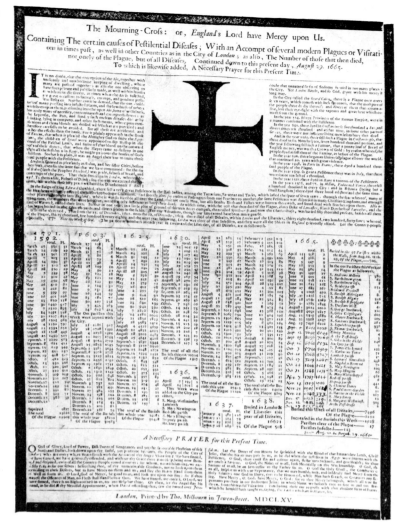

was assailed by all. An impeachment was launched against him, and he went into exile, there to complete his noble *History of the Rebellion*, which casts its broad and lasting illumination on the times through which he lived. The growing discontents of the Cavalier Parliament at the morals and expense of the Court made it necessary to broaden the basis of the government, and from 1668 five principal personages began to be recognised as the responsible Ministers. There had been much talk of Cabinets and Cabals; and now, by chance, the initials of these five men, Clifford, Arlington, Buckingham, Ashley, and Lauderdale, actually spelt the word "CABAL".

The dominant fact on the continent of Europe, never realised by Cromwell, was the rise of France at the expense of Spain and Austria. Charles and the Cabal, aided by their envoy Sir William Temple at The Hague, concluded a triple alliance with Holland and Sweden against France. The Protestant combination was hailed with delight by the whole country. This, the first of the long series of coalitions against France, checked Louis XIV for a while. He addressed himself to England and in 1670 began secret negotiations with Charles II. Above all things Charles needed money. He pointed out to Louis that Parliament would give him ample funds to oppose France; how much would Louis pay him not to do so? Here was the basis of the shameful Treaty of Dover. Besides the clauses which were eventually made public, there was a secret clause upon which Arlington and Clifford were Charles's only confidants. "The King of Great Britain being convinced of the truth of the Catholic Faith, is determined to declare himself a Catholic . . . as soon as the welfare of his realm will permit." The King was also to receive a subvention of £166,000 a year.

The Treaty of Dover contemplated a third Dutch War, in which France and England would combine when Louis XIV felt the moment opportune. In March 1672 Louis

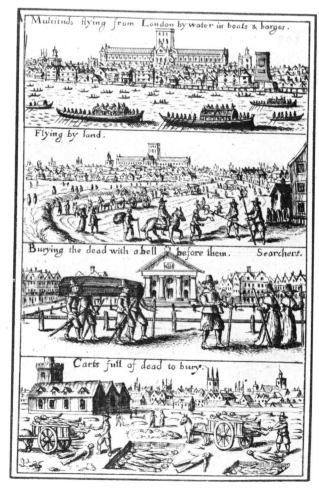

The Great Fire of London, 1666, seen from the east, upwind of the blaze. This painting is by an unknown Dutch artist who, from the detail shown, is believed to have been an eyewitness of the event. The Tower, old St Paul's, which appeared in the woodcut on the previous page, and old London Bridge, can be clearly seen. THE LONDON MUSEUM

claimed fulfilment of the pact. War began. In a great battle at Sole Bay on May 28, 1672, De Ruyter surprised the English and French, who were ten ships stronger, as they lay at anchor. Grievous and cruel was the long battle. The Suffolk shores were crowded with frantic spectators, and the cannonade was heard many miles away. The French squadron put out to sea, but the wind prevented them from engaging. The Duke of York's flagship, the *Prince*, was beset on every side. Upon her decks stood the First Company of the Guards, in which Ensign Churchill was serving. She became such a wreck that the Duke, who fought with his usual courage, was forced to shift his flag to the *St Michael*, and, when this ship was in turn disabled, to the *London*. Nevertheless, the Dutch drew off with very heavy losses of their own.

On land Louis struck with terrible force at the hard-pressed Republic. The Dutch people, faced with extermination, turned in their peril to William of Orange. The great-grandson of William the Silent, now Captain-General, did not fail them. He uttered the famous defiance, "We can die in the last ditch." The sluices in the dykes were opened; the bitter waters rolled in a deluge over the fertile land, and Holland was saved.

Resentment of the Dutch affronts at sea and jealousy of their trade were overridden

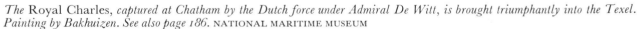

The Royal Charles, *captured at Chatham by the Dutch force under Admiral De Witt, is brought triumphantly into the Texel. Painting by Bakhuizen. See also page 186.* NATIONAL MARITIME MUSEUM

by fear and hatred of Papist France and her ever-growing dominance in Europe. The secret article in the Dover Treaty had only to be known to create a political explosion of measureless violence. Shaftesbury, though not privy to it, must have had his suspicions. Early in 1673 Arlington seems to have confessed the facts to him. With dexterity and promptitude Shaftesbury withdrew himself from the Government, and became the leader of an Opposition which was ultimately as violent as that of Pym. A Bill was forced upon the King for a Test. No man could hold office or a King's commission afloat or ashore who would not solemnly declare his disbelief in the doctrine of Transubstantiation. This purge destroyed the Cabal. All eyes were now fixed upon James, Duke of York, a convert to Rome. Very soon it was known that the heir to the throne had laid down his post of Lord High Admiral rather than submit to the Test. The strength of the forces now moving against the King and his policy rose from the virtual unanimity which prevailed between the Anglicans and the Dissenters, between the swords which had followed Rupert and the swords which had followed Cromwell. They were all on the same side now, and at their head was the second great Parliamentary tactician of the century, Shaftesbury.

Sir Thomas Osborne, a Yorkshire landowner, had gathered great influence in the Commons, and was to a large extent forced upon the King for his own salvation. He was very soon raised to the peerage as Earl of Danby, and began an administration which was based on a party organisation possessing a small but effective majority in the House of Commons. Economy, Anglicanism, and independence from France were the principal ideals of this party. In foreign affairs the new Minister publicly differed from his master. The height of his precarious popularity was reached when he contrived a marriage between Mary, the Duke of York's daughter by his first wife, and the now famous Protestant hero, William of Orange.

It was at this moment that Louis XIV, dissatisfied with his English investments and indignant at a marriage which threatened to carry England into the Dutch system and was a strong assertion of Protestant interests, resolved to ruin Danby. He revealed to the Opposition, most of whom took his bribes while opposing his interests, that the English Minister had been asking for French money. A renegade priest of disreputable character, Dr Titus Oates, presented himself as the Protestant champion. He accused the Duchess of York's private secretary, Coleman, of a conspiracy to murder the King, bring about a French invasion, and cause a general massacre of Protestants. Coleman was examined in October 1668 before a magistrate, Sir Edmund Berry Godfrey, and while the case was proceeding Godfrey was found dead one night at the foot of Greenberry Hill, now Primrose Hill. This cumulative sensation drove English society into madness. Oates rose in a few months to be a popular hero; and being as wicked as any man who ever lived, he exploited his advantage to the full. Charles, wishing to stay the capital proceedings instituted against his Minister, partly unjustly, and anyhow for actions which Danby had taken only to please the King, at length, in December 1678, dissolved the Cavalier Parliament.

As happened after the Short Parliament of Charles I, all the prominent opponents of the King were returned. The situation was not unlike that of 1640; but with one decisive difference. Both the King and the country had gone through an experience which neither wished to repeat. Charles II yielded to the wish of the nation; he bowed to the hostile Parliament. Danby, threatened by attainder, was glad to be forgotten for five years in the Tower. He had still a part to play. The brunt fell upon James, Duke of York. The King had already asked him not to attend the Privy Council, and now advised him to leave the country. Charles, thus relieved at home, faced the fury of the anti-Popish hurricane. The last five years of his reign are those most honourable to his memory. His mortal duel with Shaftesbury

The Dutch in the Medway, June 20, 1667. A painting by Jan Peters showing the four English ships of the line set on fire by the Dutch ships under Admiral De Witt. NATIONAL MARITIME MUSEUM

was a stirring episode. The struggle centred upon the Exclusion Bill. To keep the Papist heir from the throne was the main object of the majority of the nation. Shaftesbury looked to William of Orange; but he also looked, with more favour, upon the Duke of Monmouth, Charles's illegitimate son by Lucy Walters. Nothing would induce the King to betray the succession. He laboured to present a compromise. But in the prevailing temper no one would believe that any restrictions could be imposed upon a Popish King. The Exclusion Bill passed its second reading by an overwhelming vote, and the King descended upon the Parliament with another dissolution. Nevertheless this short-lived legislature left behind it a monument. It passed a Habeas Corpus Act which confirmed and strengthened the freedom of the individual

against arbitrary arrest by the executive government. The descent into despotism which has engulfed so many leading nations in the present age has made the virtue of this enactment, sprung from English political genius, apparent even to the most thoughtless, the most ignorant, the most base.

As soon as the King saw that the election gave him no relief he prorogued the meeting of the resulting Parliament for almost another year. And it is in this interval that we first discern the use of those names Whig and Tory which were to divide the British Island for nearly two hundred years. The term "Whig" had described a sour, bigoted, canting, money-grubbing Scots Presbyterian. Irish Papist bandits ravaging estates and manor-houses had been called "Tories". One can see from these expressions of scorn and hatred how narrowly England escaped another cruel purging of the sword.

Charles was now in full breach with Louis XIV, who scattered his bribes widely among the Opposition. A glorified Privy Council assembled. Shaftesbury, the leader of the Opposition, was appointed its President by the King. When Parliament met in October 1680 Shaftesbury again championed the Exclusion Bill, and at this moment he reached his zenith. The Exclusion Bill was carried through the Commons, and the struggle was fought out in the Lords. That it ended bloodlessly was largely due to the statesman who has rendered the word "Trimmer" illustrious. George Savile, Marquis of Halifax, was the opponent alike of Popery and of France. He was one of those rare beings in whom cool moderation and width of judgment are combined with resolute action. Halifax, who had been so hot against Danby, broke the Exclusion Bill in the House of Lords. In the immortal pen-pictures which Dryden has drawn of the personalities of these turbulent days none is more pleasing than that of Jotham, who

> only tried
> The worse awhile, then chose the better side,
> Nor chose alone, but changed the balance too.
> So much the weight of one brave man can do.

The fury against the Popish Plot was gradually slaked in the blood of its victims. Charles saw in this new temper the chance of a more favourable Parliament. Halifax, fresh from rendering him the highest service, opposed the dissolution. But for the third time in three years there was an electoral trial of strength. Again there was no decisive change in the character of the majority returned. Presently it was learned that Parliament was to meet in Oxford, where the King could not be bullied by the City of London and Shaftesbury's gangs of apprentices called "White Boys". He had caused Lawrence Hyde, Clarendon's son, the Duke of York's brother-in-law, a competent financier, to examine precisely the state of the normal revenue granted to the Crown for life. Hyde was next employed in negotiating with Louis XIV, and eventually £100,000 a year was obtained upon the understanding that England would not act contrary to French ambitions on the Continent. With this aid it was thought the King could manage independently of the ferocious Parliament. A private Member of importance unfolded to the House the kind of plan for a Protestant Protectorate during James's reign which the King had in mind. James, when he succeeded, should be King only in name. The kingdom would be governed by a Protector and the Privy Council. The administration should rest in Protestant hands. But Oxford was a camp in which two armed factions jostled one another. At any moment there might be an outbreak. The Commons passed a resolution for excluding the Duke of York. On the Monday following Black Rod knocked at the door and summoned them to the Peers. Most Members thought that this portended some compliance by the King with their wishes. They were surprised to see him robed, upon his throne, and astounded when the Lord Chancellor declared in his name that Parliament was again dissolved. Shaftesbury made a bid to convert the elements of the vanished Parliament into a revolutionary Convention. But the dose of the Civil War still worked in the Englishmen of 1681. Charles had hazarded rightly.

Within two months the King felt strong enough to indict Shaftesbury for fomenting rebellion. The Middlesex Grand Jury, faithful to his cause, wrote "Ignoramus" across the bill presented against him. This meant that they found the evidence insufficient. He was liberated according to law. He counselled insurrection; and it seemed that a royal murder would be one of its preliminaries. Shaftesbury at this point fled to Holland, hoping perhaps for Dutch support, and died at The Hague in a few weeks. He cannot be ranked with the chief architects of the Parliamentary system. He sought above all the triumph of his party and his tenets. His life's work left no inheritance for England. He was as formidable as Pym, but his fame sinks to a different level.

King James II (1633–1701). Portrait by Kneller. NATIONAL PORTRAIT GALLERY

The absorbing question now was whether there would be civil war. Fifty zealous Ironsides could easily overpower the small travelling escort of the King and the Duke of York on their return from their pastime of horse-racing. Above this dark design, and unwitting of it, was a general conspiracy for armed action. The lucky accident of a fire in Newmarket, by which much of the town was destroyed, led Charles and James to return some days before the expected date. They passed the Rye House in safety, and a few weeks later the secret of the plot was betrayed. When the news spread through the land it caught the Royalist reaction upon its strong upturn. Two famous men were engulfed. Neither William, Lord Russell nor Algernon Sidney had sought the King's life; but Russell had been privy to preparations for revolt, and Sidney had been found with an unpublished paper, scholarly in character, justifying resistance to the royal authority. After public trial both went to the scaffold. Martyrs for religion there had been in plenty. But here were the first martyrs for the sake of Party.

The power of Charles at home remained henceforth unchallenged. By pressure and manipulation Tory sheriffs were elected in London, and henceforth through that agency City juries could be trusted to deal severely with Whig delinquents. The Whig corporations were asked by writs of *Quo Warranto* to prove their title to their long-used liberties. Under these pressures large numbers of hitherto hostile corporations threw themselves on the mercy of the Crown and begged for new charters in accordance with the royal pleasure. Talk of excluding James from the throne died away. He resumed his functions. The King was only fifty-six, and in appearance lively and robust, but his exorbitant pleasures had undermined his constitution. Halifax, now more than ever trusted, still urged him to the adventure of a new Parliament, and Charles might have consented, when suddenly in February 1685 an apoplectic stroke laid him low. With that air of superiority to death for which all mortals should be grateful he apologised for being "so unconscionable a time in dying". James was at hand to save his soul. Apart from hereditary monarchy, there was not much in which Charles believed in this world or another. He wanted to be King, as was his right, and have a pleasant life. He was cynical rather than cruel, and indifferent rather than tolerant. His care for the Royal Navy is his chief claim upon the gratitude of his countrymen.

Eighty years of fearful events and the sharpest ups and downs of fortune had brought the monarchy, in appearance and for the practical purposes of the moment, to

A letter from the Duke of Monmouth to Christopher, Duke of Albemarle (son of George Monk), commanding the Devon militia. June 11 or 12, 1685:

"Whereas we are credibly informed that there are some horse and foot under your command for James, Duke of York: which are purposely raised in opposition to us and our Royal Authority.

"We have thought to signify to you our Royal resentment: and do promise our self that what you have transacted therein is through inadvertency and mistake and that your Grace will take other measures when you have received information of our being proclaimed King to succeed our Royal father lately deceased. We therefore have sent this messenger on purpose to intimate the same to you. And it is our Royal will and pleasure and we do hereby strictly charge and command you upon notice and receipt hereof to cease all hostility and force of arms against us and all our loving subjects and that your Grace would immediately repair to our camp where you shall not fail of kind and hearty reception from us: And in default of the premises we shall be obliged to proclaim you and all those under your command rebels and traitors and shall prosecute both them and you accordingly.

"Yet we assure our self your Grace will pay a ready obedience to our command wherefore we bid you heartily farewell.   JAMES R."

Albemarle's reply, written on the back of Monmouth's letter and returned by the same messenger, was brief:

"I have received your letter and do not doubt but you would use me very kindly if you had me and since you have given your self the trouble of an invitation this is to let you know that I never was nor will be a rebel to my lawful King who is James the Second brother to my late dear master King Charles the Second.

"If you think I am in the wrong and your self in the right, when ever we meet I do not doubt but the justice of my cause shall sufficiently convince you that you had better have let this rebellion alone and not have put the nation to so much trouble.   ALBEMARLE"

almost Tudor absolutism. For the last two years of his brother's reign James had played a leading part in the realm. All he thought he needed to make him a real king, on the model now established in Europe by Louis XIV, was a loyal Fleet and a standing Army, well trained and equipped. Behind this there swelled in the King's breast the hope that he might reconcile all his people to the old faith and heal the schism which had rent Christendom for so many generations. He was resolved that there should at least be toleration among all English Christians. It is one of the disputes of history whether toleration was all he sought. James ascended the throne with all the ease of Richard Cromwell. He tried to dispel the belief that he was vindictive or inclined to arbitrary rule. The electors returned a House of Commons loyal and friendly to the new King. They voted him a revenue for life which, with the growth of trade, amounted to nearly £2,000,000 a year.

It was at this moment, on June 11, 1685, that Monmouth landed. He entered the harbour of Lyme Regis, not far from Portland Bill. He was at once welcomed by the populace. He issued a proclamation asserting the validity of his mother's marriage and denouncing James as a usurper who had murdered Charles II. All the ruling forces rallied round the Crown. One last chance remained—a sudden night attack upon the royal army. Feversham was surprised in his camp at Sedgemoor; but an unforeseen deep ditch, called the Bussex Rhine, prevented a hand-to-hand struggle. Lord Churchill, James's long-trusted officer and agent, vigilant and active, took control. The West Country peasantry and miners, though assailed by sixteen pieces of artillery and charged in flank and rear by the Household troops, fought with Ironside tenacity. They were slaughtered where they stood, and a merciless pursuit, with wholesale executions, ended their forlorn endeavour. Monmouth escaped the field only to be hunted down a few days later. He could claim no mercy, and none did he receive.

Chief Justice Jeffreys was sent into the West to deal with the large number of prisoners. This cruel, able, unscrupulous judge made his name for ever odious by "the Bloody Assize". Between two and three hundred persons were hanged, and about eight hundred transported to Barbados, where their descendants still survive.

James was now at the height of his power. As soon as Jeffreys's "campaign", as James called it, was ended he proposed to his Council the repeal of the Test Act and the Habeas Corpus Act. Halifax was removed, not only from the Presidency of the Council, but from the Privy Council altogether; and when North died soon after, Chief Justice Jeffreys, red-handed from "the Bloody Assize", was made Lord Chancellor in his stead. Robert Spencer, Earl of Sunderland, later in the year became Lord President in the place of Halifax, as well as Secretary of State, and was henceforth James's Chief Minister. Parliament met for its second session on November 9, and the King laid his immediate purpose before it. A strong standing Army was indispensable to the peace and order of the realm. He also made it plain that he would not dismiss his Catholic officers on the morrow of their faithful services. These two demands shook the friendly Parliament to its foundations. Its most hideous nightmare was a standing Army, its dearest treasure the Established Church.

During the whole of 1686 and 1687 James held Parliament in abeyance, and used his dispensing power to introduce Roman Catholics into key positions. The Church, the bulwark of legitimacy, the champion of non-resistance, seethed with suppressed alarms, and only the powerful influence of Lawrence Hyde, now Earl of Rochester, upon the bishops and clergy prevented a vehement

Chief Justice Jeffreys, as Lord Chancellor. Portrait by an unknown artist. NATIONAL PORTRAIT GALLERY

outburst. It was plain that the King, with all the downright resolution of his nature, was actively and of set purpose subverting the faith and Constitution of the land. He now embarked upon a political manœuvre at once audacious, crafty, and miscalculated. If Whigs and Tories were combined he would match them by a coalition of Papists and Nonconformists under the armed power of the Crown. In January 1687 came the fall of the Hydes. Clarendon, the elder brother, in Ireland, had been overawed by James's faithful follower, the Roman Catholic Earl of Tyrconnel; Rochester, in Whitehall, was subdued by Sunderland. With the dismissal of Rochester began the revolutionary conspiracy. Meanwhile, James was raising and preparing his Army. Every summer a great camp was formed at Hounslow to impress the Londoners. In August 1686 this contained about ten thousand men. A year later Feversham could assemble fifteen thousand men and twenty-eight guns.

The provocations of the royal policy continued. The first Declaration of Indulgence was issued. It did precisely what James's Parliament had objected to in advance: it set aside statutory Act by Royal Prerogative.

Meanwhile, an attempt to force a Catholic President upon Magdalen College, Oxford, and the expulsion of the Fellows for their resistance, added to the stir. In July James planned the public reception of the Papal Nuncio, d'Adda. The King had, in modern parlance, set up his political platform. The second step was to create a party machine, and the third to secure by its agency a Parliament with a mandate for the repeal of the Tests. The narrow franchise could be manipulated in the country to a very large extent by the Lord-Lieutenants and by the magistrates, and in the towns and cities by the corporations. Upon these therefore the royal energies were now directed. The process of setting Papists and Dissenters over or in place of Anglicans and Cavaliers ruptured and recast the whole social structure of English life as established at the Restoration. The rich and powerful, in resisting the Crown, felt themselves upborne by the feelings of the voteless masses.

In England during the autumn of 1688 everything pointed, as in 1642, to the outbreak of civil war. At the end of April James had issued a second Declaration of Indulgence. On May 18 seven bishops, headed by the Primate, the venerable William Sancroft, protested against this use of the dispensing power. James, furious at disobedience, and apparently scandalised at this departure, by the Church he was seeking to undermine, from its doctrine of non-resistance, demanded that the bishops should be put on trial for seditious libel. As they stepped on board the barge for the Tower they were hailed by immense crowds with greetings in which reverence and political sympathy were combined. The same scenes were repeated when they were brought back to Westminster Hall on June 15, and at their trial on June 29. When on the following day the bishops were declared "Not Guilty" the verdict was acclaimed with universal joy. But the attitude of the Army was more important. The King had visited them at Hounslow, and as he departed heard loud cheering. "What is that clamour?" he asked. "Sire, it is nothing; the

The seven bishops leaving the Tower through Traitor's Gate, from a contemporary Dutch engraving. BRITISH MUSEUM

soldiers are glad that the bishops are acquitted." "Do you call that nothing?" said James. On the same night, while cannon and tumults proclaimed the public joy, the seven leaders of the party of action met at Shrewsbury's town-house, and there and then dispatched their famous letter to William of Orange. The signatories were Shrewsbury, Danby, Russell, Bishop Compton, Devonshire, Henry Sidney, and Lumley. But on June 10, while the trial of the bishops was still pending, the Queen had given birth to a son. The legend that a child had been smuggled into St James's Palace in a warming-pan was afoot even before the ashes of the official bonfires had been cleared from the streets. Up to this moment there always lived the hope that the stresses which racked the nation would die with the King. Now William, stricken in his ambition by the birth of a male Stuart heir, exclaimed, "Now or never!" and began to prepare his expedition.

Louis XIV kept all in suspense till the last moment. Had James been willing to commit himself finally to a French alliance Louis would have invaded Holland. But James had patriotic pride as well as religious bigotry. To the last he wavered so that in Holland they thought he was allied to France, and in France to Holland. Louis therefore decided that the best he could hope for would be an England impotent through civil war. At the end of September he turned his armies towards the Middle Rhine, and

from that moment William was free to set forth.

As the autumn weeks slipped by excitement and tension grew throughout the Island, and the vast conspiracy which now comprised the main strength of the nation heaved beneath the strain of affairs. Everyone watched the weathercock. All turned on the wind. Rumour ran riot. The Irish were coming. The French were coming. The Papists were planning a general massacre of Protestants. The kingdom was sold to Louis. Nothing was safe, and no one could be trusted. The laws, the Constitution, the Church—all were in jeopardy. But a deliverer would appear. He would come clad with power from over the seas to rescue England from Popery and slavery—if only the wind would blow from the east. The scale and reality of William's preparations and the alarming state of feeling throughout England had terrified Sunderland and Jeffreys. These two Ministers induced the King to reverse his whole policy. Parliament must be called without delay. But it was too late. On October 19 William set out upon the seas.

On November 5 he landed at Torbay, on the coast of Devon.

James was not at first greatly alarmed at the news. At this crisis the King could marshal as large an army as Oliver Cromwell at his height. Nearly forty thousand regular soldiers were in the royal pay. But now successive desertions smote the unhappy prince. Lord Cornbury, eldest son of the Earl of Clarendon, an officer of the Royal Dragoons, endeavoured to carry three regiments of horse to William's camp. James, warned from many quarters, meditated Churchill's arrest. On the night of November 23, having failed to carry any large part of the Army with them, Churchill and the Duke of Grafton, with about four hundred officers and troopers, quitted the royal camp. At the same time the Princess Anne, attended by Sarah Churchill, and guided by Bishop Compton, fled from Whitehall and hastened northwards. And now revolt broke out all over the country. Danby was in arms in Yorkshire, Devonshire in Derbyshire, Delamere in Cheshire. Lord Bath delivered Plymouth to William. Byng, later an admiral, representing the captains of the Fleet, arrived at his headquarters to inform him that the Navy and Portsmouth were at his disposal. City after city rose in rebellion. By one spontaneous, tremendous convulsion the English nation repudiated James.

Meanwhile, the invading army moved steadily forward towards London. James sent his wife and son out of the kingdom, and on the night of December 11 stole from the palace at Whitehall, crossed the river, and rode to the coast. The London mob sacked the foreign embassies, and a panic and terror, known as "Irish Night", swept the capital. James in his flight had actually got on board a ship, but, missing the tide, was caught and dragged ashore by the fishermen and townsfolk. He was brought back to London, and after some days of painful suspense was allowed to escape again. This time he succeeded and left English soil for ever.

CHAPTER SEVEN

England's Advance to World Power

WILLIAM of Orange was fatherless and childless. His life was loveless. As a sovereign and commander he was entirely without religious prejudices. The darkest stain upon his memory was to come from Scotland. A Highland clan whose chief had been tardy in making his submission was doomed to destruction by William's signed authority. Troops were sent to Glencoe "to extirpate that den of thieves". But the horror with which this episode has always been regarded arises from the treacherous breach of the laws of hospitality by which it was accomplished. The King had not prescribed the method, but he bears the indelible shame of the deed.

William was cold, but not personally cruel. His sole quarrel was with Louis XIV. For all his experience from a youth spent at the head of armies, and for all his dauntless heart, he was never a great commander. He had not a trace of that second-sight of the battlefield which is the mark of military genius. His inspiration lay in the sphere of diplomacy. He has rarely been surpassed in the sagacity, patience, and discretion of his Statecraft. He required the wealth and power of England by land and sea for the European war. He never was fond of England, nor interested in her domestic affairs.

A Convention Parliament was summoned by the Prince on the advice of the statesmen who had made the Revolution. Loyal Tories were alarmed by the prospect of disturbing the Divine Right in the Stuart succession. Danby got in touch with Princess Mary. An obvious solution which would please many Tories was the accession of Mary in her own

right. But other Tories, including Mary's uncle, the Earl of Clarendon, favoured the appointment of William as Regent, James remaining titular King. The whole situation turned upon the decision of William. Would he be content with the mere title of honorary consort to his wife? After protracted debates in the Convention Halifax's view was accepted that the Crown should be jointly vested in the persons of William and Mary. His triumph was complete, and it was he who presented the Crown and the Declaration of Rights to the two sovereigns on behalf of both Houses. Many honours and promotions at the time of the Coronation rewarded the Revolutionary leaders. Churchill, though never in William's immediate circle, was confirmed in his rank of Lieutenant-General,

The Pass of Glencoe. J. ALLAN CASH

William of Orange landing at Torbay, November 5, 1688. Painting by an unknown artist, now in Hampton Court Palace.
REPRODUCED BY GRACIOUS PERMISSION OF HER MAJESTY THE QUEEN

William R.

and employed virtually as Commander-in-Chief to reconstitute the English Army. He was created Earl of Marlborough, and when in May 1689 war was formally declared against France, and William was detained in England and later embroiled in Ireland, Marlborough led the English contingent in Flanders.

Cracks speedily appeared in the fabric of the original National Government. William felt that Whig principles would ultimately lead to a republic. He was therefore ready to dissolve the Convention Parliament which had given him the Crown while, as the Whigs said, "its work was all unfinished". At the election of February 1690 the Tories won.

It may seem strange that the new King should have turned to the Earl of Sunderland, who had been King James's chief adviser. But James and Sunderland had now irrevocably quarrelled, and Sunderland was henceforth bound to William's interests. His knowledge of the European political scene was invaluable to his sovereign's designs. After a brief interval he reappeared in England, and gained a surprising influence. The actual government was entrusted to the statesmen of the middle view—the Duke of Shrewsbury, Sidney Godolphin, and Marlborough, and, though now, as always, he stood slightly aloof from all parties, Halifax.

Ireland presented itself as the obvious immediate centre of action. James, sustained by a disciplined French contingent, many French officers, and large supplies of French munitions and money, had landed in Ireland in March. He was welcomed as a deliverer.

The whole island except the Protestant settlements in the North passed under the control of the Jacobites, as they were henceforth called. The loyal defence of Londonderry and its relief from the sea was the one glorious episode of the campaigning season of 1689. Had William used his whole strength in Ireland in 1689 he would have been free to carry it to the Continent in 1690; but in the new year he found himself compelled to go in person with his main force to Ireland. The Prince of Waldeck, William's Commander in the Low Countries, suffered a crushing defeat at the Battle of Fleurus. At the same time the French Fleet gained a victory over the combined fleets of England and Holland off Beachy Head. It was said in London that "the Dutch had the honour, the French had the advantage, and the English the shame". However, on July 11 King William gained a decisive victory at the Boyne and drove King James out of Ireland back to France. By the winter the French Fleet was dismantled, and the English and Dutch Fleets were refitted and again at sea. The end of 1690 therefore saw the Irish War ended and the command of the sea regained.

Thereafter a divergence grew between the King and Marlborough. He was the leading British general, and many officers of various ranks resorted to him and loudly expressed their resentment at the favour shown to the Dutch. Shrewsbury, Halifax, and Marlborough all entered into correspondence with James. There was talk of the substitution of Anne for William and Mary, and at the same time the influence of the Churchills with Princess Anne continued to be dominating. As often happens in disputes among high personages, the brunt fell on a subordinate. The Queen demanded the dismissal of Sarah Churchill from Anne's household. Anne refused with all the obstinate strength of her nature. The next morning the Earl of Nottingham, Secretary of State, delivered to Marlborough a written order to sell at once all the offices he held, civil and military, and consider himself as from that date dismissed from the Army and all public employment and forbidden the Court.

No sooner had King William set out upon the Continental war than the imminent menace of invasion fell upon the Island he had left denuded of troops. It was not until the middle of April 1692 that French designs became known to the English Government. Louis XIV planned a descent upon England. King James was to be given his chance of regaining the throne. On May 19–20, 1692, the English and Dutch Fleets met Tourville with the main French naval power in the English Channel off Cape La Hogue. The whole apparatus of invasion was destroyed under the very eyes of the former King whom it was to have borne to his native shore. The Battle of Cape La Hogue, with its consequential actions, effaced the memories of Beachy Head. It broke decisively for the whole of the wars of William and Anne all French pretensions to naval supremacy. It was the Trafalgar of the seventeenth century.

On land the campaign of 1692 unrolled in the Spanish Netherlands, which we now know as Belgium. Namur fell to the French armies. Worse was to follow. In August William marched by night with his whole army to attack Marshal Luxembourg. The French were surprised near Steinkirk in the early morning. But Luxembourg was equal to the emergency and managed to draw out an ordered line of battle. The British infantry

The siege of Londonderry in 1689 by the Jacobite army of James II. Engraving by Schoonebeck. MANSELL COLLECTION

formed the forefront of the Allied attack. Eight splendid regiments, under General Mackay, charged and broke the Swiss in fighting as fierce as had been seen in Europe in living memory. Luxembourg now launched the Household troops of France upon the British division, already strained by its exertions, and after a furious struggle, fought mostly with cold steel, beat it back. From all sides the French advanced and their reinforcements began to reach the field. Count Solms, the Dutch officer and William's relation, who had replaced Marlborough in

The Battle of the Boyne, 1690, from an engraving by Theodor Maas. William III (mounted, left foreground) sees his forces cross the river while beyond it the Jacobites are in retreat towards Drogheda. MANSELL COLLECTION

The Battle of Cape La Hogue. The scene after Admiral Rooke's attack on the morning of May 23, 1692, by A. Van Diest.
NATIONAL MARITIME MUSEUM

command of the British contingent, had already earned the cordial dislike of its officers and men. He now refused to send Mackay the help for which he begged. William, who was unable to control the battle, shed bitter tears as he watched the slaughter, and exclaimed, "Oh, my poor English!" By noon the whole of the Allied army was in retreat, and although the losses of seven or eight thousand men on either side were equal the French proclaimed their victory throughout Europe. These events infuriated the English Parliament. Against

great opposition supplies were voted for another mismanaged and disastrous year of war. In July 1693 was fought the great Battle of Landen, unmatched in Europe for its slaughter except by Malplaquet and Borodino for over two hundred years. William rallied the remnants of his army, gathered reinforcements, and, since Luxembourg neglected to pursue his victory, was able to maintain himself in the field. In 1694 he planned an expedition upon Brest, and, according to the Jacobites, Marlborough betrayed this design to the enemy.

The Continental ventures of William III now forced English statesmen to a reconstruction of the credit and finances of the country. The first war Government formed from the newly organised Whig Party possessed in the person of Charles Montagu a first-rate financier. The first essential step was the creation of some national organ of credit. In collaboration with the Scottish banker William Paterson, Montagu, now Chancellor of the Exchequer, started the Bank of England in 1694 as a private corporation. With the help of the philosopher John Locke, and William Loundes of the Treasury, he planned a complete overhaul of the coinage. It is perhaps one of the greatest achievements of the Whigs.

At the end of 1694 Queen Mary had been stricken with smallpox, and on December 28 she died, unreconciled to her sister Anne, mourned by her subjects, and lastingly missed by King William. This altered the whole position of the Princess, and with it that of the redoubtable Churchills, who were her devoted intimates and champions.

In 1695 the King gained his only success. He recovered Namur in the teeth of the French armies. This event enabled the war to be brought to an inconclusive end in 1696. In order to achieve lasting peace it was vital

that England should be strong and well armed, and thus enabled to confront Louis on equal terms. The Whigs were sensitive to the danger of the French aggression in Europe. But the Tories were now in one of their moods of violent reaction from Continental intervention. Groaning under taxation, impatient of every restraint, the Commons plunged into a campaign of economy and disarmament. In 1697 the Whig administration was driven from office upon such themes, and with such a programme Robert Harley, now the rising hope of Toryism, created his power and position in the House of Commons. Harley was supported by Sir Edward Seymour, the pre-eminent "sham good-fellow" of the age, who marshalled the powerful Tories of Cornwall and the West. In the Lords he was aided by Nottingham and the Earl of Rochester. They did all they could to belittle and undermine the strength of their country. No closer parallel exists in

Robert Harley, 1st Earl of Oxford and Mortimer. Portrait after Kneller. NATIONAL PORTRAIT GALLERY

history than that presented by the Tory conduct in the years 1696 to 1699 with their similar conduct in the years 1932 to 1937. In each case short-sighted opinions, agreeable to the party spirit, pernicious to national interests, banished all purpose from the State and prepared a deadly resumption of the main struggle.

William was so smitten by the wave of abject isolationism which swept the governing classes of the Island that he contemplated an abdication and return to Holland. His distress led him to look again to Marlborough, with whom the future already seemed in a great measure to rest. Anne's sole surviving son, the Duke of Gloucester, was now nine years old, and it was thought fitting to provide the future heir apparent to the Crown with a Governor of high consequence and with an establishment of his own. In the summer of 1698 William invited Marlborough to be Governor of the boy-prince. From this time forth William seemed to turn increasingly towards the man of whose aid he had deprived himself during the most critical years of his reign. The untimely death in 1700 of the little Duke of Gloucester, who succumbed to the fatal, prevalent scourge of smallpox, deprived Marlborough of his office. There was now no direct Protestant heir to the English and Scottish thrones. By an Act of Settlement the House of Hanover, descended from the gay and attractive daughter of James I who had briefly been Queen of Bohemia, was declared next in succession after William and Anne. The Act laid down that every sovereign in future must be a member of the Church of England. It also declared that no foreign-born monarch might wage Continental wars without the approval of Parliament; he must not go abroad without consent, and no foreigners should sit in Parliament or on the Privy Council. Thus were recorded in statute the English grievances against William III.

No great war was ever entered upon with more reluctance on both sides than the War of the Spanish Succession. Over all Europe hung the long-delayed, long-dreaded, ever-approaching demise of the Spanish Crown. William cast himself upon the policy of partitioning the Spanish Empire. There were three claimants, whose pretensions are set out in the accompanying table. The first was France, represented either by the Dauphin, or if the French and Spanish Crowns could not be joined, by his second son, the Duke of Anjou. The next was the Emperor, who was willing to transfer his claims to the Archduke Charles. Thirdly, there was the Emperor's grandson, the Electoral Prince of Bavaria. The essence of the new Partition Treaty of September 24, 1698, was to recognise the Electoral Prince as heir to Charles II of Spain. This plan concerted between Louis XIV and William III was vehemently resented by the Emperor. As it became known it also provoked a fierce reaction in Spain. Spanish society now showed that it cared above all things for the integrity of the Spanish domains.

But now a startling event occurred. In February 1699 the Electoral Prince of Bavaria, the child in whose chubby hands the greatest States had resolved to place the most splendid prize, suddenly died. Why and how he died at this moment did not fail to excite dark suspicions. By great exertions William and Louis arranged a second Treaty of Partition on June 11, 1699, by which the Archduke Charles was made heir-in-chief. Meanwhile, the feeble life-candle of the childless Spanish King burned low in the socket. Charles had now reached the end of his torments. But within his diseased frame, his clouded mind, his superstitious soul, trembling on the verge of eternity, there glowed one Imperial thought—the unity of the Spanish Empire. In the end he was persuaded to sign a will leaving his throne to the Duke of Anjou, and couriers galloped with the news from the Escorial to Versailles. On November 1 Charles II expired.

Louis XIV had now reached one of the great turning-points in the history of France. Should he reject the will, stand by the treaty, and join with England and Holland in enforcing it? On the other hand, should he repudiate the treaty, endorse the will, and

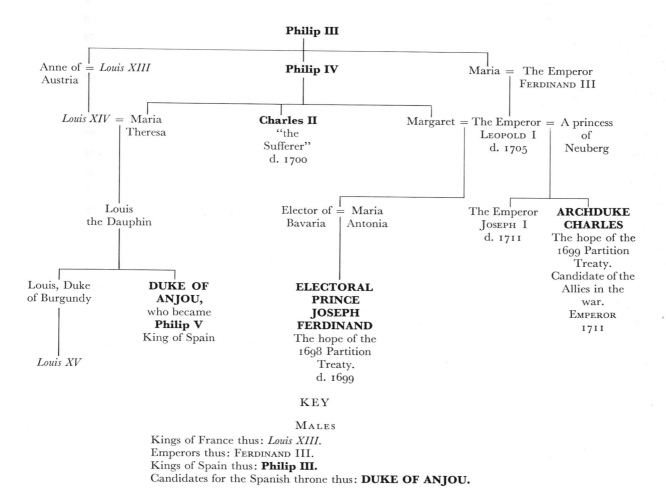

KEY

MALES

Kings of France thus: *Louis XIII.*
Emperors thus: FERDINAND III.
Kings of Spain thus: **Philip III.**
Candidates for the Spanish throne thus: **DUKE OF ANJOU.**

defend his grandson's claims in the field against all comers? It was decided to repudiate the treaty and stand upon the will. On November 16 a famous scene was enacted at Versailles. Louis XIV, at his levee, presented the Spanish Ambassador to the Duke of Anjou, saying, "You may salute him as your King." The Ambassador gave vent to his celebrated indiscretion, "There are no more Pyrenees." Confronted with this event, William felt himself constrained to recognise the Duke of Anjou as Philip V of Spain. The House of Commons was still in a mood far removed from European realities. They eagerly accepted Louis XIV's assurance that, "content with his power, he would not seek to increase it at the expense of his grandson". A Bourbon prince would become King of Spain, but would remain wholly independent of France. But now a series of ugly incidents broke from outside upon the fevered complacency of English politics. A letter from Melfort, the Jacobite Secretary of State at Saint-Germain, was discovered in the English mail-bags, disclosing a plan for the immediate French invasion of England in the Jacobite cause. It appeared that the Spaniards had now offered to a French company the sole right of importing Negro slaves into South America. It also became apparent that the freedom of the British trade in the Mediterranean was in jeopardy. But the supreme event which roused all England to an understanding of what had actually happened in the virtual union of the Crowns of France and Spain was a tremendous military operation effected under the guise of brazen legality. A line of fortresses in Belgium, garrisoned under treaty rights by the Dutch, constituted the main barrier of the Netherlands against a French invasion. During the month of February 1701 strong French

John Churchill, Duke of Marlborough. Portrait after Kneller. NATIONAL PORTRAIT GALLERY

forces arrived before all the Belgian cities. The Spanish commanders welcomed them with open gates. The Dutch garrisons, over-awed by force, and no one daring to break the peace, were interned. All that the Grand Alliance of 1689 had defended in the Low Countries in seven years of war melted like snow at Easter. Europe was roused, and at last England was staggered.

William felt the tide had set in his favour. On May 31 he proclaimed Marlborough Commander-in-Chief of the English forces assembling in Holland. In June he appointed him Ambassador Extraordinary to the United Provinces. On September 16, 1701, James II died. Louis visited in State his death-bed at Saint-Germain, and announced to the shadow Court that he recognised James's son as King of England and would ever sustain his rights. All England was roused by the insult to her independence. King William was able to sever diplomatic relations with France. The Emperor had already begun the war, and his famous general, Prince Eugene of Savoy, was fighting in the North of Italy.

At this moment death overtook King William. On February 20, 1702, he was rid-ing in the park round Hampton Court on Sorrel, a favourite horse. Sorrel stumbled in the new workings of a mole, and the King was thrown. The broken collar-bone might well have mended, but in his failing health the accident opened the door to a troop of lurking foes. William died at fifty-two, worn out by his labours. Marlborough at the same age strode forward against tremendous odds upon the ten years of unbroken victory which raised the British nation to a height in the world it had never before attained.

There was at that time an extraordinary wealth of capacity in the English governing class. It was also the Augustan Age of English letters. Addison, Defoe, Pope, Steele, Swift, are names which shine today. Art and science flourished. The work of the Royal Society, founded in Charles II's reign, now bore a largesse of fruit. Sir Isaac Newton in mathe-matics, physics, and astronomy completed the revolution of ideas which had begun with the Renaissance. Architecture was led to noble achievements by Wren, and to massive monuments by Vanbrugh.

In March 1702 Anne ascended the throne. The new reign opened in a blaze of loyalty. It was the "sunshine day" for which the Princess Anne had long waited with placid attention. Marlborough was made Captain-General of her armies at home and abroad. The office of Stadtholder and Commander-in-Chief was allowed to pass into abeyance and Marlborough was appointed Deputy Captain-General of Holland. He was thus in supreme command of the armies of the two Western Powers. But although the highest title and general deference were accorded to the English General his authority could only

Queen Anne (1665–1714), from a portrait by Dahl. NATIONAL PORTRAIT GALLERY

assert itself at every stage by infinite patience and persuasiveness. Moreover, he was never head of the government in London. The Tories regarded with aversion the sending of large armies to the Continent. They declared that the country gentlemen were being mulcted while the City of London, its bankers and its merchants, established an ever-growing mortgage upon the landed estates. The Whigs, on the other hand, though banished from office, were ardent advocates of the greatest military efforts. The issue was radical, and much to his regret Marlborough found it necessary to use his paramount influence with the Queen against the leaders of the Tory Party.

For the year 1702 Louis had decided to set his strongest army against Holland. The valiant but fruitless efforts of King William were replaced by the spectacle of substantial advances, and the hitherto aggressive French were seen baffled, hesitating, and in retreat. When after the storm of Liège, Marlborough, narrowly escaping an ambuscade upon the Meuse, returned to The Hague he was received with intense public joy by the Dutch, and on his arrival in England he was created Duke by the Queen. A powerful fleet and army sailed for Cadiz at the end of July under the Duke of Ormonde and Admiral Sir George Rooke. The commanders lacked the nerve to force the harbour upon the first surprise, and a prolonged series of desultory operations ensued. After a month it was decided to re-embark the soldiers and sail for home. The ignominy was relieved by a lucky windfall. News was brought that the Spanish Treasure Fleet with millions from the Indies aboard had run into Vigo Bay. It was decided to raid the harbour. The entire enemy fleet was sunk, burned, or captured. Had they shown at Cadiz one-half of the spirit of Vigo Bay the sea-Powers would have been masters of the Mediterranean in 1703.

For the campaign of 1703 Marlborough was able to concentrate the "Grand Army" of the Alliance around Maastricht, eighty miles south of Nimwegen, the starting-point of the previous year. He deferred to Dutch opinion and began the siege of Bonn on the Rhine. When Bonn fell he made the attempt upon Antwerp, and very rapid manœuvring and hard marching followed. The "great design", as he called it, did not succeed because the Dutch were not willing to·consent to the very severe offensive battle which Marlborough wished to fight. Both at home and abroad the fortunes of the Grand Allies

sank to a low ebb in the winter of 1703. Queen Anne here rose to her greatest height. "I will never forsake," she wrote to Sarah, "your dear self, Mr Freeman [Marlborough], nor Mr Montgomery [Godolphin]." With this support Marlborough during the winter months planned the supreme stroke of strategy which turned the whole fortune of the war. But before he could proceed to the Continent it was essential to reconstitute the government of the High Tories. Rochester was already dismissed and Nottingham was soon to go. The combination became Marlborough, Godolphin, and Harley, with the Queen and Sarah as before.

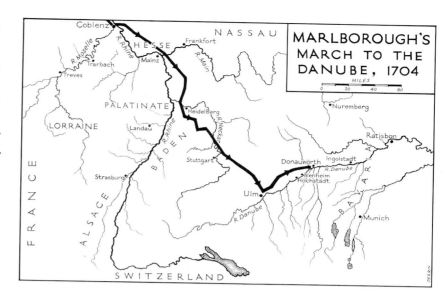

The annals of the British Army contain no more heroic episode than Marlborough's march from the North Sea to the Danube. Here for the first time began that splendid comradeship of the Duke and Eugene which for seven years continued without jealousy or defeat. The twin captains—"one soul in two bodies" as they were described—fell upon the French and Bavarian armies at Höchstädt, on the Danube, early in the morning of August 13. The battle was fought with the greatest fury on both sides. Eugene commanded the right and Marlborough the left and centre. The English attack upon the village of Blindheim—or Blenheim, as it has been called in history—was repulsed, and for several hours the issue hung in the balance; but Marlborough, as dusk fell on this memorable day, was able to write his famous letter to his wife: "I have not time to say more, but to beg you will give my duty to the Queen, and let her know her army has had a glorious victory."

The victory of Blenheim almost destroyed the French and Bavarian armies on the Danube. Over forty thousand men were killed, wounded, captured, or dispersed. Ulm surrendered after a brief siege, and Marlborough marched rapidly westward to the angle of the Rhine, where he was soon able to concentrate nearly a hundred thousand men. Finally, unwearied by these superb exertions,

the Duke marched during October from the Rhine to the Moselle, where he closed a campaign ever a classic model of war by the capture of Treves and Trarbach. The whole force of the Grand Alliance was revived and consolidated. England rose with Marlborough to the summit, and the Islanders, who had never known such a triumph since Crécy and Agincourt, four centuries earlier, yielded themselves to transports of joy. The same year had seen remarkable successes at sea. In May a powerful Anglo-Dutch fleet under Admiral Rooke entered the Mediterranean. Reinforced by a squadron under Sir Cloudesley Shovell, Rooke turned his attention in July to the Rock of Gibraltar.

Prince Eugene of Savoy. MANSELL COLLECTION

The Battle of Vigo Bay, October 12, 1702. The 80-gun Torbay *sails in to break the boom and lead the fleet into the bay, while in the foreground Lord Ormonde and his soldiers land to attack the fort from the rear. Painting by Luolf Bakhuizen.* NATIONAL MARITIME MUSEUM

After bombardment the Rock was taken on August 4, in the same month as Blenheim, by a combined assault, led on land by Prince George of Hesse-Darmstadt.

Just as the brilliant campaign of 1702 was succeeded by the disappointments of 1703, so the grand recovery of 1704 gave place to disunity in 1705. The Duke, unsupported, was forced to abandon his plan of fighting a decisive battle at the head of a hundred thousand men and advancing towards Paris. The triumph of Blenheim seemed overclouded.

Wearied with the difficulties of co-operating with the Dutch and with the Princes of the Rhine, Marlborough planned through the winter an even more daring repetition of his 'march to the Danube in 1704. He schemed to march across Europe with about twenty-five thousand British and British-paid troops by Coblenz, Stuttgart, and Ulm, through the passes of the Alps, to join Eugene in Northern Italy. There the two great captains would strike into France from the south. But the earliest events of the campaign of 1706 destroyed the Italian project. The key fortress of Landau was threatened. Marlborough's hopes were dashed. It was with

Plan of the Battle of Blenheim, 1703, by Thomas Brodrick. (See also the engraving by Huchtenburg, below.) BRITISH MUSEUM

The Battle of Blenheim, an engraving by J. van Huchtenburg. (See also the plan by Thomas Brodrick, above.) MANSELL COLLECTION

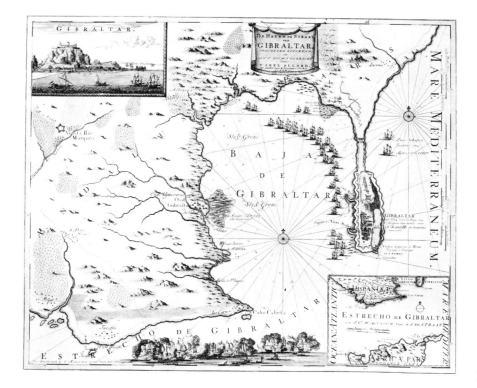

loss of less than five thousand men, destroyed and defeated his opponents with great slaughter and thousands of captives.

The consequences of Ramillies were even more spectacular than those which had followed Blenheim. If, as was said, Blenheim had saved Vienna, Ramillies conquered Belgium. These immense successes were enhanced by the victories of Prince Eugene in Northern Italy. At the same time in Spain the Allies had achieved much to their credit and come near to a striking success. The Earl of Galway, assisted by a Portuguese army two or three times the size of his own small force of about five thousand British and Dutch, reached the Spanish capital from Portugal in June. The "Year of Victory", as it was called in London, may close on this.

Britain's military prowess and the sense of the Island being at the head of mighty

melancholy thoughts that he began his most brilliant campaign. Fortune, whom Marlborough had so ruefully but sternly dismissed, returned importunate, bearing her most dazzling gift.

Louis XIV had convinced himself that a defensive war could not be maintained against such an opponent. At dawn on May 23 the two armies were in presence near the village of Ramillies. Marlborough, having deployed, about noon began a heavy but feigned attack upon the French right with the British troops. Availing himself of the undulations of the ground, he hurled the whole mass of the Dutch, British, and Danish cavalry, over twenty-five thousand strong, upon the finest cavalry of France. After furious fighting, in which forty thousand horsemen were engaged, he broke the French line, drove their right from the field, and compromised their centre. His main infantry now broke attack upon the village of Ramillies, while his victorious cavalry, forming at right angles to the original front, swept along the whole rear of the French line. All the Allied troops now advanced, and the French army fled from the field in utter ruin. In this masterpiece of war, fought between armies almost exactly equal in strength and quality, the military genius of the English General, with a

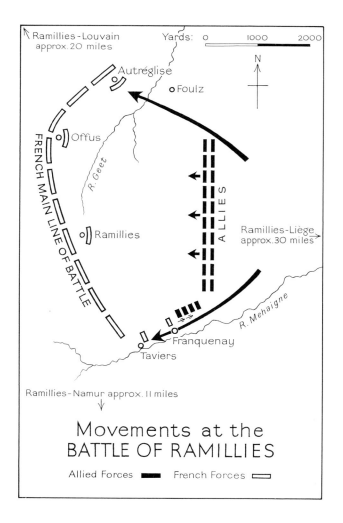

Movements at the BATTLE OF RAMILLIES

Allied Forces ▬▬▬   French Forces ▭▭▭

Europe now bore more lasting fruit. At last England was prepared to show some financial generosity to the Scots, and they in turn were willing to accept the Hanoverian succession. The Act of Union was finally passed in 1707, and in spite of some friction was generally accepted. The Union has grown in strength the longer it has lasted.

About this time Sarah's relations with the Queen entered on a perilous phase. She had brought a poor relation, Abigail Hill, into the Queen's life as a "dresser" or lady's maid. Abigail, by the beginning of 1707, had acquired an influence of her own with the Queen destined to deflect the course of European history. Abigail was a cousin of Sunderland's. She was at the same time a cousin of Harley's. Harley was much disconcerted by the arrival of the Whig Sunderland in the Cabinet. Anne loathed the Whigs from the bottom of her heart, but her Ministers could not see how it was possible to carry on the war without the Whigs and with only half the Tory Party at their back. One day a gardener handed Harley a secret letter from the Queen. She appealed for his help. Forthwith he set himself to plan an alternative Government based on the favour of the Queen, comprising Tories and moderate Whigs and sheltered by the renown and, he hoped, the services of Marlborough.

Everything went wrong in 1707. Marlborough's design was that Eugene should debouch from Italy into France and capture Toulon. Meanwhile, Marlborough faced and held the superior forces of Marshal Vendôme in a holding campaign in the North. The campaign in the North reduced itself to stalemate. The great enterprise against Toulon, to which Marlborough had subordinated all other interests, ended in failure. The French concentrated powerful forces not only to defend but to relieve Toulon. After several costly assaults the siege failed. Great misfortunes happened in Spain. A bloody defeat

was sustained at Almanza by the Allies, and the whole Spanish scene, so nearly triumphant in 1706, was now completely reversed.

Marlborough returned from these tribulations to a furious party storm in England. Harley's designs were now apparent, and his strength nourished itself upon the military misfortunes. Marlborough and Godolphin together resolved to drive him from the Cabinet. But a true Stuart and daughter of

Her Majesties
MOST GRACIOUS
SPEECH
To both Houses of
PARLIAMENT

My Lords and Gentlemen.

IT is with the greatest satisfaction, that I have given my assent to a Bill, for the Uniting *England* and *Scotland* into one Kingdom.

I consider this UNION as a Matter of the greatest Importance to the Wealth, Strength and Safety of the whole Island; And at the same time, as a Work of so much Difficulty and Nicety, in its own nature; That till now, all Attempts, which have been made toward it, in the course of above 100 Years have proved ineffectual: And therefore I make no doubt, but it will be remembred and spoke of hereafter, to the Honour of those who have been instrumental in bringing it to such a happy Conclusion.

I desire and expect from all my Subjects of both Nations, that from henceforth, they act with all possible Respect and Kindness to one another, That so it may appear to all the World, they have Hearts disposed to become one People.

This will be a great pleasure to Me, and will make us all quickly sensible of the good effect of this UNION.

And I cannot but look upon it as a particular Happiness, That in my Reign so full a Provision is made, for the Peace and Quiet of my People, and for the Security of Our Religion, by so firm an Establishment of the Protestant Succession, throughout *Great-Brittain:*

Gentlemen of the House of Commons,

I have this occasion to remind you of making effectual Provision for the Payment of the *Equivalent* to *Scotland,* within the time appointed by this Act; And I am perswaded you'll show as much readiness in this particular, as you have done in all the other parts of this great Work.

My Lords and Gentlemen.

The Season of the Year being now pretty far advanced, I hope you will continue the same Zeal which has appeared throughout this Session, in dispatching what yet remains unfinished of the Publick Business before you.

March 6. 1707.

Edinburgh, Printed by the Heirs and Successors of Andrew Anderson, Printer to the Queens most Excellent Majesty 1707.

The Battle of Oudenarde, from a tapestry at Blenheim Palace. COURTESY: HIS GRACE THE DUKE OF MARLBOROUGH

MONTES HANNONIÆ

The Battle of Malplaquet, from a tapestry at Blenheim Palace. COURTESY: HIS GRACE THE DUKE OF MARLBOROUGH

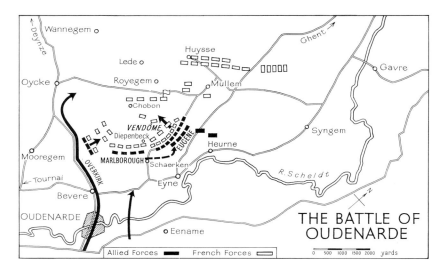

James II would not let Harley go. He advised the Queen to accept his resignation. With him went Henry St John, whom Marlborough had regarded almost as an adopted son.

This struggle gave Marlborough a final lease of power. It was on these perilous foundations that he embarked upon the campaign of 1708. For the only time in the Duke's career he bent and bowed under the convergent strains at home and in the field. Eugene, arriving with only a cavalry escort, found him near Brussels in the deepest depression. Eugene sustained his comrade. Marlborough rose from his sick-bed, mounted his horse, and the Army was set in motion. As the Allies poured across the Scheldt the French army wheeled to their left to face them. The Battle of Oudenarde was in every aspect modern. It more nearly resembled Tannenberg in 1914 than any great action of the eighteenth century. Marlborough, giving Eugene command of the right wing, held the centre at heavy odds himself while the rest of the Army was prolonging its line to the left. This long left arm reached out continually, and the battle front flared and flamed as it grew. The operation of crossing the river corps by corps in the face of an army equal in strength was judged most hazardous by the military opinion of that age of strife. The pace of the battle and its changes prevented all set arrangement. The French fought desperately but without any concerted plan, and a large part of their army was never

engaged. At length the Dutch, under the veteran Overkirk, traversed the Oudenarde bridges and swung round upon the heights to the north. At the same time Eugene broke through on the right. The opposite wings of the Allies almost met. In furious anger and consternation Vendôme ordered a retreat on Ghent. A quarter of his army was destroyed or dispersed. The Allies had recovered the initiative. It was resolved to attack Lille, the strongest fortress of France. The siege of Lille was not only the largest but the most complicated operation of its kind known to the eighteenth century. In many ways it is unique in military annals. Marshal Boufflers with fifteen thousand men defended the city. Eugene conducted the siege, and Marlborough with the covering army held off the largely superior forces which, both from the neighbourhood of Ghent and from France itself, sought to relieve the city or sever the communications of the besiegers. Sixteen thousand horses drew Marlborough's siege-trains from Brussels to the trenches. The heavy batteries played upon the town, and a succession of bloody assaults was delivered week after week upon the breaches. The citadel of Lille fell in December. Bruges was recaptured at the end of December, and Ghent in the first days of January. At the same time the capture of Minorca, with its fine harbour at Mahon, gave to the English Navy at last a secure, permanent base in the Mediterranean. The power of France was broken. The Great King was humbled.

Meanwhile, in England the Whigs had at last achieved their long purpose. They drove the remaining Tories from the Cabinet, and installed a single-party administration, above which still sat the two super-Ministers, Marlborough and Godolphin. The Whigs, ardent, efficient masters of the Parliamentary arts, arrived in power at the very moment when their energy and war spirit were least needed. When we look upon the long years of terror and spoliation to which the Princes of the Grand Alliance had been subjected by Louis XIV great allowances must be made for their suspicions in the hour of victory. Nevertheless, the offers now made by France were so ample as to satisfy all reasonable demands of the Allies. In Spain alone did French fortunes prosper. The negotiations broke on the article that Louis must himself become responsible for expelling his grandson from Spain on the pain of having the Allies renew the war against him from the bases and fortresses he was to surrender in guarantee. The drums beat in the Allied camps, and the greatest armies those war-worn times had seen rolled forward to the campaign of 1709 and the carnage of Malplaquet.

Justice quite suddenly gathered up her trappings and quitted one cause for the other. From this moment France, and to a lesser degree Spain, presented national fronts against foreign inroad and overlordship. By swift movements Marlborough and Eugene invested Mons, and, advancing south of it, found themselves confronted by Marshal Villars in the gap between the woods in which the village of Malplaquet stands, almost along the line of the present French Frontier. On September 11 a hundred and ten thousand Allied troops assaulted the entrenchments, defended by about ninety thousand French. Marlborough in the main repeated the tactics of Blenheim. At length the French cavalry were mastered. Their infantry were already in retreat. The Allies had lost over twenty thousand men, and the French two-thirds as many. There were hardly any prisoners. Indeed Malplaquet, the largest and bloodiest battle of the eighteenth century, was surpassed only by Napoleon's barren victory at Borodino a hundred years later.

The great armies faced one another for the campaign of 1710. Their actual numbers were larger than ever before, but Marlborough and Eugene could not or did not bring Villars to battle. While Marlborough was at these toils the political crisis of Queen Anne's reign moved steadily to its climax. Dr Sacheverell, a High Church divine, delivered a sermon in London in violent attack upon the government, the Whigs, and the Lord Treasurer. With great unwisdom the government ordered a State prosecution in the

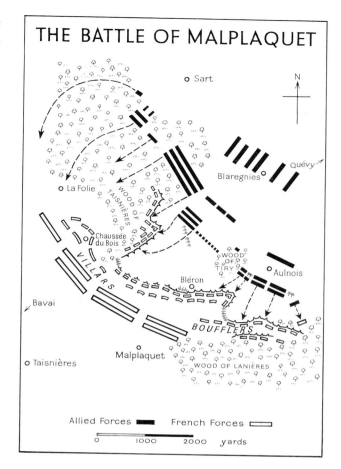

THE BATTLE OF MALPLAQUET

Allied Forces ■■■ French Forces ☐☐☐

0   1000   2000   yards

form of an impeachment. By narrow majorities nominal penalties were inflicted upon Sacheverell. He became the hero of the hour. Queen Anne, advised by Harley, now felt strong enough to take her revenge for what she considered the insult inflicted on her by the Whig intrusion into her Council. Whig Ministers were relieved of office. Harley formed a predominantly Tory government, and at his side Henry St John became Secretary of State. The General Election, aptly launched, produced a substantial Tory majority in the House of Commons.

Yet Marlborough remained the most precious possession of the hostile government and vengeful Queen. Terms were made between the Tory Ministers and Marlborough for the proper upkeep of the armies at the Front, and the Captain-General for the tenth year in succession took the field. During the winter Villars had constructed an enormous system of entrenchments and inundations stretching from the sea through the fortress of Arras and Bouchain to Maubeuge, on the

Sambre. He called these lines "Ne Plus Ultra". Marlborough prepared to pierce this formidable barrier. By subtle arts and stratagems he convinced Villars that he intended to make another frontal attack on the scale of Malplaquet south of Arras. On August 4 the Duke in person conducted a reconnaissance along the whole of Villars's front. Villars was filled with hope.

At length tattoo beat and darkness fell. Orders came to strike tents and stand to arms. Soon staff officers arrived to guide the four columns, and in less than half an hour the whole army was on the march to the left. All through the moonlit night they marched eastward. They traversed those broad undulations between the Vimy Ridge and Arras which two centuries later were to be dyed with British and Canadian blood. A sense of excitement filled the troops. It was not after all to be a bloody battle. Before five o'clock on the morning of the 5th they reached the Scarpe near Vitry. Here the Army found a series of pontoon bridges already laid, and as the light grew they saw the long columns of their artillery now marching with them. Marlborough sent his aides-de-camp and staff officers down the whole length of the marching columns with orders to explain to the officers and soldiers of every regiment what he was doing and what had happened, and to tell them that all now depended upon their marching qualities. "My Lord Duke wishes the infantry to step out." As the light broadened and the day advanced the troops could see upon their right, across the marshes and streams of the Sensée, that the French were moving parallel to them within half cannon-shot. But they also saw that the head of the French horse was only abreast of the Allied foot. In the result Marlborough formed a front beyond the lines, and cast his siege-grip on the fortress of Bouchain. The forcing of the "Ne Plus Ultra" lines and the siege and capture of Bouchain were judged by Europe to be outstanding manifestations of the military art. There is no finer example of Marlborough's skill. For ten years he had led the armies of the Grand Alliance, and during all that period he never fought a battle he did not win or besieged a town he did not take. Nothing like this exists in the annals of war.

It was now impossible to conceal any longer the secret peace negotiations which had all this while been in progress. The Tory leaders were sure they could carry the peace if Marlborough would support it. The Duke, who was in close association with the Elector George of Hanover, the heir to the throne, and still enjoyed the support of the King of Prussia and the Princes of the Grand Alliance, would not agree to a separate peace in any circumstances. The Whigs used their majority in the House of Lords. But Harley, strong in the support of the House of Commons, and using to the full the favour of the Queen, met this assault with a decisive rejoinder. He loosed charges of peculation upon Marlborough, and procured from the Queen an extraordinary creation of twelve peers to override the adverse majority in the Lords. Marlborough was dismissed from all his offices and exposed to the censure of the House of Commons.

England was now riven in twain upon the issue of peace. Harley and St John could not avoid the campaign of 1712. They appointed the Duke of Ormonde, the splendid magnifico who had failed at Cadiz, to the command. St John sent secret restraining orders to Ormonde not to "partake in any siege in a way to hazard a battle"—as if such tactics were possible. Upon a dark day the British Army, hitherto the most forward in the Allied cause and admired by all, marched away from the camp of the Allies in bitter humiliation and amid the curses of their old comrades. Villars, advancing rapidly, fell upon Eugene's magazines at Denain and inflicted upon him a cruel defeat in which many of his troops were driven into the Scheldt and drowned. After these shattering defeats all the States of the Grand Alliance were compelled to make peace on the best terms possible.

What is called the Treaty of Utrecht was in fact a series of separate agreements between individual Allied States with France

The House of Commons in session, 1710, Sir Richard Onslow in the Speaker's chair. From a painting by Peter Tillemans in the Houses of Parliament. The Commons met in St Stephen's Chapel, Westminster, from 1547 until its destruction by fire in 1834. See also the picture of Pitt addressing the Commons in Chapter Nine. REPRODUCED BY KIND PERMISSION OF THE RT HON. THE SPEAKER

and with Spain. In the forefront stood the fact that the Duke of Anjou, recognised as Philip V, held Spain and the Indies, thus flouting the unreasonable declaration to which the English Parliament had so long adhered. With this out of the way the British Government gained their special terms; the French Court recognised the Protestant succession in Britain, and agreed to expel the Pretender from France, to demolish the fortifications of Dunkirk, and to cede various territories in North America and the West Indies, to wit, Hudson Bay, Newfoundland, Nova Scotia, which had been captured by an expedition from Massachusetts, and St Christopher. With Spain the terms were that England should hold Minorca and Gibraltar, thus securing to her, while she remained the chief sea-Power, the entry and control of the Mediterranean. Commercial advantages, one day to provoke another war, were obtained in Spanish South America, and in particular the Asiento, or the sole right for thirty years to import African Negroes as slaves into the New World.

Marlborough was so much pursued by the Tory Party and harassed by the State prosecutions against him for his alleged peculation that at the end of 1712 he left the country and lived in self-imposed exile in Holland and Germany till the end of the reign. The final phase of the Tory triumph was squalid.

EUROPE AFTER THE TREATY OF UTRECHT 1713
AUSTRIAN POSSESSIONS

St John, raised to the peerage as Viscount Bolingbroke, became involved in a mortal quarrel with Harley, Earl of Oxford. Anne was now broken with gout and other ailments. No one knows whether she wished to make her half-brother, the Pretender, her heir or not. The Whigs, strong in the Act of Succession and in the Protestant resolve of the nation, prepared openly to take arms against a Jacobite restoration. The Elector of Hanover, supported by the Dutch and aided by Marlborough, gathered the forces to repeat the descent of William of Orange. The declaration of the "Pretended Prince of Wales" that he would never abandon the Roman Catholic faith made his imposition upon the British throne impracticable.

Many accounts converge upon the conclusion that the final scene in the long duel between Oxford and Bolingbroke at the Cabinet Council of July 27, 1714 brought about the death of Queen Anne. Bolingbroke remained master of the field and of the day— but only for two days. The Privy Council pressed upon the death-bed of the Queen; they urged her to give to Lord Shrewsbury the White Staff of Lord Treasurer, which Oxford had delivered. With fleeting strength Anne, guided by the Lord Chancellor, passed the symbol to him, and then sank into a coma. Vigorous measures were taken to ensure the Hanoverian succession. When Queen Anne breathed her last at half past seven on August 1 it was certain that there would be no Popery, no disputed succession, no French bayonets, no civil war.

Thus ended one of the greatest reigns in English history. It had been rendered glorious by Marlborough's victories and guidance. The Union and the greatness of the Island had been established. The power of France to dominate Europe was broken, and only Napoleon could revive it. The last of the Stuart sovereigns had presided over a wonderful expansion of British national strength, and in spite of the moral and physical failures of her closing years she deserved to bear in history the title of "the Good Queen Anne".

CHAPTER EIGHT

The First British Empire

Duric the late summer of 1714 all England awaited the coming of King George I. On September 18 he landed at Greenwich. Here on English soil stood an unprepossessing figure, an obstinate and humdrum German martinet with dull brains and coarse tastes. Yet the rigidity of his mind was relieved by a slow shrewdness and a brooding common sense. He owed his Crown to the luck of circumstance, but he never let it slip from his grasp.

Foremost among those now in acute anxiety was Bolingbroke. His fall was relentless and rapid. The first Parliament of the new reign demanded his impeachment. A few months later he took the plunge and became Secretary of State to the Pretender. His great rival Robert Harley, Earl of Oxford, was meanwhile imprisoned in the Tower of London. No condign punishment was inflicted on him; but when he emerged from the Tower he was a broken man. George I had come peacefully to the throne. The Tory Party was shattered, and England settled down, grumbling but safe, under the long rule of Whiggism. A new generation of statesmen—Walpole, Stanhope, Carteret, and Townshend—were to ensure the peaceful transition from the age of Anne to the age of the Georges.

On September 6 the Earl of Mar raised the Jacobite standard at Perth. But the Whig Ministers, though nervous, took good precautions. In the North of England a small band of gentry, led by Lord Derwentwater, rose in support of the Stuarts. The Duke of Marlborough was consulted by the military authorities. "You will beat them", he said,

King George I (1660–1727), studio of Kneller. NATIONAL PORTRAIT GALLERY

marking Preston with his thumbnail on the map, "there." And on November 13 beaten there they were. The Government forces in Scotland, led by the Whig Duke of Argyll, met the Jacobite army at Sheriffmuir on the same day. The battle was indecisive, but was

Paragraphs from the Daily Courant, *September 5, 1720.* BRITISH MUSEUM

Sir Robert Walpole, from a contemporary cartoon. BRITISH MUSEUM

In 1710 a Tory Ministry had granted a charter to a company trading with the South Seas, and had arranged for it to take over part of the National Debt. Financial speculation was encouraged. By June 1721 the South Sea stock stood at 1050. At every coffee-house in London men and women were investing their savings in any enterprise that would take their money. There was no limit to the credulity of the public. Promoters invited subscriptions for making salt water fresh, for constructing a wheel of perpetual motion, for importing large jackasses from Spain to improve the breed of English mules, and the boldest of all was the advertisement for "a company for carrying on an undertaking of Great Advantage, but no one to know what it is". The Government took alarm, and the process of suppressing these minor companies began. The South Sea Company was only too anxious to exterminate its rivals, but the pricking of the minor bubbles quickened and precipitated a slump. The brief hour of dreamed-of riches closed in wide-eyed misery. Bringing order to the chaos that remained was the first task of Britain's first Prime Minister.

One man only amid the crash and panic of 1721 could preserve the Whig monopoly. He was Robert Walpole, now established as the greatest master of figures of his generation. Walpole, on becoming head of the Government, immediately turned to financial reconstruction. The political crisis was quickly ended. A Jacobite plot was swiftly and silently suppressed. At the same time

followed by desertion and discouragement in the Jacobite ranks. The collapse was followed by a batch of treason trials and about thirty executions. Despite the incompetence of the rising, the Government perceived and feared the unorganised opposition throughout the country to the new régime. A Septennial Act prolonged the life of the existing House of Commons for another four years, and decreed septennial Parliaments henceforth. This was the boldest and most complete assertion of Parliamentary sovereignty that England had yet seen.

Political power was henceforth founded on influence: in the dispensation of Crown patronage; stars, sinecures, pensions; the agile use of the Secret Service fund; jobs in the Customs for humble dependants; commissions or Church livings for younger sons. Thus the Whigs established control of the Parliamentary machine.

Walpole did not prevent the pardon and return of Bolingbroke.

Walpole's object was to stabilise the Hanoverian régime and the power of the Whig Party within a generation. Taxation was low; the land tax, which was anxiously watched by the Tory squires, was reduced by economy to one shilling. The National Debt decreased steadily, and an overhaul of the tariff and the reduction of many irksome duties stimulated and expanded trade. But men remembered the great age that had passed and scorned the drab days of George I. A policy of security, prosperity, and peace made small appeal to their hearts, and many were ready to attack the degeneration of politics at home and the futility of England abroad.

A high-poised if not sagacious or successful opposition to Walpole persisted throughout the twenty-one years of his administration. It drew its force from the association of those Whigs who either disliked his policy or were estranged by exclusion from office with the Tories in the shades. The younger Whigs, like William Pulteney and John Carteret, were too clever to be allowed to shine in Walpole's orbit. Nor could they weaken his hold on the House of Commons while he exercised the patronage of the Crown. The Parliamentary Opposition gathered round the Prince of Wales. It was the Hanoverian family tradition that father and son should be on the worst of terms, and the future George II was no exception. But for the strong support of Caroline, Princess of Wales, Walpole would have been in serious danger. Indeed, on the accession of George II in 1727 he suffered a brief eclipse. The new King dismissed him. But, secure in the confidence of Queen Caroline, Walpole returned to office and entrenched himself more firmly than before.

He meant to do as little as possible: to keep the peace, to stay in office, to juggle with men, to see the years roll by. But others responded to more lively themes. Walpole was forced to quarrel. His own brother-in-law, Charles Townshend, was dismissed at the end of 1729. He then entered into close co-operation with

King George II (1683–1760), portrait after Kneller. NATIONAL PORTRAIT GALLERY

a man of limited intelligence and fussy nature, but of vast territorial and electoral wealth— Thomas Pelham Holles, Duke of Newcastle. Newcastle became Secretary of State because, as Walpole said, he himself "had experienced the trouble that a man of parts gave in that office". However, in 1733 a storm broke. Walpole proposed an excise on wines and tobacco, to be gathered by Revenue officers in place of a duty at the ports. Every weapon at their command was used by the Opposition. Defeated by one of the most unscrupulous campaigns in English history,

219

Walpole withdrew his Excise reform. The violence of his critics recoiled upon themselves, and the Opposition snatched no permanent advantage. At long last the Opposition discerned the foundation of Walpole's ascendancy, namely, the avoidance of any controversy which might stir the country as a whole. The country was bored. It rejected a squalid, peaceful prosperity. The crack came from a series of incidents in Spanish America.

Such was the inefficiency of Spanish administration that it was easy to run contraband cargoes of Negroes in defiance of what was called the "Asiento contract", and the illicit trade grew steadily in the years of peace. But when the Spanish Government at last began to reorganise and extend its colonial government English ships trading unlawfully in the Spanish seas were stopped and searched by the Spanish coastguards. Walpole and Newcastle hoped for a peaceful settlement. The preliminary Convention of Prado was settled and negotiated at Madrid in January 1739. But the Opposition would have none of it. On October 19, 1739, war was declared. By sure degrees, in the confusion and mismanagement which followed, Walpole's power, as he had foreseen, slipped from him. The one success, the capture of Portobello, on the isthmus of Panama, was achieved by Admiral Vernon, the hero of the Opposition. Meanwhile, the tide of national feeling ran high.

In February 1741 an Opposition Member, Samuel Sandys, proposed an address to the King for the dismissal of Walpole. To the amazement of all, the Jacobites voted for him. But under the Septennial Act elections were due. The Prince of Wales spent lavishly in buying up seats, and his campaign, managed by Thomas Pitt, brother of William, brought twenty-seven Cornish seats over to the Opposition. The electoral influence of the Scottish earls counted against Walpole, and when the Members returned to Westminster his Government was defeated on an election petition (contested returns were in those days decided by the House on purely party lines)

and resigned. It was February 1742. He had kept England at peace for nearly twenty years. Now he went to the House of Lords as Earl of Orford. He was the first Chief Minister to reside at Number Ten, Downing Street. The sovereign had ceased after 1714 to preside in person over the Cabinet, save on exceptional occasions—a most significant event, though it was only the result of an accident. Walpole had created for himself a dominating position in this vital executive committee, now deprived of its titular chairman. But he founded no convention of collective Ministerial responsibility. One of the charges against him after his fall was that he had sought to become "sole and Prime Minister".

The war between Britain and Spain, which the Opposition had forced upon Walpole, was soon merged in a general European struggle. In October 1740 the Habsburg Emperor Charles VI died, leaving his broad domains, though not his Imperial title, to his daughter Maria Theresa. East of the Elbe the rising kingdom of Prussia acquired a new ruler. Frederick II, later called the Great, ascended his father's throne. He attacked and seized the Austrian province of Silesia, which lay to the south of his own territories. France, ever jealous of the Habsburgs, encouraged and supported him.

In London, after Walpole's fall, King George's Government was managed by Henry Pelham, First Lord of the Treasury, and his brother, the Duke of Newcastle, long a Secretary of State. They were skilled in party manoeuvre, but inexpert in the handling of foreign or military affairs. George II turned for help and advice to the Pelhams' rival, Lord Carteret. Carteret wanted Hanover and England to preserve and promote a balance of power in Europe. To meet the combination of France, Spain, and Frederick the Great, he negotiated a treaty with Maria Theresa and renewed the traditional agreements with the Dutch. Carteret, to his misfortune, lacked both the personal position and the political following to put his decisions to good effect. Foremost among his critics was William Pitt, Member for the ancient but uninhabited borough of Old Sarum. Pitt made a withering speech against the subsidies proposed for raising Hanoverian troops, which gained him the lasting displeasure of the King. These attacks on Carteret were not unwelcome to Pelham and Newcastle.

Thirty thousand British troops, under the command of one of Marlborough's old officers, the Earl of Stair, fought on the Continent. In the spring of 1743 the King himself, accompanied by his younger son, the Duke of Cumberland, left England to take part in the campaign. The Battle of Dettingen raised a brief enthusiasm in London, but opinion slowly hardened against the continuance of a major European war. At the end of 1744 Carteret, now Lord Granville, was driven from office.

For the campaign of 1745 the King made Cumberland Captain-General of the forces on the Continent. He had to face the most celebrated soldier of the day, Marshal Saxe. The French army concentrated against the barrier fortress line, the familiar battleground of Marlborough's wars, now held by the Dutch. Having masked Tournai, Saxe took up a strong position centring upon the village of Fontenoy, near the Mons road. Cumberland drew up his army in battle order, and marched it under fire to within fifty paces of the French army. He was outnumbered by nearly two to one. Lieutenant-Colonel Lord Charles Hey, of the First (Grenadier) Guards, stepped from the front ranks, took out a flask, raised it in salute to the French Household troops, and declared, "We are the English Guards, and hope you will stand till we come up to you, and not swim the Scheldt as you did the Main at Dettingen." Cheers rang out from both sides. The English advanced, and at thirty paces the French fired. The murderous fusillade did not halt the Allied infantry, and they drove the enemy from their positions. For hours the French cavalry tried to break the Allied columns, and, watching the Irish Brigade of the French army sweeping into action, Cumberland exclaimed, "God's curse on the laws that made those men our enemies." It is a more generous remark than is usually recorded of him.

The set battle-pieces of Dettingen and Fontenoy were perhaps useless, but certainly the most creditable engagements in which English troops took part in the middle eighteenth century. At any rate England played no further part in the War of the Austrian Succession. In October 1745 Cumberland withdrew his men to meet the Young Pretender's invasion of England, and our Continental allies were beaten on every front. The only good news came from across the Atlantic. English colonists, supported by a naval squadron, captured the strongest French fortress in the New World, Louisburg, on Cape Breton.

The Pelham régime, built up upon the support of Whig family groups, was artificial, but it had its merits. Henry Pelham was a good administrator, economical and efficient, but he was a lesser Walpole faced with a major European war. Newcastle, in his own whimsical way, looked upon the work of government as the duty of his class, but he had no clear ideas on how to discharge it. For ten years the Pelham brothers made constant and frantic efforts to create a stable Government. Fumbling and out of date in Europe, and unmindful of the great future overseas, the Broad-bottomed Administration of the 1740's was a painful affair.

In the inaccessible Highlands, where the writ of English government hardly ran, there was a persistent loyalty to the House of Stuart and the Jacobite cause. After the failure of the rising in 1715 the Jacobites had stayed quiet, but once England was involved in war upon the Continent their activities revived. The Old Pretender was now living in retirement, and his son, Prince Charles Edward, was the darling of the impecunious exiles who clustered round him in Rome and Paris. Nothing daunted, he sailed from Nantes in June 1745 with a handful of followers and landed in the Western Isles of Scotland. Thus began one of the most audacious and irresponsible enterprises in British history.

Lieutenant-Colonel Lord Charles Hey of the First Guards, gives his salute at the Battle of Fontenoy. From a print, the property of the First or Grenadier Regiment of Foot Guards. COURTESY: THE OFFICER COMMANDING, THE GRENADIER GUARDS

Twelve hundred men under Lord George Murray raised the Jacobite standard at Glenfinnan. About three thousand Government troops gathered in the Lowlands under Sir John Cope. The rebels marched southwards; Prince Charles entered the palace at Holyrood, and Cope was met and routed on the battlefield of Prestonpans. By the end of September Charles was ruler of most of Scotland in the name of his father, "King James VIII"; but his triumph was fleeting. With five thousand men the Young Pretender crossed the Border. Plundering as they went, they marched due south, occupying Carlisle, Penrith, Lancaster, and Preston. The number of English adherents that came in was de-

pressingly small. Many Highlanders deserted and returned home during the southward march. At Derby Charles gave the signal to retreat. Murray showed great skill in the withdrawal, and in rearguard actions his troops were invariably successful. They turned and mauled their pursuers at Falkirk. But with Teutonic thoroughness the Duke of Cumberland concentrated the English armies for a decision, and in April 1746 on Culloden Moor the last chances of a Stuart restoration were swept into the past for ever. Charles Edward escaped over the moors with a few faithful servants. Disguised as a woman, he was smuggled across to the island of Skye by that heroine of romance, Flora Macdonald.

Thence he sailed for the Continent, to drink out his life in perpetual exile.

In April 1746 Pitt became Paymaster of the Forces, an office of immense emolument in time of war. Pitt refused to accept a penny beyond his official salary. A born actor, by this gesture he caught the eye of the people, and held it as no statesman had held it before

him. The dismal war on the Continent ended with the Treaty of Aix-la-Chapelle in 1748. Nothing was settled between Britain and France by this peace. Pitt now spent many hours in earnest discussion with Newcastle on the need for a new foreign policy. The French menace obsessed his mind. Pitt fretted, impotent to control or to criticise the policy of the administration of which he was a member. But in the interlude of peace between 1748 and 1754 the issues were too confused and the intrigues too virulent for a dramatic move. Hope of a great political career seemed at an end for William Pitt. After a great speech in the Commons he was dismissed from the Pay Office in November 1755. Two months later a diplomatic revolution took place towards which the four main Powers of Europe had for some time been groping. A convention was signed between Britain and Prussia, shortly followed by a treaty between the French and the Austrians. The mismanagement of the early years of the struggle, which had been precipitated by the bellicose Cumberland, gave Pitt his chance. The loss of the island of Minorca raised a national outcry. The Government

The Battle of Culloden, April 16, 1746, from a contemporary print. The Scots, held in their frontal assault on the English infantry, were then attacked on both flanks by the English cavalry (Kerr and Cobham's Dragoons are seen passing through a breach made for them in a covering wall) and put to rout. In the foreground the Duke of Cumberland directs his commanders.
BRITISH MUSEUM

shifted the blame on to Admiral Byng, whose ill-equipped fleet had failed to relieve the Minorca garrison. By one of the most scandalous evasions of responsibility that an English Government has ever perpetrated Byng was shot for cowardice upon the quarterdeck of his flagship. Pitt pleaded for him with the King. "The House of Commons, Sir, is inclined to mercy." "You have taught me", the King replied, "to look for the sense of my people elsewhere than in the House of Commons."

Pitt's hour had almost come.

We must now survey the scene presented by the American colonies, which had been quietly and steadily growing for the past hundred and fifty years, often on the initiative of the men on the spot rather than by planned direction from London. English commerce was expanding. The Hudson's Bay Company, launched in 1669, had set up its first trading posts and was building up its influence in the northern territories of Canada. On the coasts of Newfoundland English fishermen had revivified the earliest colony of the Crown. On the American mainland the British occupation of the entire eastern seaboard was almost complete. The capture of New York and the settlement of New Jersey had joined in contiguity the two existing groups of colonies that lay to the north and south. Inland the State of Pennsylvania was beginning to take shape as an asylum for the persecuted of all countries under the guidance of its Quaker proprietor, William Penn. To the south the two Carolinas had been founded and named in honour of the King.

While distracted by the Civil War the Mother Country left them alone, and although Cromwell's Commonwealth asserted that Parliament was supreme over the whole of the English world its decree was never put into practice, and was swept away by the Restoration. But after 1660 the home Government had new and definite ideas. For the next fifty years successive English administrations tried to enforce the supremacy of the Crown in the American colonies and to

William Pitt the Elder, Earl of Chatham, after Brompton.
NATIONAL PORTRAIT GALLERY

strengthen royal power and patronage in the overseas possessions. The English Revolution of 1688 changed the whole position. Hitherto the colonies had regarded the Parliament in England as their ally against the Crown. But the time was to come when Parliament, victorious over the Crown in the constitutional struggles at home, would attempt to enforce its own sovereignty over America.

The early eighteenth century saw the foundation of the last of the Thirteen Colonies. The philanthropist James Oglethorpe had been painfully moved by the horrible condition of the small debtors in English prisons. After much thought he conceived the idea of allowing these people to emigrate to a new colony. The polyglot community, named Georgia, soon attracted ardent missionaries, and it was here that John Wesley began his ministering work. This colony was the last foundation of the Mother Country in the territories that were later to become the United States.

Emigration from England had now dwindled to a trickle, but new settlers arrived from other parts. Towards the end of the seventeenth century there had been an influx of Scottish-Irish refugees, whose industrial and commercial endeavours at home had been stifled by the legislation of the English Parliament. They formed a strong English-hating element in their new homes. Pennsylvania received a steady flow of immigrants from Germany, soon to number over two hundred thousand souls. Hard-working and prosperous Huguenots arrived from France in flight from religious persecution. There was a teeming diversity of human types. On the Western farms which bordered the Indian country were rugged pioneers and sturdy yeomen farmers, and in the New England colonies assertive merchants, lawyers, and squires, and the sons of traders.

From his office in Cleveland Row Pitt designed and won a war which extended from India in the East to America in the West. The whole struggle depended upon the energies of this one man. Whether Pitt possessed the strategic eye, whether the expeditions he launched were part of a considered combination, may be ques-

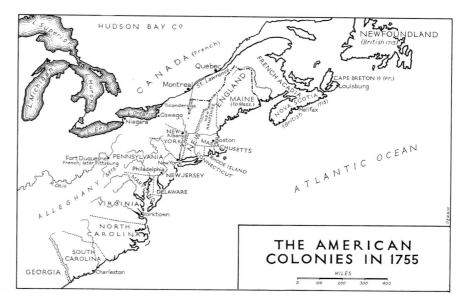

THE AMERICAN
COLONIES IN 1755

tioned. Now, as at all times, his policy was a projection on to a vast screen of his own aggressive, dominating personality. But Pitt's success was not immediate. In April 1757 he was dismissed by the King. Nevertheless, he had already made his mark with the nation. For three months there was no effective Government, though Pitt gave all the orders and did the day-to-day work. A stable war Ministry was not formed until June, but for the next four years Pitt was supreme.

The taking of Quebec, September 13, 1759, from a print based on a drawing by Captain Henry Smyth, aide-de-camp to General Wolfe. That face of the Heights of Abraham which was scaled by the first wave of the assaulting troops is indicated by the figures on the cliffs. BRITISH MUSEUM

Unless France were beaten in Europe as well as in the New World and in the East she would rise again. Both in North America and in Europe she was in the ascendant. At sea she was a formidable enemy. In India it seemed that if ever a European Power established itself on the ruins of the Mogul Empire its banner would be the lilies and not the cross of St George. On the Continent Britain had one ally, Frederick of Prussia, facing the combined power of Austria, Russia, and France. Never did a war open with darker prospects. Before the year was out it seemed as if Fortune, recognising her masters, was changing sides. Frederick, supported by the subsidies which Pitt had spent the eloquence of his youth in denouncing, routed the French at Rossbach and the Austrians at Leuthen.

So the great years opened, years for Pitt and his country of almost intoxicating glory. The French were swept out of Hanover; the Dutch, fishing in the murky waters of Oriental intrigue, were stopped by Clive and made to surrender their ships at Chinsura; Cape Breton was again taken, and the name of the "Great Commoner" stamped on the map at Pittsburg, Pennsylvania. France's two main fleets, in the Mediterranean and in the Channel, were separately defeated. Between these victories Wolfe had fallen at Quebec, leaving Amherst to complete the conquest of Canada, while Clive and Eyre Coote were uprooting the remnants of French power in India. Even more dazzling prizes seemed to be falling into British hands. Pitt proposed to conquer the Spanish Indies, West and East, and to seize the annual Treasure Fleet. But at this supreme moment in his career, when world peace and world security seemed within his grasp, the Cabinet declined to support him and he resigned.

Pitt's very success contributed to his fall. Just as Marlborough and Godolphin had been faced by a growing war-weariness after Malplaquet, so now Pitt, an isolated figure in his own Government, confronted an increasing dislike of the war after the great victories of 1759. His Imperial war policy had succeeded only too well, leaving him with the detested and costly subsidies to Prussia which he knew were essential to the final destruction of French power. In October 1760 George II died. He had never liked Pitt, but had learnt to respect his abilities. The temper of the new ruler was adverse. George III had very clear ideas of what he wanted and where he was going.

Pitt hoped that war with Spain would rouse the same popular upsurge as in 1739. His proposal for the declaration of war was put to the Cabinet. He found himself isolated. He had no choice but resignation. William Pitt ranks with Marlborough as the greatest Englishman in the century between 1689 and 1789. He was not the first English statesman to think in terms of a world policy and to broaden on to a world scale the political conceptions of William III. But he is the first great figure of British Imperialism.

Unsupported by the fame of Pitt, the Duke of Newcastle was an easy victim, and the administration slid easily into the hands of Lord Bute. His sole qualification for office, apart from great wealth and his command of the Scottish vote, was that he had been Groom of the Stole to the King's mother. For the first time since the assassination of the Duke of Buckingham the government of England was committed to a man with no political experience, and whose only connection with Parliament was that he had sat as a representative peer of Scotland for a short time twenty years before. Within three months of Pitt's resignation the Government were compelled to declare war on Spain. This led to further successes in the West Indies and elsewhere. These achievements were largely cast away. Britain's acquisitions under the terms of the Peace of Paris in 1763 were nevertheless considerable. In America she secured Canada, Nova Scotia, Cape Breton, and the adjoining islands, and the right to navigate the Mississippi, important for Red Indian trade. In the West Indies Grenada, St Vincent, Dominica, and Tobago were acquired. From Spain she received Florida. In Africa she kept Senegal. In India, as will be related, the East India Company preserved its extensive conquests, and although

Whitehall, looking towards Charing Cross, from Richmond House. A painting by Canaletto, circa 1746. The Holbein Gate, on the left, was the northern gate of two spanning King Street, which is now part of Whitehall. The Privy Gardens are in the foreground, and in the background can be seen the spire of St Martin-in-the-Fields. COURTESY: HIS GRACE THE DUKE OF RICHMOND AND GORDON; THE TRUSTEES OF THE GOODWOOD COLLECTION

their trading posts were returned the political ambitions of the French in the sub-continent were finally extinguished. In Europe Minorca was restored to England, and the fortifications of Dunkirk were at long last demolished.

Historians have taken a flattering view of a treaty which established Britain as an Imperial Power, but its strategic weakness has been smoothly overlooked. The naval power of France had been left untouched. Spain regained the West Indian port of Havana, which controlled the maritime strategy of the Caribbean. She also received back Manila, an important centre for the China trade. In Africa, in spite of Pitt's protests, France got back Goree—a base for privateers on the flank of the East Indian trade routes. Moreover, the treaty took no account of the interests of Frederick the Great. This ally was left to shift for himself. Vain was it that Pitt denounced the treaty and prophesied war.

"The peace was insecure, because it restored the enemy to her former greatness. The peace was inadequate, because the places gained were no equivalent for the places surrendered."

The accession of George III caused a profound change in English politics. In theory and in law the monarchy still retained a decisive influence and power in the making of policy, the choice of Ministers, the filling of offices, and the spending of money. Both George I and George II were aliens in language, outlook, upbringing, and sympathy; George III was, or thought he was, an Englishman born and bred. The times were opportune for a revival of the royal influence. In 1761 elections were held throughout England, in which Newcastle was not allowed to control all the royal patronage and many offices in the gift of the Crown were bestowed

229

King George III (1738–1820), by Gainsborough. REPRODUCED BY GRACIOUS PERMISSION OF HER MAJESTY THE QUEEN

on supporters of the new monarch. In March Bute was appointed Secretary of State, and Newcastle was shuffled querulously out of office in the following spring. Within two years of his accession the "King's Friends" predominated in the House of Commons.

The first decade of his reign passed in continual and confused manœuvring between the different Parliamentary groups, some of them accepting the new situation, some making passive resistance to the new tactics of the Crown.

Many people shared Dr Johnson's opinion of the Scots, and Bute, who was much disliked, fell from power early in 1763. His successor, George Grenville, was a mulish lawyer, backed by the enormous electoral power of the Duke of Bedford. On April 23, 1763, a newspaper called *The North Briton* attacked Ministers as "tools of despotism and corruption". George was incensed. A week later his Secretary of State issued a warrant commanding that the authors, printers, and publishers of "*The North Briton*, No. 45", none of whom was named,

should be found and arrested. Searches were made, houses were entered, papers were seized, and nearly fifty suspects were put in prison. Among them was John Wilkes, a rake and a Member of Parliament. He protested that the warrant was illegal and claimed Parliamentary privilege against the arrest. The legality of "general" warrants which named no actual offender became a constitutional question of the first importance. Wilkes was charged with seditious libel and outlawed. But his case became a national issue when he returned to fight his Parliamentary seat. The radical-minded Londoners welcomed this rebuff to the Government, and in March 1768 he was elected for Middlesex. The next February he was expelled from the House of Commons and there was a by-election. Wilkes stood again, and obtained 1,143 votes against his Government opponent, who polled 296. Finally his opponent in Middlesex was declared duly elected. When Wilkes was released from gaol in April 1770 London was illuminated to greet him. After a long struggle he was elected Lord Mayor, and again a Member of Parliament.

The whole machinery of eighteenth-century corruption was thus exposed to the public eye. By refusing to accept Wilkes the Commons had denied the right of electors to choose their Members and held themselves out as a closed corporation of privileged beings. Pitt himself, now Earl of Chatham, in blistering tones attacked the legality of general warrants and the corruption of politics, claiming that more seats in the counties would increase the electorate and diminish the opportunities for corruption, so easy in the small boroughs. His speeches were indeed the first demands for Parliamentary reform in the eighteenth century. Wilkes and the other victims sued the officials who had executed the warrants. The judges ruled that the warrants were illegal. Wilkes obtained £4,000 damages from the Secretary of State himself. Here indeed was a potent weapon against overbearing Ministers and zealous officials. The lesson bit deep. Not until the world wars of the twentieth century was the mere word of a Minister of the Crown

John Wilkes, by R. E. Pine. BRITISH MUSEUM

The repeal of the 1765 Stamp Act by Rockingham's Government was welcomed in England as in America. This contemporary cartoon depicts Grenville carrying the coffin of the infant "Miss Americ-Stamp" to her grave, attended by few mourners, while in the background commerce flourishes once more. BRITISH MUSEUM

enough to legalise the imprisonment of an Englishman. Freedom of the Press and freedom of speech developed by much the same unspectacular, technical, but effective steps. History will not deny some share in the credit for this achievement to Alderman John Wilkes.

The contest with America had meanwhile begun to dominate the British political scene. Vast territories had fallen to the Crown on the conclusion of the Seven Years War. From the Canadian border to the Gulf of Mexico the entire hinterland of the American colonies became British soil, and the parcelling out of these new lands led to further trouble with the colonists. George III was also determined that the colonies should pay their share in the expenses of the Empire and in garrisoning the New World. The results were unsatisfactory on both sides of the Atlantic. Indirect taxation of trade being so unfruitful, Grenville and his lieutenant Charles Townshend consulted the Law Officers about levying a direct

THE REPEAL. ___ or the Funeral Procession, of MISS AMERIC-STAMP.

tax on the colonies. There were no protests, although the colonists had always objected to direct taxation, and in 1765 Parliament passed the Stamp Act. The personality of George III was now exercising a preponderant influence upon events. He was one of the most conscientious sovereigns who ever sat upon the English throne. He possessed great moral courage and an inveterate obstinacy, and his stubbornness lent weight to the stiffening attitude of his Government. His responsibility for the final breach is a high one.

In July 1765 the Marquis of Rockingham, a shy, well-meaning Whig who was disturbed at George's conduct, undertook to form a Government, and brought with him as private secretary a young Irishman named Edmund Burke, already known in literary circles as a clever writer and a brilliant talker. He was much more. He was a great political thinker. He had to overcome the notion, widely prevalent, that party was in itself a rather disreputable thing, a notion which had been strengthened by Pitt's haughty disdain for party business and organisation. A consistent programme, to be advocated in Opposition and realised in office, was Burke's conception of party policy, and the new issues arising plainly required a programme. On Ireland, on America, on India, Burke's attitude was definite. He stood, and he brought his party to stand, for conciliation of the colonies, relaxation of the restraints on Irish trade, and the government of India on the same moral basis as the government of England. He was perhaps the greatest man that Ireland has produced. The same gifts, with a dash of English indolence and irony—he could have borrowed them from Charles James Fox, Henry Fox's famous son, who had plenty of both to spare—might have made him Britain's greatest statesman.

Rockingham's Government, which lasted thirteen months, passed measures that went far to soothe the animosities raised by Grenville on both sides of the Atlantic. But the King was determined to be rid of them, and

Pitt, whose mind was clouded by sickness, was seduced by royal flattery and by his own dislike of party into lending his name to a new administration formed on no political principle whatever. The conduct of affairs slipped into other hands: Charles Townshend, the Duke of Grafton, and Lord Shelburne. In 1767 Townshend, against the opposition of Shelburne, introduced a Bill imposing duties on American imports of paper, glass, lead, and tea. There was rage in America. The Cabinet was not seriously apprehensive, but perturbed. It agreed to drop the duties, except on tea. Suddenly by some mysterious operation of Nature the clouds which had gathered round Chatham's intellect cleared. Ill-health had forced him to resign in 1768, and he had been succeeded in office by Grafton. The scene on which he reopened his eyes was lurid enough to dismay any man. But George III, after twelve years' intrigue, had at last got a docile, biddable Prime Minister. Lord North became First Lord of the Treasury in 1770. A charming man, of good abilities and faultless temper, he presided over the loss of the American colonies.

Here Samuel Adams, fertile organiser of resistance and advocate of separation, saw the struggle was now reaching a crucial stage.

In March 1770 the persistent snowballing by
Boston urchins of an English sentry outside
the custom-house caused a riot. In the confusion and shouting some of the troops opened
fire and there were casualties. This "massacre" was just the sort of incident that
Adams had hoped for. Virginian agitators,
led by the young Patrick Henry, created a
standing committee of their Assembly to
keep in touch with the other colonies, and a
chain of such bodies was quickly formed.
Thus the machinery of revolt was quietly and
efficiently created. Nevertheless, the Radicals
were still in a minority and there was much
opposition to an abrupt break with England.
In spite of the Boston "massacre", the violence
on the high seas, and the commercial
squabbles, the agitations of Adams and his
friends were beginning to peter out, when
Lord North committed a fatal blunder. The
East India Company was nearly bankrupt,
and the Government had been forced to
come to its rescue. An Act was passed
through Parliament, attracting little notice
among the Members, authorising the Company to ship tea, of which it had an enormous surplus, direct to the colonies, without
paying import duties, and to sell it through
its own agents in America. The outcry
across the Atlantic was instantaneous. The
Radicals, who began to call themselves
"Patriots", seized their opportunity to force
a crisis. In December 1773 the first cargoes
were lying in Boston. Rioters disguised as Red
Indians boarded the ships and destroyed the
cases. "Last night", wrote John Adams,
Samuel's cousin, and later the second President of the United States, "three cargoes of
Bohea tea were emptied into the sea. . . .
This is the most magnificent movement of all.
There is a dignity, a majesty and sublimity
in this last effort of the Patriots that I greatly
admire. . . ." When the news reached London
the cry went up for coercion and the reaction-
aries in the British Government became
supreme. In September 1774 the colonial
assemblies held a Congress at Philadelphia.
A Declaration of Rights demanded the

rescinding of some thirteen commercial Acts
passed by the British Parliament since 1763.
The tone of this document, which was dispatched to London, was one of respectful
moderation. The petition was rejected with
contempt.

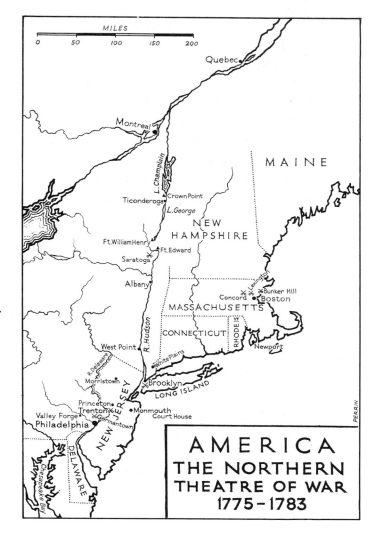

AMERICA
THE NORTHERN
THEATRE OF WAR
1775-1783

A contemporary impression of the scene on Lexington Green, where the first shot was fired in the War of Independence.
RADIO TIMES HULTON PICTURE LIBRARY

Events now moved swiftly. The Patriots had about ten thousand men in the colonial militia. Agents were sent abroad to buy weapons. The Patriots began accumulating these warlike stores at Concord, a village twenty miles from Boston, where the Massachusetts Assembly, which Parliament had declared illegal, was now in session. General Thomas Gage, the Massachusetts Military Governor, decided to seize their ammunition and arrest Samuel Adams and his colleague John Hancock. On April 18, 1775, eight hundred British troops set off in darkness along the Concord road. But the secret was out. Paul Revere, warned by lantern signals from the steeple of the North Church, mounted his horse and rode hard to Lexington, rousing Adams and Hancock from their beds and urging them to flight. At five o'clock in the morning the local militia of Lexington, seventy strong, formed up on the village green. The colonial committees were very anxious not to fire the first shot, and there were strict orders not to provoke open conflict with the British regulars. But in the confusion someone fired. A volley was returned. Brushing aside the survivors, the British column marched on to Concord. The news of

Lexington and Concord spread to the other colonies, and Governors and British officials were expelled. The War of Independence had begun.

In May 1775 a Congress of delegates from the American colonies met in the Carpenters' Hall of the quiet Pennsylvanian town of Philadelphia. Many of them still hoped for peace with England. Yet British troops under General Sir William Howe were on their way across the Atlantic, and armed, violent, fratricidal conflict stared them in the face. The centre of resistance and the scene of action was Boston, where Gage and the only British force on the continent were hemmed in by sixteen thousand New England merchants and farmers. To the north, across a short tract of water, lay a small peninsula connected by a narrow neck with the mainland. Here Breed's Hill and Bunker Hill dominated the town. If the colonists could occupy and hold these eminences they could cannonade the English out of Boston. On the evening of June 16 Gage determined to forestall them, but next morning a line of entrenchments had appeared upon the heights across the water. Patriot troops, warned by messages from Boston, had dug themselves in during the night. On the hot afternoon of the 17th the redcoats moved slowly towards the summit of Breed's Hill. The whole of Boston was looking on. At the third rush the regulars drove the farmers from their line. Over a thousand Englishmen had fallen on the slopes. Of the three thousand farmers who had held the crest a sixth were killed or wounded. The British had captured the hill, but the Americans had won the glory. On both sides of the Atlantic men perceived that a mortal struggle impended.

It was now imperative for the Patriots to raise an army. Two days before the action at Breed's Hill Congress had agreed. Adams's eye centred upon a figure in uniform, among the dark brown clothes of the delegates. He was Colonel George Washington, of Mount Vernon, Virginia. He was the only man of

On previous pages: *The presentation of the Declaration of Independence to the Congress of the American Colonies at the Pennsylvania State House by (standing, centre, left to right) John Adams, Roger Sherman, Robert Livingston, Thomas Jefferson, and Benjamin Franklin. Painting by John Trumbull.* COURTESY: THE ARCHITECT TO THE CAPITOL, WASHINGTON, D.C.

any military experience at the Congress, and this was limited to a few minor campaigns on the frontier. The colonies contained about two hundred and eighty thousand men capable of bearing arms, but at no time during the war did Washington succeed in gathering together more than twenty-five thousand. Congress nevertheless resolved on an offensive. An expedition was dispatched to Canada under Benedict Arnold, who was to be for ever infamous in American history, and Richard Montgomery, who had once served under Wolfe. French Canadians were on the whole content with life under the British Crown. Soon Canada was to harbour many refugees from the United States who were unable to forswear their loyalty to George III.

Meanwhile, Howe was still confined to Boston. He now set himself the task of overawing the Americans. This however needed extensive help from England, and as none arrived, and Boston itself was of no strategic importance, he evacuated the town in the spring of 1776 and moved to the only British base on the Atlantic seaboard, Halifax, in Nova Scotia. Patriot resistance was stiffening, and although the moderate elements in Congress had hitherto opposed any formal Declaration of Independence the evacuation of Boston roused them to a sterner effort. But it was the British Government which took the next step towards dissolving the tie of allegiance between England and America. Early in 1776 it put into force a Prohibitory Act forbidding all intercourse with the rebellious colonies and declaring a blockade of the American coast. A large-scale British invasion was feared. Many of the colonists felt that a formal defiance would wreck their cause and alienate their supporters. But at last a committee was appointed, a paper was drafted by Thomas Jefferson, and on July 4, 1776, a Declaration of Independence was unanimously accepted by the Congress of the American colonies. This historic document was in the main a restatement of the principles which had animated the Whig struggle against the later Stuarts and the English Revolution of 1688, and it now became the symbol and rallying centre of the Patriot cause.

The Battle of Bunker Hill. UNITED STATES INFORMATION SERVICE

In June 1776 Howe moved to New York, and began to invest the city, and in July his brother, Admiral Howe, arrived from England with a fleet of over five hundred sail and reinforcements. Howe was now in command of some twenty-five thousand men. From the British camp on Staten Island the American lines could be seen across the bay on the spurs of Long Island, and on the heights of Brooklyn above the East River. In August Howe attacked. Washington was compelled to retreat into New York City. It seemed impossible to make a stand in New York, yet to abandon it would dismay the Patriots. But Congress agreed that he should evacuate the city without fighting, and after skirmishing on the Harlem heights he withdrew slowly northwards. At this juncture victory lay at Howe's finger-tips. If he had pursued Washington with the same skill and vigour as Grant was to pursue Lee eighty-eight years later he might have captured the colonial army. But for nearly a month Washington was unmolested. Howe resolved to move on Philadelphia. He turned south, capturing as he went the forts in the neighbourhood of New York, and the delegates at Philadelphia fled. Thousands of Americans flocked to the British camp to declare their loyalty. The only hope for the Patriots seemed a mass trek across the Alleghanies into new lands, a migration away from British rule like that of the Boers in the nineteenth century. The Patriot cause seemed lost. But Washington remained alert and undaunted and fortune rewarded him. With an imprudence which is difficult to understand, and was soon to be punished, outposts from the British army were flung about in careless fashion through the New Jersey towns. The year ended with the British in winter quarters in New Jersey, but confined to the east of the Delaware. Meanwhile, Benjamin Franklin and Silas Deane, first of American diplomats, crossed the Atlantic to seek help from France.

Posterity should not be misled into thinking that war on the American colonies received the unanimous support of the British people. Indeed, but for the violence of the Opposition, which far outran the country's true feelings, it is probable that Lord North's administration would have fallen much sooner. Though technically responsible as First Lord of the Treasury and

Chancellor of the Exchequer, he had no grip on the conduct of affairs and allowed the King and the departmental Ministers to control the day-to-day work of government. Rarely has British strategy fallen into such a multitude of errors. Every maxim and principle of war was either violated or disregarded. The objective was to destroy Washington's army and kill or capture Washington. If he could be brought to battle and every man and gun turned against him, British victory was almost certain. But these obvious truths were befogged and bedevilled by multiplicity of counsel. The Government were well aware that Howe intended to move in the opposite direction to General Burgoyne, namely, southwards against Philadelphia, but did nothing to dissuade him.

Washington, from his winter quarters at Morristown, on the borders of New Jersey, moved hastily south-westwards to screen Philadelphia. At the beginning of September Howe advanced with about fourteen thousand men. His tactics went like clockwork. On September 26 his advance-guards entered Philadelphia. Burgoyne, with a few hundred Indians and seven thousand regulars, of whom half were German, was moving through the Canadian forests expecting to join with the British forces from New York. All concerned were confident that after capturing Philadelphia Howe could quickly return to New York and reach out to the expedition from Canada. He failed to do so, and Burgoyne paid the price. As Burgoyne advanced the New England militia gathered against him. General Clinton's garrison there had been halved, since Howe had called upon him for reinforcements. Nevertheless, Clinton marched north and captured two forts below West Point, but as the autumn rains descended Burgoyne was cornered at Saratoga, and the New Englanders, their strength daily increasing, closed in. Days of hard fighting in the woodlands followed. The German mercenaries refused to fight any longer, and on

George Washington, from a painting made on a parchment drumhead by John Trumbull of Salem, Massachusetts, in 1776. PHOTO: TURNER, NEWCASTLE. COURTESY: THE NATIONAL TRUST, WASHINGTON OLD HOUSE COMMITTEE

October 17, 1777, Burgoyne surrended to the American commander, Horatio Gates.

At this point in the struggle the Old World stepped in to aid and comfort the New. Although militarily indecisive in America, Saratoga had an immediate effect in France. There was consternation in London, where the Whig Opposition had long warned the Government against harsh dealings with the colonists, and the British Ministry formulated a generous compromise. It was too late. On February 6, 1778, before the Congress could be apprised of the new offer, Benjamin Franklin signed an alliance with France. Thus began another world war, and Britain was now without a single ally. In the agony all minds except the King's turned to Chatham. On April 7 Chatham dragged himself upon crutches to make his last speech against an Opposition address for recalling the Army in America. He had always stood for conciliation and not for surrender. In whispering sentences, shot through with a sudden gleam of fierce anger, he made his attack "against the dismemberment of this ancient and most noble monarchy". He scourged his countrymen for their inhumanity. "My lords, if I were an American as I am an Englishman, while a foreign troop was landed in my country I never would lay down my arms—never, never, never." Burke's was a fitting memorial: "The means by which Providence raises a nation to greatness are the virtues infused into great men." Such men were very few in the England of Lord North.

While Washington could not count on provisions for his men even a day in advance, Howe danced and gambled in Philadelphia. Unnerved perhaps by the carnage at Bunker Hill, and still hoping for conciliation, he did nothing. Some inkling of his reluctance may have reached the ears of the Government; at any rate, when news of the French alliance with the rebels reached England at the beginning of the New Year his resignation was accepted. Howe's successor was Sir Henry Clinton, the former Commander of New York, who held very different views on the conduct of hostilities. The solution, he thought, was

AMERICA
THE SOUTHERN
THEATRE OF WAR
1775-1783

to occupy and settle the whole country. He resolved to abandon the offensive in the North and begin the process of reduction by subduing the South. Much could be said for all this, and much might have been achieved if he had been allowed to try it out, but there now appeared a new force which abruptly checked and in time proved deadly to the realisation of these large plans. In April 1778 twelve French ships of the line, mounting, with their attendant frigates, over eight hundred guns, set sail from Toulon. News of their approach reached Clinton and it became his immediate and vital task to stop them seizing his main base at New York. On June 18 he accordingly abandoned Philadelphia and marched rapidly across New Jersey with ten thousand troops. Washington, his army swollen by spring recruiting to about equal strength, set off in parallel line of pursuit. Clinton beat off the Americans, not without heavy loss, and did not reach New York till the beginning of July. He was only

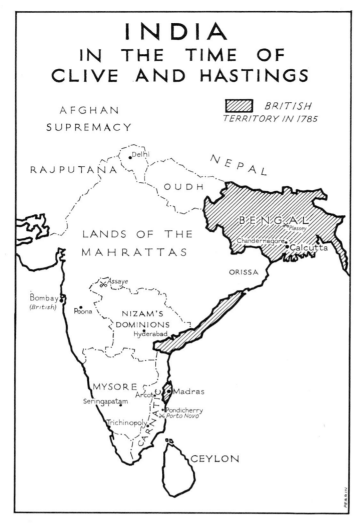

INDIA
IN THE TIME OF
CLIVE AND HASTINGS

AFGHAN
SUPREMACY

⬚ BRITISH
TERRITORY IN 1785

RAJPUTANA

Delhi

N E P A L

OUDH

LANDS OF THE
MAHRATTAS

BENGAL
Plassey
Chandernagore
Calcutta

ORISSA

Assaye

Bombay
(British)

Poona

NIZAM'S
DOMINIONS
Hyderabad

MYSORE

Arcot Madras

Seringapatam

CARNATIC

Pondicherry
Porto Novo

Trichinopoly

CEYLON

five thousand Patriot troops surrendered in the biggest disaster yet sustained by American arms. Clinton had gained a valuable base, but he was confronted with civil war. It became evident that a huge army would be needed to occupy and subdue the country. But again sea-power intervened. Rumours that French troops were once more crossing the Atlantic made Clinton hasten back to New York, leaving Cornwallis, his second-in-command, to do the best he could in the South. This was little enough. Washington sent a small force against him under Gates, Cornwallis defeated Gates, the victor of Saratoga, at the Battle of Camden and marched into North Carolina, routing the guerrillas as he went, but the countryside rose in arms behind him.

In the North Clinton for the second time found himself in great peril. Over five thousand French troops under the Comte de Rochambeau had disembarked in July at Newport, in Rhode Island. New York, Clinton's base and harbour, seemed lost. But events, in the form of treachery, ran for a time with the British. Benedict Arnold had long been dissatisfied with the conduct of the Patriots, and he had recently married a Loyalist lady. His discontent and his doubts were deepened by the news of Gates's defeat at Camden, and he now offered to surrender West Point to Clinton for the sum of £20,000. Arnold's act of betrayal, though discovered in time, had a marked, if temporary, effect on the sentiment and cohesion of the Patriots.

Strategic divergences between Clinton and Cornwallis now brought disaster to the British and Loyalist cause. Clinton judged that the holding of South Carolina was the main object of the war in the South, and that any inland excursions depended on naval control of the coast. Cornwallis on the other hand was eager to press forward. There is no doubt he was wrong. In spite of the Loyalists' unpromising behaviour in the previous campaign, and in spite of the nomination of Washington's ablest general, Nathanael Greene, to command the Patriot forces in the South, Cornwallis resolved to advance. In

just in time. Military operations in America came slowly to a standstill, and although three thousand of Clinton's troops occupied Savannah in Georgia on December 29 his plans for subduing the rebels from a Loyalist base in the South were hampered and curtailed. Stalemate continued throughout 1779, and for a time the main seat of war shifted from the New World. Fear of invasion gripped the British Government and troops intended for Clinton were kept in the British Isles. French diplomacy brought Spain into the war.

In December Clinton decided to try his hand once more at subduing the South. He resolved to capture Charleston, and on the 26th sailed for South Carolina with eight thousand men. For a time he prospered, heartened by news that the French fleet in the West Indies had been beaten by Admiral Rodney. Bad weather delayed him and the main siege did not begin till the end of March, but in May 1780 the town fell and

January 1781 he moved towards the borders of North Carolina. His forward detachments clashed with the Americans at Cowpens on the morning of the 17th. The American commander had placed his ill-organised and ill-disciplined militia with the Broad River behind them to stop them dispersing. But this time, stiffened by Continental troops, they mauled the British. Cornwallis nevertheless pressed on. His only hope was to bring Greene to battle and destroy him. They met at Guilford Court House on March 15. The American militia proved useless, but the trained nucleus of Greene's troops drawn up behind a rail fence wrought havoc among the British regulars. Cornwallis had no choice but to make for the coast and seek reinforcements from the Navy. Greene let him go. He lost the battles, but he won the campaign.

Cornwallis in the meantime, starved of supplies, and with ever-lengthening lines of communication, marched to the coast, where he hoped to make direct contact with Clinton by sea. In August he arrived at Yorktown, on Chesapeake Bay, and began to dig himself in. Nearly nine thousand Americans and eight thousand French assembled before Yorktown, while De Grasse blockaded the coast with thirty ships of the line. At the end of September the investment of Yorktown began, and the bombardment of the French siege artillery shattered the earth redoubts. On October 19, 1781, the whole army, about seven thousand strong, surrendered. On the very same day Clinton and the British squadron sailed from New York, but on hearing of the disaster they turned back. Sea-power had once more decided the issue, and but for the French blockade the British war of attrition might well have succeeded. Two years were to pass before peace came to America, but no further military operations of any consequence took place.

The surrender at Yorktown had immediate and decisive effects in England. In March North informed the Commons that he would resign. Rockingham made his terms with the King: independence for the colonies and some lessening of the Crown's influence in politics. George III was forced to accept, and

The arms of the East India Company. RADIO TIMES HULTON PICTURE LIBRARY

Robert Clive, by Dance. NATIONAL PORTRAIT GALLERY

Rockingham took office. It fell to him and his colleague, Lord Shelburne, to save what they could from the wreckage of the First British Empire.

The eighteenth century saw a revolutionary change in the British position in India. The English East India Company, founded simply as a trading venture, grew with increasing speed into a vast territorial Empire. About the year 1700 probably no more than fifteen hundred English people dwelt in India, including wives, children, and transient seamen. They lived apart in a handful

241

of factories, as their trading stations were called, little concerned with Indian politics. A hundred years later British officials and soldiers in their thousands, under a British Governor-General, were in control of extensive provinces. This remarkable development was in part a result of the struggle between Britain and France, which filled the age and was fought out all over the globe.

The acquisition of territory played little part in the thoughts and plans of either nation, and indeed the Directors of the English East India Company had long been reluctant to own any land or assume any responsibilities beyond the confines of their trading stations. About 1740 events forced them to change their tune. The Mahrattas slaughtered the Nawab, or Imperial Governor, of the Carnatic, the five-hundred-mile-long province on the south-eastern coast. It was becoming impossible for the European traders to stand aside. They must either fight on their own or in alliance with Indian rulers or quit. The Government was never involved as a principal in the Indian conflict, and while Pitt, who justly appreciated the ability of Robert Clive, supported him with all the resources at his command, his influence on events was small. Of India it has been well said that the British Empire was acquired in a fit of absence of mind.

The "Westminster Election, 1796" by Robert Dighton, showing the hustings at St Paul's, Covent Garden. The candidates were Charles James Fox (right foreground) and Sir Alan Gardner, who were elected, and Horne Tooke, one of the shrewdest agitators in the John Wilkes case, who was defeated. THE LONDON MUSEUM

CHAPTER NINE

Napoleon

THE Marquis of Rockingham had waited long for his opportunity to form a Government, and when at last it came in March 1782 he had but four months to live. He died in July, and Lord Shelburne was entrusted with the new administration. Shelburne sought to form a Government by enlisting politicians of the most diverse views and connection. Of great ability, a brilliant orator, and with the most liberal ideas, he was nevertheless, like Carteret before him, distrusted on all sides. Shelburne himself had the support of those who had followed Chatham, including his son, the young William Pitt, who was appointed Chancellor of the Exchequer. But North still commanded a considerable faction, and, smarting at his sovereign's cold treatment after twelve years of faithful service, coveted a renewal of office. The third group was headed by Charles James Fox, vehement critic of North's régime, brilliant, generous-hearted, and inconsistent. Hostility to Shelburne grew and spread. Nevertheless, by negotiations in which he displayed great skill, the Prime Minister succeeded in bringing the world war to an end on the basis of American independence. The difficulty was the Canadian frontier. After months of negotiation a frontier was agreed upon which ran from the borders of Maine to the St Lawrence, up the river, and through the Great Lakes to their head. Everything south of this line, east of the Mississippi and north of the borders of Florida, became American territory. This was by far the most important result of the treaty. France now made her terms with England. An armistice was declared in January 1783, and the final peace treaty was signed at Versailles later in the year. The French kept their possessions in India and the West Indies. They were guaranteed the right to fish off Newfoundland, and they reoccupied the slave-trade settlements of Senegal on the African coast. The important cotton island of Tobago was ceded to them, but apart from this they gained little that was material. Their main object however was achieved. The Thirteen Colonies had been wrested from the United Kingdom, and England's position in the world seemed to have been gravely weakened. Spain was forced to join in the general settlement. Her American ambitions had melted away, her one gain in this theatre being the two English colonies in Florida; but this was at the expense of the English retention of Gibraltar, the main Spanish objective. She had conquered Minorca, the English naval station in the Mediterranean during the war, and she kept that at the peace. Thus ended what some then called the World War.

England's emergence from her ordeal was the work of Shelburne. He resigned after eight months, in February 1783. Shelburne's Government was followed by a machine-made coalition between North and Fox. It was said that this combination was too much even for the agile consciences of the age. Within nine months this Ministry also collapsed. Party and personal issues alike being exhausted by the weight of the disaster, George III saw his opportunity if he could find the man. By what was certainly the most outstanding domestic action of his long reign, in December 1783, the King asked Pitt to form a Government.

The revolt of the American colonies had shattered the complacency of eighteenth-century England. Men began to study the root causes of the disaster and the word "reform" was in the air. England was silently undergoing a revolution in industry and agriculture, which was to have more far-reaching effects than the political tumults of the times. An ever-expanding and assertive industrial community was coming into being. The religious revival of John Wesley had broken the stony surface of the Age of Reason. Demand for some reform of the representation in Parliament began to stir; but the agitation was now mild and respectable. The main aim of the reformers was to increase the number of boroughs which elected Members of Parliament, and thus reduce the possibilities of Government corruption. Many of the early reform schemes were academic attempts to preserve the political power and balance of the rural interest. The individualism of eighteenth-century England assumed no doctrinaire form. The enunciation of first principles has always been obnoxious to the English mind.

The elections which carried Pitt into power were the most carefully planned of the century. His majority rested on a number of elements—Pitt's personal following; the "Party of the Crown", put at his disposal by George III; the independent country gentlemen; the East India interest, alienated by Fox's attempt to curb their political power; and the Scottish Members, marshalled by Dundas. Thus from the outset Pitt was overcome by the dead hand of eighteenth-century politics. He failed to abolish the slave trade. He failed to make a settlement in Ireland. He failed to make Parliament more representative of the nation, and the one achievement in these early months was his India Act, which increased rather than limited the opportunities for political corruption. He saw quite clearly the need and justification for reform, but preferred always to compromise with the forces of resistance. The greatest orators of the age, Fox and Burke, were Pitt's opponents. They dwelt eloquently

William Pitt the Younger. Detail from a portrait by Hoppner. NATIONAL PORTRAIT GALLERY

on the broad themes of reform. Yet it was Pitt, aided by Dundas, who in a quiet, business-like way reconstructed the practical policies of the nation.

It was in the most practical and most urgent problem, the ordering and reconstruction of the country's financial structure, that Pitt achieved his best work, and created that Treasury tradition of wise, incorruptible management which still prevails. It is to Pitt that we owe the modern machinery of the "Budget". By gathering around him able officials he reorganised the collection and disbursement of the revenue. The National Debt stood at two hundred and fifty million pounds, more than two and a half times as great as in the days of Walpole. Pitt resolved to acquire a surplus in the revenue and apply it to the reduction of this swollen burden. In 1786 he brought in a Bill for this purpose. Each year a million pounds would be set aside to buy stock, and the interest would be used to reduce the National Debt. Here was the famous oft-criticised Sinking Fund. In this same year, 1786, the Customs and Excise were amalgamated, and a reconstituted Board of Trade established in its modern form. But perhaps the most striking achievement of Pitt's management was the negotiation of the Eden treaty with France—the first Free Trade treaty according to the new

244

economic principles. In 1776 Adam Smith had published *The Wealth of Nations*, which quickly became famous throughout educated circles. Pitt was deeply influenced by his book. He was the first English statesman to believe in Free Trade, and for a while his Tory followers accepted it.

Fully aware of the economic changes in eighteenth-century England, Pitt was less sensitive to signs of political disturbance abroad. He believed firmly in non-intervention, and the break-up of the Old Régime in France left him unimpressed. The First Minister was deaf to the zealous campaign of the Whig Opposition in favour of the French Revolutionaries, and ignored the warnings of Burke and others who believed that the principles of monarchy, and indeed of civilised society, were endangered by the roar of events across the Channel.

In England the Whigs, and especially the reformers and Radicals, had at first welcomed the French Revolution. They were soon repelled by its excesses. In his Budget speech of 1792 Pitt had announced that he believed in fifteen years of peace for Europe. Non-intervention was his policy. Something more vital to Britain than a massacre of aristocrats or a speech in the Convention, something more concrete than a threat of world revolu-

tion, had to happen before he would face the issue of war. The spark, as so often in England's history, came from the Netherlands. On the last day of January 1793 the French Convention, with Danton's defiant speech in their ears, decreed the annexation of the Austrian Netherlands to the French Republic. The next day France declared war on Great Britain and Holland, firm in the belief that an internal revolution in England was imminent. Pitt now had no choice.

If Britain had possessed even a small effective army it would not have been difficult, in concert with allies moving from the Rhine, to strike from the French coast at Paris and overthrow the Government responsible for provoking the conflict. But Pitt was barely able to send five thousand men to help his Dutch allies protect their frontiers from invasion. By 1795 the British forces on the Continent were driven back upon the mouth of the Ems on the German border, whence they were evacuated home. Great hopes had been founded in London upon the French Royalists, who launched daring schemes to arrest the Revolution by civil war in France. In 1793 they seized Toulon, and but for the fact that Dundas had already assigned all available troops to the West Indies a vital base for future invasion might have been secured. Something else happened

Pitt addressing the House of Commons, a painting by K. A. Hickel. In the Speaker's chair is Dr Henry Addington, who was himself to become Prime Minister. The Commons met in St Stephen's Chapel, Westminster, from 1547 until 1834, when it was destroyed by fire. NATIONAL PORTRAIT GALLERY

at Toulon. A young lieutenant of the French Army, sprung from a leading Corsican family, well versed in artillery and other military matters, happening to be on leave from his regiment, looked in on the camp of General Carteaux, who commanded the Jacobin besieging army. Orders arrived from Paris prescribing the method of siege according to customary forms, for which however the necessary material resources were lacking. None dared dispute the instructions of the terrible Committee of Public Safety which was now at the head of French affairs. Nevertheless, at the council of war, held in daylight, on bare ground, the expert lieutenant raised his voice. The orders, he said—or so he claimed later—were foolish, and all knew it. There was however a way of taking Toulon. He placed his finger on the map where Fort l'Aiguillette on its promontory commanded the entrance to the harbour. "There is Toulon," he said, and all, taking their lives in their hands, obeyed him. He organised and led the assault upon Fort l'Aiguillette. After a hot fight it fell. The whole wide front of the Toulon defences remained intact, but on the morning after Fort l'Aiguillette fell the British Fleet was seen to be leaving the harbour. Once the British Fleet had departed all resisting power perished. The lieutenant had understood not only the military significance of the captured fort, but the whole set of moral and political forces upon which the Royalist defence of Toulon hung. His name was Napoleon Bonaparte. He became the sword of the Revolution, which he was determined to exploit and to destroy.

In England the Government had been forced to take repressive measures of a sternness unknown for generations. Republican lecturers were swept into prison. The Habeas Corpus Act was suspended. The mildest criticism of the Constitution brought the speaker under danger from a new Treason Act. Few victories came to brighten these dark years. In 1794 the French Channel Fleet, ill-equipped and under-officered, was half-heartedly engaged by Admiral Howe.

Three years later, off Cape St Vincent, the Spanish Fleet—Spain being now in alliance with France—was soundly beaten by Jervis and Nelson. But such had been the neglect of conditions of service in the Navy that the ships at Spithead refused to put to sea. Some slight concessions satisfied the mutineers, and they retrieved their honour in a handsome victory off Camperdown over the Dutch, who were now satellites of France. France, dominant in Western Europe, firmly planted in the Mediterranean, safeguarded against attack from Germany by a secret understanding with Austria, had only to consider what she would conquer next. A sober judgment might have said England, by way of Ireland. Bonaparte thought he saw his destiny in a larger field. In the spring of 1798 he sailed for Egypt.

During the afternoon of August 1 a scouting vessel from Nelson's fleet signalled that a number of French battleships were anchored in Aboukir Bay, to the east of Alexandria. The French Admiral Brueys was convinced that not even an English admiral would risk sailing his ship between the shoals and the French line. But Nelson knew his captains. Five British ships passed in succession on the land side of the enemy, while Nelson, in the *Vanguard*, led the rest of his fleet to lie to on the starboard of the French line. Relentlessly the English ships, distinguished by four lanterns hoisted in a horizontal pattern, battered the enemy van, passing from one disabled foe to the next down the line. At ten o'clock Brueys's flagship, the *Orient*, blew up. The five ships ahead of her had already surrendered; the rest, their cables cut by shot, or frantically attempting to avoid the inferno of the burning *Orient*, drifted helplessly. In the morning hours three ran ashore and surrendered, and a fourth was burned by her officers. Of the great fleet that had convoyed Napoleon's army to the adventure in Egypt only two ships of the line and two frigates escaped. Nelson's victory of the Nile cut Napoleon's communications with France and ended his hopes of vast Eastern conquests. In 1799 he escaped back to France, leaving his army behind him. The British Fleet was once again supreme in the Mediterranean Sea. This was a turning-point. With the capture of Malta in 1800 after a prolonged siege Britain had secured a strong naval base in the Mediterranean, and there was no further need to bring the squadrons home for the winter as in the early part of the war. But still the British Government could conceive no co-ordinated military plan upon the scale demanded by European strategy. Their own resources were few and their allies seldom dependable. Meanwhile, Napoleon again took charge of the French armies in Italy. In June 1800 he beat the Austrians at Marengo, in Piedmont, and France was once more mistress of Europe.

Union with Scotland had been a success. Why not with Ireland too? The shocks and alarums of the previous years determined Pitt to attempt some final settlement in that troubled island. But the prime requisite for any agreement must be the emancipation of Irish Catholics from the disabilities of the penal laws. Pitt had committed himself to the cause of Catholic freedom without extracting a written agreement from the King. When George refused his assent, on March 14, 1801, Pitt felt bound to resign. Catholic emancipation was delayed for nearly thirty years. The Act of Union had meanwhile been carried through the Irish Parliament by wholesale patronage and bribery against vehement opposition. Bitter fruits were to follow from this in the later nineteenth century. Pitt was succeeded by a pinchbeck coalition of King's Friends and rebels from his own party. Masquerading as a Government of National Union, they blundered on for over three years. Their leader was Henry Addington, an amiable former Speaker of the House of Commons whom no one regarded as a statesman. In March 1802 Addington's Government made terms with Napoleon by the Treaty of Amiens, and for a time there was a pause in the fighting. In May 1803 war was renewed, and once more mismanaged.

Pitt was in retirement at Walmer, in Kent.

The strain of the past years had broken his health. He was prematurely aged. He had lived a lonely, artificial life, cheered by few friendships. The only time that he ever came in contact with the people was during this brief interval from office, when as Warden of the Cinque Ports he organised the local militia against the threat of invasion. Few things in England's history are more remarkable than this picture of an ex-Prime Minister, riding his horse at the head of a motley company of yokels, drilling on the fields of the South Coast, while a bare twenty miles away across the Channel the Grand Army of Napoleon waited only for a fair wind and a clear passage.

In 1804 Pitt was recalled to power. Since the renewal of war Britain had found herself alone against Napoleon, and for two years she maintained the struggle single-handed during one of the most critical periods in her history.

At the crest of his hopes Napoleon had himself crowned by the Pope as Emperor of the French. One thing alone was lacking to his designs—command of the sea. As before and since in her history, the Royal Navy alone seemed to stand between the Island and national destruction. Day in, day out, winter and summer, British fleets kept blockade of the French naval bases of Brest and Rochefort on the Atlantic coast and Toulon in the Mediterranean. In May 1803 Nelson had returned to the Mediterranean to resume command of his fleet. He kept a screen of frigates watching Toulon, and himself with his battleships lay off Sardinia, alert for interception. Twice in the course of two years the French attempted a sortie, but retired.

In May 1804 the Emperor had confided the Toulon fleet to Admiral Villeneuve, an excellent seaman, who realised that his ships, except for the luck of circumstance, could only play a defensive part. Spain was dragged into his schemes, her Fleet being a necessary adjunct to the main plan. In the early months of 1805 Napoleon made his final arrangements. Over ninety thousand assault troops, picked and trained, lay in the camps round

Boulogne. The French Channel ports were not constructed to take battleships, and the French fleets in the Atlantic and Mediterranean harbours must be concentrated elsewhere to gain command of the Channel. The Emperor fixed upon the West Indies. Here, after breaking the Mediterranean and Atlantic blockades, and drawing off the British Fleet, as he thought, into the waters of the Western Atlantic, his ships were ordered to gather. The combined French and Spanish Fleets would then unite with Ganteaume, the Admiral of the Brest Squadron, double back to Europe, sail up the Channel, and assure the crossing from Boulogne.

Nelson was lying in wait off the Sardinian coastline in April 1805 when news reached him that Villeneuve was at sea, having slipped out of Toulon on the dark night of March 30, sailing, as Nelson did not yet know, in a westerly direction with eleven ships of the line and eight frigates. The fox was out and the chase began. Nelson, picking up scattered reports from frigates and merchantmen, pieced together the French design. Villeneuve and his Spanish allies reached Martinique on May 14. Nelson made landfall at Barbados on June 4. Meanwhile, news of his arrival alarmed the French Admiral, who was promptly out again in the Atlantic by June 8, heading east. Before leaving the islands Nelson sent a fast sloop back to England with dispatches, and on June 19 it passed Villeneuve's fleet, noting his course and position. The commander of the sloop

saw that Villeneuve was heading north-eastwards for the Bay of Biscay, and raced home, reaching Plymouth on July 8. Nelson was sailing rapidly eastwards after Villeneuve, believing he would catch him at Cadiz and head him off the Straits, while the French Fleet was making steadily on a more northerly course in the direction of Cape Finisterre. Villeneuve intended to release the Franco-Spanish squadron blockaded at Ferrol, and, thus reinforced, join with Ganteaume from Brest. But Ganteaume, in spite of peremptory orders from Napoleon, failed to break out. Admiral Cornwallis's fleet in the Western Approaches kept him in port. Meanwhile, on orders from the First Lord of the Admiralty, Lord Barham, Admiral Calder intercepted Villeneuve off Finisterre, and here in late July the campaign of Trafalgar opened. Calder's action was indecisive, and the French took refuge in Ferrol.

Nelson meanwhile had reached Cadiz on July 18. Realising that Villeneuve must have gone north, he replenished his fleet in Morocco and sailed for home waters on the 23rd. On the same day Napoleon arrived at Boulogne. Calder joined Cornwallis off Brest on August 14, and on the next day Nelson arrived with twelve more ships, bringing the main fleet up to a total of nearly forty ships of the line. Thus was the sea-barrier concentrated against the French. Nelson went on alone with his flagship, the *Victory*, to Portsmouth. In the following days the campaign

Nelson's prayer before Trafalgar, from his Journal. NATIONAL MARITIME MUSEUM

The Battle of Trafalgar, by Clarkson Stanfield. The members of the United Service Club, many of whom had fought at Trafalgar, commissioned Stanfield to record the events of the action. The progress of the picture was watched by many of Nelson's old companions, who assisted the artist with information, a very special interest being taken by Sir Thomas Hardy. The picture represents the centre of the combined fleet at 2.30 p.m.—about an hour after Nelson was shot. The Victory, after sustaining a heavy fire

from four of the enemy's ships, is in the act of disengaging herself from the Redoutable *(a French 74) at that time lashed alongside the* Téméraire *(a British 78) at the moment the* Fougueux *(a French 74) became the prize of the latter. On the right of the* Victory *is the* Bucentaure *(a French 80) with her main and mizzen masts shot away.* COURTESY: THE COMMITTEE OF MANAGEMENT OF THE UNITED SERVICE CLUB, PALL MALL, LONDON

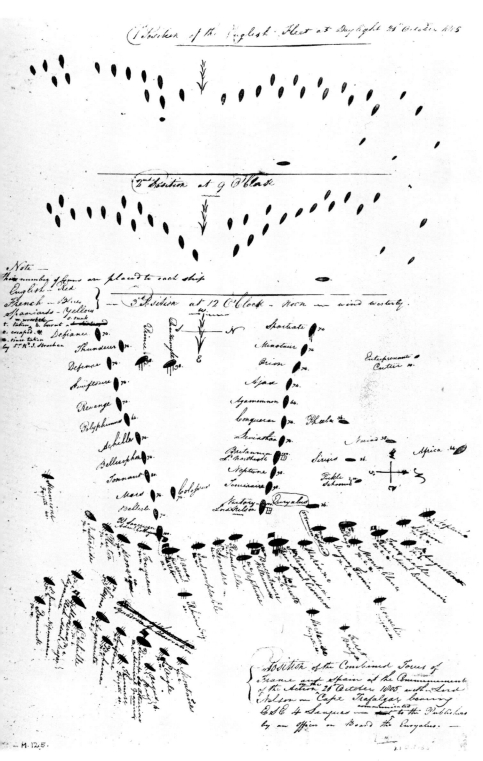

leaving harbour, but Cornwallis closed in with his whole force and the French turned back. Meanwhile, Villeneuve, having edged out into the Atlantic, had changed his mind. The threat of invasion was over.

Early in September dispatches reached London telling that Villeneuve had gone south. Nelson, summoned from his home at Merton, was at once ordered to resume his command. Amid scenes of enthusiasm he rejoined the *Victory* at Portsmouth and sailed on September 15. A fortnight later he joined the Fleet off Cadiz, now numbering twenty-seven ships of the line. His object was to starve the enemy Fleet, now concentrated in Cadiz harbour, and force it out into the open sea and to battle. To gain a decisive victory, he was resolved to abandon the old formal line of battle, running parallel to the enemy's Fleet. He would break Villeneuve's line, when it came out of port, by sailing at right angles boldly into it with two main divisions. While the enemy van was thus cut off and out of touch his centre and rear would be destroyed. At daybreak on the 21st he saw from the quarterdeck of the *Victory* the battle line of the enemy, consisting of an advance-squadron of twelve Spanish ships under Admiral Gravina and twenty-one French ships of the line under Villeneuve. Nelson signalled his ships to steer east-north-east for the attack in the two columns he had planned. The enemy turned northwards on seeing the advancing squadrons, and Nelson pressed on with every sail set. The clumsy seamanship of his men convinced Villeneuve that flight was impossible, and he hove to in a long sagging line to await Nelson's attack. Nelson signalled to Collingwood, who was at the head of the southern column in the *Royal Sovereign*, "I intend to pass through the van of the enemy's line, to prevent him getting into Cadiz." Nelson went down to his cabin to compose a prayer. "May the Great God whom I worship grant to my country and for the benefit of Europe in general a great and glorious Victory. . . . For myself individually I commit my life to Him who made me, and may His blessing light upon my endeavours for serving my country faithfully."

reached its climax. Villeneuve sailed again from Ferrol on August 13 in an attempt to join Ganteaume and enter the English Channel, for Napoleon still believed that the British fleets were dispersed and that the moment had come for invasion. On August 21 Ganteaume was observed to be

The Fleets were drawing nearer and nearer. Another signal was run up upon the *Victory*, "England expects every man will do his duty."

A deathly silence fell upon the Fleet as the ships drew nearer. Each captain marked down his adversary, and within a few minutes the two English columns thundered into action. The *Victory* smashed through between Villeneuve's flagship, the *Bucentaure*, and the *Redoutable*. The three ships remained locked together, raking each other with broadsides. Nelson was pacing as if on parade on his quarterdeck when at 1.15 p.m. he was shot from the mast-head of the *Redoutable* by a bullet in the shoulder. His backbone was broken, and he was carried below amid the thunder of the *Victory*'s guns. By the afternoon of October 21, 1805, eighteen of the enemy ships had surrendered and the remainder were in full retreat. Eleven entered Cadiz, but four more were captured off the coast of Spain. In the log of the *Victory* occurs the passage, "Partial firing continued until 4.30, when a victory having been reported to the Right Hon. Lord Viscount Nelson, K.B. and Commander-in-Chief, he then died of his wound."

Napoleon meanwhile was attracted to other fields. He determined to strike at the European coalition raised against him by Pitt's diplomacy and subsidies. The campaign that followed wrecked Pitt's hopes and schemes. A personal sorrow now darkened Pitt's life. The House of Commons by the casting vote of the Speaker resolved to impeach his close colleague and lifelong companion, Henry Dundas, now Lord Melville, for maladministration in the Admiralty and for the peculations of certain of his subordinates. The decisive speech against Dundas was made by none other than Wilberforce, the friend of Pitt's Cambridge days, and the only person who enjoyed his confidence. It was this disgrace, rather than the news of Austerlitz, which finally broke the spirit and energy of the Prime Minister. In January 1806 he died.

"In an age", runs the inscription on his monument in Guildhall, "when the con-tagion of ideals threatened to dissolve the forms of civil society he rallied the loyal, the sober-minded, and the good around the venerable structure of the English monarchy." This is a fitting epitaph.

The three years between the death of Pitt in January 1806 and the rise of Wellington in 1809 were uncheered by fortune. In 1806 and 1807 there was a brief Ministry of "All the Talents" under Lord Grenville. The Government's tenure of office was redeemed by Fox's abolition of the slave trade, a measure which ranks among the greatest of British achievements, and from which Pitt had always shrunk. It was Fox's last effort. For forty years his warm-hearted eloquence had inspired the Whigs. Almost his whole Parliamentary life was spent in Opposition. He died as Secretary of State, nine months after his great rival, Pitt, had gone to the grave. In 1807 the Whigs fell. They were succeeded by a mixed Government of Tory complexion under the nominal leadership of the Duke of Portland. Its object was to hold together the loyalties of as much of the nation as it could command. In this it was remarkably successful.

The Franco-Russian Alliance, signed at Tilsit on July 7, was the culmination of Napoleon's power. Only Britannia remained, unreconciled, unconquered, implacable. There she lay in her Island, mistress of the seas and oceans, ruled by her proud, stubborn aristocracy, facing this immense combination alone, sullen, fierce, and almost unperturbed. Secure throughout the rest of Europe, Napoleon turned his attention to the Spanish Peninsula. Powerless at sea, he realised that to destroy his one outstanding rival he must turn the weapon of blockade against the Island. English goods must be kept out of the markets of Europe by an iron ring of customs guards stretching from the borders of Russia round the coasts of Northern Europe and Western France and sealing the whole Mediterranean coastline as far as the Dardanelles. In reply to Napoleon's Continental System the British Government issued an Order in Council declaring a sea blockade of all French and French-allied

The quarter-deck of H.M.S. Victory, *from a drawing made by Turner while the ship was under repair after Trafalgar. The mast is the jury mizzen rigged after the action. It is thought that the swivel guns on the poop-rail were fitted after Nelson's death; they would be used to clear sharpshooters from the tops and rigging of enemy ships. Turner's notes are:*

1 *"Splinter netting marked in pencil";*
2 *"9 inches thick" (the mizzen shrouds);*
3 *"Rail shot away during the action"; and "Guns* $\frac{lb:rs}{12}$ *used in the ports mark: x".* BRITISH MUSEUM

The quarter-deck of the Victory *today, looking forward from beneath the awning. Her rails and splinter netting have been restored, and her 12-pounders are back at their ports.* PHOTO: BASIL LAVIS. COURTESY: MRS MARY LAVIS

Right: *Nelson, by Lemmel Abbott.* NATIONAL PORTRAIT GALLERY

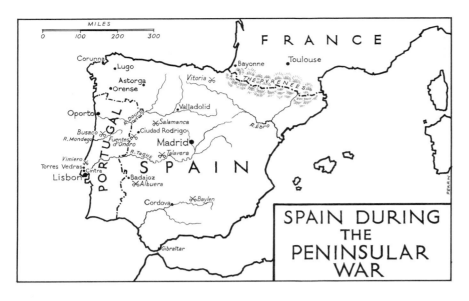

Map: SPAIN DURING THE PENINSULAR WAR

ports—in other words, of almost the whole of Europe. Napoleon's decrees and the English Orders wounded the merchant shipping of the neutral countries. The results of this trade war were far-reaching for both sides. The commerce of Europe was paralysed and the nations stirred beneath the French yoke. Interference by British ships with neutral vessels raised with the United States the question of the freedom of the seas. It was a grievous dispute, not to be settled without recourse to war.

Napoleon, insatiable of power, and seeking always to break England and her intangible blockade, resolved to seize the Spanish Crown. He placed his own brother Joseph on the throne of Spain as a vassal of the French Empire. As soon as the Spaniards realised what had happened and that their country was practically annexed to France they rose everywhere in spontaneous revolt. Nothing like this universal uprising of a numerous, ancient race and nation, all animated by one thought, had been seen before. This country, which Napoleon had expected to incorporate in his Empire by a personal arrangement with a feeble Government, by a trick, by a trap, without bloodshed or expense, suddenly became his main military problem. Canning and his colleagues decided to send an army to the Peninsula to aid the Spanish insurgents. At the head of the first troops to land appeared Sir Arthur Wellesley, whose conduct of

Sir John Moore, after Lawrence. NATIONAL PORTRAIT GALLERY

the Mahratta War in India had been distinguished. He did not wait for the rest of the army, but immediately took the field. The French columns of assault were broken by the reserved fire of the "thin red line", which now began to attract attention. Junot retreated upon Lisbon. Wellesley's wish to seize the pass of Torres Vedras and thus cut Junot's line of retreat was frustrated by his seniors. But the French commander now offered to evacuate Portugal if the British would carry him back to France. The Convention of Cintra was signed, and punctiliously executed by the British. History has endorsed Byron's line, "Britannia sickens, Cintra! at thy name".

Napoleon now moved a quarter of a million of his best troops into Spain. An avalanche of fire and steel broke upon the Spanish Juntas, who, with ninety thousand raw but ardent volunteers, had nursed a brief illusion of freedom regained. The Emperor advanced upon Madrid, driving the Spanish army before him in a series of routs, in which the French cavalry took pitiless vengeance. But the Spanish people were undaunted, and all around the camps of the victorious invaders flickered a horrible guerrilla.

A new English general of high quality had succeeded the commanders involved in the Convention of Cintra. Sir John Moore advanced from Lisbon through Salamanca to Valladolid. His daring thrust cut or threatened the communications of all the French armies, and immediately prevented any

French action in the south of Spain or against Portugal. But Napoleon, watching from Madrid, saw him a prey. Moore, warned in time, and invoking amphibious power, dropped his communications with Portugal and ordered his transports to meet him at Corunna, on the north-west tip of Spain. The retreat of the British through the rugged, snow-bound hill country was arduous. The French pressed heavily. It was now resolved to slip away in the night to Corunna, where the army arrived on January 14, 1809. But the harbour was empty. Contrary winds had delayed the Fleet and transports. On the 16th Soult assaulted Moore with twenty thousand against fourteen thousand. He was everywhere repulsed, and indeed counter-attacked. But both Sir John Moore and his second-in-command, Sir David Baird, had fallen on the field. Moore's countrymen may well do him justice. By daring, skill, and luck he had ruptured Napoleon's winter campaign and had drawn the Emperor and his finest army into the least important part of Spain, thus affording protection and time for movements to get on foot in all the rest of the Peninsula. His campaign had restored the military reputation of Britain, which had suffered increasing eclipse since the days of Chatham; he had prepared the way for a new figure, destined to lead the armies of Europe upon the decisive field.

When the British sailed away from Corunna no organised forces remained in Spain to hinder Napoleon's Marshals. Soult now entered Portugal and established himself at Oporto. Few observers were then convinced that effective success could be won in distant Spain and Portugal. These doubts were not shared by Arthur Wellesley. In April he was reappointed to take command in Lisbon. The passage of the Douro, the surprise of Oporto, and the discomfiture of Soult constituted a brilliant achievement for the new British General and paved the way for further action. Wellesley now resolved to penetrate into the centre of Spain along the valley of the Tagus, and, joining the Spanish army under Cuesta, to engage Marshal Victor. Wellesley's position at Talavera, a hundred miles south-west of Madrid, became pre-

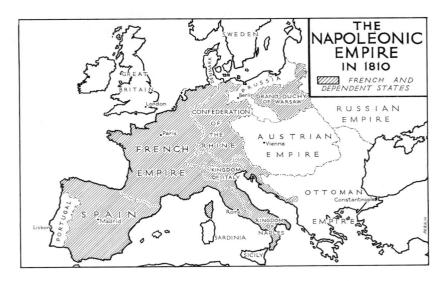

carious, and his soldiers were near starvation. Marshal Victor conceived himself strong enough to attack without waiting for the arrival of Soult. On the afternoon of July 27, 1809, the armies engaged. Victor's attacks, which began in earnest on the 28th, were ill-concerted, and were repulsed with heavy loss after fierce mass-fighting with the bayonet. In the afternoon the crisis of the battle was reached. By nightfall Marshal Victor accepted defeat and withdrew towards Madrid. The ferocity of the fighting may be judged from the British losses. Nearly six thousand men out of Wellesley's total of twenty thousand had fallen, killed or wounded; the French had lost seven thousand five hundred and twenty guns. The Spaniards claimed to have lost one thousand two hundred men. Wellesley was in no condition to pursue. He withdrew unmolested along the Tagus back to Portugal. In England there was unwonted satisfaction. Sir Arthur Wellesley was raised to the peerage as Viscount Wellington, and, in spite of Whig opposition, was granted a pension of £2,000 a year for three years.

The disgrace of the Convention at Cintra had sharpened the rivalry and mutual dislike of Canning and Castlereagh. Now the two Ministers were at loggerheads over the disaster that threatened the expedition to Walcheren. Tempers were sharpened by the ill-defined and over-lapping functions of the Foreign Secretary and the Secretary for War. A duel was fought between them, in which Canning was wounded. Both resigned office, and so did Portland. Spencer Perceval,

Nelson's funeral procession from Greenwich to Whitehall. An engraving by I. Hill from a painting by C. A. Pugin. NATIONAL MARITIME MUSEUM

hitherto Chancellor of the Exchequer, took over the Government. Wellington's cause in Spain was favoured by the new administration. In 1810 the King's renewed madness provoked a fresh crisis. George, Prince of Wales, became Regent.

These were testing years for Wellington. He commanded Britain's sole remaining army on the continent of Europe. The French had always bent every effort to driving the British into the sea. In 1810 they were massing for a fresh attempt. The ablest of Napoleon's Marshals, Masséna, now headed the French Army of Portugal. In September there was a stiff battle at Busaco. The French were badly mauled and beaten. Wellington's withdrawal

nevertheless continued. Suddenly the forward flow of the French came to a halt. Ahead of them rose the formidable lines of Torres Vedras, manned by the undefeated British, and all around extended a countryside deliberately laid waste. This was the hinge of the whole campaign. The French paused and dug into winter quarters. In the following spring Masséna gave up. He retreated into Spain, leaving behind him seventeen thousand dead and eight thousand prisoners.

Rejoicing in London and Lisbon however was mingled with a certain impatience. Wellington himself was unperturbed by cries for haste. He must have in his hands the frontier fortresses of Badajoz and Ciudad

258

Right: *The Duke of Wellington, by Lawrence.* WELLINGTON MUSEUM, APSLEY HOUSE

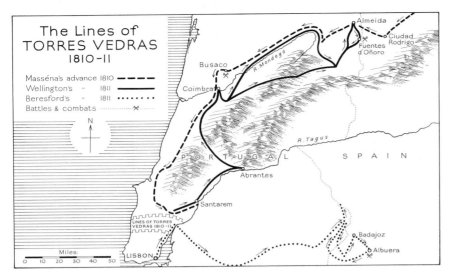

Rodrigo, which guarded the roads to Madrid. Two French armies confronted him. Masséna, later replaced by Marmont, held the northern front in the province of Leon. Soult lay to the south in Andalusia. The Battles of Fuentes and Albuera, which was fought by Wellington's lieutenant, Beresford, were not decisive, but the British remained masters of the field. In fact Wellington was already laying his plans for the day when he would drive the French back over the Pyrenees and carry the conflict into their own country. Amid the snows of January 1812 he was at last able to seize Ciudad Rodrigo. Four months later Badajoz fell to a bloody assault. The cost in life was heavy, but the way was opened for an overpowering thrust into Spain. Wellington and Marmont manœuvred about one another, each watching for the other to make a mistake. It was Marmont who erred, and at Salamanca Wellington achieved his first victory on the offensive in the Peninsular War. King Joseph Bonaparte fled from Madrid, and the British occupied the capital amid the pealing of bells

and popular rejoicing. But there was still Soult to be dealt with. He outnumbered the British commander by nearly two to one, and he was careful to offer no opening for promising attack. Wellington fell back once more on the Portuguese frontier. In the year's campaign he had shattered one French army and enabled the whole of Southern Spain to be freed from the French. But meanwhile heavier shadows from the East were falling upon Napoleon's Empire. It was the winter of the retreat from Moscow.

On the southern front Wellington's achievement surpassed all expectations. At the Battle of Vitoria on June 21 he routed Marshal Jourdan and drove his forces over the Pyrenees. News of this victory heartened the Czar and for the first and only time in history the success of British arms was greeted by a *Te Deum* sung in Russian. Tenaciously Wellington pursued his purpose of reducing, as he put it, "the power and influence of the grand disturber of Europe". By spring of 1814 he was on French soil and had occupied Bordeaux. In early April he sought out and defeated his old antagonist, Soult, at Toulouse. For Napoleon the end had already come. In the south the front had crumpled; to the east Prussians, Russians, and Austrians were reaching into the heart of France. Napoleon was never more brilliant in manœuvre than during his brief campaign of 1814. But the combined strength of Europe was too much for him. The forces of opposition to his rule in France openly rose against him. On April 3 Napoleon abdicated and retired to the island of Elba. The long, remorseless tides of war rolled back, and at the Congress of Vienna the Powers prepared for the diplomatic struggle of the peace.

The confused and tumultuous issues of European politics reached America in black and white, becoming less theoretical and much more vehement as soon as American commercial interests were affected. Tempers rose as American ships and merchandise endured the commerce-raiding and privateering

Napoleon's Deed of Abdication, dated April 6, 1814.
BRITISH MUSEUM

The opening shots of the action between the Chesapeake (*right*) *and H.M.S.* Shannon, *June 1, 1813. A coloured lithograph by Hagje after Schetky.* NATIONAL MARITIME MUSEUM.

of France and Britain. But, as the Battle of Trafalgar had proved, the Royal Navy was much more powerful than the French, and it was at the hands of the British that American shipping suffered most. Anglo-American relations grew steadily worse.

The unofficial trade war with the United States was telling heavily upon England. The loss of the American market and the hard winter of 1811–12 had brought widespread unemployment and a business crisis. Petitions were sent to Parliament begging the Government to revoke the Orders in Council. After much hesitation Castlereagh, now at the Foreign Office, announced in the House of Commons that the Government had done so. But it was too late. The Atlantic crossing took too long for the news to reach America in time. On June 18, 1812, two days after Castlereagh's announcement, Congress declared war on Great Britain.

The root of the quarrel, as American historians have pointed out, lay not in rival interpretations of maritime law, but in the problems of the Western frontier. The seaboard States, and especially New England, wanted peace. But on the frontiers, and especially in the North-West, men were hungry for land, and this could be had only from the Indians or from the British Empire. Trouble with the Indians had been brewing for some time. As the Western territories of America filled up, pressure mounted for a farther north-westerly move. In 1811 the Red Indians bordering on the Ohio united under their last great warrior-leader, Tecumseh. It is one of the legends of American history that the resistance of the Indians was encouraged

and organised from Canada—a legend created by the war party of 1812. A new generation was entering American politics, headed by Henry Clay from Kentucky and John C. Calhoun from South Carolina. They had no conception of affairs in Europe; they cared nothing about Napoleon's designs, still less about the fate of Russia. Their prime aim and object was to seize Canada and establish American sovereignty throughout the whole Northern continent. A short expedition of pioneers would set things right, it was thought, and dictate peace in Quebec in a few weeks. Congress adjourned without even voting extra money for the American Army or Navy.

The first American expedition ended in disaster. By August the British were in Detroit, and within a few days Fort Dearborn, where Chicago now stands, had fallen. The remainder of the year was spent on fruitless moves upon the Niagara front, and operations came to an inconclusive end. The British in Canada were forced to remain on the defensive while great events were taking place in Europe. The war at sea was more colourful, and for the Americans more cheering. They had sixteen vessels, of which three surpassed anything afloat. Within a year they had won more successes over the British than the French and Spaniards in two decades of

On following pages: *The Highlanders in square at Waterloo, June 18, 1815. A painting by Felix Philippoteaux.* VICTORIA AND ALBERT MUSEUM; CROWN COPYRIGHT RESERVED

warfare. But retribution was at hand. On June 1, 1813, the American frigate *Chesapeake*, under Captain Laurence, sailed from Boston harbour with a green and mutinous crew to accept a challenge from Captain Broke of H.M.S. *Shannon*. After a fifteen-minute fight the *Chesapeake* surrendered. Other American losses followed, and command of the ocean passed into British hands. American privateers, however, continued to harry British shipping throughout the rest of the war.

The Americans set about revising their strategy. By land they made a number of raids into the province of Upper Canada, now named Ontario. Towns and villages were sacked and burnt. In October, the United States were established on the southern shores of the Great Lakes and the Indians could no longer outflank their frontier. But the invasion of Upper Canada on land had been a failure, and the year ended with the Canadians in possession of Fort Niagara.

Hitherto the British in Canada had lacked the means for offensive action. Troops and ships in Europe were locked in the deadly struggle against Napoleon. But by the spring of 1814 a decision had been reached in Europe. Napoleon abdicated in April and the British could at last send adequate reinforcements.

Peace negotiations had been tried throughout the war, but it was not until January 1814 that the British had agreed to treat. The American Commissioners, among them Henry Clay, reached Ghent in June. The previous November Wellington had been asked to take command in America. He realised that victory depended on naval superiority upon the Lakes. He saw no way of gaining it. He held moreover that it was not in Britain's interest to demand territory from America on the Canadian border. Both sides therefore agreed upon the *status quo* for the long boundary in the North. Other points were left undetermined. Naval forces on the Great Lakes were regulated by a Commission in 1817, and the disputed boundary of Maine was similarly settled later.

Thus ended a futile and unnecessary con-

Viscount Castlereagh. Detail from a portrait by Lawrence.
NATIONAL PORTRAIT GALLERY

flict. The results of the peace were solid and enduring. The British Army and Navy had learned to respect their former colonials. Canadians took pride in the part they had played in defending their country, and their growing national sentiment was strengthened. Henceforward the world was to see a three-thousand-mile international frontier between Canada and the United States undefended by men or guns. On the oceans the British Navy ruled supreme for a century to come, and behind this shield the United States were free to fulfil their continental destiny.

Britain was represented at the Congress of Vienna by Castlereagh. In 1812 the Prime Minister, Perceval, had been shot dead by a madman in the lobby of the House of Commons. His colleague, Lord Liverpool, took over the administration, and remained in power for fifteen years. Castlereagh rejoined the Government as Foreign Secretary, an office he was to hold until his death. Castlereagh believed in the Balance of Power. This is a concept that became unpopular in the twentieth century during the interval between the World Wars. On the Continent the main preoccupation of the Powers was to draw a *cordon sanitaire* around France to protect Central Europe from the infections and dangers of revolution. The British were principally concerned with the colonial settlement. Many conquests were returned, yet the Peace of Paris, which was the outcome of the Congress, marks another stage in the establishment of the new Empire which was replacing the lost American colonies. The captured French colonies were surrendered, with the exception of Mauritius, Tobago, and St Lucia. The Dutch recovered their possessions in the East Indies. At the price of three millions sterling Britain acquired part of Guiana from the Dutch. The Government, however, was most concerned with those possessions which had a strategic value as ports of call. For that reason it held on to Malta, and the key of the route to India, the Cape of Good Hope. From this acquisition in South Africa a troubled saga was to unfold. Dutch Ceylon was kept, and Danish Heligoland, which had proved a fine base for breaking the Continental System and smuggling goods into Germany. These gains were scattered and piecemeal, but, taken together, they represented a powerful consolidation of the Imperial structure.

Napoleon had for nine months been sovereign of Elba. In February 1815 he saw,

or thought he saw, that the Congress of Vienna was breaking up. The Allies were at odds, and France, discontented, beckoned to him. On March 1 he landed near Antibes. The drama of the Hundred Days had begun, and a bloodless march to Paris ensued. The British Government, which had led the country and the world against the Corsican, realised that they would have to bear the brunt of a whirlwind campaign. Prussia was the only main ally then in readiness. Within a month of the escape from Elba Wellington took up his command at Brussels.

As the summer drew near Wellington assembled a mixed force of eighty-three thousand men, of whom about a third were British. Napoleon could not afford to waste a day. Nor did he do so. Wellington waited patiently in Brussels for a sign of the Emperor's intention. He and his great opponent were to cross swords for the first time. They were both in their forty-sixth year. Quietly on June 15 Napoleon crossed the Sambre at Charleroi and Marchiennes, driving the Prussian forward troops before him to within twenty-five miles of Brussels.

Wellington resolved to concentrate on the strategic point of Quatre-Bras. For the French everything depended upon beating the Prussians before forcing Wellington north-westwards to the coast. Leaving Ney with the French left, the Emperor swung with sixty-three thousand men and ninety-two guns to meet the main Prussian army, centred in Ligny. Realising that so far only a small force held the position at Quatre-Bas, he ordered Ney to attack, and then meet him that evening in Brussels. At two o'clock in the afternoon of the 16th the French went into action on a two-mile front. There was little tactical manoeuvre in the fierce struggle which swayed backwards and forwards on that June afternoon at the cross-roads on the way to Brussels. It was a head-on collision in which generalship played no part, though leadership did. Wellington was always at his coolest in the hottest of moments. In this battle of private soldiers the fire-power of the British infantry prevailed. Out of thirty thousand men engaged by nightfall on their side the

THE WATERLOO CAMPAIGN

Allied Forces ■ French Forces ▭

BRUSSELS

Waterloo

Mont St. Jean

WELLINGTON

NAPOLEON

Hougoumont

La Haye Sainte

BLÜCHER'S position on the afternoon of June 18

La Belle Alliance

BATTLE OF JUNE 18

NAPOLEON June 17

BLÜCHER June 17

Genappe

Wavre

WELLINGTON

NEY

Quatre Bras

BATTLES OF JUNE 16

BLÜCHER

Ligny

NAPOLEON

Gembloux

Direction of GROUCHY'S Force

Mons 13 miles

Namur 7 miles

R. Sambre

CHARLEROI

265

The meeting of Wellington and Blucher after Waterloo, by Maclise. "Mein lieber Kamerad," said Blucher, "quelle affaire!"

Allies lost four thousand six hundred; the French somewhat less. But Ney had not gained his objective. Brussels was not in his grasp. Napoleon had gained the advantage at the opening of the campaign, but he had not intended that both wings of his army should be in action at once. At Ligny, however, he won a striking success. Marshal Blücher was out-generalled, his army split in two, battered by the magnificent French artillery, and driven back on Wavre. The crisis of the campaign was at hand.

Wellington himself had inspected this Belgian countryside in the autumn of 1814. He had noted the advantages of the ridge at Waterloo. There he would accept battle, and all he asked from the Prussians was the support of one corps. Throughout the night of the 16th and 17th a carefully screened retreat began, and by morning the Waterloo position, a line of defence such as Wellington had already tested in the Peninsula, was occupied. Late in the morning of the 18th of June the French attacked both flanks of the Allied position, of which the key points were the fortified Château of Hougoumont on the right and the farm of La Haye Sainte in the middle. The battle swayed backwards and forwards upon the grass slopes, and intense fighting centred in the farm of La Haye Sainte, which eventually fell to the French. At Hougoumont, which held out all day, the

fighting was heavier still. In the early afternoon one of the most terrific artillery barrages of the time was launched upon Wellington's infantry as preparation for the major cavalry advance of fifteen thousand troopers under Ney. Under the hail of the French guns Wellington moved his infantry farther back over the ridge of Waterloo to give them a little more shelter. On seeing this Ney launched his squadrons in a series of attacks. Everything now depended upon the British muskets and bayonets. But the French cuirassiers never reached the infantry squares. As one eyewitness wrote: "As to the so-called charges, I do not think that on a single occasion actual collision occurred. I many times saw the cuirassiers come on with boldness to within some twenty or thirty yards of a square, when, seeing the steady firmness of our men, they invariably edged away and retired." No visible decision was achieved. Napoleon, looking through his glasses at the awful *mêlée*, exclaimed, "Will the English never show their backs?" "I fear," replied Soult, "they will be cut to pieces first."

Wellington too had much to disturb him. Although the Prussians had been distantly sighted upon the roads in the early afternoon, they were slow in making their presence felt upon the French right. But by six o'clock in the evening Ney's onslaughts had failed and the Prussians were beating relentlessly upon the wing. They drew off fourteen thousand men from the forces assailing Wellington. The French made a final effort, and desperate fighting with no quarter raged again round the farms. The Imperial Guard itself, with Ney at its head, rolled up the hill, but again the fury of British infantry fire held them. The long-awaited moment to counterattack had come. Wellington had been in the forefront of danger all day. Now he rode along his much-battered line and ordered the advance. "Go on, go on!" he shouted. "They will not stand!" His cavalry swept from the ridge and sabred the French army into a disorganised mass of stragglers. Ney, beside himself with rage, a broken sword in his hand, staggered shouting in vain from one band to another. It was too late.

Wellington handed over the pursuit to the Prussians. The day had been almost too much even for a man of iron. The whole weight of responsibility had fallen on him. Only the power and example of his own personality had kept his motley force together. The strain had been barely tolerable. "By God!" as he justly said, "I don't think it would have been done if I had not been there."

On July 26 the Emperor sailed to his sunset in the South Atlantic. He never permitted himself to understand what had happened at Waterloo. The event was everybody's fault but his own. Six years of life in exile lay before him. He spent them with his small faithful retinue creating the Napoleonic legend of invincibility which was to have so powerful an effect on the France of the future.

It remained for the emissaries of the Powers to assemble in Paris and compose a new peace with France. The Prussians pressed for harsh terms. Castlereagh, representing Britain, saw that mildness would create the least grievance and guard best against a renewal of war. In this he had the hearty support of Wellington, who now exerted a unique authority throughout Europe. In the moderation of the settlement with France the second Treaty of Paris had its greatest success. Castlereagh, with his sombre cast of mind, thought the treaty would be justified if it kept the peace for seven years. He had built better than he knew. Peace reigned for forty years between the Great Powers, and the main framework of the settlements at Vienna and Paris endured until the twentieth century.

CHAPTER TEN

Recovery and Reform

AFTER a generation of warfare peace had come to Europe in the summer of 1815. The English political scene succumbed to stagnation. The principal figures in the Government were Lord Liverpool, Lord Castlereagh, and, after 1818, the Duke of Wellington. Castlereagh and Wellington towered above their colleagues. The rest of the Cabinet were Tories of the deepest dye, such as the Lord Chancellor, Eldon; Addington, now Viscount Sidmouth, once Prime Minister and now at the Home Office; and Earl Bathurst, Colonial Secretary, whom Lord Rosebery has described as "one of those strange children of our political system who fill the most dazzling offices with the most complete obscurity". Liverpool was the son of Charles Jenkinson, organiser of Government patronage under George III and close colleague of the younger Pitt. In 1812 he became Prime Minister, and for fifteen years presided over the affairs of the realm with tact, patience, and laxity. Castlereagh was a specialist in foreign and Wellington in military affairs. The others were plain Tory politicians resolved to do as little as possible as well as they could.

Britain was a world-Power whose strength lay in her ranging commerce and in her command of the seas. Her trade flourished and multiplied independently of the reigning ideas in Europe. Moreover, her governing classes, long accustomed to public debate, did not share the absolutist dreams that inspired, and deluded, the Courts of the autocrats. Although Tory opinion even in the day of triumph was fearful of Continental commitments, Castlereagh resolved that Britain should not abandon the position of authority she had won during the war. To him the Quadruple Alliance and the Congress at Vienna were merely pieces of diplomatic machinery for discussing European problems. On the other hand, the Austrian Chancellor Metternich and his colleagues regarded them as instruments for preserving the existing order. In spite of these differences the Congress of Vienna stands as a monument to the success of classical diplomacy. Castlereagh was pre-eminent as the genius of the conference. He reconciled opposing views, and his modest expectation that peace might be ensured for seven years was fulfilled more than fivefold. He represented, with its faults and virtues, the equable, detached and balanced approach to Continental affairs that was to characterise the best of British foreign policy for nearly a century.

Earlier than her neighbours Britain enjoyed the fruits and endured the rigours of the Industrial Revolution. She gained a new domain of power and prosperity. At the same time the growing masses in her ill-built towns were often plunged into squalor and misery, the source of numerous and well-grounded discontents. Machinery, the rise of population, and extensive changes in employment all presented a formidable social problem. The Government were by their background and upbringing largely unaware of the causes of the ills which they had to cure. They concentrated upon the one issue they understood, the defence of property. Napoleon had closed the Continent to British commerce, and the answering British blockade had made things worse for industry at home.

There was much unemployment in the industrial North and the Midlands. Smashing of machinery during the Luddite riots of 1812 and 1813 had exposed the complete absence of means of preserving public order. Bad harvests now added to the prevailing distress. Extremist Radical leaders came out of hiding and kept up a perpetual and growing agitation. Their organisations, which had been suppressed during the French Revolution, now reappeared, and began to take the shape of a political movement, though as yet scarcely represented in the House of Commons. The violence of language used by the Radicals frightened Tories and Whigs alike. It stiffened the resistance of the upper middle classes, both industrial and landed, to all proposals for change. English political tradition centred in Parliament, and men still looked to Parliament to cure the evils of the day. If Parliament did nothing, then the structure of Parliament must be changed. Huge meetings were held, and protests vociferously made. The Cabinet was thoroughly perturbed. Habeas Corpus was suspended, and legislation passed against the holding of seditious meetings. These alarms and excursions revealed the gravity of conditions. Not only was there grinding poverty among the working population, but also a deep-rooted conflict between the manufacturing and agricultural classes. The economy of the country was dangerously out of balance.

In 1819 an incident took place which increased the unpopularity and quickened the fears of the Government. A meeting of protest was held at St Peter's Fields, in mid-Manchester, attended by over fifty thousand people, including women and children. The local magistrates lost their heads, and, after reading the Riot Act, ordered the yeomanry to charge. Eleven people were killed, two of them women, and four hundred were injured. This "massacre of Peterloo", as it was called in ironic reference to the Battle of Waterloo, aroused widespread indignation, which was swelled still further when the Government took drastic steps to prevent the recurrence of disorder. Soon afterwards a conspiracy was discovered against the whole Cabinet. A small gang of plotters was arrested in Cato Street, a turning off the Edgware Road, where they had met to plan to murder all the Ministers at a dinner-party and seize the Bank of England. Yet compared with most Continental countries, Britain came lightly out of these years of disturbance.

Once again in English history the personal affairs of the royal family now exploded into public view. In 1810 the old King finally sank into incurable imbecility. He lived for another ten years, roaming the corridors of Windsor Castle with long white beard and purple dressing-gown. The Prince of Wales became Regent, with unrestricted royal prerogatives. To the consternation of his old Whig friends, he had kept his Tory advisers in power and prosecuted the war with vigour. Whatever the faults of George IV, his determination as Regent to support Wellington and Castlereagh and to stand up to Napoleon should earn him an honourable place in his country's history.

In 1784 the Prince had fallen in love. The Prince's Whig friends were alarmed when the heir to the most Protestant throne in Europe insisted on marrying a Roman Catholic widow who had already survived two husbands. Under the Royal Marriages Act the union was illegal, and George's behaviour was neither creditable to himself nor to his position. Mrs Fitzherbert, prim and quiet, was not the woman to hold him for long. At the bidding of his parents in 1795 he was wedded to Caroline of Brunswick, a noisy, flighty, and unattractive German princess. A high-spirited, warm-hearted girl was born of their brief union, Princess Charlotte, who found her mother quite as unsatisfactory as her father. In 1814 George banned his wife from Court, and after an unseemly squabble she left England for a European tour, vowing to plague her husband when he should accede to the throne. The Government were perturbed about the problem of the succession. Princess Charlotte married Prince Leopold of Saxe-Coburg, later King of the Belgians, but in 1817 she

King George IV (1762–1830) and his train-bearers at his Coronation, July 19, 1821. A drawing by J. or P. Stephanoff. VICTORIA AND ALBERT MUSEUM; CROWN COPYRIGHT RESERVED

died in childbirth. Her infant was stillborn. George's brothers, who were all in different ways eccentric, were thoroughly unpopular; as Wellington said, "the damnedest millstone about the necks of any Government". They lacked not only charm, but lawful issue. In 1818 however the obliging Dukes of Clarence and Kent did their royal duty— for a sum. Kent made a German marriage, and retired to Gibraltar to exercise his martial talents upon the Rock. The offspring of this alliance was the future Queen Victoria.

The Prince of Wales had long played with the idea of divorcing his itinerant wife. He got a commission appointed to inquire into the Princess's conduct. It posted to Italy to collect evidence from the unsavoury entourage of Caroline. In July 1819 the Government received a report producing considerable circumstantial evidence against her. The Princess's chief legal adviser was Henry Brougham, the ablest of the younger Whigs. He entered into confidential relations with the Government, hoping for a compromise

The Imperial State Crown, entirely encrusted with precious stones, was made for Queen Victoria's Coronation in 1838. In the front is the Black Prince's ruby, given him by Pedro the Cruel in 1367 and said to have been worn by Henry V at Agincourt. Below the ruby, in the circlet, is the second largest portion of the Star of Africa (Cullinan) diamond. In the centre of the cross pattée on the top of the crown is the sapphire of Edward the Confessor, and at the intersection of the arches are the four large pearls which are said to have been the ear-rings of Queen Elizabeth I. REPRODUCED BY KIND PERMISSION OF THE CONTROLLER OF HER MAJESTY'S STATIONERY OFFICE. CROWN COPYRIGHT RESERVED

George Canning, an engraving after Lawrence. BRITISH MUSEUM

which would bring advancement to himself. But in January 1820 the mad old King died and the position of the new sovereign's consort had to be determined. George IV fell seriously ill, but his hatred of Caroline sustained and promoted his recovery. In April 1820 an open letter appeared in the London Press, signed by her, and recounting her woes. Brougham was sent to intercept the Queen on her journey to England. But nothing would stop the infuriated woman, whose obstinacy was inflamed by Radical advice. In June she landed, and she drove amid stormy scenes of enthusiasm from Dover to London. The Government reluctantly decided that they must go through with the business. A Secret Committee of the Lords was set up, and their report persuaded Liverpool to agree to introduce a Bill of Pains and Penalties if the Queen were proved guilty of adultery. In July the hearing of the charges was opened in Westminster Hall. In lengthy sessions the Attorney-General put the case for the Government, producing unreliable Italian witnesses from Caroline's vagabond Court. Stories of keyholes, of indecorous costumes and gestures, regaled the public ear. Brougham led the defence. The peers thought the Queen guilty, but doubted the wisdom of divorce, and the Bill passed through their House by only nine votes. The Whigs, when compromise had become impossible, voted against the Government. The Cabinet now decided that there was small chance of forcing the Bill through the

Commons. They withdrew it and the affair was dropped. The London mob rioted in joy; the whole city was illuminated. One political result of the crisis was the resignation of George Canning, who had been on friendly terms with the Queen. In July 1821 George IV was crowned in pomp at Westminster Abbey. Caroline attempted to force her way into the Abbey, but was turned away because she had no ticket. A month later she died.

The agitation over the Queen had been essentially the expression of discontent. It marked the highest point of the Radical movement in these post-war years. Towards the end of 1820, however, industry and trade revived and popular disturbances subsided. The mass of the country was instinctively Royalist and the personal defects of the sovereign had little effect upon this deep-rooted tradition.

Modern scholars, delving deeply into family connections and commercial interests, have sought to show that there was no such thing as a two-party system in eighteenth-century Britain. It is not much of a conclusion to come to about a great age of Parliamentary debate. The ins and outs might as well have names, and why not employ the names of Whig and Tory which their supporters cast at one another? At any rate, in the 1820's a Government of Tory complexion had been in power almost without interruption for thirty years. This Government had successfully piloted the country through the longest and most dangerous war in which Britain had yet been engaged. It had also survived, though with tarnishing reputation, five years of peace-time unrest. But the Industrial Revolution posed a set of technical administrative problems which no aristocratic and agricultural party, Whig or Tory, was capable of handling.

The younger Tories, headed by George Canning and supported by William Huskisson, spokesman of the merchants, advocated

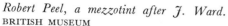

The Great Seal of King William IV, "Sailor William" (1765–1837). BRITISH MUSEUM

Robert Peel, a mezzotint after J. Ward.
BRITISH MUSEUM

Earl Grey, by Lawrence. NATIONAL
PORTRAIT GALLERY

a return to Pitt's policy of Free Trade and intelligent commercial legislation. But even they were disunited. Meanwhile, Peel became Canning's rival for the future leadership of the Tories. Personalities added their complications. Canning had played a leading part in the conception and launching of the Peninsular War. His chief interest lay in foreign affairs. But this field seemed barred to him by his quarrel with Castlereagh. The older Members distrusted him. Brilliant, witty, effervescent, he had a gift for sarcasm which made him many enemies. Early in 1822 Canning was offered the post of Governor-General of India. His political life seemed at an end. But then Fate took a hand. In August while he was waiting to take up his post in the East, Castlereagh, his mind unhinged by overwork, cut his throat in the dressing-room of his home. Canning's presence in the Government was now essential: he was appointed Foreign Secretary, and in this office he dominated English politics until his death five years later. The Ministry had recently been joined by Peel at the Home Office and now Huskisson went to the Board of Trade. Canning, Peel, and Huskisson pursued bold policies which in many respects were in advance of those propounded by the Whigs. The penal code was reformed by Peel, and the London police force is his creation. But on one issue Canning was firm. He was a stubborn defender of the existing franchise. He believed that by far-sighted commercial

measures and a popular foreign policy the problems of Parliamentary Reform could be evaded. Length of years was not given him in which to perceive himself mistaken.

Up and down the whole length of the Andes campaigns were fought for South American liberation. By Canning's time at the Foreign Office most of the republics that now figure on the map had come into separate if unstable existence. In the meanwhile British commerce with these regions had trebled in value since 1814. Canning urged the United States to join Britain in opposing European interference in the countries across the Atlantic. As he later declared in a triumphant phrase, he had "called the New World into existence to redress the balance of the Old". The New World meanwhile had something of its own to say. The United States had no wish to see European quarrels transferred across the ocean. Hence there was propounded on December 2, 1823, in the President's annual message to Congress a purely American doctrine, the Monroe Doctrine, which has often since been voiced in transatlantic affairs. "The American continents," President Monroe said, "by the free and independent condition they have assumed and maintain, are henceforth not to be considered as subjects for future colonisation by any European Powers. . . . We should consider any attempt on their part to extend their [political] system to any portion of this hemisphere as dangerous to our peace and safety." These were resounding claims. Their acceptance by the rest of the world depended on the friendly vigilance of the British man-of-war, but this was a fact seldom openly acknowledged. For the best part of a century the Royal Navy remained the stoutest guarantee of freedom in the Americas. So Canning's view prevailed. His stroke over South America may probably be judged his greatest triumph in foreign policy.

His colleagues had become increasingly critical of the activities of their Foreign Secretary. The two wings of the administration were only held together by the conciliatory character of the Prime Minister, and in February 1827 Liverpool had a stroke. A major political crisis followed. Canning abroad and Huskisson at home had alienated the old Tories in the party. The choice of Prime Minister still lay with the Crown, and George IV hesitated for a month before making his decision. It soon became plain that no Government could be constructed which did not include Canning and his friends, and that Canning would accept all or nothing. His final argument convinced the King. "Sire," he said, "your father broke the domination of the Whigs. I hope your Majesty will not endure that of the Tories." "No," George IV replied, "I'll be damned if I do." In April 1827 Canning became Prime Minister, and for a brief hundred days held supreme political power. Canning's Ministry signalled the coming dissolution of the eighteenth-century political system. He held office by courtesy of a section of the Whigs. The only able Tory leader in the House of Commons whom he had lost was Robert Peel. Peel resigned partly for personal reasons and partly because he knew that Canning was in favour of Catholic Emancipation. Had Canning been granted a longer spell of life the group he led might have founded a new political allegiance. But on August 8, after a short illness, Canning died. He was killed, like Castlereagh, by overwork.

Canning's death at a critical moment at home and abroad dislocated the political scene. A makeshift administration composed of his followers, his Whig allies, and a group of Tories struggled ineptly with the situation. Its leader was the lachrymose Lord Goderich, formerly Chancellor of the Exchequer. There had been a hitch in carrying out Canning's policy of non-intervention in the Greek revolt against the Turks. Admiral Codrington, one of Nelson's captains, who had fought at Trafalgar and was now in command of the Allied squadron in Greek waters, had on his own initiative destroyed the entire Turkish Fleet in the Bay of Navarino. The Government, rent by Whig intrigues, abruptly disappeared.

Wellington became Prime Minister, with Peel as Home Secretary and Leader of the House of Commons. The old Tories were to fight one more action. Peel was one of the ablest Ministers that Britain has seen. But his was an administrative mind. General ideas moved him only when they had seized the attention of the country and become inescapable political facts. The Government's first retreat was the carrying of an Opposition measure repealing the Test and Corporation Acts which nominally excluded the Noncomformists from office. After a long struggle they at last achieved political rights and equality. Not so the Catholics. The greatest failure of British Government was in Ireland. A main dividing line in politics after 1815 was upon this issue of Catholic Emancipation. But the patience of the Irish was coming to its end. They were organising under Daniel O'Connell for vehement agitation against England. If the English Government refused to enfranchise the Catholics there would be revolution in Ireland, and political disaster at home. As a general Wellington knew the hopelessness of attempting to repress a national rising. The only opponents of Emancipation were the English bishops, the old-fashioned Tories, and the King. The bishops and the Tories could be outvoted; but the King was a more serious obstacle. Wellington and Peel had had a most unsatisfactory interview with him at Windsor. Peel was growing more and more uncomfortable, but the attitude of the King would dictate his own. Wellington could not carry the measure without Peel, and the Whigs could not carry

Queen Victoria (1819–1901) in her Coronation robes, 1838. Portrait by Hayter.
NATIONAL PORTRAIT GALLERY

it without the King. This determined Peel. His offer to stand by Wellington finally persuaded George IV, who dreaded a Whig administration. Peel himself introduced the Bill for Catholic Emancipation into the House of Commons, and it was carried through Parliament in 1829 with comfortable majorities. Revolution in Ireland was averted.

In June 1830 King George IV died, with a miniature of Mrs Fitzherbert round his neck. His extravagance had become a mania, and his natural abilities were clouded by years of self-indulgence. "The first gentleman of Europe" was not long mourned by his people.

George IV was succeeded on the throne by his brother, the Duke of Clarence, the most eccentric and least obnoxious of the sons of George III. He had been brought up in the Navy, and had passed a life of total obscurity, except for a brief and ludicrous interval when Canning had made him Lord High Admiral in 1827. It had been expected that the new King might prefer a Whig administration. As Duke of Clarence he had been dismissed from the Admiralty by the Duke of Wellington. But on his accession William IV welcomed and retained the Duke. His reputation for fairness proved to be of political value. "Sailor William" needed every ounce of fairness. There were heavy seas ahead.

In 1830 the Liberal forces in Europe stirred again. At the polls the Whigs made gains, but the result was indecisive. The Whig leader was Earl Grey, a friend and disciple of Fox. He and his colleagues perceived that the agitation which had shaken England since Waterloo issued from two quite separate sources—the middle classes, unrepresented, prosperous, respectable, influenced by the democratic ideas of the French Revolution, but deeply law-abiding in their hunger for political power; and on the other side a bitter and more revolutionary section of working men, smitten by the economic dislocation of war and its aftermath, prepared to talk of violence and perhaps even to use it. Parliament met in November. There were some

who hoped that the Tories would do again what they had done over Catholic Emancipation and, after a rearguard action, reform the franchise themselves. But Wellington was adverse. To the House of Lords he said, "I have never read or heard of any measure . . . which can in any degree satisfy my mind that the state of the representation can be improved. . . ." When he sat down he turned to his Foreign Secretary, the Earl of Aberdeen. "I have not said too much, have I?" He received no direct answer, but in reporting the incident later the Foreign Secretary described Wellington's speech briefly. "He said that we were going out." A fortnight later the Tories were defeated and King William IV asked Grey to form a Government.

Only Parliamentary Reform could maintain the Whig Government, and to this they now addressed themselves. A secret Cabinet committee was appointed to draft the scheme, and in March 1831 Lord John Russell rose in the House of Commons to move the first Reform Bill. Amid shouting and scornful laughter he read out to their holders a list of over a hundred and fifty "pocket" borough seats which it was proposed to abolish and replace with new constituencies for the

Lord John Russell, a photograph taken in 1861

unrepresented areas of the Metropolis, the industrial North, and the Midlands. To the Tories this was a violation of all they stood for, an affront to their deepest political convictions, a gross attack on the rights of property. Radical leaders were disappointed by what they conceived to be the moderation of the Bill, but in their various ways they supported it.

The Government was by no means sure of its majority, and although a small block of Irish votes controlled by O'Connell, leader of the emancipated Catholics, was cast for Grey the Bill was defeated. A roar of hatred and disappointment swept the country. Grey asked the King for a dissolution, and William IV had the sense to realise that a refusal might mean revolution. Excited elections were held on the single issue of Reform. It was the first time a mandate of this kind had been asked of the British people. They returned an unmistakable answer. The Tories were annihilated in the county constituencies and the Whigs and their allies gained a majority of 136 in the House of Commons. When Parliament reassembled the battle was shifted to the House of Lords. The Bill was defeated and a new constitutional issue was raised—the Peers against the People. In December Russell introduced the Bill for the third time, and the Commons carried it by a majority of two to one. In the following May it came again before the Lords. It was rejected by thirty-five votes. There was now no question of another dissolution and Grey realised that only extreme remedies would serve. He accordingly drove to Windsor and asked the King to create enough new peers to carry the Bill. The King refused and the Cabinet resigned. William IV asked Wellington and Peel to form an administration to carry Reform as they had carried Catholic Emancipation, and thus avoid swamping the Lords. But Peel would not comply; he was not prepared to assume Ministerial responsibility for a measure of which he disapproved. Feeling in the country became menacing. Radical leaders declared they would paralyse any Tory Government which came to power, and after a week the Duke admitted

Lord Melbourne, by Partridge. NATIONAL PORTRAIT GALLERY

defeat. On the afternoon of May 18 Grey and Brougham called at St James's Palace. The King authorised them to draw up a list of persons who would be made peers and could be counted on to vote for the Whigs. When the Bill was again introduced the Opposition benches were practically empty. It was carried by an overwhelming majority, and became law on June 7, 1832.

The Whigs became more and more uncomfortable, and Grey, feeling he had done enough, retired in 1834. The new leaders were Lord Melbourne and Lord John Russell. Russell was a Whig of the old school, sensitive to any invasion of political liberty and rights. He saw the need for further reforms in the sphere of government, but the broadening paths of democracy did not beckon him. Melbourne in his youth had held advanced opinions, but his lack of any guiding aim and motive, his want of conviction, his cautious scepticism, denied him and his party any theme or inspiration. He accepted the office of Prime Minister with reluctance, genuinely wondering whether the honour was worth while. One of Melbourne's ablest colleagues was Lord Palmerston, who held the Foreign Office for nearly eleven years. Under Melbourne Palmerston did much as he pleased in foreign affairs. His leading beliefs were two: that British interests must everywhere be stoutly upheld, if necessary by a show of force, and that Liberal movements in the countries of Europe should be encouraged

The Royal Family in 1846, by Winterhalter, a painting now in Buckingham Palace. Queen Victoria has her arm round Edward, Prince of Wales. Prince Alfred, Princess Alice, the Princess Royal and the infant Princess Helena are in the foreground.

whenever it was within Britain's power to extend them sympathy or even aid.

With the passing of the Reform Bill the Whig Party had done its work. Its leaders neither liked nor understood the middle classes. Some quarter of a million voters had been added by the Reform Bill to the electorate, which now numbered nearly 700,000 persons. However, they by no means gave their undivided support to the Whigs. The strange habit of British electors of voting against Governments which give them the franchise now made itself felt, and it was with great difficulty that the Whig administrations preserved a majority. Nevertheless, the legislation and the commissions of these years were by no means unfruitful. The slaves in the West Indies were finally emancipated in 1833. For the first time in English history the Government made educational grants to religious societies. The Poor Law was reformed on lines that were considered highly advanced in administrative and intellectual circles, though they did not prove popular among those they were supposed to benefit. The first effective Factory Act was passed, though the long hours of work it permitted would horrify the twentieth century and did not satisfy the humanitarians of the time. The whole system of local government was reconstructed and the old local oligarchies abolished. A large mass of the country still remained unenfranchised. The relations of capital and labour had scarcely been touched by the hand of Parliament, and the activities of the early trade unions frightened the Government into oppressive measures. The most celebrated case was that of the Tolpuddle "Martyrs" of 1834, when six labourers from that Dorsetshire village of curious name were sentenced to transportation for the technical offence of "administering unlawful oaths" to members of their union. Sir Robert Peel, on the other hand, was not slow to adjust the Tories to the new times and a speedy reorganisation of their machinery was set on foot. In 1837 King William IV died. Humorous, tactless, pleasant, and unrespected, he had played his part in lowering esteem for the monarchy, and indeed the vices and eccentricities of the sons of George III had by this time almost destroyed its hold upon the hearts of the people. The new sovereign was a maiden of eighteen. The country knew nothing of either her character or her virtues. "Few people", wrote Palmerston, "have had opportunities of forming a correct judgment of the Princess; but I incline to think that she will turn out to be a remarkable person, and gifted with a great

deal of strength of character." He was right. On the eve of her accession the new Queen wrote in her diary: "Since it has pleased Providence to place me in this station, I shall do my utmost to fulfil my duty towards my country; I am very young, and perhaps in many, though not in all things, inexperienced, but I am sure that very few have more real good will and more real desire to do what is fit and right than I have." It was a promise she was spaciously to fulfil.

By the time Queen Victoria came to the throne the Whigs had shot their bolt. Conditions in the industrial North soon became as bad as after Waterloo, and in May 1838 a group of working-class leaders published a "People's Charter". Chartism, as it was called, in which some historians discern the beginnings of socialism, was the last despairing cry of poverty against the Machine Age. Agitation revived from time to time in the years that followed, culminating in the revolutionary year of 1848. But in the end the whole muddled, well-intentioned business came to nothing. In 1839 Melbourne offered to resign, but for another two years Victoria kept him in office. His charm had captured her affections. He imparted to her much of his wisdom on men and affairs, without burdening her with his scepticism, and she

The Crystal Palace, erected in Hyde Park as the centre of the Great Exhibition of 1851. A coloured engraving by G. Baxter. GUILDHALL LIBRARY

refused to be separated from her beloved Prime Minister. In February of the following year a new figure entered upon the British scene. The Queen married her cousin, Prince Albert of Saxe-Coburg. The Prince was an upright, conscientious man with far-ranging interests and high ideals. At first the Prince found his presence in England resented by the political magnates of the time. Eventually the party leaders in England learnt to value his advice, especially on foreign affairs, though they did not always pay heed to it. Together the Queen and the Prince set a new standard for the conduct of monarchy which has ever since been honourably observed.

Peel, unlike Melbourne, had given the Queen an impression of awkwardness and coldness of manner; but at last in 1841 a General Election brought him to power. His abilities now came into full play. In 1843 trade began to revive, prosperity returned, and the demand for political reform was stilled. But a storm was gathering in Ireland.

The Tory Party leaned heavily on the votes of the landowners, who had invested much capital in their properties during the Napoleonic Wars. Peace had brought cheaper corn from abroad, and the cry for Protection had led in 1815 to a prohibition of the import of foreign grain except when the price in the home market was abnormally high. Hostility to the Corn Laws had grown during the depression of 1838–42. An Anti-Corn Law League was formed at Manchester to press for their abolition. Cobden and Bright's thundering speeches against the landed classes reverberated through the nation. Peel, like Cobden and Bright, came from the middle class, and their arguments bit deeply into his mind. England's trade and prosperity demanded the abolition of the Corn Laws, but at least half his supporters were landowners, and such a step would wreck the Conservative Party. Then in August 1845 the potato crop failed in Ireland. Famine was imminent and Peel could wait no longer, but when he put his proposals to the Cabinet several of his colleagues revolted and in December he had to resign. The Whig leader Russell refused to form an administration, and Peel returned to office to face and conquer the onslaught of the Tory Protectionists. Their spokesman, the hitherto little-known Benjamin Disraeli, denounced him not so much for seeking to abolish the Corn Laws as for betraying his position as head of a great party.

On June 25, 1846, with the help of Whig

Disraeli

and Irish votes, the Corn Laws were repealed. Disraeli immediately had his revenge. Turmoil in Ireland destroyed Peel's Government, and by a vote on the same night the great Ministry, one of the strongest of the century, came to an end. Peel had been the dominating force and personality in English politics since the passing of the great Reform Bill. The age over which he presided was one of formidable industrial advance. It was the Railway Age. By 1848 some five thousand miles of railroads had been built in the United Kingdom. Coal and iron production had doubled. Free trade seemed essential to manufacture, and in manufacture Britain was entering upon her supremacy. All this Peel grasped.

Lord John Russell's Government, with a few upsets, survived for six years. It achieved little of lasting note, but it piloted Britain through a restless period when elsewhere in Europe thrones were overturned and revolutions multiplied. The Tories for their part were irreconcilably split. The faithful followers of Peel and Free Trade, who included in Aberdeen and Gladstone two future Prime Ministers, were content to let the Whigs bear the heat of the day. The Liberal Party, which would presently arise from the coalition of Whigs, Peelites, and Radicals, was not yet foreseen. The opponents of the Peelites, the old Tories, were led by Lord Stanley, soon to be Lord Derby, whose forbears had played a rôle in the kingdom for even longer than the Russells. Derby was increasingly assisted in the House of Commons by his lieutenant Disraeli, whose reputation for brilliance was growing rather faster than his capacity for inspiring trust. It was Disraeli's gradual task over these years to persuade the Tories to abandon their fidelity to the Corn Law tariff and to work out a new and more broadly based Conservative policy.

In 1851 the Great Exhibition was opened in Hyde Park. In spite of prophecies of failure, the Exhibition was a triumphant success. The Queen paid many visits to the Crystal Palace, where her presence aroused in the scores of thousands of subjects with whom she mingled a deep loyalty and a sense of national pride. Never had the Throne been so firmly grounded in the affections of the people. The mid-century marks the summit of Britain's preponderance in industry. In another twenty years other nations, among whom industrial progress had started later, had begun to cut down her lead. Critics were not wanting of the age of mass production that was now taking shape. Charles Dickens in his novels revealed the plight of the poor, holding up to pity the conditions in which many of them dwelt and ridiculing the State institutions that crudely encompassed them. John Ruskin was another. His heart lay in the Middle Ages, which he imagined to be peopled by a fraternity of craftsmen harmoniously creating works of art. Peering out upon the Victorian scene, this prophetic figure looked in vain for similar accomplishment.

Foreign affairs and the threat of war now began to darken the scene. Turkey had troubled the statesmen of Europe for many years. The need to resist Russia was plain to most British observers, though Radicals like Cobden strongly opposed this view. At home Lord Derby, after a brief spell in office, had been succeeded by Lord Aberdeen, who

"*The Thin Red Line*". *The painting by Robert Gibb, F.S.A., of the stand of the 93rd Highlanders at Balaclava.* COURTESY: THE REGIMENTAL HEADQUARTERS OF THE ARGYLL AND SUTHERLAND HIGHLANDERS. *The description of the action, and of the Charge of the Light Brigade on page 285, are from William Russell's dispatch of October 25, 1854, printed in* The Times *of November 14 of that year.* COURTESY: THE TIMES

THE TIMES, TUESDAY, NOVEMBER 14. 1854.

the Highlanders. As the Russian cavalry on the left of their line crown the hill across the valley they perceive the Highlanders drawn up at the distance of some half mile, calmly waiting their approach. They halt, and squadron after squadron flies up from the rear, till they have a body of some 1,500 men along the ridge—Lancers and Dragoons and Hussars. Then they move *en echelon* in two bodies, with another in reserve. The cavalry who have been pursuing the Turks on the right are coming up to the ridge beneath us, which conceals our cavalry from view. The heavy brigade in advance is drawn up in two lines. The first line consists of the Scots Grays and of their old companions in glory, the Enniskillens; the second of the 4th Royal

Irish, of the 5th Dragoon Guards, and of the 1st Royal Dragoons. The Light Cavalry Brigade is on their left, in two lines also. The silence is oppressive; between the cannon bursts one can hear the champing of bits and the clink of sabres in the valley below. The Russians on their left drew breath for a moment, and then in one grand line dashed at the Highlanders. The ground flies beneath their horses' feet; gathering speed at every stride, they dash on towards that thin red streak topped with a line of steel. The Turks fire a volley at 800 yards, and run. As the Russians come within 600 yards, down goes that line of steel in front, and out rings a rolling volley of Minié musketry. The distance is too great; the Russians are not checked, but still sweep onwards with the whole force of horse and man, through the smoke, here and there knocked over by the shot of our batteries above. With breathless suspense every one awaits the bursting of the wave upon the line of Gaelic rock; but ere they come within 150 yards, another deadly volley flashes from the levelled rifle, and carries death and terror into the Russians. They wheel about, open files right and left, and fly back faster than they came. "Bravo, Highlanders! well done," shout the excited spectators; but events thicken. The Highlanders and their splendid front are soon forgotten, men scarcely have a moment to think of this fact, that the 93d never altered their formation to receive that tide of horsemen. "No," said Sir Colin Campbell, "I did not think it worth while to form them even four deep!" The ordinary British line, two deep, was quite sufficient to repel the attack of these Muscovite cavaliers. Our

Sebastopol from the north; a lithograph of 1885. The Redan is the diamond-shaped construction in the eastern (left) line of defences covering the port; the Malakhov is to the left of the Redan. At the top left is shown the scene of the Charge of the Light Brigade. BRITISH MUSEUM

presided over a coalition Government of Whigs and Peelites, far from united in their opinions. The Prime Minister himself and his Foreign Secretary, Lord Clarendon, were hesitant and favoured appeasement. In early July 1853 Russian troops crossed the River Pruth and entered Turkish Moldavia. On October 4 the Sultan declared war on Russia, and soon afterwards attacked the Russians beyond the Danube. Palmerston sent in his resignation in December on a domestic issue, but his action was interpreted as a protest against the Government's Eastern policy and Aberdeen was accused of cowardice. Thus England drifted into war. In February 1854 Nicholas recalled his Ambassadors from London and Paris, and at the end of March the Crimean War began, with France and Britain as the allies of Turkey.

The operations were ill-planned and ill-conducted on both sides. With the exception of two minor naval expeditions to the Baltic and the White Sea, fighting was confined to Southern Russia, where the great naval fort of Sebastopol, in the Black Sea, was selected as the main Allied objective. Unable to complete

their investment of the town, the Allies had to beat off fresh Russian field armies which arrived from the interior. At Balaclava in October the British cavalry distinguished themselves by two astonishing charges against overwhelming odds. The second of these was the celebrated charge of the Light Brigade, in which 673 horsemen, led by Lord Cardigan, rode up the valley under heavy fire, imperturbably, as if taking part in a review, to attack the Russian batteries. They captured the guns, but only a third of the brigade answered the first muster after the charge. Lord Cardigan calmly returned to the yacht on which he lived, had a bath, dined, drank a bottle of champagne, and went to bed. His brigade had performed an inspiring feat of gallantry. But it was due, like much else in this war, to the blunders of commanders. Lord Raglan's orders had been badly expressed and were misunderstood by his subordinates. The Light Brigade had charged the wrong guns.

The Battle of Inkerman followed, fought in the mists of a November dawn. It was a desperate infantry action, in which the

THE CAVALRY ACTION AT BALAKLAVA.

OCTOBER 25.

If the exhibition of the most brilliant valour, of the excess of courage, and of a daring which would have reflected lustre on the best days of chivalry can afford full consolation for the disaster of to-day, we can have no reason to regret the melancholy loss which we sustained in a contest with a savage and barbarian enemy.

I shall proceed to describe, to the best of my power, what occurred under my own eyes, and to state the facts which I have heard from men whose veracity is unimpeachable, reserving to myself the exercise of the right of private judgment in making public and in suppressing the details of what occurred on this memorable day.

When Lord Lucan received the order from Captain Nolan and had read it, he asked, we are told, "Where are we to advance to?" Captain Nolan pointed with his finger to the line of the Russians, and said, "There are the enemy, and there are the guns, sir, before them; it is your duty to take them," or words to that effect, according to the statements made since his death. Lord Lucan, with reluctance, gave the order to Lord Cardigan to advance upon the guns, conceiving that his orders compelled him to do so. The noble Earl, though he did not shrink, also saw the fearful odds against him. Don Quixote in his tilt against the windmill was not near so rash and reckless as the gallant fellows who prepared without a thought to rush on almost certain death. It is a maxim of war, that "cavalry never act without a support," that "infantry should be close at hand when cavalry carry guns, as the effect is only instantaneous," and that it is necessary to have on the flank of a line of cavalry some squadrons in column, the attack on the flank being most dangerous. The only support our light cavalry had was the reserve of heavy cavalry at a great distance behind them, the infantry and guns being far in the rear. There were no squadrons in column at all, and there was a plain to charge over, before the enemy's guns were reached, of a mile and a half in length. At 11.10 our Light Cavalry Brigade rushed to the front. They numbered as follows, as well as I can ascertain:—

				Men.
4th Light Dragoons	...	...	...	118
8th Irish Hussars	...	...	...	104
11th Prince Albert's Hussars	...	...	110
13th Light Dragoons	...	...	...	130
17th Lancers	...	...	...	145
Total	...	...	...	607 sabres.

The whole brigade scarcely made one effective regiment, according to the numbers of continental armies; and yet it was more than we could spare. As they passed towards the front, the Russians opened on them from the guns in the redoubt on the right, with volleys of musketry and rifles. They swept proudly past, glittering in the morning sun in all the pride and splendour of war. We could scarcely believe the evidence of our senses! Surely that handful of men are not going to charge an army in position? Alas! it was but too true— their desperate valour knew no bounds, and far indeed was it removed from its so-called better part—discretion. They advanced in two lines, quickening their pace as they closed towards the enemy. A more fearful spectacle was never witnessed than by those who, without the power to aid, beheld their heroic countrymen rushing to the arms of death. At the distance of 1,200 yards the whole line of the enemy belched forth, from 30 iron mouths, a flood of smoke and flame, through which hissed the deadly balls. Their flight was marked by instant gaps in our ranks, by dead men and horses, by steeds flying wounded or riderless across the plain. The first line is broken, it is joined by the second, they never halt or check their speed an instant; with diminished ranks, thinned by those 30 guns, which the Russians had laid with the most deadly accuracy, with a halo of flashing steel above their heads, and with a cheer which was many a noble fellow's death-cry, they flew into the smoke of the batteries, but ere they were lost from view the plain was strewed with their bodies and with the carcasses of horses. They were exposed to an oblique fire from the batteries on the hills on both sides, as well as to a direct fire of musketry. Through the clouds of smoke we could see their sabres flashing as they rode up to the guns and dashed between them, cutting down the gunners as they stood. We saw them riding through the guns, as I have said; to our delight we saw them returning, after breaking through a column of Russian infantry, and scattering them like chaff, when the flank fire of the battery on the hill swept them down, scattered and broken as they were. Wounded men and dismounted troopers flying towards us told the sad tale—demi-gods could not have done what we had failed to do. At the very moment when they were about to retreat an enormous mass of Lancers was hurled on their flank. Colonel Shewell, of the 8th Hussars, saw the danger, and rode his few men straight at them, cutting his way through with fearful loss. The other regiments turned and engaged in a desperate encounter. With courage too great almost for credence, they were breaking their way through the columns which enveloped them, when there took place an act of atrocity without parallel in the modern warfare of civilized nations. The Russian gunners, when the storm of cavalry passed, returned to their guns. They saw their own cavalry mingled with the troopers who had just ridden over them, and, to the eternal disgrace of the Russian name, the miscreants poured a murderous volley of grape and canister on the mass of struggling men and horses, mingling friend and foe in one common ruin. It was as much as our Heavy Cavalry Brigade could do to cover the retreat of the miserable remnants of that band of heroes as they returned to the place they had so lately quitted in all the pride of life. At 11.35 not a British soldier, except the dead and dying, was left in front of these bloody Muscovite guns. Our loss, as far as it could be ascertained, in killed, wounded, and missing at 2 o'clock to-day, was as follows:—

			Went into Action. Strong.		Returned from Action.		Loss.
4th Light Dragoons	...	...	118	...	39	...	79
8th Hussars	...	...	104	...	38	...	66
11th Hussars	...	...	110	...	25	...	85
13th Light Dragoons	...	...	130	...	61	...	69
17th Lancers	...	...	145	...	35	...	110
			607		198		409

It is not certain that all these were killed, wounded, or missing; many may still come in, and about 80 wounded have already returned. Captain Nolan was killed by the first shot fired, as he rode in advance of the Hussars, cheering them on.

The Charge of the Light Brigade, after the painting by R. Caton Woodville. COURTESY: THE PARKER GALLERY

Roger Fenton's photograph of the Redan, after the abandonment of Sebastopol by the Russians on the night of September 8, 1855 (see the lithograph reproduced on page 284). Although the British assault on the Redan earlier in the day had failed, with heavy losses, the French capture of the Malakhov the same day made Sebastopol untenable for the Russians. VICTORIA AND ALBERT MUSEUM. OFFICIAL PHOTOGRAPH; CROWN COPYRIGHT RESERVED

British soldier proved his courage and endurance. Russian casualties were nearly five times as many as those of the Allies. But Inkerman was not decisive. Amid storms and blizzards the British Army lay, without tents, huts, food, warm clothes, or the most elementary medical care. Cholera, dysentery, and malarial fever took their dreadful toll.

Even the War Office was a little shaken by the incompetence and suffering. *The Times* under its great editor J. T. Delane, sent out the first of all war correspondents, William Russell, and used his reports to start a national agitation against the Government. Aberdeen was assailed from every quarter, and when Parliament reassembled in January a motion was introduced by a private Member to appoint a commission of inquiry into the state of the army before Sebastopol. Aberdeen resigned, and was succeeded by Palmerston, who accepted the commission of inquiry. By the summer of 1855 the Allied armies had been reinforced and were in good heart. In September Sebastopol at last fell. Threatened by an Austrian ultimatum, Russia agreed to terms, and in February 1856 a peace con-

ference opened in Paris. The Treaty of Paris, signed at the end of March, removed the immediate causes of the conflict, but provided no permanent settlement of the Eastern Question. Within twenty years Europe was nearly at war again over Russian ambitions in the Near East. The fundamental situation was unaltered: so long as Turkey was weak so long would her Empire remain a temptation to Russian Imperialists and an embarrassment to Western Europe.

With one exception few of the leading figures emerged from the Crimean War with enhanced reputations. Miss Florence Nightingale had been sent out in an official capacity by the Secretary at War, Sidney Herbert. The Red Cross movement, which started with the Geneva Convention of 1864, was the outcome of her work, as were great administrative reforms in civilian hospitals.

Palmerston, though now in his seventies, presided over the English scene. With one short interval of Tory government, he was Prime Minister throughout the decade that began in 1855. Not long after the signing of peace with Russia he was confronted with another emergency which also arose in the East, but this time in Asia. The scale of the Indian Mutiny should not be exaggerated. It was in no sense a national movement, or, as some later Indian writers have suggested, a patriotic struggle for freedom or a war of independence. But from now on there was an increasing gulf between the rulers and the ruled. The easy-going ways of the eighteenth century were gone for ever, and so were the missionary fervour and reforming zeal of the early Victorians and their predecessors. British administration became detached, impartial, efficient. Great progress was made and many material benefits were secured. The frontiers were guarded and the peace was kept. Starvation was subdued. The population vastly increased. The Indian Army, revived and reorganised, was to play a glorious part on Britain's side in two World Wars. The Indian Mutiny made, in some respects, a more lasting impact on England than the Crimean War. It paved the way for Empire. After it was over Britain gradually and consciously became a world-wide Imperial Power.

While these events unrolled in India the political scene in England remained confused. Palmerston was willing to make improvements in government, but large-scale changes were not to his mind. Russell hankered after a further measure of electoral reform, but that was the limit of his programme. The greatest of the European movements in these years was the cause of Italian unity. This long-cherished dream of the Italian peoples was at last realised, though only partially, in 1859 and 1860. The story is well known of how the Italians secured the military aid of Napoleon III for the price of ceding Nice and Savoy to France, and how, after winning Lombardy from the Austrians, the French Emperor left his allies in the lurch. Venice remained unredeemed; still worse, a French army protected the rump of the Papal State in Rome, and for ten years deprived the Italians of their natural capital. But as one small Italian State after another cast out their alien rulers, and merged under a single monarchy, widespread enthusiasm was aroused in England. Garibaldi and his thousand volunteers, who overturned the detested Bourbon Government in Sicily and Naples with singular dash and speed, were acclaimed as heroes in London. These bold events were welcome to Palmerston and his Foreign Secretary, Russell. At the same time the British leaders were suspicious of Napoleon III's designs and fearful of a wider war. Congratulation but non-intervention was therefore their policy. It is typical of these two old Whigs that they applauded the new Italian Government for putting into practice the principles of the English Revolution of 1688. Russell in the House of Commons compared Garibaldi to King William III. History does not relate what the Italians made of this. Radicalism in these years made little appeal to the voters. The doctrine of industrious self-help, preached by Samuel Smiles, was widely popular in the middle classes and among many artisans as well. Religious preoccupations were probably more widespread and deeply felt than at any

The inner arm of Sebastopol harbour, from the rear of the Redan, a photograph by Roger Fenton. Fort St Nicholas is prominent beyond the "Bridge of Boats", and other features can be identified from the lithograph reproduced on page 284. VICTORIA AND ALBERT MUSEUM. OFFICIAL PHOTOGRAPH; CROWN COPYRIGHT RESERVED

Lord Palmerston, from a photograph taken circa *1860*

time since the days of Cromwell. But the theory of evolution, and its emphasis on the survival of the fittest in the history of life upon the globe, was a powerful adjunct to mid-Victorian optimism. It lent fresh force to the belief in the forward march of mankind.

A sublime complacency enveloped the Government. Disraeli, chafing on the Opposition benches, vented his scorn and irritation on this last of the eighteenth-century politicians. But the Tories were little better off. Disraeli more than once sought an alliance with the Radicals, and promised them that he would oppose armaments and an aggressive foreign policy. But their chief spokesman, John Bright, was under no illusions. "Mr Disraeli", he said, "is a man who does what may be called the conjuring for his party. He is what among a tribe of Red Indians would be called the mystery-man." Thus foiled, Disraeli returned to his attack on the Whigs. He was convinced that the only way to destroy them was by extending the franchise yet further so as to embrace the respectable artisans and counter the hostility of the middle classes. Standing apart both from the Whigs and Derby's Tories were the Peelites, of whom the most notable was William Gladstone. Having started his Parliamentary career in 1832 as a strict Tory, he was to make a long pilgrimage into the Liberal camp. In 1859, aged nearly fifty, Gladstone joined the Whigs and the pilgrimage was over. In 1865, in his eighty-first year, Palmerston died. The eighteenth century died with him. Gladstone, like Disraeli, wanted to extend the franchise to large

sections of the working classes: he was anxious to capture the votes of the new electorate. He prevailed upon the Government, now headed by Russell, to put forward a Reform Bill, but it was defeated on an amendment and the Cabinet resigned. Minority administrations under Derby and Disraeli followed, which lasted two and a half years.

Disraeli now seized his chance. He introduced a fresh Reform Bill in 1867, which he skilfully adapted to meet the wishes of the House, of which he was Leader. There was a redistribution of seats in favour of the large industrial towns, and nearly a million new voters were added to an existing electorate of about the same number. The carrying of the second Reform Bill so soon after the death of Palmerston opened a new era in English politics. In February 1868 Derby resigned from the leadership of the party and Disraeli was at last Prime Minister—as he put it, "at the top of the greasy pole". He had to hold a General Election. The new voters gave their overwhelming support to his opponents, and Gladstone, who had become leader of the Liberal Party, formed the strongest administration that England had seen since the days of Peel.

The long struggle against France had stifled or arrested the expansion of the English-speaking peoples, and the ships and the men who might have founded the second British Empire had been consumed in twenty years of world war. Once more the New World offered an escape from the hardships and frustrations of the Old. The result was the most spectacular migration of human beings of which history has yet had record and a vast enrichment of the trade and industry of Great Britain. The increasing population of Great Britain added to the pressure. The numbers grew, and the flow began: in the 1820's a quarter of a million emigrants, in the 1830's half a million, by the middle of the century a million and a half, until sixty-five years after Waterloo no fewer than eight million people had left the British Isles.

Of the new territories Canada was the most familiar and the nearest in point of

distance to the United Kingdom. Pitt in 1791 had sought to solve the racial problems of Canada by dividing her into two parts. In Lower Canada the French were deeply rooted, a compact, alien community, holding stubbornly to their own traditions and language. Beyond them, to the north-west, lay Upper Canada, the modern Province of Ontario, settled by some of the sixty thousand Englishmen who had left the United States towards the end of the eighteenth century rather than live under the American republic. These proud folk had out of devotion to the British Throne abandoned most of their possessions, and been rewarded with the unremunerative but honourable title of United Empire Loyalists. The Mohawk tribe, inspired by the same sentiments, had journeyed with them. French, English, and Red Indians all fought against the Americans, and repulsed them in the three-year struggle between 1812 and 1814. Then trouble began. The French in Lower Canada feared that the immigrants would outnumber and dominate them. The Loyalists in Upper Canada welcomed new settlers who would increase the price of land but were reluctant to treat them as equals. Moreover, the two Provinces started to quarrel with each other. Differences over religion added to the irritations. From about 1820 the Assembly in Lower Canada began to behave like the Parliaments of the early Stuarts and the legislatures of the American colonies, refusing to vote money for the salaries of royal judges and permanent officials. Liberals wanted to make the executive responsible to the Assembly and talked wildly of leaving the Empire, and in 1836 the Assembly in which they held a majority was dissolved. In the following year both Provinces rebelled, Lower Canada for a month and Upper Canada for a week. The Whig leaders in London were wiser than George III. They perceived that a tiny minority of insurgents could lead to great troubles, and in 1838 Lord Durham was sent to investigate, assisted by Edward Gibbon Wakefield. Durham stayed only a few months. His high-handed conduct aroused much criticism at Westminster. Feeling himself deserted by Lord Melbourne's Government, with which he was personally unpopular, but which should nevertheless have stood by him, Durham resigned and returned to England. He then produced the famous report in which he diagnosed and proclaimed the root causes of the trouble and advocated responsible government, carried on by Ministers commanding the confidence of the popular Assembly, a united Canada, and planned settlement of the unoccupied lands. These recommendations were largely put into effect by the Canada Act of 1840, which was the work of Lord John Russell. Thereafter Canada's progress was swift and peaceful.

The British North America Act of 1867 created the first of the self-governing British Dominions beyond the seas. The Provinces of Ontario, Quebec, New Brunswick, and Nova Scotia were the founding members. Manitoba became a Province of the Dominion in 1870, and in the next year British Columbia was also admitted. The challenging task that faced the Dominion was to settle and develop her empty Western lands before the immigrant tide from America could flood across the 49th parallel. The answer was to build a transcontinental railway. When the Maritime Provinces joined the federation they had done so on condition they were linked with Ontario by rail, and after nine years of labour a line was completed in 1876. British Columbia made the same demand and received the same promise. The Canadian Pacific Railway was opened in 1885. Canada had become a nation, and shining prospects lay before her.

South Africa, unlike America, had scanty attractions for the early colonists and explorers. The establishment of a permanent settlement was discussed, but nothing was done till 1652, when, at the height of their power and in the Golden Age of their civilisation, the Dutch sent Jan van Riebeek, a young ship's surgeon, with three ships to take possession of Table Bay. Throughout the eighteenth century the colony prospered and grew. In 1760 the first European crossed the Orange River, and by 1778 the Fish River had been made its eastern boundary. Napoleon's wars ruined the Dutch trade, swept the Dutch ships from the seas, and overthrew the Dutch State. Holland had no longer the power to protect her possessions, and when the Dutch were defeated by the French and the puppet-State of the Batavian Republic was established the British seized Cape Colony as enemy territory. It was finally ceded to them under the peace settlement of 1814 in return for an indemnity of £6,000,000. They decided that the only way to secure the line of the Fish River was to colonise the border with British settlers, and between 1820 and 1821 nearly five thousand of them were brought out from Great Britain. This emigration coincided with a change of policy. Convinced that South Africa was now destined to become a permanent part of the

British Empire, the Government resolved to make it as English as they could. Thus was born a division which Canada had surmounted. British methods of government created among the Boers a more bitter antagonism than in any other Imperial country except Ireland. By 1857 there were five separate republics and three colonies within the territory of the present Republic of South Africa. The old colony of the Cape meanwhile prospered, as the production of wool increased by leaps and bounds, and in 1853 an Order in Council established representative institutions in the colony, with a Parliament in Cape Town, though without the grant of full responsible government. Here we may leave South African history for a spell of uneasy peace.

Australia has a long history in the realms of human imagination. The extent of the continent was not accurately known until the middle of the eighteenth century, when Captain James Cook made three voyages between 1768 and 1779, in which he circumnavigated New Zealand, sailed inside the Australian Barrier Reef, sighted the great Antarctic icefields, discovered the Friendly Islands, the New Hebrides, New Caledonia, and Hawaii, and charted the eastern coastline of Australia. English

convicts had long been transported to America, but since the War of Independence the Government had nowhere to send them and many were now dying of disease in the hulks and gaols of London. The younger Pitt's administration shrank from colonial ventures after the disasters in North America, but delay was deemed impossible, and in January 1788 seven hundred and seventeen convicts, of whom one hundred and ninety-eight were women, were anchored in Botany Bay. The region had been named by Captain Cook after South Wales.

There were of course a few free settlers from the first, but the full migratory wave did not reach Australia till the 1820's. Driven by the post-war distress in Great Britain and attracted by the discovery of rich pasture in the hinterland of New South Wales, English-speaking emigrants began to trickle into the empty sub-continent and rapidly transformed the character and life of the early communities. The population changed from about fifteen thousand convicts and twenty-one thousand free settlers in 1828 to twenty-seven thousand convicts and over a hundred thousand free settlers in 1841. Free men soon demanded, and got, free government. Transportation to New South Wales was finally abolished in 1840, and two years later a Legislative Council was set up, most of whose members were elected by popular vote.

Long before 1850 the settlement of other parts of Australia had begun. The first to be made from the mother-colony of Port Jackson was in the island of Tasmania, or Van Diemen's Land as it was then called; at Hobart in 1804; and two years later at Launceston. The third offspring of New South Wales was Queensland. It grew up round the town of Brisbane, but developed more slowly and did not become a separate colony until 1859. By then two other settlements had arisen on the Australian coasts, both independently of New South Wales and the other colonies. In 1834 a body known as "the Colonisation Commissioners for South

Australia" had been set up in London, and two years later the first settlers landed near Adelaide. The city was named after William IV's Queen. South Australia was never a convict settlement. The other colony, Western Australia, had a very different history. Founded in 1829, it nearly died at birth. Convicts, which the other colonies deemed an obstacle to progress, seemed the only solution, and the British Government, once again encumbered with prisoners, eagerly accepted an invitation to send some out to Perth. In 1849 a penal settlement was established, with much money to finance it. Thus resuscitated, the population trebled within the next ten years, but Western Australia did not obtain representative institutions until 1870, after the convict settlement had been abolished, nor full self-government till 1890.

Australia, as we now know it, was born in 1901 by the association of the colonies in a Commonwealth, with a new capital at Canberra. Federation came late and slowly to the southern continent, for the lively, various, widely separated settlements cherished their own self-rule. Even today most of the Australian population dwells in the settlements founded in the nineteenth century. The heart of the country, over a million square miles in extent, has attracted delvers after metals and ranchers of cattle, but it remains largely uninhabited. The silence of the bush and the loneliness of the desert are only disturbed by

the passing of some transcontinental express, the whirr of a boomerang, or the drone of a pilotless missile.

Twelve hundred miles to the east of Australia lie the islands of New Zealand. Here, long before they were discovered by Europeans, a Polynesian warrior race, the Maoris, had sailed across the Pacific from the northeast and established a civilisation notable for the brilliance of its art and the strength of its military system. Soon after Cook's discovery a small English community gained a footing in the Bay of Islands in the far north, but they were mostly whalers and sealers, ship-wrecked mariners, and a few escaped convicts from Australia, enduring a lonely, precarious, and somewhat disreputable existence. They constituted no great threat to Maori life or lands. Resistance to English colonisation was fortified by the arrival of Christian missionaries. A move to colonise the islands had nevertheless long been afoot in London, impelled by a group of men around Gibbon Wakefield, who had already so markedly influenced the future of Canada and Australia. But the Government was hostile. Wakefield, however, was resolute, and in 1838 his Association formed a private joint stock company for the colonisation of New Zealand, and a year later dispatched an expedition under his younger brother. Over a thousand settlers went with them, and they founded the site of Wellington in the North Island. News that France was contemplating the annexation of New Zealand compelled the British Government to act. Instead of sanctioning Wakefield's expedition they sent out a man-of-war, under the command of Captain Hobson, to treat with the Maoris for the recognition of British sovereignty. In February 1840 Hobson concluded the Treaty of Waitangi with the Maori chiefs. By this the Maoris ceded to Great Britain all the rights and powers of sovereignty in return for confirmation in "the full and exclusive possession of their lands and estates". Two powers were thus established, the Governor at Auckland at the top of the North Island, which Hobson had chosen as the capital, and the Company at Wellington. The Company wanted land, as much and as soon as possible. The treaty and the Colonial Office said it belonged to the Maoris. Nevertheless, by 1859 the settlers had occupied seven million acres in the North Island and over thirty-two million acres in the South, where the Maoris were fewer. The result was the Maori Wars, a series of intermittent local conflicts lasting from 1843 to 1869. But by 1869 the force of the movement was spent and the risings were defeated. Thereafter the enlightened policy of Sir Donald MacLean, the Minister for Native Affairs, produced a great improvement. The Maoris realised that the British had come to stay.

Despite a depression in the eighties, the prosperity of New Zealand has continued to grow ever since. New Zealand's political development was no less rapid. Indeed her political vitality is no less astonishing than her economic vigour. The tradition and prejudices of the past weighed less heavily than in the older countries. Many of the reforms introduced into Great Britain by the Liberal Government of 1906, and then regarded as extreme innovations, had already been accepted by New Zealand. Industrial arbitration, old-age pensions, factory legislation, State insurance and medical service, housing Acts, all achieved between 1890 and the outbreak of the First World War, and State support for co-operative production, testified to the survival and fertility even in the remote and unfamiliar islands of the Pacific, of the British political genius.

CHAPTER ELEVEN

The Victorian Age

WE now enter upon a long, connected, and progressive period in British history—the Prime Ministerships of Gladstone and Disraeli. Both men were at the height of their powers, and their skill and oratory in debate gripped and focused public attention on the proceedings of the House of Commons. When Gladstone became Prime Minister in 1868 he was deemed a careful and parsimonious administrator who had become a sound Liberal reformer. But this was only one side of his genius. What gradually made him the most controversial figure of the century was his gift of rousing moral indignation both in himself and in the electorate. Such a demand, strenuously voiced, was open to the charge of hypocrisy when, as so often happened, Gladstone's policy obviously coincided with the well-being of the Liberal Party. But the charge was false; the spirit of the preacher breathed in Gladstone's speeches. To face Gladstone Disraeli needed all the courage and quickness of wit with which he had been so generously endowed. Many Tories disliked and distrusted his reforming views, but he handled his colleagues with a rare skill. He has never been surpassed in the art of party management. In all his attitudes there was a degree of cynicism; in his make-up there was not a trace of moral fervour. He never became wholly assimilated to English ways of life, and preserved to his death the detachment which had led him as a young man to make his own analysis of English society. Nothing created more bitterness between them than Gladstone's conviction that Disraeli had captured the Queen for the Conservative Party and endangered the Constitution by an unscrupulous use of his personal charm. Gladstone, though always respectful, was incapable of infusing any kind of warmth into his relationship with her. She once said, according to report, that he addressed her like a public meeting. Disraeli did not make the same mistake. He wooed her from the loneliness and apathy which engulfed her after Albert's death, and flattered her desire to share in the formulation of policy. She complained that Gladstone, when in office, never told her anything. But in fact little harm was done; Gladstone grumbled that "the Queen is enough to kill any man", but he served her patiently, if not with understanding.

Gladstone came in on the flood; a decisive electoral victory and a country ready for reform gave him his opportunity. He began with Ireland and, in spite of bitter opposition and in defiance of his own early principles, which had been to defend property and the Anglican faith, he carried, in 1869, the disestablishment of the Protestant Church of Ireland. This was followed next year by a Land Act which attempted to protect tenants from unfair eviction. After the Electoral Reform of 1867 Robert Lowe, now Chancellor of the Exchequer, had said that "We must educate our masters." Thus the extension of the franchise and the general Liberal belief in the value of education led to the launching of a national system of primary schools. This was achieved by W. E. Forster's Education Act of 1870, blurred though it was, like all education measures for some decades to come, by sectarian passion and controversy. At the same time patronage was finally destroyed in the home Civil Service. In the following year all religious tests at Oxford and Cambridge were abolished. The Judicature Act marked the culmination of a lengthy process of much-needed reform. A single Supreme Court was set up, with appropriate divisions, and procedure and methods of appeal were made uniform.

Reforms were long overdue at the War Office. They were carried out by Gladstone's Secretary of State, Edward Cardwell, one of the greatest of Army reformers. The Commander-in-Chief, the Duke of Cambridge, was opposed to any reform whatever, and the first step was taken when the Queen, with considerable reluctance, signed an Order in Council subordinating him to the Secretary of State. Flogging was abolished. An Enlistment Act introduced short service, which would create an efficient reserve. In 1871 Cardwell went further, and after a hard fight with Service opinion the purchase of commissions was prohibited. The infantry were rearmed with the Martini-Henry rifle, and the regimental system was completely reorganised on a county basis. The War Office was overhauled, though a General Staff was not yet established.

All this was achieved in the space of six brilliant, crowded years, and then, as so often happens in English history, the pendulum swung back. Great reforms offend great interests. The working classes were

The cutting of the Suez Canal across the Isthmus of Suez. RADIO TIMES HULTON PICTURE LIBRARY

offered little to attract them apart from a Ballot Act which allowed them to exercise the newly won franchise in secret and without intimidation. The settlement for fifteen million dollars of the *Alabama* dispute with the United States, though sensible, was disagreeable to a people long fed on a Palmerstonian diet.[1] An unsuccessful Licensing Bill, prompted by the Temperance wing of the Liberal Party, estranged the drink interest and founded an alliance between the brewer and the Conservative Party. Gladstone fought the election on a proposal to abolish the income tax, which then stood at threepence in the pound, and to the end of his life he always regretted his failure to achieve this object. But the country was now against him and he lost. He went into semi-retirement, believing that the great reforming work of Liberalism had been completed.

Disraeli's campaign began long before Gladstone fell. He concentrated on social reform and on a new conception of the Empire, and both prongs of attack struck Gladstone at his weakest points. Disraeli proclaimed that "the first consideration of a Minister should be the health of the people". Liberals tried to laugh this off as a "policy of sewage". In his first full session after reaching office Disraeli proceeded to redeem his pledge. He was fortunate in his colleagues, among whom the Home Secretary, Richard Cross, was outstanding in ability. A Trade Union Act gave the unions almost complete freedom of action, an Artisan's Dwelling Act was the first measure to tackle the housing problem, a Sale of Food and Drugs Act and a Public Health Act at last established sanitary law on a sound footing. Disraeli succeeded in persuading much of the Conservative Party not only that the real needs of the electorate included healthier conditions of life, better homes, and freedom to organise in the world of industry, but also that the Conservative Party was perfectly well fitted to provide them. The second part of the new Conservative programme, Imperialism, had

[1] The *Alabama* was a Confederate commerce-raider built in Britain which sailed out of the Mersey under a false name in June 1862, at the height of the American Civil War, in spite of the protests of the American Minister in London.

also been launched before Disraeli came to power. At first Disraeli was brilliantly successful. The Suez Canal had been open for six years, and had transformed the strategic position of Great Britain. In 1875, on behalf of the British Government, Disraeli bought, for four million pounds, the shares of the Egyptian Khedive Ismail in the Canal. In the following year Queen Victoria, to her great pleasure, was proclaimed Empress of India. Disraeli's purpose was to make those colonies which he had once condemned as "a millstone round our necks" sparkle like diamonds. New storms in Europe distracted attention from this glittering prospect.

In 1876 the Eastern Question erupted anew. The nice choice appeared to lie between bolstering Turkish power and allowing Russian influence to move through the Balkans and into the Mediterranean by way of Constantinople. In a famous pamphlet, *The Bulgarian Horrors and the Question of the East*, Gladstone delivered his onslaught on the Turks and Disraeli's Government. After this broadside relations between the two great men became so strained that Lord Beaconsfield (as Disraeli now was) publicly described Gladstone as worse than any Bulgarian horror.

At the end of the year a conference of the Great Powers was held in Constantinople at which Lord Salisbury, as the British representative, displayed for the first time his diplomatic talents. Salisbury's caustic, far-ranging common sense supplemented Disraeli's darting vision. A programme of reform for Turkey was drawn up, but the Turks, sustained in part by a belief that Salisbury's zeal for reform did not entirely reflect the views of his Prime Minister and the British Cabinet, rejected it. The delegates returned to their capitals and Europe waited for war to break out between Russia and Turkey. When it came in the summer of 1877 the mood of the country quickly changed. Gladstone, whose onslaught on the Turks had at first carried all before it, was now castigated as a pro-Russian. Public opinion reached fever-point. The music-hall song of the hour was:

We don't want to fight, but by jingo if we do
We've got the ships, we've got the men,
   we've got the money too!
We've fought the Bear before, and while
   we're Britons true
The Russians shall not have Constantinople.

In February 1878, after considerable prevarication, a fleet of British ironclads steamed into the Golden Horn. They lay in the Sea of Marmora, opposite the Russian army, for six uneasy months of truce.

In March Turkey and Russia signed the Treaty of San Stefano. It gave Russia effective control of the Balkans, and was obviously unacceptable to the other Great Powers. War again seemed likely, and Lord Derby, who objected to any kind of military preparations, resigned. He was replaced at the Foreign Office by Lord Salisbury, who immediately set about summoning a conference of the Great Powers. They met at the Congress of Berlin in June and July. The result was that Russia gave up much of what she had momentarily gained at San Stefano. Beaconsfield returned from Berlin claiming that he had brought "peace with honour".

The following weeks saw the zenith of Beaconsfield's career. But fortune soon ceased to smile upon him. Thrusting policies in South Africa and Afghanistan led, in 1879, to the destruction of a British battalion by the Zulus at Isandhlwana and the massacre of the Legation staff at Kabul. These minor disasters, though promptly avenged, lent fresh point to Gladstone's vehement assault upon the Government, an assault which reached its climax in the autumn of 1879 with the Midlothian Campaign. His constant theme was the need for the nation's policy to conform with the moral law. This appeal to morality infuriated the Conservatives, who based their case on the importance of defending and forwarding British interests and responsibilities wherever they might lie. But the force of Gladstone's oratory was too much for the exhausted Ministry. Moreover, their last years in office coincided with the onset of an economic depression, serious enough for industry but ruinous for agriculture. When Beaconsfield dissolved in March 1880 the electoral result was decisive.

After the massacre at Isandhlwana in January 1879, the Zulu impis moved on to the mission house and hospital at Rorke's Drift on the Buffalo River, Zululand, held by some eighty men under the command of Lieutenants Chard and Bromhead. Although between thirty and forty men of the tiny garrison, drawn in the main from the 24th Regiment, were hospital cases, the post was held against six attacks by an estimated force of four thousand Zulus during the afternoon and night of the 22nd–23rd. Eight Victoria Crosses were awarded to the defenders. The photograph below shows the survivors of the action. RADIO TIMES HULTON PICTURE LIBRARY

Beaconsfield died a year later. He made the Conservatives a great force in democratic politics. The large-scale two-party system with its "swing of the pendulum" begins with him. Such was the work of Disraeli, for which his name will be duly honoured.

The emergence of a mass electorate called for a new kind of politics. Of the two leaders Gladstone was slow to see the implications of the new age. Disraeli, on the other hand, produced both a policy and an organisation. The Central Office was established and a network of local associations was set up, combined in a National Union. In the Liberal camp the situation was very different. Gladstone's coolness and Whig hostility prevented the building of a centralised party organisation. The impulse and impetus came not from the centre, but through the provinces. In 1873 Joseph Chamberlain had become Mayor of Birmingham. Aided by a most able political adviser, Schnadhorst, he built up a party machine which, although based on popular participation, his enemies quickly condemned as a "caucus".

Gladstone and Disraeli had done much to bridge the gap between aristocratic rule and democracy. Elections gradually became a judgment on what the Government of the day had accomplished and an assessment of the promises for the future made by the two parties. By 1880 they were being fought with techniques which differ very little from those used today.

When Gladstone in 1880 became Prime Minister for the second time his position was not the comfortable one he had held twelve years before. In the first Gladstone Government there had been little discord. But the old Whig faction thought that reform had gone far enough, and Gladstone himself had some sympathy with them. He disliked intensely the methods of the Radical "caucus" and scorned their policies of social and economic reform. But the Liberals, or rather the Whigs, were not alone in their troubles and anxieties. Shocked by the onset of democracy and its threat to old, established interests, the Tory leaders proceeded to forget the lessons which Disraeli had tried so long to teach them. Into the breach stepped a small but extremely able group whose prowess at Parliamentary guerrilla fighting has rarely been equalled, the "Fourth Party"—Lord Randolph Churchill, A. J. Balfour, Sir Henry Drummond Wolff, and John Gorst. Conflict was fierce, but often internecine. Chamberlain and Lord Randolph, though sometimes in bitter disagreement, had far more in common than they had with their own leaders.

One of the first troubles sprang from South Africa. There the Boer Republic of the Transvaal had long been in difficulties, threatened by bankruptcy and disorders within and by the Zulu warrior kingdom upon its eastern border. To save it from ruin and possible extinction Disraeli's Government had annexed it, an action which at first met with little protest. As soon as British arms had finally quelled the Zulus in 1879, a fierce desire for renewed independence began to stir among the Transvaal Boers. At the end of 1880 they revolted and a small British force

Lord Randolph Churchill. RADIO TIMES HULTON PICTURE LIBRARY

was cut to pieces at Majuba Hill. The outcome was the Pretoria Convention of 1881, which, modified in 1884, gave virtual independence to the Transvaal. This application of Liberal principles provided the foundation of Boer power in South Africa.

As Gladstone had foreseen at the time, Disraeli's purchase of shares in the Suez Canal, brilliant stroke though it was, soon brought all the problems of Egypt in its wake. On June 11, 1882, fifty Europeans were killed in riots in Alexandria. A few days later the Cabinet decided to dispatch an army under Sir Garnet Wolseley to Egypt. The decision was crowned by military success, and Arabi's army was decisively defeated at Tel-el-Kebir on September 13. Intervention in Egypt led to an even more perplexing entanglement in the Sudan. During the same year that the Egyptians revolted against France and Britain the Sudanese rebelled against the Egyptians. Either the Sudan must be reconquered or it must be evacuated, and the Government in London chose evacuation. On January 14, 1884, General Charles Gordon left London charged by the Cabinet with the task. He arrived in Khartoum in February, and once there he judged that it would be wrong to withdraw the garrisons and abandon the country to the mercy of the Mahdi's Dervishes. He was resolved to remain in Khartoum until his self-imposed mission was accomplished. His strength of will, often capricious in its expression, was pitted against Gladstone's determination not to be involved in fresh colonial adventures. Eventually, upon the insistence of Lord Hartington, then Secretary of State for War, who made it a matter of confidence in the Cabinet, the

Government were induced to rescue Gordon. In September Wolseley hastened to Cairo, and in less than a month he had assembled a striking force of ten thousand men. In October he set out from the borders of Egypt upon the eight-hundred-mile advance to Khartoum. His main strength must proceed steadily up-river until, all cataracts surmounted, they would be poised for a swoop upon Khartoum. In the meantime he detached the Camel Corps under Sir Herbert Stewart to cut across a hundred and fifty miles of desert and rejoin the Nile to the north of Gordon's capital. On January 21 steamers arrived from Khartoum, sent down-river by Gordon. On the 24th a force of 26 British and 240 Sudanese sailed south on two of the steamers, assailed by Dervish musketry fire from the banks. On the 28th they reached Khartoum. It was too late. Gordon's flag no longer flew over the Residency. He was dead; the city had fallen two days before, after a prodigious display of valour by its defender. He had fallen alone, unsuccoured and unsupported by any of his own countrymen. In the eyes of perhaps half the nation Gladstone was a murderer. Thirteen years went by before Gordon was avenged.

While the nation thought only of Gordon the Government was pressing ahead with its one considerable piece of legislation, a Reform Bill which completed the work of democratising the franchise in the counties. Almost every adult male was given a vote. Another Act abolished the remaining small boroughs and, with a few exceptions, divided the country into single-Member constituencies.

Further speculation about the future of English politics was abruptly cut short by the announcement of Gladstone's conversion to the policy of Home Rule. In the years since the Great Famine of the 1840's Ireland had continued in her misery. In the forty years before 1870 forty-two Coercion Acts were passed. During the same period there was not a single statute to protect the Irish peasant from eviction and rack-renting. This was deliberate; the aim was to make the Irish peasant a day-labourer after the English pattern. But Ireland was not England; the Irish peasant clung to his land; he used every means in his power to defeat the alien landlords. It must not be supposed that the Irish picture can be seen from Britain entirely in black and white. The landlords were mostly colonists from England and of long standing; they believed themselves to be, and in many ways were, a civilising influence in a primitive country. They had often had to fight for their lives and their property. The deep hold of the Roman Catholic Church on a superstitious peasantry had tended on political as well as religious grounds to be hostile to England. In 1870 Isaac Butt had founded the Home Rule League. Effective leadership of the movement soon passed into the hands of Charles Stewart Parnell. A patrician in the Irish party, he was a born leader, with a power of discipline and a tactical skill that soon converted Home Rule from a debating topic into the supreme question of the hour. The root of Parnell's success was the junction of the Home Rule cause with a fresh outburst of peasant agitation. This process was just beginning when, in 1877, Michael Davitt came

The last page of General Gordon's diary. RADIO TIMES HULTON PICTURE LIBRARY out of prison after serving a seven-year sentence for treason. It was Davitt's belief that Home Rule and the land question could not be separated, and, in spite of opposition from the extreme Irish Nationalists, he successfully founded the Land League in 1879. Its objects were the reduction of rack-rents and the promotion of peasant ownership of the land. When Parnell declared his support for the League the land hunger of the peasant, the political demand for Home Rule, and the hatred of American emigrants for their unforgotten oppressors were at last brought together in a formidable alliance.

At the time none of this was immediately clear to Gladstone; his mind was occupied by the great foreign and Imperial issues that had provoked his return to power. His Government's first answer was to promote an interim Compensation for Disturbance Bill. When this was rejected by the House of Lords in August 1880 Ireland was quick to reply with Terror. The Government then decided both to strike at terrorism and to reform the land laws. In March 1881 a sweeping Coercion Act gave to the Irish Viceroy the power, in Morley's phrase, "to lock up anybody he pleased and to detain him for as long as he pleased". The Coercion Act was followed immediately by a Land Act which conceded almost everything that the Irish had demanded. This was far more generous than anything the Irish had expected, but Parnell, driven by Irish-American extremists and by his belief that even greater concessions could be extracted from Gladstone, set out to obstruct the working of the new land courts. The Government had no alternative, under the Coercion Act, but to arrest him. Crime and murder multiplied, and by the spring of 1882 Gladstone was convinced that the policy of coercion had failed. In April therefore what was called the "Kilmainham Treaty" was concluded, based on the understanding that Parnell would use his influence to end crime and terror in return for an Arrears Bill which would aid those tenants who, because they owed rent, had been unable to take advantage of the Land Act. W. E. Forster, Chief Secretary for Ireland

and advocate of coercion, and the Viceroy, Lord Cowper, resigned. They were replaced by Lord Frederick Cavendish and Lord Spencer. On May 6 Lord Frederick Cavendish landed in Dublin. A few hours after his arrival he was walking in Phoenix Park with his under-secretary, Burke, when both men were stabbed to death. Gladstone did what he could to salvage a little from the wreck of his policy.

Thus we return to 1885. On June 8 the Government was defeated on an amendment to the Budget, and Gladstone promptly resigned. After some hesitation and difficulty Lord Salisbury formed a Government which was in a minority in the House of Commons. A most significant appointment was that of the Earl of Carnarvon as Viceroy of Ireland. It was well known that Carnarvon favoured a policy of Home Rule, and on August 1 he met Parnell in a house in Grosvenor Square. He left Parnell with the impression that the Government was contemplating a Home Rule measure. When the election came in November Parnell, unable to extract a clear promise of support from Gladstone, ordered the Irish in Britain to vote Conservative. In the new House of Commons the Liberal majority over the Conservatives was eighty-six. But Parnell had realised his dream. His followers, their ranks swollen by the operation of the Reform Act in the Irish counties, also numbered eighty-six. In these circumstances Gladstone continued to hope that the Parnellite-Conservative alliance would hold fast and that Home Rule would pass as an agreed measure without undue opposition from the House of Lords.

It is doubtful whether there had ever been substance in Gladstone's hopes. Carnarvon represented himself and not his party or the Cabinet. His approach to Parnell had been tentative and the Government was uncommitted. Salisbury, for his part, was naturally content to have the Irish vote in a critical election, but his Protestantism, his belief in the Union, his loyalty to the landowners and to the Irish minority who had put their faith in the Conservative Party, were all far too strong for him ever to have seriously considered Home Rule. Carnarvon resigned in the New Year, and on January 26 Salisbury's Government announced that it would introduce a Coercion Bill of the most stringent kind. Without hesitation, almost without consultation with his colleagues, Gladstone brought about its defeat on an amendment to the Queen's Speech. There was no doubt that the new Government would be a Home Rule Government, and Hartington and the other leading Whigs refused to join. This was probably inevitable, but Gladstone destroyed any remaining hope of success by his treatment of Chamberlain. In the eyes of the country Chamberlain now stood next to his leader in the Liberal Party. But he was not consulted in the preparation of the Home Rule Bill, and his own scheme for local government reform was ignored. He resigned on March 26, to become Gladstone's most formidable foe. The Home Rule Bill was introduced into the Commons on April 8, 1886, by Gladstone in a speech which lasted for three and a half hours. The Bill was defeated on the second reading two months after its introduction. Ninety-three Liberals voted against the Government. Gladstone had a

Lord Salisbury. RADIO TIMES HULTON PICTURE LIBRARY

difficult decision to make. He could resign or dissolve. He chose the latter course and fought the election on the single issue of Home Rule. The new House contained 316 Conservatives and 78 Liberal Unionists, against 191 Gladstonians and 85 Parnellites. Gladstone resigned immediately, and Salisbury again took office.

The long period of Liberal-Whig predominance which had begun in 1830 was over. The turn of the wheel had brought fortune to the Conservatives, whose prospects had seemed so gloomy in 1880. The opponents whom they had feared as the irresistible instruments of democracy had delivered themselves into their hands.

Salisbury's Government depended upon the support of the Liberal Unionists, led by Hartington, though their most formidable figure, both in Parliament and in the country, was Joseph Chamberlain. Inside the Cabinet there was little harmony. Lord Randolph's ideas on Tory Democracy struck no spark in Salisbury's traditional Conservatism. The differences between the two men, both in character and policy, were fundamental. The final collision occurred over a comparatively trivial point, Lord Randolph's demand for a reduction in the Army and Navy Estimates. He resigned on the eve of Christmas 1886 at the wrong time, on the wrong issue, and he made no attempt to rally support. Salisbury made George Goschen, a Liberal Unionist of impeccable Whig views, his Chancellor of the Exchequer, thus proclaiming that Tory Democracy was now deemed an unnecessary encumbrance. Thereafter his Government's record in law-making was meagre in the extreme. The main measure was the Local Government Act of 1888, which created county councils and laid the basis for further advance. Three years later school fees were abolished in elementary schools, and a Factory Act made some further attempt to regulate evils in the employment of women and children. It was not an impressive achievement. Even these minor measures were largely carried out as concessions to Chamberlain.

Salisbury's interest and that of a large

section of public opinion lay in the world overseas, where the Imperialist movement was reaching its climax of exploration, conquest, and settlement. Livingstone, Stanley, Speke, and other travellers had opened up the interior of darkest Africa. Their feats of exploration paved the way for the acquisition of colonies by the European Powers. It was the most important achievement of the period that this partition of Africa was carried out peacefully. The credit is largely due to Salisbury, who in 1887 became Foreign Secretary as well as Prime Minister, and who never lost sight of the need to preserve peace while the colonial map of Africa was being drawn. His foreign policy was largely swayed by these colonial affairs. When Salisbury took office he himself promoted no great schemes of Imperial expansion, but he was prepared to back up the men on the spot. The key to his success lay in his skilful handling of the innumerable complications that arose between the Powers in an age of intense national rivalries. He once said that "British policy is to drift lazily downstream, occasionally putting out a boat-hook to avoid a collision". No British Foreign Secretary has wielded his diplomatic boat-hook with greater dexterity.

The relentless question of a sullen and embittered Ireland over-shadowed domestic politics. "What Ireland wants", Salisbury had asserted before the election campaign, "is government—government that does not flinch, that does not vary", and in his nephew, A. J. Balfour, who became Irish Secretary in 1887, he found a man capable of putting into practice the notion that all could be solved by "twenty years of resolute government". Balfour stretched his authority to the limit and acted with a determination that fully matched the ruthlessness of his Irish opponents. Parnell stood aloof from these tumults. But his adherence to cautious and constitutional action was stricken by the publication in *The Times* on April 18, 1887, of a facsimile letter, purporting to bear his signature, in which he was made to condone the Phoenix Park murders. Parnell, while denouncing the letter as a forgery, refused to bring an action in an English court. But in the following year the Government set up a commission of three judges to investigate the whole field of Irish crime. They had been sitting for six months when, in February 1889, they at last began to probe the letters. They discovered that they had been forged by a decrepit Irish journalist named Richard Piggot. For a few months Parnell rode the crest of the wave. A General Election was approaching, the Government was out of favour, and nothing, it seemed, could prevent a victory for Gladstone and Home Rule. But the case was altered. On November 13, 1890, the suit of O'Shea *v*. O'Shea and Parnell opened in the Divorce Court. A decree *nisi* was granted to Captain O'Shea. Parnell, as co-respondent, offered no defence. The Nonconformist conscience, powerful in the Liberal Party, reared its head. Tremendous pressure was put on the Irish leader. As a last measure Gladstone wrote to Parnell that he would cease to lead the Liberal Party unless the Irishman retired. After Parnell had made a bitter attack upon Gladstone the Catholic Church declared against him, and he was disavowed by most of his party. Within a year he died.

Gladstone. RADIO TIMES HULTON PICTURE LIBRARY

303

Liberal prospects, which had been so bright in 1889, were now badly clouded. They were not improved by the adoption of the comprehensive "Newcastle Programme" of 1891. When the election came in the summer of the following year the result was a Home Rule majority of only forty, dependent on the Irish Members. Gladstone was resolute. Work began immediately on a second Home Rule Bill, and in February 1893 he introduced it himself. At the age of eighty-three he piloted the Bill through eighty-two sittings against an Opposition led by debaters as formidable as Chamberlain and Balfour. There have been few more remarkable achievements in the whole history of Parliament. It was all in vain. Passing through the Commons by small majorities, the Bill was rejected on the second reading in the Lords by 419 votes to 41. Thus perished all hope of a united, self-governing Ireland, loyal to the British Crown. After the defeat of the Home Rule Bill Gladstone fell increasingly out of sympathy with his colleagues. He resigned on

March 3, 1894, fifty-two and a half years after his swearing in as a Privy Counsellor. He died in 1898. His career had been the most noteworthy of the century, leaving behind innumerable marks on the pages of history. Few of his conceptions were unworthy. Gladstone's achievements, like his failures, were on the grand scale.

In January 1893 the Independent Labour Party had been founded at a conference at Bradford, with J. Keir Hardie, the Scottish miners'

J. Keir Hardie. RADIO TIMES HULTON PICTURE LIBRARY

leader, as its chairman. The aims of the I.L.P., as it was called, were the popularisation of Socialist doctrine and the promotion of independent working-class candidates at Parliamentary elections. Of far greater importance in England was the emergence about the same time of the Fabian Society, run by a group of young and obscure but highly gifted men, Sidney Webb and George Bernard Shaw among them. They damned all revolutionary theory and set about the propagation of a practical Socialist doctrine. They were not interested in the organisation of a new political party. Most working men knew little of these higher intellectual activities. They were absorbed in efforts to raise their standards of living. During the mid-Victorian years Trade Union organisation had been largely confined to the skilled and relatively prosperous members of the working class. But in 1889 the dockers of London, a miserably underpaid group, struck for a wage of sixpence an hour. The dockers' victory, made possible by much public sympathy and support, was followed by a rapid expansion of Trade Union organisation among the unskilled workers. Throughout the country small groups of Socialists began to form, but they were politically very weak. Their sole electoral success had been the return for West Ham in 1892 of Keir Hardie, who created a sensation by going to the House for his first time accompanied by a brass band and wearing a cloth cap. Keir Hardie patiently toiled to woo the Unions away from the Liberal connection. The outcome was a meeting sponsored by the Socialist societies and a number of Trade Unions which was held in the Memorial Hall, Farringdon Street, London, on February 27, 1900. It was there decided to set up a Labour Representation Committee, with Ramsay MacDonald as its secretary. The aim of the committee was defined as the establishment of "a distinct Labour group in Parliament who shall have their own Whips and agree upon policy". The Labour Party had been founded. MacDonald in the twentieth century was to become the first Labour Prime Minister. He was to split his party at a moment of national crisis, and die amid the execrations of the Socialists whose political fortunes he had done so much to build.

Gladstone had been succeeded as Prime Minister by Lord Rosebery. His was a bleak, precarious, wasting inheritance. Rosebery had the good luck to win the Derby twice during his sixteen months of office. Not much other fortune befell him. Rosebery had a far-ranging mind, above the shifts and compromises indispensable in political life. He was the Queen's own choice as Prime Minister, and his Imperialist views made him unpopular with his own party. The Lords continued to obstruct him. At this moment the Chancellor of the Exchequer, Sir William Harcourt, included in his Budget proposals a scheme for the payment of substantial death duties. The Cabinet was rent by clashes of personality and the quarrels of Imperialists and "Little Englanders". When the Government was defeated on a snap vote in June 1895 it took the opportunity to resign.

At the General Election the Conservative-Liberal Unionist alliance won a decisive victory. Its majority over the Opposition, including the Irish Nationalists, was 152. Lord Salisbury thereupon formed a powerful administration. His deputy and closest adviser was his nephew, Arthur Balfour, who became First Lord of the Treasury. But the man who in the public eye dominated the Government was the Liberal Unionist leader, Joseph Chamberlain, now at the height of his powers and anxious for the office which had been denied to him for so long by the events of 1886. By his own choice Chamberlain became Colonial Secretary. His instinct was a sure one. Interest in home affairs had languished. In its five years of office the Government passed only one substantial reforming measure, the Workmen's Compensation Act of 1897. The excitement of politics lay in the clash of Imperial forces in the continents of Africa and Asia, and it was there that Chamberlain resolved to make his mark. A great change had taken place in him. The Municipal Socialist and Republican of his Birmingham years was now the architect of Empire. "It is not enough", he declared,

Left: *Joseph Chamberlain*. RADIO TIMES HULTON PICTURE LIBRARY

Right: *Sir Herbert Kitchener (later Lord Kitchener), Sirdar of the Egyptian Army*. RADIO TIMES HULTON PICTURE LIBRARY

"to occupy certain great spaces of the world's surface unless you can make the best of them —unless you are willing to develop them. We are landlords of a great estate; it is the duty of a landlord to develop his estate."

From the moment he took office projects of reform were pushed into the background by the constant eruption of questions inseparable from a policy of expansion. The first was that of the Ashanti, who terrorised much of the Gold Coast; by January 1896 the Ashanti kingdom had been crushed. The situation in Nigeria was much more difficult, since the French were attempting to confine the British to the coastal areas by using their superior military strength. Chamberlain's skilful diplomacy backed resolute action, and the Anglo-French Convention of June 1898 drew boundary lines in West Africa which were entirely satisfactory to the British. A few months later a far more dangerous dispute

The charge of the 21st Lancers at Omdurman. RADIO TIMES HULTON PICTURE LIBRARY

broke out between Britain and France over the control of the Upper Nile. Since the death of Gordon the Dervishes had held unquestioned sway in the Sudan. In 1896 French moves towards the sources of the Nile were already taking place, and must be forestalled. In March Sir Herbert Kitchener, Sirdar of the Egyptian Army, launched his campaign for the avenging of Gordon and the reconquest of the Sudan. It was largely an engineers' war, enlivened by many short, fierce, gallant actions. After two and a half years the Dervish Army was finally confronted and destroyed outside Khartoum at the Battle of Omdurman on September 2, 1898. This, as described at the time by a young Hussar who took part in the battle, was "the most signal triumph ever gained by the arms of science over barbarians". The French gave way, and by the Convention of March 1899 the watershed of the Congo and the Nile was fixed as the boundary separating British and French interests. The Sudan then entered upon a period of constructive rule.

Britain entered the twentieth century in the grip of war. The Transvaal had been transformed by the exploitation of the extremely rich goldfields on the Witwatersrand. This was the work of foreign capital and labour, most of it British. The Uitlanders —or Outlanders, as foreigners were called— equalled the native Boers in number, but the Transvaal Government refused to grant them political rights, even though they contributed all but one-twentieth of the country's taxation. Paul Kruger, the President of the Republic, who was now past his seventieth year, determined to preserve the character and independence of his country. The political and economic grievances of the Uitlanders made an explosion inevitable, and Chamberlain by the end of 1895 was ready to meet it. Unknown to him however Rhodes had worked out a scheme for an uprising of the British in Johannesburg to be reinforced by the invasion of the Transvaal by a force led by the Administrator of Rhodesia, Dr Leander Starr Jameson. It was, in Chamberlain's words, "a disgraceful

Paul Kruger. RADIO TIMES HULTON PICTURE LIBRARY

exhibition of filibustering", and it ended in the failure which it deserved. The raid was a turning-point; the entire course of South African history was henceforth violently diverted from peaceful channels.

The next three years were occupied by long-drawn-out and arduous negotiations, Chamberlain's determination being more than matched by Kruger's tortuous obstinacy. In March 1897 Sir Alfred Milner, an

Cecil Rhodes. He was resolved to create a vast, all-embracing South African dominion, and was endowed by nature with the energy that often makes dreams come true. RADIO TIMES HULTON PICTURE LIBRARY

outstanding public servant, became High Commissioner in South Africa. He was an administrator of great talents, but he lacked the gift of diplomacy. The climax was reached in April 1899, when a petition, signed by more than 20,000 Uitlanders, arrived in Downing Street. A conference at Bloemfontein in June between Kruger and Milner settled nothing. On October 9 the Boers delivered an ultimatum while the British forces in South Africa were still weak. Three days later their troops moved over the border.

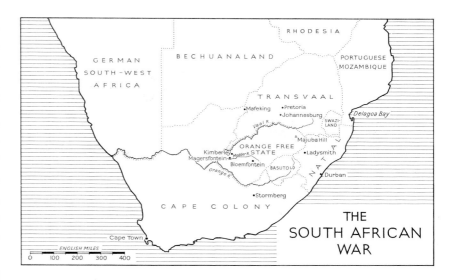

At the outbreak of the war the Boers put 35,000 men, or twice the British number, in the field, and a much superior artillery derived from German sources. Within a few weeks they had invested Ladysmith to the east, and Mafeking and Kimberley to the west. World opinion was uniformly hostile to the British. Meanwhile a British army corps of three divisions was on the way as reinforcement, under the command of Sir Redvers Buller, and volunteer contingents from the Dominions were offered or forthcoming. The British army corps, as it arrived, was distributed by Buller in order to show a front everywhere. One division was sent to defend Natal, another to the relief of Kimberley, and a third to the north-eastern district of Cape Colony. Within a single December week each of them advanced against the rifle and artillery fire of the Boers, and was decisively defeated with, for those days, severe losses in men and guns. Although the losses of under a thousand men in each case may seem small nowadays, they came as a startling and heavy shock to the public in Britain and throughout the Empire, and indeed to the troops on the spot. But Queen Victoria braced the nation in words which have become justly famous. "Please understand", she replied to Balfour when he tried to discuss "Black Week", as it was called, "that there is no one depressed in *this* house. We are not interested in the possibilities of defeat. They do not exist." Lord Roberts of Kandahar, who had won fame in the Afghan Wars, was made the new

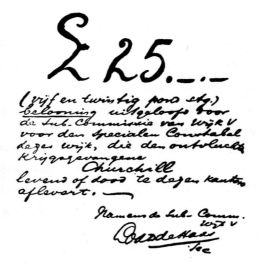

The twenty-five-year-old war correspondent of the Morning Post *after his capture by the Boers on November 1899, and the reward notice posted after his escape from the State Model Schools at Pretoria.*

Translation:

£25

(*Twenty-five pounds stg.*) reward *is offered by the Sub-Commission of the fifth division, on behalf of the Special Constable of the said division, to anyone who brings the escaped prisoner of war*

Churchill

dead or alive to this office.
For the Sub-Commission of the fifth division
Lodk. de Haas
Sec.

RADIO TIMES HULTON PICTURE LIBRARY

A Boer commando, manning trenches before Mafeking. RADIO TIMES HULTON PICTURE LIBRARY

Commander-in-Chief, Lord Kitchener of Khartoum was appointed his Chief of Staff, and in a few months the two already illustrious generals with an ever-increasing army transformed the scene.

Piet Cronje at Mafeking was deceived into thinking that the main blow would fall on Kimberley, and he shifted the larger portion of his troops to Magersfontein, a few miles south of the diamond centre. Kimberley indeed was one of Roberts' objectives, but he gained it by sending General French on a long encirclement, and French's cavalry relieved it on February 15. The threat from the rear now compelled Cronje to quit his earthworks and fall back to the north-east. Twelve days later, after fierce frontal assaults by Kitchener, he surrendered with four thousand men. Thereafter all went with a rush. On the following day Buller relieved Ladysmith; on March 13 Roberts reach Bloemfontein, on May 31 Johannesburg, and on June 5 Pretoria fell. Mafeking was liberated after a siege which had lasted for two hundred and seventeen days, and its relief provoked unseemly celebrations in London. Kruger fled. The Orange Free State and the Transvaal were annexed, and in the autumn of 1900 Roberts went home to England. At this Lord Salisbury, on Chamberlain's advice, fought a General Election and gained another spell of power with a large majority.

On January 22, 1901, Queen Victoria died. In England during the Queen's years of withdrawal from the outward shows of public life there had once been restiveness against the Crown, and professed republicans had raised

their voices. By the end of the century all this had died away. The Sovereign had become the symbol of Empire. At the Queen's Jubilees in 1887 and 1897 India and the colonies had been vividly represented in the State celebrations. The Crown was providing the link between the growing family of nations and races which the former Prime Minister, Lord Rosebery, had with foresight christened the Commonwealth. The Queen herself was seized with the greatness of her rôle. She represented staunchness and continuity in British traditions, and as she grew in years veneration clustered round her. The Victorian Age closed in 1901, but the sense of purpose and confidence which had inspired it lived on through the ordeals to come.

The War in South Africa meanwhile continued. Botha, Kritzinger, Hertzog, De Wet, De la Rey, to name only five of the more famous commando leaders, soon faced Kitchener with innumerable local battles and reverses which were not to end for another seventeen months. Each of these leaders wanted an amnesty for the Cape rebels; but Milner, the High Commissioner, was adverse, and the Cabinet in London supported him. Thus frustrated, and much against his judgment and personal inclination, Kitchener was driven to what would nowadays be called a "scorched earth" policy. Blockhouses were built along the railway lines;

Piet Cronje, after his surrender to Lord Roberts in February, 1900. RADIO TIMES HULTON PICTURE LIBRARY

fences were driven across the countryside; then more blockhouses were built along the fences. Movement within the enclosures thus created became impossible for even the most heroic commandos. Then, area by area, every man, woman, and child was swept into concentration camps. Such methods could only be justified by the fact that most of the commandos fought in plain clothes, and could only be subdued by wholesale imprisonment, together with the families who gave them succour. Nothing, not even the incapacity of the military authorities when charged with the novel and distasteful task of herding large bodies of civilians into captivity, could justify the conditions in the camps themselves. By February 1902 more than twenty thousand of the prisoners, or nearly one in every six, had died, mostly of disease. An Englishwoman, Miss Emily Hobhouse, exposed and proclaimed the terrible facts. Chamberlain removed them from military control; conditions thereupon speedily improved, and at last, on March 23, 1902, the Boers sued for peace. Thirty-two commandos remained unbeaten in the field. Two delegates from each met the British envoys, and after much discussion they agreed to lay down their arms and ammunition. None should be punished except for certain specified breaches of the usages of war; self-government would be accorded as soon as possible, and Britain would pay three million pounds in compensation. Upon the conclusion of peace Lord Salisbury resigned. The last Prime Minister to sit in the House of Lords, he had presided over an unparalleled expansion of the British Empire. He died in the following year, and with him a certain aloofness of spirit, now considered old-fashioned, passed from British politics. All the peace terms were kept, and Milner did much to reconstruct South Africa.

We have now reached in this account the end of the nineteenth century. Nearly a hundred years of peace and progress had carried Britain to the leadership of the world. She had striven repeatedly for the maintenance of peace, at any rate for herself,

Queen Victoria, Empress of India. A photograph taken in 1887. RADIO TIMES HULTON PICTURE LIBRARY

and progress and prosperity had been continuous in all classes. The franchise had been extended almost to the actuarial limit, and yet quiet and order reigned. There was endless work to be done. It did not matter which party ruled: they found fault with one another, as they had a perfect right to do. None of the ancient inhibitions obstructed the adventurous. If mistakes were made they had been made before, and Britons could repair them without serious consequences. Active and vigorous politics should be sustained. To go forward gradually but boldly seemed to be fully justified.

The future is unknowable, but the past should give us hope.

Acknowledgements

THE publishers wish to acknowledge the assistance given them in the production of *The Island Race* by John R. Freeman & Co. (Photographers) Ltd., Newman Street, London, who undertook much of the necessary illustration research and were responsible for photographing or collecting transparencies and photographs of most of the material reproduced in the book.

They wish also, with John R. Freeman & Co., to express their gratitude to the staffs of all the museums, libraries, private collections, etc., acknowledged in the captions, for their enthusiastic co-operation in suggesting and supplying illustrative material, often at very short notice.

Coins, seals and medallions, unless otherwise acknowledged, are reproduced by courtesy of the British Museum. Signatures by courtesy of the British Museum and the Mansell Collection.

Short quotations in the text are by courtesy of Messrs. William Heinemann Ltd. (*Dio's Roman History*, the Loeb Classical Library) and Messrs. John Murray, Ltd. (*Tacitus' Annals*). In the original *A History of the English-speaking Peoples*, the author acknowledged his debt to George Harrap & Co. Ltd., the publishers of his *Marlborough; His Life and Times*.

On previous pages: *The Houses of Parliament*. JARROLD AND SONS LTD